CATARINO GARZA'S REVOLUTION ON

THE TEXAS-MEXICO BORDER

American Encounters/Global Interactions

A SERIES EDITED BY GILBERT M. JOSEPH
AND EMILY S. ROSENBERG

This series aims to stimulate critical perspectives and fresh interpretive frameworks for scholarship on the history of the imposing global presence of the United States. Its primary concerns include the deployment and contestation of power, the construction and deconstruction of cultural and political borders, the fluid meanings of intercultural encounters, and the complex interplay between the global and the local. American Encounters seeks to strengthen dialogue and collaboration between historians of U.S. international relations and area studies specialists.

The series encourages scholarship based on multiarchival historical research. At the same time, it supports a recognition of the representational character of all stories about the past and promotes critical inquiry into issues of subjectivity and narrative. In the process, American Encounters strives to understand the context in which meanings related to nations, cultures, and political economy are continually produced, challenged, and reshaped.

Catarino Garza's Revolution on the Texas-Mexico Border

ELLIOTT YOUNG

DUKE UNIVERSITY PRESS

Durham & London

2004

© 2004 Duke University Press. All rights reserved.
Printed in the United States of America on acid-free paper ∞
Designed by Rebecca Giménez. Typeset in Sabon by Keystone
Typesetting. Library of Congress Cataloging-in-Publication
Data appear on the last printed page of this book.

Para Isabel, Zulema, y Perdido

Y la memoria de mi maestro, amigo,

y compañero Michael F. Jiménez

*History is the fruit of power, but power
itself is never so transparent that its analysis
becomes superfluous. The ultimate mark of
power may be its invisibility; the ultimate
challenge, the exposition of its roots.*
— Michel-Rolph Trouillot,
Silencing the Past

CONTENTS

MAPS AND FIGURES

MAPS

FIGURES

ACKNOWLEDGMENTS

In my first semester of graduate school at the University of Texas, Austin, I happened upon Catarino Garza's autobiography "La lógica de los hechos" in the Benson Latin American Collection. That same afternoon I sat down to read Américo Paredes's *With His Pistol in His Hand*, and I noticed Catarino Garza's name in the epigraph. The spark eventually turned into a seminar paper, grew into a master's thesis, exploded into a dissertation, and finally, after radical surgery, has become this book. My advisors Neil Foley and David Montejano, the yin and the yang of my academic world, inspired me to keep at it and supported me through the long process. I would like to thank the other members of my dissertation committee, who were also teachers, friends, and occasional comrades: Harry Cleaver, Susan Deans-Smith, Alan Knight, and Mauricio Tenorio.

There have been many scholars who gave generously of their minds, and in some cases their sources, and helped me to bring this project to completion. At times I felt like the last runner in a long relay race. Here are some of the other runners who passed the baton: Arnoldo De León, Celso Garza Guajardo, José Limón, Jerry Thompson, Paul Vanderwood, David Weber, and Emilio Zamora. A special thanks to the late Américo Paredes, who read and commented on my master's thesis, gently correcting my grammar and spelling in both English and Spanish. Friends and colleagues not only read and commented on papers and chapters along the way, but they helped to keep me relatively sane and happy during the interminable process of research and writing: Seth Fein, Benjamin Johnson, Laura Lomas, Andres Reséndez, Richard Ribb, Michael Snodgrass, Alex Stern, Sam Truett, and Justin Wolfe. Un abrazo for the participants of the urban guerrilla seminar on modernity — Tito Bracamonte, Fanny Muñoz Cabrejo, Pablo Piccato, and Pamela Voekel — conducted in various safe houses throughout Mexico City in 1995. Thanks also to present and former colleagues and students at Lewis & Clark College whose conversations about Latin America and the borderlands have made me feel closer to the border than a map might indicate: Laura Benson, Monica DeHart, Diane Nelson, Angela Rosen, Juan Carlos Toledano, and José Villalobos. Isabel Toledo reviewed all of the Spanish quotes, spending long nights trying to decipher the meaning and unorthodox orthography of late-nineteenth-century Border Spanish.

This book could not have been produced without the goodwill and diligence of the staffs of the Benson Latin American Collection and the Center for American History at the University of Texas at Austin, the Texas State Archives, the National Archives in Washington, D.C., the library at the U.S. Military Academy at West Point, the Archivo Historico de la Secretaría de Relaciones Exteriores de México, the Centro de Estudios de Historia de México Condumex, the Colección de Porfirio Díaz at the Universidad Iberoamericana, and the Archivo Nacional de Costa Rica.

Un abrazo fuerte for Homero Vera who helped me to gain access to Garza's personal letters and to interview Garza's grandson. Homero put me in touch with Garzista families, tracked down information in local archives, and he always called me with the latest news about Garzista flags found in attics, gold discovered under floorboards, and the TV pilot program about Garza's life. My most sincere thanks to Garza's grandson, the late Carlos Pérez, and his family, who opened their homes, their personal letters and photographs, and their hearts to a New Yorker with a lot of questions. Carlos, who died a couple of months after I interviewed him in late July 1999, kept the memory of Catarino Garza alive. I hope that this book can do a small part to continue Carlos's work of remembering Catarino.

Although ideas are essential, we do not live by spirit alone. Material sustenance for my long journey has been provided by the following institutions and grants: the García-Robles Fulbright dissertation fellowship (1995); the Fulbright-Hays dissertation fellowship (1996); the Clara Driscoll and Texas Sesquicentennial fellowships, given by the Daughters of the Republic of Texas; a Recovering the U.S.-Hispanic Literary Heritage grant; a Southwest Council of Latin American Studies scholarship award; research and travel funding by the history department at the University of Texas at Austin; and continuing support by Lewis & Clark College.

My manuscript has been on a long and winding road from one coast to the other. I would like to thank Gil Joseph, who wisely advised me to send my manuscript to Duke University Press, and although I neglected his advice at first, I saw the error of my ways. Valerie Millholland and Miriam

Angress at Duke University Press kept things moving along and coaxed reviews out of readers at just the right moments, and for that I am deeply thankful. The diligent critique and analysis of the two anonymous Duke readers helped me to focus the narrative and improve this book more than I can say. The copy editor's keen eye for detail humbled me. My department chair, Jane Hunter, has read more versions of this manuscript than she may remember; I thank her for her insightful comments, her support, and her epistolary skills through these years.

Finally, I have to acknowledge the person who is most responsible for sending me along the path that led to my academic career and this book: my undergraduate mentor, teacher, and comrade at Princeton University, Michael F. Jiménez. More than just providing me with an excellent training in Latin American history and intellectual curiosity, Michael made me believe that history and politics matter. I have tried to follow his example in my research, my teaching, and my life.

After returning from the archive or the library at the end of the day, it was Isabel Toledo, our daughter Zulema, and our dearly departed dog, Perdido, who provided meaning. It is to them that I dedicate this book, in the hope that otro mundo es posible.

INTRODUCTION

Nadie es profeta en su tierra. (No one

is a prophet in their homeland.) — Catarino

Garza, from exile in Costa Rica, 1894

Catarino Erasmo Garza stood on the bank of the Rio Grande, a Winchester rifle in one hand and a revolutionary proclamation in the other. The harsh sunlight was just beginning to soften on this day of September 15, 1891, the eve of Mexico's Independence Day, when Catarino led his band across the Rio Grande from Texas to Mexico. He had come to overthrow Porfirio Díaz, the tyrannical president who had ruled over Mexico for fifteen years. "The last of the independent journalists, the most humble of all," Garza wrote with typical hyperbole, "today abandons the pen to seize the sword in defense of the people's rights."[1]

After several incursions into Mexico, skirmishes with troops from both countries, and scores of casualties, Garza's rebellion was finally crushed. The two-year revolt raised doubts about the durability of the *pax porfiriana* (Porfirian peace), long heralded as the salvation for Mexico's incessant problems of economic stagnation and political chaos. Just as important, the insurrection graphically demonstrated the lack of control that Anglo Americans exercised in South Texas, a region that the United States had occupied just forty years earlier during the Mexican-American War. Although not a great military threat to Mexico or the United States, Garza's rebellion was an expression of broader, and potentially more destructive, racial and class antagonisms.

Years later, border people would remember Catarino as the one who stood up to Porfirio Díaz, the one who defended Mexicans in Texas, the one who outsmarted the Rangers and the armies, and the one who kept

1. Portrait of Catarino Garza used for identification
by detective agencies. (Courtesy of Archivo Historico de
la Secretaría de Relaciones Exteriores de México)

riding and writing until fate caught up with him in a small town on the
coast of Panama (fig. 1). Even at the dawn of the new century, five years
after the deadly bullets finally found their mark, men on the border still
gathered around and sang their melancholy verses of farewell to the revolution that never was and to the man who never stopped believing that it
could be.

> A donde fue Catarino
> Con sus planes pronunciados
> Con su lucha insurgente
> por el mexicoamericano
>
> (Where did Catarino go
> With his insurrectionary plans
> With his insurgent struggle
> for the Mexican American.)[2]

This is a book about the formation of the U.S.-Mexico border at the end of the nineteenth century. It is also a story about Catarino Garza, a Mexican journalist who gathered the support of his compatriots living in the South Texas–Mexico border region to overthrow a dictator in Mexico. A few members of Garza's group fought to realize the long-postponed promise of liberalism, others took up arms for a chance to win a piece of land after the revolution triumphed, and some poor souls joined the rebels just for a daily meal and wages of a dollar a day. With hundreds of men under arms and support from northern Mexican military *caudillos* (strongmen) and wealthy South Texas ranchers and merchants, the revolt seemed like a good bet. It wasn't.

The combined efforts of the U.S. military, the Texas Rangers, local sheriffs, and the Mexican Army proved too much for this guerrilla force. Within six months, Catarino Garza had gone into exile, and after two years the few remaining armed rebels were scattered in small groups, spending all of their energies just trying to avoid capture. Porfirio Díaz would manage to hold power for another twenty years until a wave of rebellions swept the aging dictator from the country in 1911. But none of this was clear at the time. The border itself, so vivid in the contemporary popular imagination and well policed on the ground, was at the end of the nineteenth century still an unfinished project, a line on a map more than a barrier between people or nations. To understand how the border came into being, we must return to the moment when the borderland was still a coherent space, being torn asunder by the emergence of two strong national identities. Catarino Garza launched his revolution on the cusp of this great transformation, and in doing so the rebellion helped to make the border. It is perhaps not a coincidence that the memory of Garza's revolt "flashes up" in this, our present moment of danger when national boundaries are being transgressed by global commerce and reinforced to regulate the movement of migrants.[3] By seizing on this memory and rescuing it from historical amnesia, I want to expose the process through which nationalism and its preeminent symbol, the border, were forged.

Garza's rebellion had very concrete goals: to topple Díaz and reinstate the 1857 liberal constitution in Mexico. The revolutionary plan called for an absolute prohibition on the reelection of public officers, freedom for all political parties, removal of all obstacles to commerce and industry, redistribution of vacant lands, and establishment of sovereignty of state and municipal governments. The plan also warned about the dangers of foreign investment in Mexico, particularly of English and Spanish loans and the

Introduction   3

proposal in the U.S. Congress to buy Baja California.[4] Like other nineteenth-century Mexican liberals, Garza was long on his critique of the present regime's faults and short on proposing detailed alternatives. In any case, the causes and meaning of the revolt go beyond its nationalist aims and are deeply rooted in the fabric of the borderland society that gave birth to it. By exploring these roots one can begin to see how Garza's revolt signified more than a simple change of government in Mexico. The cross-border nature of the rebel army and the battles fought on both sides of the national boundary line questioned the notion of the inviolability and integrity of national borders. In spite of the fact that the Garzistas articulated their desires in the framework and language of Mexican nationalism, the real danger Garza posed for both governments was the transnationality that he and his movement represented. To understand the meaning of the revolt, we must also try to understand its leader. Who was Catarino Garza? The evidence illustrates that Garza was clearly not "the wife-beater, defaulting sewing-machine agent, blackmailing editor, and hater of the Gringos," that his opponents depicted, but neither was he the perfect, courageous revolutionary hero that he and his supporters wrote about in their promotional literature.[5] One Laredo newspaper, the *Gate City*, suggested that Garza had become "a monomaniac on the subject of raising a revolution against the Díaz government," but rejected the *San Antonio Express's* characterization of Garza as a "famous bandit" and "well known border ruffian." In the *Gate City*'s view, Garza was a "journalist of more than ordinary ability," and he was "possessed of great personal courage, and daring enough to attempt almost any enterprise."[6] By sifting through the many versions of Garza recorded by his enemies, his supporters, and himself we can begin to understand this man who inspired such confidence in some and such enmity in others.

While I seek to explain Garza's motivations and reconstruct his political and personal life, this volume is not a biography in the traditional sense. In other words, I am reading and analyzing the sources not only to explain Garza's life and "what happened," but to understand how the texts themselves functioned as part of a broader ideological battle. Therefore, throughout this book I stress the importance of narratives and stories to struggles over land, cultural acceptability, political control, and identity.[7] From the first few months after his arrival in Brownsville in 1877 until his death in Panama in 1895, Garza wrote as a way to understand his own life, the collective experience of Mexicans in the United States, and the wider relationship between Latin America and the United States. He also self-consciously took up the pen as a weapon against the Díaz dictatorship, U.S. imperialism and in defense of Mexicans in the United States. The struggle over narrative and how to interpret the meaning of the revolt was also explicitly played out in the columns of local and national newspapers and journals. While it was not true, as some opponents asserted, that Garza's revolution was a fantasy created by overly imaginative journalists to sell newspapers, it is true that Garza understood the significance of the press for creating public opinion, and he used it to garner support for his cause. At the same time, Mexican diplomats like Matías Romero and U.S. Army officers like John Gregory Bourke employed the press to control the Garza story and to aid their efforts to crush the revolt. By juxtaposing these different narratives I am able to explore the crucial question of how and why particular narratives about the rebellion persisted over others.

Although I am interested in getting at the "truth" by uncovering blatant misrepresentations of events, I also acknowledge the difficulty if not impossibility of this task. By recovering alternative or silenced narratives about the rebellion, and setting those aside the dominant ones, I hope to present a fuller, and, dare I say it, more truthful, picture of the past. However, as Michel-Rolph Trouillot argues in his suggestive book *Silencing the Past*, "power is constitutive of the story. Tracking power through various 'moments' simply helps emphasize the fundamentally processual character of historical production, to insist that what history is matters less than how history works; that power itself works together with history."[8] The history of the silences may therefore not get us exactly to the "Truth," but it will help us to see the inner workings of the mechanisms that produce historical "truth." I am aware of how much my own construction of the history of the revolt is part of that field of power.

Literary analysis is one of the lenses I employ to view the intricate machinery that produces history. Scholars often acknowledge the connection between literature (the word) and politics (the deed), but rarely do they bring the two genres of literary and historical analysis together or try to show explicitly the complex relationship between "word" and "deed."[9] I have tried here to reflect the interwoven reality of "narrative" and "action" by transgressing the artificial academic disciplinary boundaries that place literature in one box and history in another.

Borderlands studies is an obvious place to undertake a project of disciplinary border crossing, and it is not surprising that this field has produced some of the best examples of such scholarship, beginning with Américo

Paredes's *With His Pistol in His Hand* (1956) through Gloria Anzaldúa's *Borderlands/La Frontera* (1987).[10] The veritable explosion in recent years of books with the words "border" or *frontera* in the title indicates that the "border," at least as a concept, has gone from a marginal field of specialization to the center of academic debate across several disciplines in the social sciences and the humanities.[11] There is, however, an important analytic distinction to be made between the border as a concept on the one hand, and as a physical place on the other. Abstract borders exist everywhere, between cultures, races, cities, bodies, genders, and sexualities. The geographical boundary between the United States and Mexico is a temporally and physically specific manifestation of the more general, abstract borders. I hope to show here the dialectical relationship between metaphysical and physical borders without allowing one to stand in for the other. The history of this particular national contact zone also raises interesting questions about similar processes of cultural, racial, class, and gender interaction that are far removed from the U.S.-Mexico boundary line. Although it would be presumptuous and misguided to argue that the Texas-Mexico border provides a universal template of cultural interaction, the heightened complexity and ambiguity of identity on this border helps us to appreciate the subtle shadings and gray zones that characterize cross-cultural relationships more generally.

The U.S.-Mexico border established in 1848 cut straight through preexisting political, economic, and cultural communities. The nation-state project of severing these communities, however, remains even today only partially completed. The establishment of the Berlin Wall and the U.S. economic embargo on Cuba are two of the most dramatic cases in the twentieth century of state attempts to disrupt radically relationships across a political boundary. However, even in these extreme cases, directed by the Soviet Union and the United States, respectively, the boundaries proved porous to culture and people, and have either disintegrated (Berlin in 1989) or are in the process of disintegrating (Cuba in 1991 to the present).[12] Unlike the extreme Cuban and German examples, however, the U.S.-Mexico border was not meant to completely block passage but rather to regulate and manage the flows of people, capital, and ideas. While the border clearly divides communities, it also unites them in relation to the two central states. Paradoxically, the very act of establishing the border created similar structural conditions on either side of the boundary in relation to the central state, thereby reinforcing a broader borderlands community that remained distant from, and oftentimes at odds with, the power of the nation-state. In order to keep these two dialectically related meanings of the "border" clear, I use the term "borderlands" to refer to the cultural and ethnoracial community that remains unified across imperial or national boundary lines, and I use the term "border" to refer to the political and ideological boundary that produces differences that are then used to forge national identity.[13] In short, borderlands unite and borders divide.

Historians have virtually ignored Garza's cross-border insurrection because it fits neither wholly within either Mexican or U.S. national history and because it failed. Yet, it is precisely this type of story that allows us to move beyond the confines of "national" history and begin to explore the lives of those people who lived between and betwixt boundaries. The Garzistas moved in a space that the cartographers had not yet mapped, even if statesmen had already imagined such lines. The Mexican and U.S. governments had experience putting down borderlands rebellions, but winning each of these battles would not prevent future insurrections. The war to incorporate the borderlands into each nation-state and to forge the border required the central governments to map the region physically and ethnographically. More than merely stopping this particular revolt, the U.S. and Mexican armies took advantage of the opportunity to make the area "legible" to outsiders, thus rendering it susceptible to both state control and capitalist penetration.[14]

The Garzistas rode into battle with their hatbands emblazoned with the motto *"libres fronterizos"* (free border people).[15] Although Garza's revolution aimed to be national in scope, the motto of the Garzistas makes it clear that they identified themselves as border people. The adjective *libres* (free) invokes a common theme in nineteenth-century liberal ideology, namely the sacredness of individual freedom and liberty. For border people, freedom specifically meant preventing central-government interference in a region that had been relatively isolated and semiautonomous for its entire history. The centralist versus federalist struggles in Mexico that ultimately resulted in Texas independence in 1836 were part of this long history of fighting for autonomy. The Garzistas fought to overthrow Díaz, but they were motivated by their desire to maintain their freedom and autonomy as border people, and that is what ultimately brought them into open warfare with both the Mexican and U.S. governments.

Aside from the story of Garza's insurrection itself being fascinating and virtually unknown, the issue of what such a rebellion can reveal about racial and national relations on the border at a moment of dramatic structural change is of particular interest here. After an extensive investigation, it became clear to me that Garza's rebellion was not, as some of the contemporary press and later historians contended, a quixotic adventure pursued by a misguided bandit, or an anachronistic ripple on an otherwise placid *pax porfiriana*.[16] Rather, Garza's movement reflected a longer struggle of borderlands people to maintain their autonomy in the face of two powerful and encroaching nation-states, and of borderlands Mexicans in particular to protect themselves from being economically and socially displaced by Anglo Americans.

Garza's revolution has been the subject of sporadic interest by Mexicanist and Chicano historians, but until now there has been no full-length analysis of the movement and its significance. Mexican historiography virtually ignores the rebellion, perhaps because so much of it took place in South Texas or because it failed. In his weighty multivolume *Historia moderna de México*, Daniel Cosío Villegas devotes only one paragraph to the revolt, concluding that it was insignificant and definitively "forgotten" after Garza's death in 1895.[17] In 1943, Mexican historian Gabriel Saldívar published a collection of Garza documents he discovered in the private archive of Ignacio Mariscal, Porfirio Díaz's foreign minister. In a three-page introduction, Saldívar concluded that the movement was a "completely justified democratic and revolutionary movement," but one that lacked leadership and commitment.[18] In spite of this neglect, a few scholars from the border region have studied the movement and have published articles and Garzista documents, thereby keeping alive the memory of the revolution. In 1974, Gilbert Cuthbertson published in *Texana* the lengthiest scholarly treatment in English of the rebellion up to that date. In 1989, Celso Garza Guajardo, a chronicler from northeastern Mexico, put together a transcription of Garza's autobiography and selected Garzista documents in a book entitled *En busca de Catarino Garza*. The historical memory of Garza has also been kept alive by Chicano historians such as David Montejano and Arnoldo De León, who saw in Garza a border hero in the tradition of Juan Cortina and Gregorio Cortez.[19]

Where academic memory has largely failed, popular culture succeeded. During the first half of the twentieth century, at a time when there was virtually no written study of Garza's revolt, the memory of the rebellion was passed down in the form of *corridos* (Mexican ballads), but by the 1990s this form of popular memory had mostly faded. In this book I build on these previous efforts to rescue this border rebellion from oblivion and to correct the image of Garza as a bandit who organized a "worthless" revolution. However, more important than simply recovering this event and its main protagonist from the dustbin of history, I want to explore the moment when the border was simultaneously being fortified and transgressed, because that time resembles very much our present moment of free trade and militarized borders.

A TRANSNATIONAL PERSPECTIVE

I have tried here to write a history of the U.S.-Mexico border from a transnational perspective. Until now, most border histories have either adopted a North-South or South-North vantage point, and with few exceptions these rely either on sources in U.S. archives or on those in Mexico. The coherence of the transnational border region throughout the nineteenth century requires an approach that mines sources in both countries and addresses the particular history of each, while at the same time recognizing the need to move beyond either national perspective. Moving beyond the national perspective means more than simply using archives in different countries, an approach that is not new.[20] It means, instead, focusing on both stories and processes that do not fit easily into national historiographical frameworks. And it also means recasting familiar stories, like those of nineteenth-century labor migration and the 1898 war, in new ways. The point is to ask not only how a revolt like Garza's affected the development of a particular country or set of countries, but also how it simultaneously created and altered spaces and realities that lay beyond the nation. In many ways, Garza's revolution represents this transnationality, illustrating for us a less obvious and partially hidden alternative space and community that superceded the nation.

Although by the end of his life Garza became somewhat of an internationalist, or at least a pan–Latin Americanist, he thoroughly embraced Mexican nationalism in his revolution, employing its myths and symbols for his own political ends. Garza's nationalism echoes other nineteenth-century Mexican liberals, yet the same language was used differently on the border to represent and defend the particular interests of Mexicans living in Texas. While cross-border organizing continued, and continues to this day, Garza's rebellion was the last concerted effort to unify the region against intervention by both the U.S. and Mexican governments. A major insurrection known as the Plan de San Diego rocked the Texas border in 1915, but in this case the rebels directed their attacks not at Mexico but at the U.S. government, Anglo Americans, and elite Texas

Mexicans.[21] Beginning at the close of the nineteenth century and gaining speed in subsequent years, the power of the central state in each nation grew, pulling the "frontier" zones closer to their respective orbits and thereby tearing at the social fabric that had previously bound the region. Although continuing to resist easy categorization, the strong currents of nationalism in both countries forced many to choose, at least publicly, between Mexico and the United States. The Texas Mexicans who fought with Garza refused such a limited choice by temporarily creating in their cross-border struggle an interstitial space between the two nations: a borderlands space. The border today continues to be a zone of ambivalence and ambiguity, but those in-between spaces have been rapidly eroding in the shadow of ever-higher walls and greater militarization.[22]

Garza began his political life defending Mexicans in Texas, then later struggled against an authoritarian regime in Mexico, helped the Cuban independence movement, and finally died trying to defeat Conservatives in Colombia. All of these moments in Garza's short life, between 1859 and 1895, were part of a broader Latin American movement for liberalism and against imperialism. The best-known symbol of this movement was the Cuban independence leader and modernist writer José Martí. Like Garza, Martí was a journalist, a revolutionary, and a Mason. Both lived in exile in the United States for fifteen years, both led liberal nationalist struggles as well as advocating broader pan–Latin American unity, both criticized U.S. imperialism on the domestic and overseas fronts, both defended the rights of racial minorities in the United States, and both were killed in spring 1895 fighting for their cause.[23] The point here is that Garza's political trajectory emerged in a particular historical context, one that helped produce Martí as well as other less well-known writers and revolutionaries. Although they continued to articulate their political goals in the framework of nationalism, these late-nineteenth-century thinkers began to conceive of broader communities of cultural affinity that stretched beyond national borders.

This basic contradiction, beginning with the birth of the modern nation, is that the strengthening of national boundaries and identity came at the same time as transnational commerce increasingly transgressed those lines and blurred that identity. In their much-celebrated book *Empire*, Michael Hardt and Antonio Negri argue that the present-day concept of empire fundamentally differs from late-nineteenth-century imperialism because the sovereignty of nation-states has declined and power is no longer territorially centered nor reliant on fixed boundaries.[24] Garza's story reminds us that even at the height of nineteenth-century imperialism, power did not rest exclusively in the nation-state but rather was to a large degree already transnational, hybrid, and decentered. Power continues, then as now, to be exercised largely, although not solely, through the nation-state. One only need look to the wars of the late twentieth and early twenty-first centuries to recognize just how much the nation-state remains the locus of power, and how that power is increasingly concentrated in just one nation: the United States of America.

This global reach of the nation was evident to Garza, who despite having gone all the way to Panama could not escape from the long tentacles of U.S. empire. At the end of the nineteenth century, the U.S.-Mexico border was only one node in an intricate web that linked the Americas. One century later, those webs have only grown stronger. The ties that bind the northern and southern parts of the continents are not, however, all part of the imperial project. Garza's story reminds us that the struggle against empire and authoritarianism has itself been transnational. The cooperation on which Garza depended — between Mexicans on either side of the border, between Anglos and Mexicans in Texas, and between Cubans, Colombians, and Mexicans in Florida and Central America — illustrates the flip side of empire's drive beyond national boundaries. These types of transnational alliances continue today with cross-border labor organizing efforts as well as utopian artistic expressions of a "new world border" where "no centers remain" and "hybridity is the dominant culture."[25]

BRIDGING HISTORIOGRAPHIES

In trying to understand how people moved beyond and between borders, it is essential for historians to replicate this process by bridging the traditional nationally bounded historiographies. Border historians are well positioned to make this leap because the study of the U.S.-Mexican border is inherently a comparative and transnational field, lying in the overlapping space between U.S. western, northern Mexican, and Spanish borderlands historiography. Until the 1980s, triumphalist narratives of Anglo, Spanish, and Mexican conquest and settlement of their respective "frontiers" dominated these three fields. Shared conceptions about the "savagery" of nomadic and seminomadic indigenous groups led to strikingly similar national myths about Mexico's northern and the U.S. western frontiers. While Mexico's frontier myth may not have quite the same importance as the imagined West has in the United States, both regions have been characterized with similar adjectives. Like U.S. westerners, the culturally distinct Mexican *norteños* (northerners) are viewed as hard-working, patriotic, pioneering, courageous, and aggressive, and they have also figured prominently in Mexican history as leaders of the 1910 revolution, as architects of the recent neoliberal restructuring (Carlos Salinas de Gortarí), and even as a masked Zapatista rebel leader (Subcomandante Marcos).[26]

Chicano history led the way, at least for U.S. historiography, toward a critical interpretation of "civilization" and "progress" narratives. Following in this tradition, scholars since the late 1980s have revolutionized the study of the borderlands. Innovative historical analyses by Ramón Gutiérrez, Sara Deutsch, David Montejano, and Neil Foley, among others, have examined social relations in the borderlands, painting a much richer and more multidimensional portrait of the complexity of border society than previously existed.[27] All of these efforts, combined with a growing literature in New Western history, has not only brought discussions of race, class, and gender to the center of histories of the U.S. West but also has forced us to rethink the Anglocentric East-West paradigm of most U.S. history.[28]

The painstaking historical research by Emilio Zamora, Armando Alonzo, and Gilberto Hinojosa, among others, on Mexican workers, land tenancy, and the demographic changes on the South Texas border has helped me to understand the context of the border in which Garza operated.[29] Compared to the extensive literature on the U.S. West and the growth of U.S. border studies, the historiography of Mexico's northern frontier is small. The regionalization of Mexican history, especially after the 1960s, sparked an interest in the northern area and has also created a much more heterogeneous view of the country that is less centered on the capital city.[30] However, until recently, and with few exceptions, the best studies of northern Mexico focused on industrialization, mining, land, and governmental politics while paying little attention to culture, race, or gender.[31] Since the 1990s books exploring these cultural relations in greater depth suggest the beginnings of a new northern Mexican history. Of particular interest are the anthropologically based microhistories of Namiquipa, Chihuahua, by Ana Alonso and by Daniel Nugent; the culturally sensitive labor history of mining in Chihuahua by William French; and the richly detailed history of the Tomochic rebellion by Paul Vanderwood.[32] However, although these books are set in the border region they do not explicitly grapple with the meaning or development of the border. In contrast, Juan Mora-Torres's book on the mining industry in Nuevo

León, a state in northeastern Mexico, demonstrates that historians of Mexico's northern regions are also beginning to engage the borderlands as a concept.[33]

The folklorist and literary critic Américo Paredes foreshadowed and blazed the trail for the innovations in borderlands history that have begun to emerge since the late 1980s. His seminal work, *With His Pistol in His Hand* (1958), about an early twentieth-century border battle between a Mexican ranchero, Gregorio Cortez, and the Texas Rangers pioneered popular cultural criticism and brought to a wider audience a history that had not yet made its way into the history books. *With His Pistol in His Hand* also provided to me the original spark of recognition for this study: it was Paredes's inscription in his book to his father "who rode a raid or two with Catarino Garza," combined with my encounter with Garza's autobiography in the Benson Latin American Collection at the University of Texas, that set me off on this long intellectual journey. Anthropologist and cultural critic José Limón continued in Paredes's distinguished footsteps, bringing poststructural perspectives to his analysis of South Texas borderlands culture. Limón's insightful discussion of John Gregory Bourke, the U.S. Army captain who led the military campaign against Garza, helped me to recognize the significance of the ideological struggle over narrative that permeated Garza's revolt and its suppression.[34] Both Paredes's and Limón's imaginative analyses of borderlands expressive culture and its relationship to history inspired my work.

A distinguished and growing literature on the history of border rebellions, both preceding and following Garza's revolt, has allowed me to place Garza in a broader historical context. Although there have been several essays and short books exploring Juan Nepomuceno Cortina's border rebellions (1859–1870s), a full-length treatment of this important figure and his movement has yet to be written.[35] The analyses of the 1915 Plan de San Diego and the political activities of the anarchist Magón brothers in the United States (1904–1920s) by Dirk Raat, Juan Gómez Quiñones, and James Sandos have helped to put these crucial early-twentieth-century radical rebellions on the larger map of U.S. and Mexican history.[36] And finally, Linda Hall and Don Coerver's work on border rebellions and militarization during the first phase of the Mexican Revolution (1910–1920) explores the impact of this major event on the border region. Their book is also noteworthy for its use of U.S. as well as Mexican archives, and of both Spanish- and English-language sources, which provided the binational research model that I have tried to emulate here.[37]

Catarino Garza's revolt in 1891, which falls chronologically in the middle of this longer history of border rebellion (1859–1920), comes at a key moment in the transition of borderlands into border zones, from a semi-autonomous and coherent region to two regions increasingly incorporated into the activities, imaginations, and politics of nation-states. The history of Garza's revolt is a crucial link in the chain that can help us to understand how the border was made. The innovative and culturally sensitive histories of northern Mexico, the U.S. West, and the borderlands, and the simultaneous boom in borderlands literary criticism, have laid tracks on either side of the border, opening pathways to begin writing transnational histories such as this one on the Garza revolt.

Crossing these boundaries has not only changed border history but also influenced a simultaneous transnationalization of both Latin American and U.S. American studies. These new histories, which owe a great debt to the field of Chicano/a studies, have contributed to what literary critic José David Saldívar calls the "worlding" of American studies.[38] Latin American studies is undergoing a similar process where transnational connections, especially to the United States, are being studied and analyzed in original ways. While examining U.S.-Latin American relations is not new to diplomatic historians, what is new is the focus on culture.[39] This book follows along this promising path by exploring power relations in a particularly salient and contested space of American empire: the Texas-Mexico border.

In addition to crossing the national border, New Western and Mexicanist historians have been attempting to bridge the chronological divide that separated the study of colonial "frontier" regions from that of national border zones. In the early 1980s, Mexicanist historian Friedrich Katz proposed a "frontier to border" notion to explain the transition of northern Mexican states like Sonora, Chihuahua, and Coahuila from relatively isolated regions to ones that were "within the reach of two countries at once."[40] New Western historians have developed a similar framework for linking colonial and national historiographies, but they have been unable thus far to move beyond the confines of U.S. national boundaries and show the intricate links between the histories of the United States and Mexico.[41]

The establishment of national borders changes the context within which borderlanders act and interact, but transnational linkages do not evaporate or even necessarily diminish over time. Rather, it is the inability to theorize transnational relationships that has led to a dichotomous view where a region is either seen as a frontier or a border. As Jeremy Adelman and Stephen Aron argue, once the colonial borderlands gave way to national borders, "borderlanders became 'ethnics' — minorities distinguished by phenotype or language from the 'national' majority."[42] The ongoing and increasingly tight economic, political, and cultural connections between the United States and Mexico (and the rest of the Americas as well) shows us that rather than borderlanders becoming ethnics and ceasing to be borderlanders, they maintain hybrid borderland identities even after national borders have been established.[43] Garza's roles as a Mexican who struggled against U.S. imperialism and fought for Texas Mexican rights in the United States and for liberalism in Latin America exemplify the multidimensionality of borderlands identity — even forty years after the border was drawn. During the periodic moments of heightened nationalism and xenophobia (such as occurred in the United States in the 1910s, 1930s, 1950s, and 1990s), legal coercion and violence has been deployed to make "ethnics" choose "America" both in terms of citizenship and cultural assimilation.[44] In the face of a conservative anti-immigrant backlash to the 1990s, Mexicans (and other immigrants) have been rushing in record numbers to INS offices to fill out their U.S. citizenship applications. Such official declarations of national identity say a great deal about structural incentives, but they say almost nothing about people's lived identity. The vibrancy of a transnational borderlands identity, however, even amidst this xenophobic onslaught and militarization of the border, testifies to its strength and resilience.[45]

FORGING THE BORDER IN AN AGE OF EMPIRE

The rise of the nation-state and the expansion of imperialism in the late eighteenth and nineteenth centuries came hand in hand. In this era of modern mapmaking, men in the world's capital cities dragged their thin pens across small pieces of white paper, attached names to blank spaces, and defined entire continents. Cultural communities were carved up and divided and newly imagined communities were defined as nations. By the middle of the twentieth century, nationalism grew to be one of the most powerful forces in the world.[46] Even though the sentiment originated from above, it also took root from below. This global process of colonization and nation building had an especially profound impact on the Texas-Mexico border region. Not only does the drawing of this particular boundary stand out as one of the great geographical amputations of all times, but the continued crossings of the border illustrate the limits of erecting barriers through the middle of cultural and economic communities. A century and a half after the boundary line was established, the Mexicanization of the United States and the Americanization of Mexico continues apace. Culture, just like capital, has proven to be far more transnational than nationalist imaginations could have predicted.

Although several empires and nations laid claim to the borderlands region throughout its history, it was not until the early twentieth century that the United States and Mexico were able to make the boundary line an effective marker of difference. The Spanish Crown ruled over Texas and what is today the U.S. West for several hundred years until 1821 when Mexico gained its independence. In spite of this lengthy colonization process New Spain's northern frontier never gained the prominence of central Mexico, and for the most part it remained a defensive outpost, especially Texas, which suffered from anemic population growth.[47] In 1836, Anglo and Mexican settlers in Texas joined together to fight against Santa Anna's centralist government in Mexico. Desiring more autonomy and the continuation of slavery, Texans declared independence from Mexico and established their own republic. The southern boundaries of the republic, and later the state of Texas after it was annexed by the United States in 1845, extended only to the Nueces River (map 1). Nonetheless, with his eye on the rest of the continent, President James Polk sent troops to contest the strip of land between the Nueces and the Rio Grande in 1846. In the ensuing war, the U.S. Army occupied both Monterrey and Mexico City. Mexico's prostrate government was forced to sign the Treaty of Guadalupe Hidalgo in 1848, establishing the boundary line at the Rio Grande and ceding the entire northern half of its territory for the paltry sum of fifteen million dollars. While the official border was fixed by midcentury, the region between the Nueces and Rio Grande (what is today South Texas) remained thoroughly Mexicanized throughout the rest of the century, in terms of both its culture and economy. By the beginning of the twentieth century, however, the gravitational pull of both Mexico and the United States began to tear apart this transnational region.

When Catarino Garza was born on November 25, 1859, on a small farm outside of Matamoros, Benito Juárez was leading the country's greatest era of liberal reform. It was a tumultuous time marked by a bitter civil war between liberals and conservatives and punctuated by revolving-door presidents. The French, under Napoleon III, invaded and installed the Hapsburg Maximilian as emperor of Mexico in 1862. Although Juárez defeated

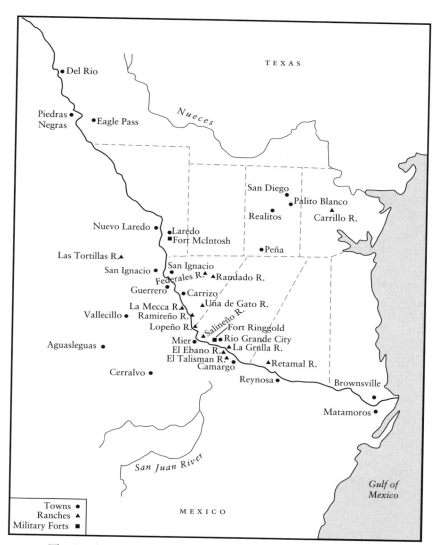

MAP 1. The South Texas–Mexico border region, early 1890s. Although the rail lines had linked up the United States and Mexican networks through Laredo in the early 1880s, the whole lower Rio Grande Valley was still not reachable by train, thus impeding efforts to track down and capture the Garzistas.

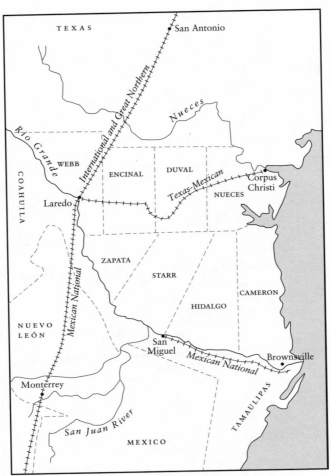

MAP 2. Railroads and political boundaries in
the South Texas–Mexico border region, early 1890s.

the French in 1867, another more powerful nation — the one that had
already taken half of Mexico's territory — loomed menacingly to the
north. Within Mexico, internecine squabbles among liberals kept the
country in turmoil for a decade until Díaz brought "peace" and stability in
1876. It was this authoritarian peace that Garza and other liberals rejected, especially when it became clear in the beginning of the 1890s that
Díaz intended to ignore his no-reelection pledge and install himself as
perpetual dictator of Mexico.[48]

Garza launched his rebellion in 1891 amid political and economic upheaval on the border. His revolt was bracketed by two other major border

insurrections: Juan Cortina's raids on Texas beginning in 1859 and an ill-fated 1915 revolt in South Texas led by Mexicans.[49] Juan Cortina was a Mexican who was active along the South Texas border from 1859 through the 1870s. Cortina's killing of Anglo Americans who had abused Mexicans, along with his repeated raids into Texas, expressed the frustration of a community whose displacement began when the U.S. Army invaded the region. Like other legendary folk heroes such as Joaquín Murieta in California, Cortina was seen as a "bandit" by Anglos and a Robin Hood–type hero by Mexicans.[50] Cortina even briefly served as governor of the Mexican border state of Tamaulipas. His ability to continue his raiding for nearly two decades illustrates how little control central governments in either the United States or Mexico had over this remote region. It was not until Díaz came to power in 1876 that Cortina was jailed in Mexico City.[51]

The 1915 revolt, sparked by a manifesto entitled the Plan de San Diego, also sought to redress Mexican grievances against Anglos in Texas. The targeting of Anglos during the raids and the manifesto's call to kill adult North American males, suggests a racial aspect to this rebellion. However, as Benjamin Johnson shows in *Revolution in Texas*, many of the victims of rebel violence were Texas Mexican elites.[52] Furthermore, the acts of tearing up railroad tracks and burning irrigation pumping stations constituted a clear attack on capitalist development. Indeed, it is difficult to separate the racial and class aspects of this revolt. One leader of the revolt, Aniceto Pizaña, was active in the anarchist Partido Liberal Mexicano (PLM) of the Flores Magón brothers, and there is speculation that the Plan itself may have been inspired if not planned by the PLM.[53] The Plan aimed to reclaim the territory taken by the United States from Mexico in 1848, to create an independent republic for Latinos, to restore ancestral lands to indigenous people, and to kill every North American male over sixteen years old.[54] The radical and impractical aims of the Plan de San Diego represented a last desperate gasp to resolve Mexican grievances in the United States through armed rebellion. However, whereas Cortina's raids lasted nearly two decades, the Plan de San Diego was discovered before it was even launched, and the wave of repression that followed put an end to any further armed insurrections.

Between 1859 and 1915, the border was transformed. Anglos had taken over most of the land base in South Texas, northeastern Mexico's caudillos had been tamed by the central government, and the entire regional economy was in the process of full-scale industrialization and commercialization. It was in this context of dramatic economic and political change that the South Texas–northeastern Mexico border region became the preeminent staging ground for many of Mexico's major rebellions in the second half of the nineteenth century. The availability of weapons in the United States and the political geography that provided would-be revolutionaries and counterrevolutionaries in Texas with some degree of protection from the reigning powers in Mexico helps explain why such rebellious activity came from the Texas border. That said, the political and economic changes that caused resentment and impoverishment among Mexicans also created a pool of potential recruits for their insurrections. From this small corner of Texas, Benito Juárez and Melchor Ocampo organized their liberal revolt against the conservative Santa Anna in the early 1850s, Porfirio Díaz launched his revolt against President Lerdo de Tejada in 1876, and Lerdo de Tejada in turn rebelled against Díaz one year later.[55] Mexican rebellions spanning the entire ideological spectrum continued to be launched from the Texas border in the early twentieth century. Incursions by anarchist Magonistas and liberal Maderistas, followers of Mexico's first postrevolution president, Francisco Madero, set in motion a full-scale social revolution by 1911, and the Porfirista General Bernardo Reyes organized his counterrevolutionary movement, all from the same region of Texas.[56] Out of this long process of conflict, violence, miscegenation, and social bonding, the border finally emerged as both a barrier and a bridge between nations.

Eminent historian Friedrich Katz has argued that the northern region of Mexico played such a large role in the revolution because it was the only area that was able to forge a multiclass anti-Díaz movement. This coalition of hacendados, middle-class professionals, miners, and peasants allowed northerners to not only topple Díaz but hold onto the reins of government through at least twenty years of spasmodic insurrections. The tradition of frontier independence and cooperation between hacendados and peasants that had developed from a century of fighting Apaches created the conditions for revolution in a way that the paternalistic bonds linking peons and hacendados in the rest of Mexico did not. While the northern peasantry joined anti-Díaz hacendados like Madero, they were also quite willing to abandon recalcitrant landowners like Terrazas to join revolutionary armies. Porfirian development ultimately undermined the balance that had held frontier society together and kept it loyal to the center. The disproportionate investment of foreign capital in the North, the close links to the U.S. economy, and the concentration of land in a few hands resulted in losses for peasants, workers, and the middle classes, especially after the 1907 economic crisis. Encroachment on peasant land-holdings sparked sporadic peasant revolts in the North throughout the late nineteenth century, including the large-scale rebellion in Tomochic in Chihuahua (1891) and the Yaqui Indian rebellions in Sonora. Katz argues that such outbursts did not assume "revolutionary proportions" because the nonrural classes, who were benefiting from the Porfirian economy up until 1900, did not join them.[57] The multiclass support for Garza's 1891 insurrection, including some of northern Mexico's wealthiest caudillos and military generals, foreshadows the sort of alliance that ultimately crystallized in 1910. As Garza's revolt got underway, many of Garza's backers, especially the caudillos, generals, and large landowners, decided that the revolution's debut was premature. For the next twenty years, this multiclass coalition would continue to rehearse in the shadows until the curtain was finally raised in 1910 on what became the first social revolution of the twentieth century.

RACE, NATION, AND GENDER

Officially, Garza's revolt was directed against Díaz, but in practice the Garzistas organized and ended up fighting most of their battles on Texas soil against U.S. authorities. Thus, what was ostensibly a political struggle in Mexico also expressed Anglo-Mexican tensions in Texas over land and political power. While only Juan Cortina's raids and the 1915 Plan de San Diego specifically targeted Anglos in Texas in their official proclamations, there was an undeniable racial element to Garza's movement. When the Garzistas turned their guns on the U.S. military and the Texas Rangers, they were in part venting their frustrations at being dispossessed by Anglos. At a more abstract level, the Garzistas turned their weapons against both governments because both were engaged in a similar project of capitalist development and nation building that cut directly into the autonomy and power of borderlanders. The Garzistas's literal and metaphorical crisscrossing of the boundary line exposed the limits of a border that was supposed to divide Mexico from the United States and Mexicans from "Americans." The everyday practices of walking or swimming across the border, smuggling contraband, maintaining family ties and keeping up on politics in both countries created an alternative reality to that imposed by the treaty makers and cartographers.[58]

The border not only separated two nations but also fundamentally divided two ethnoracial groups, Mexicans and Anglo Americans. Although they had a distinctive identity, the Tejanos who had lived in the region before the border was established were slowly being lumped by Anglos into the Mexican category as the border became more of a reality. Just as nations are imposed from above and resisted from below, so too are ethnoracial labels. The inability to fit border people into the American (read Anglo)/Mexican, white/brown polarity constantly frustrated U.S. Army officers. The most common nomenclature in the United States continues to locate people in an ethnoracial pentagon consisting of five discrete units: white (northern European), black (African), red (Indian), yellow (Asian), and brown (Latin).[59] While these categories have been used in both scholarly discourse and everyday practice and therefore cannot easily be dismissed, they do not reflect the complexity and heterogeneity within each group or the overlapping between them. The situation is further complicated by the fact that on the border two distinct racial discourses, one from Mexico and the other from the United States, functioned simultaneously. In Mexico, the presence and legitimacy of a *mestizo* (mixed) identity, generally understood as a mixture of Spaniards and Indians, allowed for more flexibility than the rigid black-white-Indian triad that held sway in most of the United States. That said, a racial heirarchy continued to exist in Mexico that located "whiter" people with European phenotypes higher on the social, material, and political ladder than darker people with Indian, African, or Asian features. Mexican and U.S. racial discourses thus shared some key assumptions, such as the glorification of whiteness and the denigration of blackness, but they also differed in fundamental ways, especially in terms of how mestizaje was viewed.[60] In short, the location of Mexicans (and Latin Americans in general) in the U.S. racial scheme caused much confusion in the late nineteenth century, just as it does today.

On one level, there was a simple ethnoracial distinction on the late-nineteenth-century border between Anglo Americans (white) and Mexicans (brown). Yet much is glossed over and hidden by such a stark dichotomy. Many elite Mexicans and Tejanos, for instance, considered themselves and were considered by others to be white. Similarly, Irish, Italian, and French Americans do not fit well into either side of the Anglo/Mexican polarity.[61] The Mexican label also hides the true diversity of a community that included recent immigrants, U.S. and non-U.S. citizens, and families whose Tejano roots stretched back to the Spanish colonial era. In spite of these limitations, in this volume I will employ the shorthand terms Anglo and Mexican because this duality existed and was perceived by border people even if it did not accurately represent their complex mestizaje.[62] Further, by the beginning of the twentieth century the flexibility and complexity of the borderlands racial paradigm was eroding and being replaced by a simple hierarchy: Anglo Americans on top, Mexicans on the bottom. When relevant, I try to qualify these crude labels by providing a more complete picture of an individual's ethnic background and class status. For instance, it is important to note that Captain Bourke of the U.S. Army was Catholic and of Irish descent in order to understand his particular relationship to Mexicans, but he still served the broader Anglo American project of capitalist development and "Americanization" of the lower Rio Grande Valley. The finer distinctions of ethnoracial identity often were lost in the desperate moments of barroom brawls and backcountry shoot-outs when one was most likely to be lumped into one of two categories: "gringo" or "greaser."[63]

Although Garza invoked race as a motivating factor for his personal and political activities, he and his opponents staked their claim to honor even more frequently. Honor was at the center of Garza's political battle for borderlands autonomy, for liberalism in Mexico, and in defense of the rights of Mexicans in the United States. Honor was also the main category he used to claim respectability in his personal relationships with women and men and in his career as a journalist. Garza's autobiography, which he started writing two years before his insurrection, highlighted the importance of masculine honor to his personal and political struggles. For Garza, having honor meant being strong, protecting women from brutish men (often Anglo Americans in his stories), and defending the nation from foreign invasion (again from Anglo Americans). Although Garza recognized that women played important supporting roles in his political movement, the leading roles, the protagonists, were supposed to be played by men. These same notions of honor and cultural respectability, and the emphasis on being *gente culta* (a cultured person), figured prominently in northern Mexican society and politics.[64] While there were a whole host of structural economic and political reasons why Garza launched his revolution when he did, his public attack in a newspaper on General Bernardo Reyes's mother provided the spark that led to the conflict. Maintaining masculine honor was therefore not just a reflection of other political battles but was itself a central part of the political struggle. Honor was the coin of the realm by which one measured one's wealth, poverty, and manliness.

The border is a place of confusion where cultures collide, where races meet, where nations rub up against each other with barbed-wire fences and well-guarded bridges. To capture this border reality requires a twilight perspective, one that allows for the ambiguities and complexities of identity and resists assumed categories of race, nation, gender, or class. My aim here is to evoke the evolving shades that have too often been blanched by the floodlights of social science, and to allow the reader to become part of the interpretive act.[65] The good guys do not wear white or black hats in this story, and many characters switch their hats with a frequency that would make the most cynical double agent blush. So many of the accounts of the Garza rebellion fall into an easy dichotomy of good and evil, revolutionary hero and opportunistic bandit, that it is tempting to just choose sides and erase the complexity. While I do want to show that Garza was a revolutionary and not a bandit, I also want to portray him as he was — a human with personal shortcomings, a developing political consciousness, hints of racist and sexist attitudes, and an overblown sense of his own importance. Yet, with all of these human frailties, Garza showed remarkable consistency in remaining true to a liberal political project for his entire adult life and ultimately dying for his beliefs.

Without a nation to build monuments to him and inscribe him into its mythology, Garza's memory has faded like many others whose stories do not fit easily into national narratives or boundaries. Garza and his thousands of followers may have lost their battles in the early 1890s, but their struggle, which continues today, helped forge a transnational borderlands society that over a century later is stronger than ever.

1. THE MAKING OF A REVOLUTIONARY

Mi pluma no sabe pintar, pero si reproducir,

fotografiar y estampar verdades. (My pen

knows not how to paint, rather it reproduces,

photographs and prints truths.) — Catarino

Garza, "La lógica de los hechos"

Catarino Garza did not become a revolutionary by picking up a gun, but rather by writing himself into the role. Along with his explicitly political activities and writings (manifestos, newspaper articles, etc.) he wove his life story into a narrative that proclaimed himself as a revolutionary protagonist. While only brief traces of Garza's speeches and journalism have survived, a full-length unpublished autobiography, which he was working on when his revolt broke out, has been preserved at the Benson Latin American Collection at the University of Texas, Austin. In this chapter I highlight Garza's autobiography as a site of struggle. Nonnarrative activities, including barroom brawls, fence cutting, train derailing, lynching, and armed revolts, were also decisive and powerful expressions of political power. My argument here is that the stories that border people told about themselves and about Anglo Americans, Europeans, and "others" were central to their own political struggles.

Edward Said makes a similar observation about the importance of the novel to imperialism and anticolonial struggles. "Stories," Said contends, "are at the heart of what explorers and novelists say about strange regions of the world; they also become the method colonized people use to assert their own identity and the existence of their own history. The main battle of imperialism is over land, of course; but when it came to who owned the land, who had the right to settle and work on it, who kept it going, who won it back, and who now plans its future—these issues were reflected, contested and even for a time decided in narrative."[1] Before rushing on to look at the physical battles over land, however, let us pause to analyze the narrative struggle.

There is a complex relationship between narrative (novels, travel accounts, autobiography, journalism) and political action (armed revolts, strikes, public protest), which is similar to that between culture and economic structures. Mechanical causal explanations that view narrative as a mere reflection of politics, or vice versa, obscure more than they reveal. Academic disciplinary boundaries that separate and analyze word and deed in isolation from one another contribute to the inability to see the subtle and multifaceted connections between the two. Although disciplinary borders have become more porous of late, literary and art critics still tend to read and comment on texts and art objects in isolation from their political and historical contexts, while historians and sociologists cite novels and other artistic expressions merely as reflections of a preexisting sociopolitical reality. My aim here is to bridge the artificial divide between literary and historical analysis, and between art and politics, by showing the web of relationships that tie Garza's literary work to his political action and vice versa.

There is a moment in the long road to revolution when the oppressed finally raise picket signs, hurl rocks, or fire guns. This is the moment of open rebellion, and it does not happen often. When Garza declared his revolution on the banks of the Rio Grande in September 1891, it was just such a gesture of liberation. It would be mistaken, however, to seek the meaning of Garza's revolution, or any revolution for that matter, by only analyzing the actual event—that is, the armed actions, the manifestos, and the constitutions that may follow. The outbreak of violence in any revolt is like the tip of an iceberg. Most of an iceberg lies beneath the water, and thus one must dive beneath the surface in order to get a sense of its size and shape. Similarly, to see the foundations of a rebellion one must dive beneath the surface of society. I am not proposing a materialist analysis where one focuses on the foundation, usually conceived of as an economic structure, and then assumes that the cultural superstructure merely reflects the material base. Rather, I am suggesting that this is a false dichotomy and that the art of remembering and analyzing the past is a necessary foundation for revolution or for any other extraordinary activity.

The histories that all individuals make for themselves, often not in written form, serve as a guide to present action by making a coherent narrative out of past experiences and knowledge. Garza's analysis of border society and his organic links to its communities enabled him to forge a coalition of anti-Porfirian Mexicans in South Texas and to begin to imagine himself as a political leader. As a founder of several *mutualistas* (mutual aid societies), and as a public orator and a journalist, Garza helped to construct the vibrant late-nineteenth-century working-class culture that historian Emilio Zamora has described so vividly.[2] At the same time, Garza was as much a product of this broader cultural context as he was its initiator. Masonic lodges, mutualistas, and small Spanish-language newspapers created a social network that formed the basis for political organization. Even though many mutualistas explicitly prohibited political discussions in their meetings, Garza communicated his anti-Díaz message and his defense of Mexicans in the United States, as well as organized his armed rebellion through these networks. The multiclass nature of these Texas Mexican organizations, including workers, merchants, lower-middle-class professionals, and other prominent members of the community, mirrored the coalition that Garza would ultimately cobble together for his revolt.

One of the key characteristics of both the mutualistas and Garza's writing is the emphasis on the need to inculcate a developmentalist ethic stressing middle-class values of thrift, sobriety, hygiene, hard work, and patriarchal roles. As William French shows in his analysis of northern Mexico, the emerging Porfirian middle class employed this developmentalist ideology to discipline workers and to distinguish themselves, the gente culta, from the growing floating population of rural and urban laborers. At the same time, artisans and employees organized in mutualistas claimed their status as gente culta as well; they were proud to be workers but they went to great lengths to distinguish themselves from the floating population of unskilled laborers. This ideology also attempted to reinforce patriarchal gender relationships that were being challenged as more and more women worked in urban and industrial settings. In particular, the Porfirian educational project hoped to produce good daughters, wives, and mothers, but it also emphasized practical vocational training in what were considered "feminine" pursuits: typing, sewing, dressmaking, and household duties.[3] Garza carried this developmentalist ethic with him to South Texas, where it violently clashed with a masculinist and racially discriminatory Anglo worldview. At the same time that Garza was trying to assert his cultural respectability and masculinity in the face of a rapidly changing northern Mexican society, he was also confronting Anglo Texans who saw him as uneducated, uncultured, and less virile simply because he was Mexican. Garza's autobiography describes his defense of honor and masculinity in order to legitimize himself to a northern Mexican audience, to respond to the discrimination faced by Mexicans in Texas, and to justify revolt and political action.

Garza's autobiography begins with a description of his arrival in 1877 in Brownsville, Texas, and covers the twelve subsequent years he spent living and working in different towns along the border and in St. Louis, Missouri. In the volume's dedication and preface Garza explains that the work should not be read as art or literature but as history or the narration of actual events. "I am basing my hopes," he writes, "not in the aptitude of my pen, but in the security that I faithfully fulfill my duty as a Mexican on foreign soil of narrating the circumstances of our nationals in this country."[4] His autobiography, titled "La lógica de los hechos: O sean observaciones sobre las circunstancias de los mexicanos en Texas, desde el año de 1877 hasta 1889" (The logic of events: Observations on the circumstances of Mexicans in Texas, from 1877 until 1889) served as part of his ongoing defense of Mexicans in Texas (fig. 2). In 1888, he felt the urgency to write a history of the last twelve years of his life because he was afraid that he would be killed, either by agents of Porfirio Díaz or by hostile Anglos. His autobiography, he believed, would allow his voice and his explanation of events to resonate even after his death. More immediately, he hoped that it would publicize the difficult plight of Mexicans in Texas and "arouse the zeal of the representatives of my country."[5] The 431-page handwritten manuscript stops abruptly in 1888, leaving unfinished chapters and blank pages where Garza intended to include photographs. John Gregory Bourke, the U.S. Army captain who led the campaign against Garza, discovered the manuscript under Garza's bed in one of his raids on Garza's headquarters in Palito Blanco. Years after the revolt, Captain Bourke derided the autobiography for its "sickening tone of eulogy."[6] Such a harsh judgment must be put in perspective as the bitter recriminations of a man who had failed in his campaign to capture Garza, and who was ultimately chased out of South Texas by Garza's supporters.

In spite of its incomplete form and the fact that it was never published, "La lógica" helps to sketch out Garza's life before the revolution and, most important, it provides invaluable insight into the way Garza conceived of the world and of himself. A loose note at the back of the manuscript gives the dictionary definition of the title. "La lógica: The science

2. A page from the introduction to Catarino
Garza's autobiography, "La lógica de los hechos."
(Courtesy of the Benson Latin American Collec-
tion, University of Texas, Austin)

that teaches how to reflect and reason precisely by means of methodical
deductions. . . . Natural disposition to reflect and judge without the help of
art."[7] Rather than an imaginative literary narrative, Garza framed his
autobiography as the product of cool, methodical reasoning, a reflection
on reality without the influence of art. Thus, even though he wrote a
personal narrative as well as a collective one, Garza denied the individu-
ality of his writing by identifying himself as a "son of the people" whose
mission was to "educate the masses."[8] Effacing his own literary and artistic skills allowed him to claim that he merely reproduced a story made by
el pueblo (the people). "You will not find in all of these writings," he
proclaims, "one elegant phrase, nor delicate images, nor erudite phrases,
much less literary portrayals, because my pen does not know how to
paint, rather it reproduces, photographs and prints truths."[9] The identification of his writing with modern technologies of reproduction, pho-
tography, and printing allowed him to deny his artistry and therefore his

Making of a Revolutionary 29

subjectivity.[10] He thus insisted that his autobiography not be seen as an autonomous piece of art but as a product of a community and a historical process.

Garza's subjectivity can be seen, however, in his choosing to include particular events and to omit or downplay other episodes. Using the autobiographical form had other consequences as well, such as making his individual story dominate the collective one and allowing him space to discuss aspects of his personal life. Like the genre of Latin American *testimonio* literature, Garza's story is both a political and personal one.[11] Louis Mendoza's *Historia*, which examines the literary making of Chicana/o history, demonstrates that even as we make distinctions between literature (the imaginative reconstruction of the past) and history (the "factual" retelling of the past), the line between the two forms of narrative is exceedingly blurry.[12] While Garza rarely used the impersonal third person, he wanted his text to speak for a shared Texas Mexican experience, a history of his people. Just like the framing, cropping, and composition of any photograph, Garza's autobiography did not simply reproduce the "truth" or a story made by "el pueblo." Rather, he was creating a "truth" based on a northern Mexican developmentalist ethic to promote himself as a central protagonist in an ongoing political struggle both in Mexico and in the United States. The autobiography should thus be read as both literature and history.

JOURNALIST, BUSINESSMAN, REVOLUTIONARY

Little biographical information is known about the early part of Catarino Garza's life, with the exception of the details he included in his autobiography and in a letter he wrote to his wife from exile. Nonetheless, that information combined with other accounts by relatives, friends, and even enemies yields a fairly good picture of his background before the revolution. All versions agree that Garza was not born into privilege. For the first ten years of his life he had apparently not even picked up a book because he was helping his parents, Encarnación and Doña María de Jesús Rodríguez, to raise vegetables and fruit on their farm and to run a dairy. Garza's rendition of his youth highlighted his poverty, his lack of educational opportunities, and his need to work to pay for his books and schooling. Eventually, however, it was possible for him to escape the work routine of the farm in the mornings and study for four hours a day at a nearby ranch. He exhibited such promise as a student that a respected teacher and former priest from Hualahuises, Nuevo León, agreed to tutor the young Garza. This teacher, José María Morales, also gave him some military training, and the writing and military skills that Garza picked up from the ex-priest would prove invaluable in his future career as a revolutionary journalist. On his return to Matamoros, Garza enrolled in the Colegio de San Juan and also briefly served in the Mexican National Guard at the Port Plaza.[13]

Catarino was just eighteen years old in 1877 when he crossed the border from his hometown of Matamoros in Mexico to Brownsville, located at the southeastern tip of Texas.[14] He began working as a clerk at a local drygoods store, Bloomberg and Raphael, which sold shoes, boots, and groceries. The fact that one of the owners was a Spaniard (Raphael) and the other from New York City (Bloomberg) indicates the degree to which the border was already integrated into the international market economy by the late 1870s.[15] Job opportunities on the U.S. side were certainly more attractive than in Mexico, and Garza was not alone in making this move.

Like an anthropologist describing his arrival in the field, the opening chapter of "La lógica," titled "Pluma en desorden" (Pen in disorder), begins with Garza's entry into Texas. Garza's first encounter with the "native" Anglo Texans immediately implicated him in a history that preceded his arrival.[16] As he crossed the border from Matamoros into Brownsville, a U.S. customs official stopped him and, without any cause, emptied all of his belongings onto the floor. After rifling through Garza's clothes, the customs guard simply said "all right." Garza describes this episode ironically and notes the impolite speech of the customs official by consciously mistranslating the English "all right" for the Spanish "dispense Vd. la molestia," a formal way of saying "sorry to have bothered you." In the next clause, Garza makes it clear to his readers that everything was not all right "given the disorder in which he left my clothes."[17] Although Garza claims the authoritative voice of an impartial observer who merely "reproduced and photographed" reality, it becomes readily apparent in this first episode that Garza could not extricate himself from the story, nor view it from a neutral vantage point. Throughout "La lógica" Garza stresses that he, and Mexicans in general, had better manners than the coarse and rude *americanos* (read Anglos) with whom he had contact. His insistence on the respectability, dignity, and decency of Mexicans must be understood within a context where Anglos claimed superiority on these same grounds. The middle-class ethic in northern Mexico to which Garza subscribed also emphasized cultural respectability. Thus, culture and custom became the ideological battleground on which Garza strove to prove the equality of Anglo Americans and Mexicans, if not the superiority of the latter.

Even though Garza directed his main criticism against rude Anglos, he also found fault with Mexican Americans who betrayed their Mexican culture and "sold out" to the Anglos. Mexicans living in the United States, according to this view, were contaminated by their contact with Anglos and had lost their roots and their national culture. Even though most Brownsville residents were of Mexican origin, Garza declared that "the customs of those inhabitants can be said to be neither Mexican nor American, because they are so unrefined, that they treat each other like savages."[18] Worse than having assimilated another culture, Brownsville's population lived in a third space, a savage space between or beyond national cultures. This critique of a border culture, neither Mexican nor American, illustrates just how strongly Garza, himself a product of the border, believed in the idea of national culture.

What most bothered him, however, was the servile role played by Mexican American political leaders, and the way in which the Mexican vote was manipulated. The "unity of the *razas* [race or people]" that was on display on the few days surrounding the elections glossed over, for him, the segregation of the Mexican and "American" communities during the rest of the year. Garza even accused Brownsville's political clubs, the Popular México-Texano (azul blue) and the Democrático México-Texano (colorado red), of being "presided over by people of Mexican origin and governed by different groups of Americans, who, shielded by the leaders of the people, have always made it into a servile instrument."[19] What he meant was that even though the Democratic (blue) and Republican (red) parties fielded local Mexican candidates, they were being directed behind the scenes by Anglo power brokers.[20] This criticism of machine politics and the boss system would later become a key campaign issue for both Anglo and Mexican progressive-era reformers in South Texas.[21]

Specifically, Garza complained about what he saw as the degrading practice of bringing Mexicans over to Texas a few days before an election to make them into U.S. citizens so they could vote. Aside from having to lie by saying that they had been in the United States for one year, they also had to swear to defend the United States against any enemy, even Mexico. But what was most upsetting for Garza was that these Mexican voters would show up drunk at the voting booth after a night of revelry that was paid for by the "political speculators."[22] "What a shame to have to say that Mexico has been the country of these degraded beings," he lamented; "Mexico is badly judged because of the immigrants to this country."[23] Like Garza, northern Mexican reformers also pointed to the consumption of alcohol by workers as the cause of degradation, crime, and immorality in the working class.[24] Although Garza judged these Mexicans harshly, employing the same stereotypes used by Anglo Texans and his northern Mexican counterparts, he also sought always to find the deeper causes for their apparent degradation.

Garza held Mexicans to a high standard, expecting them to be more respectable and polite than their Anglo counterparts, but he also recognized the difficult challenges they faced in Texas. In addition to his own experiences with racist insults and violence, he was well aware of the process by which Anglos had appropriated Mexican land, both legally and illegally. He thus applauded the "great number of Mexicans who have known how to maintain their nationality and who reside in this state for their interests or that of their families, suffering the unjust depravities of hundreds of ambitious Texans, who by illegal means and with the help of corrupt public officials take over their properties."[25] Therefore, while Garza, like a northern Mexican moralizing reformer, condemned aspects of Mexican American society, he moved beyond that critique and recognized that the "degraded" state of Mexicans in Texas had more to do with a history of Anglo oppression and colonization than it did with inherent Mexican depravity. Unlike many middle-class reformers, he understood that the problem was structural and could not be solved solely through education and moral regulation.

"WE MEXICANS . . . HAVE PURER BLOOD THAN THE AMERICANS"

In his autobiography Garza shows himself as a defender of Mexicans in Brownsville. His first public effort to defend Mexicans in Texas was through a letter to the editor of a local Spanish-language newspaper. According to Garza's autobiography, he became embroiled in a public scandal after he wrote the letter protesting the racial insults of an Anglo American lawyer. Ties between the twin border towns of Brownsville and Matamoros were cut after Matamoros refused to stop rail traffic from Veracruz, the site of an outbreak of yellow fever in Mexico.[26] The workers of Brownsville (presumably mostly Mexican) called a meeting to ask for free passage between the cities; some of these workers lived on the Mexican side of the river and most had families there. According to what Garza had been told about the meeting, an Anglo lawyer, Rossell, argued that the quarantine should not be lifted because of the danger that yellow fever from Matamoros would spread to Brownsville. "It does not matter to us if it hurts the working people or if they die of hunger," Rossell said, "what we should see to is that yellow fever does not invade us, because some American could die, and as 'one white is worth more than ten Mexicans'; this is why I protest against the idea of lifting the quarantine."[27] The lawyer thus racialized the yellow fever epidemic, seeing it as a distinctly Mexican invasion that threatened "white" lives. As in the fear of racial miscegenation, Mexicans were coded as a diseased population that posed a contamination risk to Anglos. Similar racial discourses backed by the ideology of scientific medicine were penetrating every corner of the globe, allowing European and Anglo American empires to assert their supremacy over less-powerful countries and populations at the most intimate level: the body.[28]

In addition to trying to illustrate the racism of Anglo Texans, Garza's description of this episode highlighted his willingness to stand up to defend Mexicans. It was only after there were no signs of protest about the lawyer's remark, according to the autobiography, that Garza responded in a Spanish-language newspaper. When he showed a draft of his letter to the Mexican consul, he was advised not to publish it because he might be punished or, at the very least, lose his job. Garza persisted, however, taking on the lawyer directly in his letter. Men like Rossell, Garza derided, "do not deserve to be admitted into *sociedad culta* [civilized society] because of course they ride roughshod over courtesy, delicacy, and their own self-respect."[29] He continued the attack, declaring that "this white lawyer who villainously lies in asserting that one American is worth more than ten Mexicans, should know that in the house of Bloomberg and Raphael there is one Mexican (without being black) who can prove in any terrain that he is worth as much as him or any other of his cohort."[30] Garza, who worked in Bloomberg and Raphael's trading company, thus challenged "this white lawyer" to a fight to defend the dignity and honor of Mexicans. Although Garza quite ably defended Mexicans with his words, he also wanted to present himself as ready and willing to fight physically for their rights. Garza expressed his desire to "throw down the glove" in his autobiography, referring to the symbolic way to initiate a challenge to a duel.[31] Resorting to this ritualized form of defending masculine honor illustrates the degree to which Garza's ethnoracial identity (his Mexican-ness) was linked to his gender identity (his masculinity).

Beyond asserting his masculine honor, his challenge also claimed racial equality with whites. However, in his response to the lawyer he inserted the parenthetical statement "(without being black)," implying that although Mexicans were on the same level as whites, he considered blacks a different matter. The parenthetical reference might also be read as a critique of a U.S. racial system that lumped white Mexicans together with African Americans, but it seems as likely that Garza was claiming his own whiteness. The parenthetical phrase here along with others elsewhere are particularly interesting because they show how Garza tried to specify racial and national categories that were often confused in common parlance. Garza repeats Rossell's comment "a white is worth more than ten Mexicans" three different times in his autobiography. The first time, referring to Rossell's speech at the meeting, he writes "un blanco" (one white). The second time, recounting his discussion with the Mexican consul, he writes, "un blanco" followed by the parenthetical explanation "(americano)." The third time, in his letter to the newspaper, he simply writes "un americano."[32] If we assume that Garza accurately quoted the lawyer and himself, then the lawyer used the racial term "white" to stand in for "American," while Garza changed it to the national term "American" for his public letter. His reference to his conversation with the Mexican consul indicates that he understood that Rossell meant "American" when he said "white," but Garza's refusal to cede the "white" label to Americans suggests that he desired to claim whiteness for certain Mexicans.

In spite of his critique of Anglo supremacy, Garza seems to have internalized some of the dominant racial ideology that valued lighter over darker skin. On one occasion when he met two Spaniards in St. Louis, he described one as a young man "with courteous manners despite being a Moro, that is to say from Morroco, Tangiers."[33] While the comment was explicitly meant as a compliment, this off-handed description suggests that Garza believed that darker people could be expected to be less civilized than their lighter counterparts. His surprise at finding a darker-complexioned person, such as the Moro, to be so friendly and courteous thus sheds light on some of Garza's own racial prejudices. The use of the term "Moro" also invokes the historical memory of the Reconquista (722–1492) in which Spain pushed the Moroccans out of the Iberian Peninsula. Such a reference would not have been lost on someone like Garza, who was born in a town called "Matamoros," literally meaning killer of Moroccans. Garza's statement could be read as a valorization of Spain's African heritage by claiming cultural equality for the "Moro" he met. However, even as he railed against racial discrimination directed toward Mexicans and spoke well of this particular "Moro," he did not radically question prevailing views of black barbarism and white superiority.

The racial tensions that had simmered ever since the U.S. occupation of the region occasionally boiled over in episodes such as the one with the lawyer, manifesting themselves in public fights between individual Anglos and Mexicans, and riots or localized rebellions against Anglo and African American authorities. As the socioeconomic basis of the region's fragile peace came undone at the end of the nineteenth century, the frequency and intensity of these incidents grew. Garza's account of this exchange with the white lawyer highlights three important elements: Anglo racism, his own subtle racial prejudice, and his role as the sole defender of Mexicans. Although the meeting had been called by Mexican workers eager to keep open the border, Garza's narration of the event turns this collective protest into one that focuses on his own courageous actions as the only leader willing to stand up to the Anglo lawyer by challenging him to a duel if necessary to defend his masculine honor and the honor of all Mexicans.

The open letter to the lawyer was Garza's first piece of published writing, and it launched his career as a journalist and community activist. Perhaps Garza responded to the "white" lawyer in a Spanish-language newspaper rather than an English-language one because he was more comfortable writing in Spanish, or because he wanted to reach a Mexican readership, or because it may have been the only outlet to which he had access. In fact, Garza even had to pay the editor five pesos to publish his letter in the paper. Publishing in Spanish did not protect Garza, however, and an English-language newspaper quickly picked up on his letter and criticized him for his ironic tone.[34] The printed exchange between English and Spanish-language border newspapers suggests that there was a degree of communication between the reading publics. It was, nevertheless, a dialogue made difficult by a gap between Spanish and English that allowed for mistranslations or misinterpretations.[35] From this auspicious start, as Garza put it, "I had a love of this harsh career of journalism."[36] Garza went on to found two mutual-aid societies in Brownsville, La Sociedad Juárez and La Sociedad Hidalgo, and to coedit a newspaper *El Bien Público*. These mutualistas, which were emerging throughout the border region, were vital institutions, providing Mexicans with health and death benefits and a space for cultural expression.[37] According to Garza, writing about corruption in the Mexican American community and about racism in the Anglo community made him and his colleagues the target of harassment. Leon A. Obregón, one of the co-editors of La Sociedad Juárez's newspaper *El Bien Público*, had even allegedly suffered an assassination attempt at the hands of the newspaper's enemies. His life was supposedly saved only because a bundle of newspapers he carried in his bag prevented the assassin's knife from puncturing his chest. Garza himself claimed cavalierly not to have been intimidated by such threats, and they certainly did not stop him from writing provocative articles such as "The Right of Citizenship," which chastised as *renegados* (renegades) those Mexicans who sold their votes for money.[38] While raising such controversial issues in their newspaper awoke "enthusiasm in some [and] curiosity in others," Garza admitted that it inspired "hate in most."[39] However, it was just this image of the underdog hero, misunderstood and hated by society, that Garza was trying so hard to paint.

In "La lógica" Garza notes that there was animosity toward him from within the Mexican community, but he highlights the obnoxious insults that he suffered at the hands of Anglo Texans. One such incident occurred at the opera house in Brownsville, where he was harassed by a group of Anglos who were throwing orange peels at him. After Garza confronted the Anglos and one admitted to having thrown the peels, Garza grabbed his arm and led him outside. As he saw the Anglo reaching for his revolver, Garza pulled out his own pistol. "When this one saw the barrel of my gun in contact with his chest," Garza boasted, "he did what most Texans do, he screamed and repented in a most cowardly manner."[40] While this may have been a typical case of rowdy Texans at the opera, Garza attributed the orange peel harassment to the work that he was doing to "socially elevate the Mexican raza."[41]

From Garza's first contact with the Brownsville customs agent all the way through his twelve years in the United States, his autobiography depicts a heroic lone defender of Mexican dignity against Anglo insults and offenses. The detailed descriptions of these incidents of racial conflict provided both the context for understanding the plight of Mexicans in Texas, as well as a story line where the Mexican always defeats the Anglo. While Garza's narrative is clearly self-serving and at times seems exaggerated, the well-documented history of Anglo racism toward Mexicans in

Texas lends credibility to his account.[42] From the corroborating evidence that exists, it appears as if Garza took real episodes and then narrated them to highlight his own role as the heroic protagonist.

Anglos were the main source of racial conflict for Mexicans on the border, but they were not the only ones. After being treated badly by the Anglo customs guard on his way into Brownsville, Garza found himself working with Spaniards who also had a low opinion of Mexicans. The autobiography recounts how one of Garza's Spanish fellow workers remarked that "if the Spaniards had not conquered Mexico they would still be running through the countryside with a diaper and a shield."[43] The Spaniards thus implied that if they had not conquered Mexico, it would still be inhabited by "savage" and infantlike Indians. Although Garza found this comment particularly insulting, he ignored it and ended up becoming the Spaniard's friend. Later in his narrative, Garza criticized the effect of colonialism on the Mexican people. "In Mexico our tradition," he asserted, "was one of servitude and mistakes, born in the colonial power that based itself or wanted to base itself on the lack of communication with the foreigner, [and] in the legitimacy of slavery." Garza thus blamed the colonial powers of Mexico's legacy of servitude and backwardness. Nonetheless, he proclaimed, "We are no longer obligated to carry the yoke of these traditions, because it is necessary to agree that these mistakes, these moral vices produce social illness at this level; also as the imbecilic classes internalize these errors they engender false opinions in front of a people who judge by appearances, and thus the American people have called us inappropriate and insulting names."[44] Mexicans thus needed to reject the problematic colonial traditions, especially if they wanted to gain the respect of the "Americans" who judge by appearances. His comment suggests, however, that at least some Mexicans, the "imbecilic classes," had "internalized these errors."

Garza's anti-Spanish sentiments were tempered by an admiration for the "mother country." On one occasion in 1885, he toasted a group of Spaniards on Mexican Independence Day, assuring them that although speakers throughout Mexico would be praising their independence leaders, nobody in Mexico would be offering "insults to the great civilized nation, the intrepid and valiant conquerors, the mother of my country, Spain. No Señores, our two nations connected beforehand by the ties of affect and sympathy, founded in your community and language of origin are called to be one. . . . Spain is Mexico and Mexico Spain. Not identical institutions, but equal customs."[45] While Garza had criticized the colonial legacy of servitude and backwardness earlier in the narrative, here he calls on Mexico to emulate its imperial "mother."[46] Having lived in the United States for eight years, suffering Anglo American discrimination and insults, Garza began to appreciate the cultural affinities that linked Spain and Mexico.

Although "La lógica" focuses on the political and racial aspects of Garza's difficulties, he also found himself beset by a series of personal and business failures that kept him roaming the border for several years. Garza's entry into Brownsville's elite political circles was facilitated when he began courting a young Irish-Mexican American woman, Caroline O'Conner. Caroline was the niece of a leader of the local Democratic (blue) political club and a long-time county clerk.[47] Ignoring the protests of family and friends, who felt that they were jumping into marriage too quickly, Caroline and Catarino were wed on June 19, 1880. Garza would later refer to this marriage, which ended in divorce several years later, as an "error of my youth."[48] Caroline's father was Irish American and her mother was Mexican.[49] Such interethnic marriages between European Americans and Mexicans were very common on the border, especially in cases where the betrothed shared a common Catholic tradition.

The newlyweds moved back to Matamoros, where Garza's father helped him open a small store, called El Tranchete. According to Garza, providing generous credit to clients who never paid him back quickly led the business into bankruptcy. He was thus forced to return to Brownsville, but not before he managed to break the noses of a Matamoros lawyer and a Mexican Army officer who had insulted him by calling him a "Texano."[50] This would not be the last time that Garza resorted to his fists to settle a dispute, leading some to view him as a hothead. However, Garza wrote about these fights because he believed they reflected well on him and helped to boost his revolutionary masculine persona.

Garza returned to Brownsville in August 1881, but after a few months he picked up again and headed northwest along the Rio Grande to Laredo. On this first trip up the Rio Grande, he passed through many of the towns and villages that would serve as the staging ground for his revolt a decade later.[51] In the decade before his rebellion Garza would crisscross the triangular zone between the Nueces River and the Rio Grande, living in Brownsville, Rio Grande City, Laredo, Eagle Pass, Corpus Christi, and Palito Blanco. Although this "frontier" region was viewed as remote and isolated by outsiders, with every passing day the world came a little closer as railroads and telegraphs were built and people moved to the border to take advantage of an economic boom.

Garza arrived in Laredo on November 24, 1881, just four days after the first train crossed the bridge between Mexico and the United States.[52] Laredo buzzed with activity because both the Texas Mexican railroad from Corpus Christi and the International Great Northern line from San Antonio had just reached the border town. In the next few years the Mexican National would complete its line from Laredo to Mexico City, thus linking the two countries' railroads systems and exponentially expanding international commerce.[53] Even though Garza favored increasing binational trade and communication, the railroad would allow both central governments far greater control over their border zones and would ultimately undermine regional autonomy. Garza remained in Laredo for a few more months, but by the beginning of 1882 he had been hired by the Singer Sewing Company and sent to Mier, Tamaulipas, as a salesman. He ended up working for Singer for a year, traveling around northern Mexico selling sewing machines. During that year, he would return to Brownsville to visit his family every one or two months, taking the steamship that ran up and down the Rio Grande. He eventually moved back to Brownsville in 1883, but it would not be long before he departed again, and this time for good. As Garza obliquely put it in his autobiography, "family problems that I am keeping to myself obliged me to abandon that population forever."[54]

One newspaper account suggested that Garza's mother-in-law was "something of a terror, and she made life wretched for her dashing son-in-law." According to this story, the mother-in-law "had the utmost contempt for [Garza] and did all she could to facilitate the divorce."[55] Although the autobiography never mentioned Garza having children with his first wife, several accounts indicate that he fathered two children with Caroline.[56] The glossing over of these important pieces of his life story, leaving his first wife and their children, suggests that his autobiography was not as complete a story of his life as he would have us believe: indeed, his autobiographical "photograph" neatly cuts out several key members of his family. The absent husband and father was not exactly the image of the responsible male hero that he was trying to construct, although this absence from his family would prove a recurring theme in his life.

Leaving his wife and Brownsville in the distance, Garza headed back to Laredo in early March 1884. After only two days in that border boom-town, he founded the Sociedad Mutualista Union No. 3 and was elected its president, according to Garza's account, by an enthusiastic crowd of over two hundred workers, businessmen, and influential politicians, including a few Anglos.[57] He always made a point of mentioning the presence of Anglos at these events and highlighting their support for his journalistic and political activities. Having some strong Anglo allies was critical for his efforts on behalf of Mexicans in Texas.

In spite of his experiences with Anglo racism, Garza admired and became close friends with several Anglos. He even referred to one Anglo woman in Laredo, Laura Jones, as "an angel in my defense." Laura Jones sat at his side as he presided over Laredo's mutual-aid society, Union Mexicana. Her presence, according to Garza, compelled the members "for respect of the fair sex to moderate the scandals a bit."[58] Garza also referred positively to Anglos in a glowing description of a Mexican Independence celebration in Eagle Pass. Although he recognized that the "harmony" of that evening where Mexicans and Americans danced together was only a temporary respite from the tempestuous race relations, such hopeful moments expressed his desire for Mexicans and Anglos to live together peacefully.[59] In his account of the celebration, Garza praised the "americano," Santiago Riddle, as one "of the most popular on the border of the state of Coahuila and one of the most loved by the working people." Although Riddle's first name, Santiago, leaves some question as to his ethnicity, Garza usually used the marker "americano" to refer exclusively to Anglos. The mixture of a hispanicized first name and anglicized last name might indicate interracial marriage, something quite common along the border, but Garza nevertheless viewed Riddle as an "americano." Garza marked five pages (which remained blank) to be set aside for a description and portrait of Riddle, his "faithful and true friend."[60] While having some "americano" friends did not erase the reality of conflict and racial hatred between Anglos and Mexicans, Garza may have included these accounts in "La lógica" to demonstrate his hope that "las dos razas" would live together in harmony and even as friends.

The few accounts of the early part of Garza's life in Texas and Mexico that were published in newspapers generally confirm his version of events. Clearly Garza's is a highly selective account, one written to accentuate his own success as a political organizer and journalist. He may have exaggerated the danger posed by his enemies who he blamed for his constant need to keep moving. Nonetheless, the fact that Garza founded several mutualistas and was an elected leader in these societies as well as a budding journalist, suggests that he did have a role as a public figure in the Mexican community. At the same time, his inability to remain in Brownsville or Laredo for very long speaks to his tenuous political and financial situation. He had neither the family connections nor personal wealth that would have helped him to consolidate his position as a power broker in South Texas or northeastern Mexico. So, like many other young enterprising Mexicans, he headed north.

THE MEXICAN CONSUL IN ST. LOUIS

Garza departed Laredo at the end of May 1884, and after stopping for a few months in San Antonio he finally ended up in St Louis, Missouri, on September 15, the eve of Mexican Independence Day.[61] Using letters of reference from friends in Texas, Garza secured employment with a Mexican trading company in St. Louis, run by an Irish American, John F. Cahill. Cahill represented himself as the Mexican consul, and he used this position, according to Garza, to take advantage of Mexicans who came to the city to buy goods. Garza accused Cahill, the middleman, of skimming off a percentage of the trade from both buyers and sellers.[62] Incensed by such blatant corruption, Garza wrote a letter of complaint to a schoolmate who was a deputy in the Mexican Congress and also the personal secretary to the minister of war. His letter resulted, or so he believed, in an offer to take over the position as Mexican consul in St. Louis. In response, Garza packed his bags at once and departed for Mexico City.[63]

On the journey south, his steamer stopped briefly at the Port of Bagdad, near his hometown of Matamoros. The young Garza took the opportunity to dash off a letter to his father with whom he had not communicated in over a year. "Destiny leads me to the capital of my *patria*," he wrote with pride, "perhaps it won't be long before I have the satisfaction of embracing a career that without doubt will open up the path to a public life." However, he reassured his father, "I do not forget that I was born in a rancho, I was educated and brought up in it; but nevertheless it is probable that the humble nature of my cradle would be a precursor star that later guides me to the point of my ambition."[64] While he may have had reason to exaggerate his poverty and humble beginnings, there is nothing to indicate that his family was wealthy. At this point, Garza could not have known how true his prediction about entering public life would become; he would not, however, gain his fame as a representative of Díaz's government.

Once in Mexico City, Garza met with minister of foreign relations, Ignacio Mariscal, who promised, according to Garza's version of events, to replace Cahill and appoint Garza consul.[65] Although Mariscal had supposedly officially offered him the post as consul, when he returned to

St. Louis, Cahill refused to relinquish the position and began petitioning Díaz to remain as Mexico's representative. After several months of both men claiming to be consul, Díaz sent a letter affirming that Cahill, not Garza, was to serve in the post.[66]

While it is impossible to know if Mariscal really offered Garza the consular position in that Mexico City meeting, we do know that eventually Díaz decided in favor of an Irish American, Cahill, over a Mexican national, Garza. The pragmatic Díaz may have simply felt more comfortable leaving a well-known English-speaking businessman in charge of building binational trade relations in St. Louis, rather than entrusting such a post to a relatively unknown and penniless border journalist. If Garza had received the position as consul in St. Louis, it is possible that he would have become a successful businessman and a content representative of the Porfirian regime. But with his career hopes dashed, Garza's future would change. It is important to remember that Díaz came to power as the representative of a liberal movement, and even by the mid-1880s he retained the support of many Mexican liberals.[67] Therefore, Garza's pro-Díaz position at this point does not indicate a lack of commitment to liberalism. It was only after 1885, by which point Díaz had violated his no-reelection pledge, assumed the presidency for the second time, and turned increasingly to repression to silence his political enemies, that liberals began to see him as an enemy.

Garza remained in St. Louis until May 1886, serving as an unofficial representative of Mexico. He hosted a delegation of Mexican journalists to the city and was also named as the official liaison in charge of inviting Mexican businessmen to a national convention of wool producers.[68] In trying to establish to his readers his authority and importance in St. Louis, Garza went to the extent of reproducing in his autobiography all of the letters he received from various Mexican officials in response to his invitation to the wool convention. Garza also demonstrated his role as defender of Mexicans by recounting an incident in which he allegedly defended the honor of Mexican journalists. The journalists had stayed at the Planter House, one of the most prestigious hotels in Chicago. According to Garza, the *Globe Democrat* published an article asking why "this mob of Mexican writers had been accepted without checking if they carried lice."[69] Garza, who had invited and hosted the journalists, noted proudly how they protested this article by refusing to accept a dinner being given in their honor by the city's newspaper. Just as on the border, Garza had not become an official political power broker in St. Louis, but in his autobiography he insists that he nonetheless became a representative of the Mexican community.

At the center of Garza's self-construction as a border hero and defender of Mexicans was the concept of masculine honor. To have masculine honor and demonstrate it in his narrative was as important as touting liberal political principles or claiming racial equality with Anglo Americans. In short, masculine honor was a requirement for political leaders on the border. Women, who by definition lacked masculine honor, were thus rarely public political leaders. Garza did not invent this gendered system, but he used it in his narrative to claim his legitimacy as a political leader.

In her book *Thread of Blood*, anthropologist Ana Alonso explores the meaning of masculinity in the Mexican border state of Chihuahua. While the small community that Alonso studied is several hundred miles west of South Texas, her definition of masculinity fits well with that articulated by Garza. Alonso argues that in order to have "masculine honor" a man must recognize "social obligations and encompass numerous qualities of the self, including honesty, generosity, the ability to reciprocate, the capacity to respect others' rights to honor, the dedication to work, and the fulfillment of responsibilities to one's family and community." A man who respects others, but lacks the ability to exercise force would be considered *tímido* (timid), and therefore not honorable. Similarly, a man who is only a macho and exercises force but does not respect others would also not have honor and would be considered a *sinvergüenza* (without shame).[70] Garza's descriptions of his use of force and violence, his duty to the larger community, and his paternal behavior toward women all served to demonstrate his masculine honor. His decision to gloss over his divorce from his first wife and completely omit mentioning his first two children suggests that Garza edited his life story to conform to these northern Mexican expectations of proper male behavior.

The autobiography demonstrates Garza's masculine honor by showing him defending and protecting women. On one occasion, Garza explained how he helped a "precious" young Anglo woman who had come to St. Louis to visit her sick mother who had died four days earlier. After hearing that she had no surviving relatives except for her brother in Philadelphia,

Garza offered to pay for her to go visit him. She refused the money but they became close friends, and she even ended up naming her children Kate (Catarino) and Erasmo after him. He thus served as a symbolic father to her children, further reinforcing his image of himself as the paternal protector. Garza expressed this familial paternalism by placing himself in the position of her brother, explaining that he loved her "like a sister."[71]

At another point in his narrative, Garza explained how he helped a Mexican woman pay for passage to Fort Worth, Texas, to visit her ill husband. When the husband died, Garza not only sent money but traveled hundreds of miles to El Paso to meet her as she disembarked from the train.[72] Garza's self-described chivalrous behavior contrasts with his depiction of Anglo American men as uncaring and selfish. As he put it, "among these cousins helping orphans and protecting widows are abolished customs."[73] This critique of Anglo males for not assuming their male responsibility to protect women and children says as much about Garza's view of women as it does about his view of Anglo American society. The explicit connection between widows and orphans equates a woman without a husband to children without parents. In this way, Garza cast women as children, and husbands as their guardians.

Along with the notion of paternal protection, Garza's concept of heroism helped him to distinguish Anglo Americans from Mexicans. One episode recounted in his autobiography illustrates how he played on gender and national identity stereotypes to boost his self-image. According to the story, as Garza was walking along a street in St. Louis he observed two young women who were injured as they tried to enter a buggy being pulled by a wild horse. The six-foot-tall Garza grabbed hold of the horse and brought it under his control. One of the women was so impressed by his gallantry, Garza boasted, that she invited him to visit her. "To risk ones life for a young woman or for a friend is nothing for a Mexican," he explained to the woman, who turned out to be the very wealthy Miss Blanche.[74] Garza concluded, "to be a hero among the Americans one needs very little, but to be one among us Mexicans, we need to die defending the patria."[75] These two statements show how gender and nationality intersected in his thinking: the first expresses the chivalrous concept of men risking their life for young women, and the second invokes the notion of the heroic male who dies "defending the patria." However, both statements specifically equate Mexicans with chivalry and heroism. Therefore, in the guise of a compliment, he delivered a critique of American nationalism and Anglo males. His portrayal of Mexican males as virile heroes willing to die defending the nation contrasts with Anglo males, who are presumably emasculated, weak, and unwilling to defend their nation or their women.

In addition to protecting women, Garza displayed his virility through stories of barroom brawls and gun fights, in which he always emerged triumphant. In telling these stories Garza portrays himself as the paradigmatic male border hero who single-handedly defended Mexicans against Anglo oppression.[76] One such incident recounted by Garza is almost comic for its exaggerated bravado. It occurred in a hotel lobby in St. Louis when he overheard an Anglo lawyer saying that "Mexicans were just like dogs, they would fight over a bone." Without missing a beat, as the story went, Garza announced that he was a Mexican, called the lawyer a "miserable defamer," and whacked him with his umbrella. According to Garza's account, the lawyer ran away screaming for help. After a local newspaper accused Garza of hitting the lawyer without cause, Garza went to see the reporter and in plain view of everyone gave him a good whipping too. While he admitted that he had reacted "too violently" in this situation, the story promoted an image of Garza as strong and virile.[77] In contrast, he always described his enemies as weak men who either ran away or screamed "in the most cowardly manner."[78] Clearly these interpretations are self-serving, and they should be read not as the literal truth but rather as a way to understand how Garza was attempting to portray himself to the public as a strong leader.

Garza's contradictory attitude toward Anglo women, respecting them as women while disrespecting them as Anglos, led him to praise their beauty on the one hand and dismiss them as unworthy on the other. According to the autobiography, a short while after the incident of beating the Anglo lawyer, the lawyer's sister approached Garza and apologized for her brother's behavior. They later became lovers. In his retelling of this story Garza boasted that she had given him several gifts, including a portrait and a ring. He then flippantly commented that he did not even remember whether he gave these gifts to another woman. While this male form of boasting, whereby he inflates his own value by showing disdain for a woman, can be seen as somewhat universal behavior for men, Garza gave the boast a nationalist twist. He concluded that because "American women love for convenience, they are as easy to love, as they are easy to forget and to abandon."[79] Thus he suggests that Mexican women are deserving of deeper and more committed love than are Anglo women. His comments not only demonstrate his insensitivity to the lawyer's sister, but also serve as a critique of all Anglo women. Garza's descriptions of Anglo women contain this ambivalence because at the same time that he felt a need to protect and praise what was feminine about them, he felt compelled to criticize and put down what was Anglo about them.

Why does Garza choose to include in his autobiography these stories about his relations with women and his brawls with men, and what do they mean? Garza recognized that these stories did not fit with the rest of his political narrative, and he felt it necessary to explain why he wrote about them. In chapter seven, Garza apologetically introduces a section, titled "A Little Bit of Everything," by stating that he thought it "necessary to distract my pen a bit to narrate events that seem to have little importance." Yet, he continued, "in my career as a historian, I remember them, and cannot do otherwise than include them with others of more interest."[80] These stories, far from being random digressions, complemented his narration of "more interesting" events by linking ideals of masculine honor to a nationalist, cultural, and racial struggle. One must remember that Garza's view of proper gender relations was neither unique to him nor to Mexicans. However, he deployed these popular conceptions of gender roles to express the more contentious claim of Mexican cultural superiority. Women, especially Anglo women, became the objects of a territorial battle between Anglo and Mexican males. Penetrating and occupying Anglo women's bodies and then discarding them had the dual purpose of asserting male control over women and Mexican control over Anglo "property." However, more than just a battle over property, it was a struggle over land: that is, dominating women's bodies metaphorically expressed control over contested territory, in this case South Texas.

Confronting a drunk cowboy in a bar, whacking a lawyer over the head, and beating up a reporter for insulting Mexicans was a sort of dress rehearsal for the more organized battles that would follow in the coming years. In short, Garza's masculinity was a key part of his political persona as a Mexican revolutionary leader. The feeling of responsibility toward women complemented his belief that he had a special responsibility to protect the Texas Mexican community and overthrow the Díaz regime. Also, as shown above, Garza's patriarchal beliefs had a racial and national inflection, and thus his view of masculinity and femininity should not be viewed as insignificant "distractions," despite his desire for readers to see them in that manner.

During Garza's almost two years in St. Louis he failed to become Mexican consul as he had hoped, but he did expand his contacts in both the United States and Mexico through his hosting of journalists in the city and his work as a representative for the national wool producers. Most important, it was during his time in St. Louis that he turned against the Díaz government. It is difficult to say whether this change of heart was due more to his feelings of betrayal over not receiving the post as consul or because Díaz was becoming increasingly authoritarian. In either case, when Garza returned to the border in May 1886 to take up residence in Eagle Pass, he began publicly to condemn the Porfirian regime.[81]

The vehicle for these attacks was a new newspaper that he cofounded, *El Comercio Mexicano* (Mexican business), which circulated on both sides of the border and had as many as six hundred subscribers by the third edition.[82] According to "La lógica," the newspaper's public condemnation of racist Anglo Texans and the Mexican police put Garza in a dangerous position. Enemies from both sides of the border sought revenge, he claimed, against the insolent journalist who dared to speak his mind. Garza described himself as being constantly pursued by enemies, including both Anglo Texans and Mexican government agents who were out to incarcerate or kill him. Several English-language newspaper accounts during this period corroborate Garza's story, and provide convincing evidence that he was the target of at least two assassination attempts.[83] According to Garza, although he was based in Eagle Pass on the Texas side of the border, on one occasion he managed to venture into Mexico yet he encountered the Mexican Rural Guards who had orders to arrest him, and he barely escaped. Rather than shrinking from the harassment, Garza depicted himself as bravely escalating his attacks on the Porfirian regime. He even began another newspaper, *El Libre Pensador* (The free thinker), "dedicated exclusively to combat the supreme abuses" of governor of Coahuila, Garza Galán.[84]

With the battle lines constantly shifting, Garza often found himself with enemies on both flanks. An incident in June 1886, in which a Mexican citizen living in Eagle Pass was illegally handed over to Mexico and then executed, prompted Garza to condemn publicly in *El Comercio Mexicano* both U.S. and Mexican authorities. The basic facts of this story, which attracted international press coverage, are as follows: Maverick County Sheriff Oglesby arrested Francisco Erresures, a twenty-year-old

Mexican citizen living in Eagle Pass. After handcuffing him, Oglesby secretly brought Erresures to Coahuila, Mexico, and handed him over to Francisco Mondragón, the county judge for the Rio Grande district. The next day Erresures was killed while in the custody of Mondragón.

Garza publicly criticized both the United States and Mexican governments' handling of this incident, calling Mondragón "a criminal" and arguing that both Sheriff Oglesby and Mondragón should have been sent to prison.[85] Garza's forthright and indelicate comments were promptly picked up by the English-language press and reprinted. According to the *San Antonio Express*, Governor Garza Galán had warned Garza to remain "north of the Rio Grande," and had also threatened journalists in Mexico with "imprisonment or perhaps worse" if they either published Garza's articles in their newspapers or criticized Garza Galán's administration. When Garza printed reports by his fellow journalists in Mexico, believing that he could "publish the truth with impunity" in the United States, Garza Galán sent a representative to Austin to try to extradite him. When he was rebuffed, Garza Galán apparently turned to Mondragón, who offered an assassin the "snug little sum of $500 [for] merely running a knife into Editor Garza in an effectual and artful manner." This would-be assassin had coincidentally been bailed out of jail in Eagle Pass by Garza not long before, and so he agreed to cooperate in exposing Mondragón's plan to kill Garza.[86] A translation of Mondragón's obliquely worded orders to kill Garza was published in the *San Antonio Express*: "This is to certify that I guarantee you the sum of $500 to put out of the way the person whose name we have given you. [signed] Francisco Mondragón."[87] Judge Kelso refused Mexico's extradition request, stating that he "acted not only according with law; but according to justice and humanity in declining to send [Garza] to his death."[88] While Garza sometimes comes across in his autobiography as paranoid, harassment by the Mexican government, including extradition proceedings, libel charges, threats, and assassination attempts, gave him good reason to fear for his life.

At the same time as he was taking flak from the Mexican regime, Garza had also inspired the wrath of the *Galveston News* and the Veteran Volunteers of Texas, who were mobilizing to fight Mexico in response to the Erresures incident. According to Garza's description of the exchange, the *Galveston News* was itching for war and it predicted that the United States could take Mexico in fifteen days. "What we are sorry about," the newspaper declared, "is that we will have to mix our blood with that of Mexicans whose lowliness does not deserve such an honor."[89] Garza responded, attacking the "stupid editors" of the *Galveston News* and the "drunk Volunteer Veterans" by reminding them how thirty young cadets held off the attack of more than three hundred "testicle-eating Yankees" in the Mexican-American War.[90] To the racist remark about the lowliness of Mexican blood, Garza retorted with his own interpretation of racial purity: "We Mexicans consider ourselves to have purer blood than the Americans, given that in our country there is only a mixture of Spanish and Indian, and they [the Americans] are generally descendants of Irish adventurers, Polish beggars, Swiss, Prussians, Russians and more than anything else filthy Africans."[91] Rather than rejecting the racism inherent in the argument made by the *Galveston News*, Garza accepted the logic and turned it around to criticize the Americans. Mexicans were superior to Americans, reasoned Garza, because they had less racial mixing and purer blood.

According to Garza's version of events, the day that this article appeared, eight armed "Americans" forced the other editor of *El Comercio Mexicano* to sign a retraction. When they showed up at Garza's office, he refused to sign, proclaiming, "I am not accustomed to contradicting my principles or convictions." The "Americans" threatened that if he did not leave the county within twenty-four hours they would not be responsible for his life. Garza replied, "I reside in a free country and I am as much a man as you to be responsible for my actions anywhere."[92] The U.S. consul intervened on Garza's behalf, allowing him to carry a pistol and promising to settle the conflict with the Volunteer Veterans of Texas. The situation was ultimately resolved peacefully, and in the end some of the Veteran Volunteers who had threatened him became, in his words, his "best friends and protectors" in a different conflict with Garza Galán.[93]

This episode exemplifies the difficulty that Garza had in trying to negotiate racial politics on the border. Aside from showing the dangers of being a journalist in Garza's position, the Erresures incident illustrates the tangled and changeable position in which Garza often found himself. He had defended Mexico in the face of Anglo offenses, yet he also attacked Mexico's government for its offenses against its own people. In this case, he antagonized all sides by criticizing everyone. The racial divide, although clearly significant, was not the only factor determining Garza's alliances on the border. The changeable political context in Mexico and Texas made for very deep divisions within the Mexican community, thus rendering friends of enemies and enemies of friends. As Garza's narrative indicates, alliances along the border constantly shifted, like the ebb and flow of the Rio Grande border itself.

Garza's criticism of both the U.S. and Mexican governments made him vulnerable to the charge of being both anti-Mexican and anti-American. An Anglo lawyer raised this issue publicly, accusing Garza of defending the country that was responsible for murdering Erresures, namely Mexico, while at the same time condemning the United States, the country that gave Garza safe haven. In response, Garza defined his antigovernment, pronationalist stance: "To defend the institutions of a country is not to go along with its government. We defend Mexico but not its current administration. We attack the American filibusters, not the dignified and honorable men."[94] Garza's situation was difficult because he had to criticize both Mexicans and Texans. In Texas he was accused of being anti-American and in Mexico he faced the charge of being anti-Mexican.

Garza's struggle to define himself against the Díaz regime yet for the Mexican people can also be seen in the way he handled a conflict with the Mexican consul in Eagle Pass. As the story is related by Garza, the two men came into direct conflict at a meeting of a mutual-aid society when the consul opposed Garza's offer to draft the bylaws for this society. The Mexican consul's own reports discussed their mutual dislike and commented on an occasion where Garza testified in court against the consul in a libel case.[95] According to Garza's autobiography, he publicly accused the consul of not representing Mexicans in the courts and of wanting "to convert that worker association into a servile instrument."[96] In spite of the opposition by the consul, the society supposedly approved Garza's idea to celebrate publicly Mexican Independence in 1886. Although both men were chosen as keynote speakers for the celebration, the consul claimed illness at the last moment, leaving the platform entirely to Garza. Taking advantage of an audience of more than four hundred, Garza once again condemned the consul, criticized the Mexican government, and raised the banner of patriotism: "Though the consul is afraid and ashamed to say that he is Mexican in these times of international political conflict, I am honored to say that I am the son of Anáhuac, from the country of Hidalgo, Morelos, Abasalo, Allende, Matamoros, and others of equal stature, which is envied by the ambitious and miserable filibusters. . . . It is said that I attack those who govern; but señores, they are not the country, nor the laws, nor the people; but are truly only servants. I defend the Mexican republic and not the tyrants who govern it."[97] In addition to making the distinction between the country and the "tyrants" who govern it, Garza ran through a brief history of Mexico, marking 1877, the year Díaz came to power, as a moment when "the sun darkened and oppression reigned."[98] In this speech,

Garza reached back into Mexico's past, both to the pre-Columbian era, Anáhuac, and to the independence period, Hidalgo and Morelos, as inspiration for a new government in Mexico. Although Garza had previously been critical of Porfirian officials, this was to this point his most vehement public attack on the Díaz regime and it came the closest to advocating the overthrow of the Mexican government.

In October 1887, Garza was serving thirty-one days in a Maverick County jail on libel charges brought by Garza Galán. Garza actually viewed the jury's decision as a blessing because it kept him safe from his enemies and it prevented his extradition to Mexico. According to Garza's autobiography, his fellow editor at *El Comercio Mexicano* tried to fire him while he was incarcerated as a way of currying favor with Mondragón. His enemies, Garza contended, took advantage of his imprisonment to sell his printing press and thereby force the closure of his newspapers. When Garza was finally set free in mid-November, several supporters offered to help him buy a new press and begin publishing again. But Garza felt that if he stayed in Eagle Pass his enemies would not stop their harassment until he was dead. After toying with the idea of moving to California for awhile, he ultimately decided to take up an offer by the former administrator of his newspaper to spend Christmas with his family in Corpus Christi.

In Corpus Christi Garza followed the same pattern as he had elsewhere. He established the Club Político Mutualista México-Texano, got himself elected president of the society, and reopened his newspaper, *El Comercio Mexicano*.[99] As before, his account glorifies his use of his fists to defend himself and the honor of Mexicans against rowdy Anglo Texans, and his intelligence and quick wit in the courtroom kept him out of jail.[100] His well-publicized run-ins with the law and his acerbic journalism had gained him a reputation throughout South Texas as an opponent of the Porfirian regime and as a defender of Mexicans. Garza's autobiography ends with a description of three invitations he received in 1888, from Palito Blanco, San Diego, and Eagle Pass, to be the featured speaker for their Cinco de Mayo celebrations. To be so honored at one of the most important Mexican national holidays, celebrating the defeat of the French at Puebla in 1862, indicates how popular Garza had become as both a speaker and a patriot.

The invitation that he accepted came from Alejandro González, a wealthy rancher at Palito Blanco, a small ranching community near San Diego.[101] González's ranch was named Palito Blanco de Zaragoza, in

3. Catarino Erasmo Garza and Concepción Gónzalez at their wedding in San Diego, Texas, on May 23, 1890. Concepción, or Chonita as she was known, was the daughter of wealthy landowner Alejandro González, who would later support Garza's rebellion with money and horses. Garza was previously married to Caroline O'Conner of Brownsville, but they separated after a short time and finally were divorced in Corpus Christi. Catarino and Concepción had one child, their daughter Amelia. (Courtesy of the Pérez and Tijerina families)

honor of the famous Mexican general Ignacio Zaragoza, who was born nearby and fought the successful battle that Cinco de Mayo celebrates. The vast ranch was reported to measure almost forty square miles. Although González shared Garza's political sentiments, he had apparently opposed Garza's earlier proposal of marriage to his daughter, Concepción. Later, after Garza had secured a divorce from his previous wife,[102] he married Concepción in 1890. In subsequent years González became one of Garza's most important backers, providing horses, arms, and money to his revolutionary son-in-law.

CONCLUSION

Whether as an individual defending Mexicans against Anglo insults, or as a journalist exposing the abuse and corruption of the Porfirian regime, Garza used remarkably similar narrative strategies to portray himself as a heroic protagonist in an epic drama. His enemies were always lurking around him ready to attack, but instead of being cowed by such threats, Garza depicted himself as standing up bravely and continuing the battle. The fact that he ended up leaving Brownsville, Laredo, St. Louis, Eagle Pass, and Corpus Christi after spending only a few years in each suggests that his courageousness was tempered with a healthy dose of self-preservation instinct. Was Garza just being paranoid about the danger these enemies posed and did he simply exaggerate such threats in order to inflate his own importance? From press accounts that corroborate Garza's story, and from what we know of other Mexican dissidents in Texas at the time along with the extensive spy network of the Díaz regime, Garza's fears do not seem unfounded. Like Garza, the liberal-turned-anarchist Flores Magón brothers would in the early twentieth century also flee the Texas border and ultimately take up residence in St. Louis to try to keep beyond the reach of Díaz's agents. Garza had seen his newspaper colleagues stabbed, apparently by Mexican government agents, he had seen the increasing extra-judicial killings in Mexico, and he had been locked up for libel and had his press sold out from under him while in jail. There is no doubt that Governor Garza Galán had pursued him, first by trying to extradite him and then by trying to have him assassinated in Texas. His autobiography wove these stories of Anglo harassment and Mexican government repression into a coherent narrative. That his "logic of events" was exaggerated is almost certain. Perhaps he manipulated details and omitted unflattering incidents. However, the essence of the story he was telling is true and can be corroborated by countless other sources that detail the racial harassment suffered by Mexicans in the United States and the repression suffered by Díaz's political enemies.

The autobiography also shows the full range of Garza's responses to racial harassment. In some cases he publicized the issue in newspapers, in another instance he boycotted the offending party, and on many other occasions he used physical violence to make his point. He always ended up victorious over Anglos whom he characterized as "cowardly" and "disgraceful." It is likely that he chose these incidents as opposed to others where Anglos won the day, or slanted the interpretation of the events, in order to encourage more Mexicans to stand up against Anglo insults. He did not merely reproduce the events as they happened, as he asserted, but molded them into a triumphant narrative to foster greater resistance to an increasingly powerful and aggressive Anglo presence. Texas Ranger autobiographies and biographies create a similarly one-sided portrait, but in their version the lone Ranger always defeats the treacherous Mexican "bandit."[103] In some ways, Garza's "La lógica" was the counterpoint to the Ranger version of history, a tale of heroism and honor, but from the Mexican point of view.

"La lógica," which questioned the U.S. expansion and occupation of northern Mexico and the subsequent dispossession of Mexicans, was also part of an anti-imperialist culture that served as a point of departure for his insurrection against Díaz. In spite of his radical questioning of U.S. imperialism and Anglo racism, however, Garza remained wedded to many dominant views of race and gender. For instance, while he overturned the Anglo/Mexican racial hierarchy the white/black hierarchy remained intact, and while male dominance took on a racial inflection it was not radically challenged.

Revolutionary declarations and manifestos come only after the protagonists have written, metaphorically or literally, their own histories. Revolutionary consciousness is thus only the end result of a long psychological process of making sense of everyday experiences and of giving those experiences new meaning. When Garza began writing his autobiography in 1888, he probably had no idea that in a couple of years he would lead an armed insurrection against Mexico's Porfirio Díaz. In retrospect, however, one can see how the chronology of events and conclusions reached in the autobiography helped him to arrive at the decision to take up arms. While the autobiography did not call for armed revolution, it provided a space in which Garza could reflect on the position of Mexicans on the border and formulate a political response. Revolution was a plausible, although not inevitable, epilogue to the autobiography. The act of writing the autobiography was an important part of the process that finally convinced Garza, in 1891, "to put down the pen and seize the sword."[104]

2. RESISTING THE PAX PORFIRIANA

Mexicanos al grito de alarma

Con prestesa el garrote empuñar

Y á trancasos matemos á Sebree,

Al instante; que al campo va a entrar.

(Mexicans [rise] to the call of alarm

Grab the garrote with haste

And let us club Sebree to death

Immediately; for he is going to the countryside.)

— Stanza dedicated to the bandit

Sebree, by Catarino Garza

In the five years preceding Garza's revolution, political assassinations, riots, and rebellions tore at the already frayed fabric of border society. Describing the accumulation of grievances, suffering, and resistance over these years helps us to recognize Garza's insurrection as part of a longer process that began before his revolutionary proclamation and continued after his death in 1895. His detractors characterized his revolt as a brief tempest in a calm sea, attributing it to the work of an isolated and confused charlatan. However, placing the revolt within its social and historical contexts shows that it was only one moment of a much longer revolutionary process. Garza succeeded in mobilizing support because his rebellion made sense to a wider border community that felt alienated from both the U.S. and Mexican governments. More than any particular *proclama*, or manifesto, these lived experiences prepare the way for Garza's revolution and for his role as its leader.

In 1885, the pax porfiriana arrived in northeastern Mexico. As in the rest of the country, it came with chilling violence and precious little peace. The regime propagated the myth of peace and stability through newspapers, official speeches, and public celebrations. This was an attractive and comforting image for foreign investors who saw Latin America as a land of exotic and turbulent Indians who regularly broke into rebellion. Even if foreign capitalists recognized the social inequality and violence that lay beneath this peaceful facade, the maintenance of the veneer allowed them to keep their enterprises running and to continue to reap handsome profits. Under Porfirio Díaz, the commercial exchange between Mexico and the United States increased dramatically from 15 million dollars in 1880 (four years after Díaz came to power) to 166 million dollars in 1910; the United States accounted for two-thirds of Mexico's total foreign commercial exchange, and most of that was directed to northern Mexico.[1] Domestically, Díaz curtailed the power of regional leaders and established authoritarian rule over a country that had functioned as a loose federation of relatively autonomous states for more than half a century. If nothing else, the dictatorship halted the chaotic revolving-door governments that had tenuously ruled over the expansive republic since its independence from Spain in 1821.

Although the pax porfiriana has been thoroughly exposed as a violent and often contentious period, the idea that peace and prosperity had come to Mexico was nonetheless widely disseminated and popularly accepted during Díaz's tenure. Thus, even though the regime regularly resorted to violence to undermine its opponents, Díaz's skillful ideological elaboration of the myth of peace was an even more effective tool to forestall widespread rebellions.[2] Furthermore, the aging dictator personally controlled the political fate of his subordinates, guaranteeing their loyalty. As the historian Alan Knight put it, "the divide-and-rule principle kept all the strings in Díaz's hands and these hands had only to twitch, at the apprehension of an over-mighty subject, for the threat to be removed."[3]

The myth of peace and Díaz's mastery as a political puppeteer did not, however, prevent the eruption of a series of armed conflicts along the border beginning in 1886 and continuing through Garza's revolution in 1891 and beyond. The anti-Díaz forces engaged in combat against the government on Mexican soil in 1886, 1890, and 1891 to 1893; Díaz agents carried the battle to Texas soil, sponsoring political assassinations in 1888 and 1891. The persistence of these movements, despite far-reaching and repeated efforts by Mexican and U.S. authorities to crush them, suggests that the roots from which they blossomed ran deep. Furthermore, the experiences of government repression and armed resistance in the region helps to explain Garza's later popularity and success in evading the U.S. and Mexican armies, local police forces, and the Texas Rangers. When Garza crossed the Rio Bravo to declare a revolution against the "eternal czar," he was not the first to have enacted such a gesture, nor would he be the last.

The series of rebellions organized on the Texas border leading up to and continuing after Catarino Garza's insurrection had their roots in liberalism and the jealously guarded state autonomy in northeastern Mexico. An electoral dispute in November 1885 in Nuevo León set the stage for an armed uprising by dissident liberals, thus providing Díaz with the perfect excuse to impose his proconsul General Bernardo Reyes as interim governor of the state. Reyes declared martial law, arrested opposition leaders, and closed their newspapers, thus extending Porfirian control to this historically independent region.[4] Regional caudillos who might have posed a challenge to the regime, such as Evaristo Madero (father of Francisco, the first president of Mexico after the revolution), Venustiano Carranza (president of Mexico, 1915–1920), and generals Gerónimo Treviño and Francisco Naranjo, were tamed. While these regional strongmen, the first two from Coahuila and the latter two from Nuevo León, were incorporated into the regime through economic incentives and political posts, Díaz made sure to limit their influence and continually remind them who was boss.[5]

The year 1885 marks the moment when Díaz extended his control over the north through Reyes, but sporadic electoral disputes, armed rebellions, an uprising of Yaqui Indians, and even a millenarian movement continued to rock the region and test the regime's strength. Díaz succeeded, at least until 1910, in playing elite factions against one another, and using the *pan y palo* (bread and stick) strategy, to co-opt with *pan* in one hand and coerce with the *palo* in the other. This strategy kept him in power for thirty-four years, but it prevented neither the elite nor the peasantry from plotting against the regime. A rebellion in 1893 against Governor Garza Galán by prominent Coahuilans, including Evaristo Madero and the Carranza brothers, illustrates both the strengths and the limits to Díaz's control over the elite. The weakness can be seen in the fact that

eight years after Reyes was installed, and seventeen years after Díaz assumed the presidency, sectors of the elite were still plotting armed coups.
On the other hand, the ability of Díaz to resolve the insurrection through
co-optation rather than force by replacing Garza Galán as governor and
allowing the insurrectionists to occupy local government posts, testifies to
his adept political skills.[6] However, not every insurrection could be settled
through co-optation. It took a massacre of over seventy men, women, and
children before the Porfirian regime could crush an 1892 millenarian
movement in Tomochic, Chihuahua.[7] And the Yaqui Indians in northwestern Mexico continued their guerrilla struggle for autonomy all the
way through the Porfiriato in spite of brutal repression and forced deportation.[8] The fact that Díaz managed to stay in power for so long does not
necessarily imply that he had the consent of the people, but rather only
that he had prevented their many challenges from ripening and bearing
fruit.

DOCTOR AND GENERAL IGNACIO MARTÍNEZ
AND THE 1886 REBELLION

Garza's revolution can be directly traced back to one of the failed challenges to Díaz. Just six months after Reyes assumed the reins of power in
Nuevo León, an insurrection erupted in the neighboring state of Tamaulipas. In June 1886, the Mexican consul in Brownsville informed the
foreign ministry that a small band of fifteen or twenty armed men were
being organized in Tamaulipas under the leadership of Pedro Davila. This
group had support among the Mexican exiles in Texas, particularly from
Ignacio Martínez who had published their manifesto in his Brownsville
newspaper *El Mundo*.[9] The Mexican government decided not to pursue a
legal case against Martínez for violation of neutrality laws, however, because they lacked evidence that he had been either recruiting revolutionaries or stockpiling weapons in Texas.[10] Further, more than just Martínez,
Díaz was worried about the reports he had received that implicated the
caudillos Treviño and Naranjo in the plot.[11]

Martínez, a medical doctor and former general in the Mexican Army,
had strong roots in Tamaulipas and was intimately involved in the liberal
movement since the time of Benito Juárez's battles against French invaders
in the early 1860s. Born in San Carlos, Tamaulipas, in the northeastern
corner of Mexico, Martínez moved as a youth to Monterrey, the intellectual and commercial capital of the region. In 1855, he entered the semi-

nary for higher education and later studied medicine. Soon after becoming a doctor, he declared himself an atheist and embraced the ideas of materialism. By 1856, he had founded a literary-philosophy club in Monterrey, the Sociedad del Trueno (Society of thunder), where the young intelligentsia met to discuss new scientific ideas such as Darwin's theory of natural selection.[12]

Martínez became involved in politics during the French invasion of Mexico (1862–1865). When the ousted liberal president Juárez visited Monterrey in 1863, Martínez gave a speech in front of him in which he condemned Santiago Vidaurri, a powerful regional caudillo, for accepting a "shameful peace" with the French: "Benito Juárez!" he declared, "Here you have your people ready and enthusiastic for war against the French invaders."[13] After serving as a major in the medical corps in the liberal army of the north, Martínez upset the local government when he refused a position offered to him by Nuevo León's interim governor, Manuel Gómez. The rejection of the governor's offer got him into trouble, including one altercation where a person shot at Martínez's feet. In response, he started a newspaper entitled *El Busca Pies* (The feet searcher).[14] On another occasion, according to a hagiographic biography, Martínez challenged his former commander, General Escobedo, to a duel after the general had insulted him at a casino in San Luis Potosí. Finally, when Juárez announced his intention to hold power for another four years in 1869, thereby violating the sacred liberal no-reelection principle, Martínez turned against Juárez.[15] Although the rebellion failed, Martínez managed to escape to New Orleans. He returned to Mexico City after being granted an amnesty, but before long he had once again upset Juárez and was forced to flee the city or go to jail.[16]

Although Martínez would become one of Porfirio Díaz's most bitter enemies by the mid-1880s, he fought on Díaz's side during the 1871 Plan de la Noria, and was even named brigadier general at that time by General Pedro Martínez.[17] In 1876, Martínez even recruited followers for the revolution of Tuxtepec, which brought Díaz to power. Martínez was known, according to one partisan biographer, for "catechizing the señoras, who with fervent perseverance turned their husbands, fathers, or brothers to Don Porfirio's side and to his no-reelection principles."[18] In 1878, with Díaz at the helm of the republic, Martínez was named military commander of Mexico City. Shortly thereafter, a dispute with the minister of war led to his resignation, and rather than accepting another post in Díaz's government, Martínez headed back to the border region to resume his private medical practice.[19] In a vein similar to Garza's autobiography, a hagiographic pamphlet published after Martínez's assassination presented him in glowing terms as a brave and unwavering liberal, while his enemies were portrayed as power-hungry opportunists. The image of Martínez as a ladies' man was meant to build him up as the prototypical dashing male revolutionary hero. This view needs to be balanced, however, with his enemies' negative descriptions of him as a cowardly and arrogant madman.

In less than fifteen years, between 1865 and 1878, Martínez had managed to join four separate rebellions and was forced to escape on four other occasions after inspiring the ire of powerful politicians. To his supporters on the border, Martínez had shown himself to be a brave and honorable defender of liberal principles, even when that meant putting his own life at risk. As a well-educated person who had both political and military experience, Martínez was an obvious candidate to lead a revolt against Díaz. The only problem was that the people did not follow his lead, because he had overestimated his own charisma and reputation or because the Porfirian regime had coerced people into submission or they actually were satisfied with the peace and stability offered by the dictator.

In typical fashion, the news reports of the July 1886 rebellion seem to have overblown its seriousness. One U.S. newspaper even declared: "The whole country in that section is up in arms, and . . . recruits are going there from the American side of the river." Some claimed that the rebels had stolen guns and horses from ranches along the river above Brownsville, while others asserted that a band of insurrectionists had attacked a train at Capote station on the Mexican side of the river. The graphic account of the assault on the train noted that a man who had refused to surrender his pistols and horse to the rebels was riddled with bullets and strung up to a tree on a roadside "as a warning to others." The revolution was gaining strength, a dispatch from Brownsville exclaimed, and "the troops in this section seem utterly unable to cope with it." From the reports it had received, the newspaper concluded that the "revolution appears to be spreading to the state of Nuevo León."[20]

Fanning the flames of rebellion, Martínez claimed victory in an extra edition of his newspaper. *El Mundo* declared that ten important towns had been taken by the revolutionists and that all of Nuevo León had risen up against the government: "To the cry of the restoration of the Constitution of 1857, the valiant Col. Francisco T. Casa, at the head of over 50 men, occupied the city. There is no limit to the enthusiasm. . . . The sons of

Nuevo León, like all of the inhabitants of the Mexican frontier, the classic land of liberty, have risen en masse to break the chains of slavery which oppress the nation."²¹ *El Mundo's* triumphant reporting about Nuevo León rising "en masse to break the chains of slavery" must be taken "with a grain of salt," as one editorial suggested, given that Martínez was both the director of this newspaper and apparently also the mastermind behind the revolt. Nonetheless, the possibility that regional caudillos backed the insurrection made the Mexican government sufficiently concerned to send 250 government troops by train from Monterrey to Nuevo Laredo.²²

Even though high government officials attempted to downplay the significance of the revolt, their keen interest indicated that they were worried. The chancellor of the Mexican Consulate publicly dismissed the movement as the work of "thieves, robbers, and smugglers." Further, he explained, although in the past, such a rebellion might have been a serious affair, "with the improved railroad systems of the country large bodies of troops can be sent to the frontier on short notice and crush any revolt before it becomes anything serious." The Chancellor's commentary inadvertently revealed that the border was still a zone of resistance, even if the protagonists were dismissed as "thieves, robbers and smugglers." The only difference was that now the railroad made it easier and faster to "crush any revolt before it becomes anything serious."²³

There were rumors that this current rebellion in Tamaulipas had some connection to the one that had occurred the previous year in Nuevo León. In that instance, several hundred men in Lampazos led by Manuel Rodríguez took up arms against the acting governor of Nuevo León. These disturbances provided the excuse for imposing Reyes as interim governor and declaring martial law in the state.²⁴ One journalist contended that, like in Nuevo León in November 1885, "the hand of the government can be seen" in this latest revolt. He predicted that "within two months Tamaulipas will be under military control."²⁵ The two movements differed in one important respect. While Rodríguez launched his rebellion only against state authorities in Nuevo León, thereby allowing him to broker a deal with Díaz and ultimately lay down his arms, the Tamaulipas revolt was explicitly aimed at Porfirio Díaz and the national government.²⁶

In August 1886, *El Mundo* published a lengthy "Plan Político," which proclaimed: "The Revolution now has a flag! Great popular enthusiasm!" The manifesto, signed by Vicente Peña in La Ensenada, Tamaulipas, on August 18, 1886, blamed both Manuel González, who occupied the presidency from 1880 to 1884, and Porfirio Díaz for "interrupting the constitutional order" and selling the country to foreigners. It went further, accusing all Porfirian officials of living in "sumptuous palaces" and "valuable haciendas" while the oppressed people lived in "the deepest misery." The sacking of the treasury that began under González continued, they asserted, when Díaz imposed "a military dictatorship." The manifesto further condemned the Porfirian regime for almost everything from imposing high taxes to looting the country and selling it to foreigners: "They continue the fraudulent concessions, the misappropriation of public property; the customs and stamp taxes have been raised to the extreme to make traffic impossible; the favored and the speculators distribute the lands in immense parcels on the pretext of settling vacant lots; the fraud of the English debt has been consummated; and [Díaz] the hero of April 2 [the day Díaz came to power in 1876] capitalizes his laurels and patriotic service in gold bars, railroad stocks and bills from the bank." In addition to the critique of Porfirian economic policies and the looting of the treasury for personal gain, the manifesto attacked the lack of political and civil liberties in Mexico. "He [Díaz] has stepped upon all of the liberties of the citizens with the infamous *leyva* [military draft], with the prisons and assassinations of journalists, with the persecution of any demonstration of discontent."[27]

After enumerating the long list of Porfirian abuses, the "Plan Político" was followed by the "Plan Restaurador," which proposed twenty-eight articles with the aim to restore the 1857 Constitution; overthrow Díaz; force restitution to the national treasury of ill-gotten gains; abolish the military draft, peonage, and internal tariffs; guarantee municipal and state autonomy; distribute *terrenos baldíos* (vacant land) to the poor (with preference given to those who participated in the revolution); and call elections fifteen days after revolutionary forces had occupied the capital.[28] These demands were strikingly similar to the ones embodied in subsequent liberal revolutionary proclamations, including those of Francisco Ruíz Sandoval (1890), Catarino Garza (1891), Francisco Benavides (1892), and even that of the leader of the successful 1910 revolution, Francisco Madero. The emphasis on municipal and state autonomy, reducing tariffs, and opening free trade, and the absence of any defense of communal landholding, marks this as a plan specifically suited to the interest of northern Mexicans. In contrast, Emiliano Zapata, the preeminent symbol of the peasant base of the 1910 Mexican Revolution, issued a very different kind of manifesto, the Plan de Ayala (1911), which guaranteed the persistence of communal landholding.[29] Whereas the northern

Mexican revolutionaries focused on free trade, the southern revolutionaries emphasized communal land.

Two years after Martínez's failed insurrection, Garza actively participated in the Starr County electoral campaign, giving speeches and writing articles in favor of one of the political clubs in Rio Grande City. Garza's involvement in this tense political race, and particularly an article he wrote about an Anglo customs inspector's killing of a Mexican, led to a shoot-out on the streets of Rio Grande City. His brush with death not only shows the dangerous political environment on the border but helps us understand the personal motivation for Garza to pick up arms against Díaz three years later. Although the struggle to defend Mexicans in Texas and to go against Díaz may be seen as separate, both issues were very much intertwined. As much as any other political education, this experience forced Garza to confront his own mortality and ultimately to steel his resolve to become a revolutionary.

On a hot afternoon in Rio Grande City in September 1888, Catarino Garza was sitting in the doorway of the local barbershop. Victor Sebree, an Anglo customs inspector with a grudge, rode up on a horse, drew a pistol, and began firing. Garza had publicly accused the customs inspector in the local newspapers of killing a Mexican named Abraham Resendez, who had been in the custody of the customs inspector when he was killed. Needless to say, this newspaper article had only added to Garza's reputation as a troublemaker. The article, together with Garza's support for the Texas Mexican Independent Party, had placed him in the center of a bitter fight that nearly cost him his life.[30] Even though the two political parties included wealthy Texas Mexicans in their ranks, the Mexicans resented the near monopoly that the Anglos held over county offices.[31] It was this brush with death that seemed to close off the opportunities for a nonviolent strategy, both to oppose Díaz and to defend Mexican rights in Texas.

The shooting was the culmination of an incident a month earlier when the Texas Rangers arrested Garza at Realitos for allegedly libeling the customs inspector. According to a romanticized pro-Ranger account of the episode that could have appeared in any number of Hollywood westerns, Ranger Captain John Hughes bravely confronted Garza, "the fiery revolutionist," as he stepped through the doors of a saloon. Everyone on the street scattered and ran for cover as the Ranger slowly approached

Garza, who "stood his ground" with a cigarette nonchalantly dangling from his fingers. With both men eyeing each other, the Ranger "quietly and calmly" stated, "Catarino, I've got a warrant for you." "Si señor—I know," Garza responded laconically, and in an instant he reached for the butt of his pistol. Ranger Hughes reacted quickly and was able to grab the gun away from the "startled editor." Later, after pleading guilty to libel, Garza was released. Outside of the court, the Ranger offered to return Garza's pistol to him, but Garza refused, saying, "Keep it—you won it."[32] This portrayal shows Ranger Hughes as fearless and chivalrous, even when confronted with a man who had, according to the Rangers, killed a half dozen men in Mexico.[33] Garza, however, is also depicted as brave, gentlemanly, and fearless in the face of adversity. If nothing else, this Ranger seemed to recognize Garza as a worthy opponent.

The libel charge for which Garza was arrested was based on an article in *El Comercio Mexicano* in which he accused U.S. customs inspector Victor Sebree of murder. Although Sebree admitted shooting Abraham Resendez while escorting him to jail on a theft charge a few months earlier, he claimed that he did so only after Resendez had attempted to escape. Many people in the Mexican community believed that Resendez was assassinated in cold blood in another case of the *ley fuga* (fugitive law), which was frequently invoked as an excuse for killing prisoners. The *San Antonio Express* argued that although the killing was justifiable because Resendez had allegedly resisted arrest, "it created great excitement among the Mexican population of the country, and a deep feeling of resentment against Americans generally."[34]

Garza's shooting and the ensuing events reflected the tensions between the two factions in Starr County's racially charged politics.[35] The Mexican leaders of one of the factions, Agustín de la Peña and his son, were said to have hired Garza "to write incendiary articles and to lecture and to speak to the Mexicans." It was one of these articles in Garza's newspaper describing Sebree as an "assassin" and a "coward" that led to the libel charges that resulted in Garza's apprehension in August.[36] The Peña faction had capitalized on four recent lynchings of Mexicans, two hung on the U.S. side of the border by a mob and two by officials on the Mexican side, blaming these killings on Sheriff Sheley and thereby "inciting Mexicans to oppose the Americans." "Their conduct," the *Express* argued, "has brought on what may well be termed a race war."[37] Garza's newspaper articles and public speeches popularized him among Texas Mexicans at the same time that they earned him political enemies.

Two hundred people waited for Garza's arrival at Peña station following his apprehension, and when Garza was finally released on $500 bail, three hundred members of the Texas Mexican club greeted him with music and speeches.[38] Martínez publicized these events in *El Mundo* and condemned Starr County Judge Kelsey for harassing Garza and for circumventing the law in the manner in which he was arrested. While the Ranger version made it look like a respectful and restrained arrest, *El Mundo* emphasized the aggressiveness of Garza's apprehension. If his arrest warrant was for a "questionable publishing crime," Martínez asked, why did the Rangers insist on handcuffing Garza "like an assassin or horse thief." And then, to make matters worse, they released him ten miles from the Ranger camp and made him walk the rest of the way to Rio Grande City. The use of handcuffs and the forced walk served to illustrate the type of humiliation that Mexicans regularly suffered, while Anglos like Sebree were released on bond after having committed murder. Furthermore, according to legal procedure, the County Sheriff and not the Rangers should have arrested Garza. "How many would not have their blood boil to see a Mexican writer treated this way?" Martínez wrote.[39] Another Spanish-language Laredo newspaper warned that Garza's life was in danger and predicted that the libel charges were a pretext for his capture and subsequent "*ley linch* [lynching law] so in vogue in this country."[40]

Lynching in the United States reached its height in 1892, which coincidentally was also in the middle of the Garza rebellion. In the U.S. South and Southwest, lynching served to police the boundaries between races, primarily between blacks and whites but also between Mexicans and Anglos. Blacks accounted for 70 percent of the 4,561 lynching victims between 1882 and 1930, but Italians, Jews, and Mexicans were also targets of mob "justice." As many as 30 percent of lynchings in the South were retribution for alleged sexual crimes, usually involving the accusation that a black man transgressed the color line and made sexual advances toward or raped a white woman.[41] The lynchings themselves were often highly eroticized and sexualized rituals, with the mob stripping victims and mutilating and displaying the victims' genitalia.[42] Extralegal killings became widespread during the Garza rebellion, and some Anglos even publicly called for rebels to be lynched, but none of the cases I have documented fit the classic example of a mob engaging in a highly public murder ritual.

The extralegal murders of suspected Garzistas in Mexico, like on the U.S. side, were generally carried out clandestinely by state authorities, the military, or the *rurales* (the Mexican equivalent of the Rangers). However,

Adolfo Duclós Salinas, who edited *El Comercio Mexicano* with Garza, distinguished between Mexican and U.S. lynchings. He argued that in Mexico, as opposed to the United States, the government was always an accomplice or the author of the killings, and they always had political ends. In contrast, he contended, lynching in the United States had a "moral end: the defense of the family's daughters against attacks by a degraded and disgusting race."[43] Leaving aside Duclós Salinas's racism and misinterpretation of U.S. lynching, which very often was sanctioned by local authorities, he makes a point of the lack of a public mob mentality in Mexican lynching. In this way, the "lynching" on both sides of the border fits the Mexican model of state-sanctioned political murders rather than the U.S. model of mob-inspired revenge killings. Although it is difficult to quantify exactly how many Mexicans were lynched on each side of the border, and even harder to distinguish legal from extralegal killings, it is clear that state authorities killed many suspected rebels without the benefit of a trial. Like the Resendez case and the many instances of the *ley fugs* in Mexico, the killers justified their actions by claiming that the suspect had attempted to escape. In none of these cases was the killer tried and found guilty of murder.

Garza arrived safely in Rio Grande City, but the newspaper's warning about Garza's life would prove prophetic. On the afternoon of September 21, 1888, Sebree, on horseback, approached Garza as he sat in a barbershop doorway. Garza had been thrown in jail before and had even survived assassination attempts, but this was the first time that he had actually been shot at. There are two versions of what transpired next. After an investigation, the Mexican consul at Rio Grande City concluded that Sebree challenged Garza to a fight but that Garza refused. Sebree then dismounted and shot several times, wounding Garza twice. According to this account, Garza had time to shoot back after being wounded.[44] The other version, published in several English-language newspapers, blamed Federico López, an associate of Garza's, for firing the first shot at Sebree. In this account Sebree and Garza shot at each other at the same time.[45] Both stories concur that Sebree approached Garza and challenged him to fight. The second account seems less plausible given that both Garza and López were wounded while Sebree escaped unscathed. After shooting Garza, Sebree mounted his horse and rode to nearby Fort Ringgold as Garza's supporters fired shots after him.[46] The next day, the *Laredo Times* reported that "up to noon today [Garza] was still alive, but hopes for his recovery are not entertained."[47] A local Spanish language newspaper, *El*

Diablo Predicador (The preaching devil) lamented Garza's assassination, commenting wryly, "Maldición! The one who does good always ends up with martyrdom as the prize."[48]

The next day, the collector of customs at Brownsville sent out an alarm by telegraph: "An armed mob has possession of Rio Grande City. . . . Civil authorities are powerless. . . . The necessity is urgent. Fighting is hourly expected. Orders have to be sent by carrier to Fort Brown. Line to Ringgold cut by mob."[49] Another telegram sent to the governor on September 22 from Starr County's judge, John Kelsey, exclaimed: "Great riot is raging in town here — armed men parading the streets — send company of rangers post haste, or apply to use the United States troops."[50] After Garza had been shot, a group of several hundred men, almost all Mexican, arrived at Fort Ringgold, demanding that Sebree be turned over to them. The officer in charge, Colonel Clendennin, refused and ordered the "mob out of the Fort under penalty of death."[51] Undeterred, the demonstrators cut the telegraph lines between the fort and department headquarters to prevent further communication and to forestall the sending of reinforcements.

Even though the telegraph lines had been cut, news of the riot had already reached Austin and the governor had ordered Sheriff Brito of Brownsville and the Rangers to "reestablish order and the supremacy of law."[52] It would have been a bloody battle if the demonstrators had attacked Fort Ringgold or if the Rangers had arrived and faced off with several hundred armed Mexicans, but cooler heads prevailed. Initially, according to the Mexican consul in Rio Grande City, the crowd attacked the judge for trying to telegraph the Rangers, and they demanded that Sebree be turned over to them. However, the county judge, the justice of the peace, and the sheriff convinced the crowd to disperse after they had promised that Sebree would be brought to trial. The consul also lauded Garza's role for trying to calm the excited mob. Garza sent the judge a protest letter asking that he "proceed in the present case strictly according to the laws of this country; in this way strict and upright justice will be done."[53] The crowd had remained in the streets from the afternoon of the shooting through that night, but by the next day they had returned to their homes. By the time the Brownsville sheriff's posse and the Rangers arrived, the "mob" had disbanded and peace had been restored.

Several weeks later Sebree was living freely, stationed in Brownsville as a customs agent; he still had not been arrested or charged with a crime. Meanwhile, Garza and his associate López, along with the leaders of the Texas Mexican Independent Party and about twenty other Mexicans, had been arrested by the Rangers and charged with conspiracy and intent to murder. After noting the irony that the victim of the shooting, Garza, was arrested while the perpetrator, Sebree, was free, *La Colonia Mexicana* sarcastically asked its readers: "Doesn't this seem like a great way to render justice?"[54]

"ANARCHY ON THE BORDER"

After receiving his orders from the governor, Sheriff Brito of Brownsville rapidly organized a posse of sixty men, "most of them leading citizens and the flowers of the young men of the city." While newspaper coverage generally labeled all Mexicans as "rioters," the *San Antonio Express* made a point of mentioning that the "better class of Mexican citizens and principal ranchers" were part of the posse sent to reestablish law and order.[55] This distinction between the "better class" of Mexicans and the *plebe* illustrates how class status qualified race. In other words, not all Mexicans were lawless rioters. English-language Texas newspapers were quick to portray the event as a "race war," running articles linking both Ignacio Martínez and Catarino Garza to an allegedly anti-American political party in Starr County. The *Express* described the "rioters" as the "lowest class of Mexicans among whom are many noted smugglers and bandits, their party being adherents of the revolutionary Mexican chief, Martínez and his gang." These were the same people, the *Express* continued, who had started a society in Starr County that "pledged to run every American out of office in that section." The newspaper thus fanned the flames of racial fear with its description of a low-class, revolutionary, anti-American Mexican mob, and its assertion that the "safety of American and foreign residents in that section" was endangered.[56]

Sensationalist reports in national newspapers screamed "anarchy on the border" and predicted a Mexican invasion of the Rio Grande Valley. The *New York Herald* proclaimed that "a Mexican mob of one thousand strong, and armed to the teeth, are in possession of Rio Grande City." "The feeling of the mob is bitter and determined," the article warned, "and fears are beginning to be felt that they will get assistance from the other side of the river. . . . It is said that all Mexicans in Starr County are now up in arms."[57] The alarmist reports circulating throughout the country inflated the numbers of the "mob" to one thousand, reflecting Anglo fears more than reality. Eyewitnesses estimated the number of people on the streets at anywhere from two hundred to five hundred.[58] Private U.S. and Mexican government communications contradicted the hyperbolic published press accounts, indicating, as one Mexican consul said, "the public peace has not been disturbed again."[59] Col. Clendennin sent word to General Stanley a few days after the incident, stating forthrightly that "no property has been destroyed or depredations committed in Rio Grande City. Affairs not so bad as represented."[60]

While the English-language press ran hysterical articles about the Mexican "mob" threatening the Rio Grande Valley, the Spanish-language press attempted to understand the frustration that led the Mexicans of Rio Grande City to take up arms. A Laredo newspaper, *La Colonia Mexicana*, argued that both the Resendez assassination and the attempt on Garza had "aroused grave difficulties, to such an extent that the patient and tolerant Mexican people decided to take up arms to punish with their hands the criminal, who in the short period of two or three months had treacherously assassinated two Mexicans, and is a constant threat to the Mexican community in Starr County."[61] The same newspaper explained that "Mexicans living on the Texas border know perfectly well the lack of guarantees that they suffer, the cynicism and exasperating audacity with which the authorities of Starr County tolerate the violations committed against Mexicans, and even indirectly help them, giving criminals the means by which to escape the punishment of justice, and to continue planting terror in the honorable people of these communities."[62]

By and large, the English-language press focused on the threat posed by the "Mexican mob," while the Spanish-language press placed the takeover of Rio Grande City within the context of the violence that Mexicans had suffered for years. Instead of a lawless mob, the Mexicans of Rio Grande City were portrayed as harbingers of popular justice. One notable exception to this general dichotomy was the English-language *Laredo Times*, which blamed the Rio Grande City riot on the "lawless" example set by the late county judge and his cohorts who had disenfranchised half of the population to keep themselves in office. "They never did count the votes of four out of seven precincts in that County," complained the *Times*, and thus "even the simplest minded voter in that County knows beyond a doubt that their rights as citizens have been ruthlessly trampled upon."[63] However, most newspapers, even those that recognized the legitimacy of the Mexican complaints, argued, as did Laredo's *Gate City*, that "mob law can in the end but lead to disastrous results, and the strong arm of the law must eventually predominate."[64]

The strong arm of the law, however, usually predominated when it was a case of Mexicans threatening Anglos, while Anglos could attack Mexicans with little fear of legal recrimination. For example, Sebree was never charged with a crime even though he had tried to kill Garza in cold blood. The Sociedad Mexicana of Laredo, presided over by Ignacio Martínez, published a flyer with a blaring "PROTESTA" at the top, condemning both the attempted murder of Garza and Sebree's impunity.[65] Cases such as these showed the Mexican community that they could not rely on the courts for justice.

The "takeover" of Rio Grande City also exposed the fault lines between the Mexican consul and Mexicans living in Texas, both U.S. and non-U.S. citizens. Following Garza's shooting, a group of twenty armed Mexicans went to ask Consul González what he planned to do about the killing of Mexicans by Anglo Americans. The consul responded: "If you are American Citizens, that is to say Texans, I do not have anything to do with you; but if among you there are some Mexican citizens, I will comply with my duties in advising you that you are gravely infringing on the laws of this country, getting involved with politics. . . . Given that you have asked me for advice, with the weight of my position, I am telling you to go home quietly and do not get involved again in the politics of a foreign country."[66] Thus, the Mexican consul refused to help the Mexicans if they were U.S. citizens and castigated them if they were Mexican citizens for getting involved with U.S. politics. While Consul González helped secure the bail bond for four Mexicans, he boasted that he had "refrained from saying one word" for the other thirty or more Texas Mexicans in jail.[67] González attempted to relieve himself of responsibility for these Mexicans by arguing that "the authorities are convinced that the individuals responsible for the riot are for the most part Texans and some Mexicans naturalized in this country, and at the most two or three true Mexicans."[68] After investigations, presumably to prove that Garza and the "rioters" were not "true Mexicans," the Mexican consul in Brownsville grudgingly admitted that Garza, having not voted in Cameron County and having registered as a Mexican citizen in the consulate on March 23, 1880, was still a Mexican citizen.[69]

While the consul justified his position to his government, Texas Mexicans lambasted him in their newspapers. An article in Garza's *El Comercio Mexicano* attacked the consul for his inactivity and complicity with the attempt on Garza's life. The author asked whether the Mexican representatives had "come here to eat and sleep the easy-life?"[70] Although it did not appear that Sebree was motivated or paid by the Mexican government, Texas Mexicans felt that Díaz was complicit, if not in the planning then certainly by his failure to defend the rights of Mexicans in Texas. One Spanish-language Laredo newspaper condemned the consul's actions as "shameful" and accused him of allying with the enemy: "The man that does this, does not deserve anything but the epithet of traitor."[71]

At the same time that the Rio Grande City "riot" exposed the divisions between the Mexican consul and Mexicans in Texas, it also brought to the surface, or to newspaper print, latent Anglo fears of a "race war" in which they would be driven from the region. The *Brownsville Times* expressed best this paranoid fear of Mexican "aliens" taking over the Rio Grande Valley: "It crops out in Webb County once in a while, is felt in Duval, and in Starr County there is a strong faction who boldly declares it their intention to, as far as practicable, raise a little republic of aliens in that section, and who propose to drive all Americans and every English speaking person out of office and run that section to suit themselves. And the late riot was an outcropping of this feeling which is emphasized in the expression often heard, and which is but thinly concealed by the writers of *Comercio Mexicano*, and like papers, 'That this section belongs to us and the d——d gringos should all be run out of it.' "[72] The *Brownsville Times* thus justified Garza's shooting because, according to the paper, Garza had been part of this movement to run the "d——d gringos" out of the area. "Violence is to be avoided where possible," stated the *Express*, "but a Colt's revolver manages to catch and hold the attention of the Mexican bandit much more readily than anything else."[73] The only way to deal with Mexican bandits, according to San Antonio's major daily newspaper, was with violence.

The *Brownsville Times* concluded that if the troops were not given free reign to capture Mexican marauders they could expect more uncontrolled Mexican mobs to "burn, rob, and murder the peaceful inhabitants." The blame fell on Mexican "aliens" who, in the author's doomsday estimation, "may attack a town, capture it, murder the sheriff and other county officers, kill American [read Anglo] citizens and rob stores and burn dwellings without the officer in charge of the troops lying in cantonments near by deeming himself authorized to interfere or to aid civil authorities in maintaining order." Given this anarchic scenario, the author argued that troops should be empowered to "seize bands of marauders believed to have entered in the country," even though not "caught in the act of invasion."[74] This attitude turned all Mexicans into suspected "alien invaders," and therefore gave the troops a free hand in arresting any of them. When

Garza's rebellion broke out three years later, the U.S. Army troops adopted the policy advocated by the *Brownsville Times*, arresting scores of Mexicans and breaking into their homes with no evidence that they were involved in any illegal activity.

"NOWISE A BOUNDARY EXCEPT IN NAME"

The assassination attempt in Rio Grande City illustrates how Texas and Mexican politics overlapped. Mexican agents continually transgressed the national boundary to spy and occasionally kill opponents on the U.S. side. Meanwhile, exiled Mexican dissidents distributed their political propaganda across the river in Mexico and also staged armed raids from Texas soil. Just as Mexicans crossed back and forth, the Texas Rangers and U.S. military frequently penetrated Mexican territory.[75] While the 1848 Treaty of Guadalupe Hidalgo definitively fixed the boundary line, the border existed more in theory than in practice. As the chief architect of the anti-Garza campaign, Captain Bourke, put it, the Rio Grande "is supposed to be the dividing line between the territory of the State of Texas and the soil of the Mexican Republic, but . . . it can in nowise be indicated as a boundary except in name."[76] Cross-border insurrections brought the border's permeability into the limelight. The ensuing public debate over the violation of the boundary ultimately served to reinforce it as a barrier and marker of national identity. Not coincidentally, it was in the late 1890s, following on the heels of Garza's rebellion, that a joint U.S.-Mexican International Water Boundary Commission surveyed the entire border, erecting concrete monuments to physically define the landscape.

While the *Brownsville Times* advocated short-sighted and simple-minded repression to deal with the "Mexican mob," Garza insisted on a contextual and historical explanation of Mexican immigration. A week after his shooting, Garza published an editorial that laid out the problems encountered by Mexicans in Texas. Mexicans came to Texas in search of work to support their families, but unfortunately, he argued, they received less compensation "than an American, than a Frenchman, and in summary, less than a man of color." He went on to condemn U.S. politicians who brought Mexicans over to vote in city, state, and federal elections. Once Mexicans had given up their "national honor," Garza reasoned, they should at least use their rights as American citizens to gain access to public office "so that they could keep safe their *hermanos de raza* [brothers of the race/people]! Why then do you allow the Americans who hate our raza so bitterly to govern? Perhaps there is no majority of Texas Mexicans in this or other districts? Or do you believe in racial superiority?"[77] His taunting questions were meant to encourage Texas Mexicans to stop voting like sheep for any party that offered them money or alcohol, and instead to run their own candidates for office. According to Evan Anders's study of South Texas politics, the practice of "corralling" Mexican voters and plying them with liquor and barbecue all night until the polls opened continued until the 1920s and 1930s.[78]

The election was not the only issue. At its root, the problem was one of power, control over land and government. "A few lawyers and some American adventurers currently possess the principal titles," Garza railed, "having left in the most complete ruin an infinity of widows and orphaned Mexicans, whose misfortune assigned their titles in the part of the land that [the Americans] usurped in the unjust war of '46 and '47." This sort of writing was what got Garza into trouble in the first place, and even after this assassination attempt, there were no signs of him easing his critique or silencing his pen. In fact, the editorial promised a series of articles so that "Mexicans in Texas and Texanos know the origin of their present circumstances, study the way to escape them and vote away with dignity the yoke that oppresses them."[79] Thus, alongside his struggle against tyranny in Mexico, Garza found himself engaged in a battle to liberate Mexicans in South Texas from the "yoke" of Anglo oppression. In a sonnet written on Mexican Independence Day, a week before the shooting in Rio Grande City, Garza proclaimed his dual struggle in the United States and in Mexico:

> Si señores, defiende a un pueblo hermano
> Mi humilde pluma ya avatida
> Y representa al pueblo mexicano
>
> (Yes, señores, it defends a brotherly people
> My already despondent humble pen.
> And it represents the Mexican people.)[80]

"YOU ARE NOT A MAN: YOU ARE ONLY A WOMAN"

In addition to his journalistic analysis, Garza attempted to memorialize the Sebree episode in a more popular form, the corrido. I found the handwritten lyrics of a corrido titled "Stanza Dedicated to the Bandit Sebree" among the correspondence that Garza's family has preserved. While there was no written music to accompany the twelve stanzas of lyrics, the nature of the subject matter, the way in which the story is narrated, and the rhyming pattern and repetition of the chorus suggest that these words were meant to be sung and not just read.[81]

Has probado asesino cobarde
Que bandido lo fuiste y serás;
Tus hazañas las haces alarde
Las cometes y pronto te vas.

(coro) Mexicanos al grito de alarma
Con prestesa el garrote empuñar
Y á trancasos matemos á Sebree,
Al instante; que al campo va a entrar.

(You have proven to be a cowardly assassin
For a bandit you have been and will be.
You publicly boast of your feats
You carry them out and quickly take leave.

(chorus) Mexicans [rise] to the call of alarm
Grab the garrote with haste
And let us club Sebree to death
Immediately; for he is going to the countryside.)[82]

The verses tell the story of Sebree's attempted assassination of Garza and his vile murder of Resendez, and the rousing chorus exhorts Mexicans to "club Sebree to death" before he runs off to the countryside. The ballad highlights Sebree's cowardice, accusing him of killing Resendez and "various other of our brothers" (otros varios de nuestros hermanos), never face to face but always with their hands and feet tied. This same idea of Sebree shooting nonaggressive Mexicans is repeated in the fourth stanza with the lines, "you shot Garza first / when he was turning backward" (Le tirastes á Garza primero / Cuando estaba boltiado hacia atras). The next stanza shows the injured Garza drawing his pistol and the frightened Sebree running away "like a hen" (como una gallina). Along with the hen reference, Sebree was portrayed as having been so frightened when he ran away and hid that he went into labor. "Wretch! Have you no shame / That Garza made you run? / Your breast does not comfort your conscience / You are not a man; you are only a woman" (¡Miserable! No tienes verguenza / De que Garza te hiciera correr / Ya tu pecho no abriga conciencia: / No eres hombre; solo eres muger [*sic*]." The ballad continued the analogy, comparing Sebree's clothes to that of a woman's:

> Crinolinas y nalgas postizas
> En lugar de muy buen pantalon
> Camisón en lugar de camisas
> Como prueba de tu gran valor
>
> (Crinoline and artificial buttocks
> Instead of very good pants
> Nightgown instead of shirts
> As evidence of your great valor.)

The final stanza implored:

> Mexicanos Texanos; no olviden
> Las hazañas del Sebree campeon
> Es preciso que siempre se cuiden
> Del que siempre asecina [*sic*] á traición
>
> (Texas Mexicans; do not forget
> The deeds of the champion Sebree
> It is necessary to always watch out
> For those who kill by betrayal.)[83]

While we don't know whether the corrido was ever sung or how widely it was disseminated, it shows that Garza tried to popularize his ideas and the history of this episode to a wider audience than just the newspaper-reading public. The corrido points to ethnic conflict between Anglos and Mexicans, especially with its chorus that amounts to a call to arms, but significantly it uses gender as the means to deliver its most severe condemnation of Sebree. Sebree may have been a cutthroat murderer but, even worse, he was a cowardly and womanly murderer.

FACING DEATH

What can be concluded from the attempted assassination and the rebellion that ensued? Although the reports of an armed uprising following Garza's shooting appear to have been exaggerated, the incident demonstrated his popular appeal on the border and the degree of Anglo racial fear. If anything, this near-death experience strengthened Garza's resolve and boosted his image as a heroic defender of Mexicans. Perhaps it was at this moment, while lying on his deathbed, that Garza decided he should mount an armed rebellion; after all, his enemies, both Anglo and Mexican, were quickly closing in. Whether he liked it or not, the political struggle that began with words and ballots was now being fought with guns and bullets. Ever since that time, Garza kept his gold pocket watch with one of Sebree's flattened Winchester bullets lodged in the chain to remind himself of his brush with death, and perhaps to underline the life-and-death urgency with which he would live out his remaining days.[84]

Garza's obituary erroneously had been published in the newspapers just after he was shot. His false obituary may have allowed him to confront death and free himself to act on his desires. And more than just his desires, the outpouring of support by the Mexican community in Rio Grande City probably strengthened his image of himself as an important leader. While Garza's life hung in the balance, *El Comercio Mexicano* addressed the Mexican consuls and made it clear that if Garza were to be killed, there would be others to take his place: "Ah! Cowards and miserable assassin. Do you think that ending Garza's existence will stop the defenders of the Mexican race? How gullible are you? After Garza there will succeed another no less bitter, and to this one another, and another until we have realized our desires."[85]

SANDOVAL'S 1890 REBELLION

Two years after Garza's attempted assassination and four years after Martínez's failed insurrection, another revolt was being organized from the Texas border. This rebellion, led by Francisco Ruíz Sandoval in 1890, foreshadowed Garza's more-sustained effort the next year. Both anti-Díaz revolts were organized among the border exile community, but while the first ended as a farce, the latter ended in tragedy. Depending on whose account you believe, Sandoval was either a seasoned Central and South American revolutionary general or a disgruntled junior officer in the Mexican Army. When Sandoval began fomenting revolution in Mexico, the government promptly deported him, a Chilean citizen, as a "pernicious foreigner." Since that time he had lived in exile in Laredo, Texas, plotting the overthrow of Díaz's government with other Mexican oppositionists.[86]

Bernardo Reyes and Porfirio Díaz's extensive spying network in South Texas gave them advanced warning of practically every organizing effort by their enemies, including Francisco Ruíz Sandoval, Ignacio Martínez, Paulino Martínez, and Catarino Garza.[87] With such intelligence they could defend themselves against an insurrection as well as prevent them from occurring by harassing oppositionists in Texas. Worried about reports of a new revolution brewing in Laredo, Reyes devised an elaborate plot to lure Sandoval across the river to Mexico and then arrest him.[88] By mid-June 1890, Reyes informed Díaz that Sandoval had fifty "bandidos" in Laredo ready to invade Mexico and had invited Catarino Garza to gather more people along the river near Eagle Pass. Mexican troops were rapidly deployed along the river, with Colonel Luis Cerón in command from Laredo to Piedras Negras, and General Lojero in charge of the rest of the border lying in Tamaulipas. While Reyes prepared for the worst, he believed that until Sandoval and Martínez had acquired arms and resources they did not pose a serious threat.[89]

Although the rebellion was being organized primarily from Texas soil, efforts were also underway to garner support from Mexico's interior. In May 1890, the Mexican government obtained a letter sent by Paulino Martínez to Silviano Gómez, called on him to second their revolutionary plan and to organize forces to join the rebellion from the state of Hidalgo in central Mexico. Paulino appealed to Gómez as a patriot, arguing that "we cannot tolerate that a horde of ruffians continue to traffic scandalously with the national interests."[90] With the letter in hand, Díaz felt that he finally had sufficient proof to ask for the extradition of Ignacio Martínez, Paulino Martínez, and Francisco Ruíz Sandoval.[91]

News from the border confirmed their worst fears. On June 21, there was "great alarm" in Nuevo Laredo, with the troops called out in the expectation that General Martínez would march across with his men. Along with his reports of excitement on the border, the Mexican consul in San Antonio also sent Reyes an announcement of an oppositionist meeting in Lampazos, Nuevo León, on June 1, held by the son of the popular regional caudillo Francisco Naranjo.[92] While it remains unclear whether Naranjo's son was involved in the Sandoval conspiracy, it would not have been too far-fetched given the family's political sympathies. Whatever degree of secrecy the movement had previously maintained, by mid-June the imminent invasion had become public knowledge.

On June 25, 1890, the *Laredo Daily Times* reported that Sandoval and a band of fifty men were ready to invade Mexico and that the U.S. military had warrants out for their arrest.[93] In fact, Sandoval had already entered Mexico the day before at Guerrero, Tamaulipas, with thirty-five armed men. In June, Paulino Martínez's Laredo newspaper, *El Chinaco*, published "a revolutionary plan outlawing Díaz and all others in authority, and calling on all who will join in revolutionizing the country."[94] The language of the plan matched Garza's subsequent 1891 Plan Revolucionario very closely. In fact, *El Correo de Laredo* would later claim that both Sandoval's and Garza's manifestos were merely edited versions of a plan drawn up by Martínez years earlier, probably during the 1886 Tamaulipas rebellion.[95]

In their brief stay in Mexico they did not engage in combat, but rather scurried back across the river when fired on by Colonel Cerón. Laredo's police chief arrested the soaking-wet insurrectionists for violation of neutrality laws as they emerged from the river in their underwear.[96] In a letter to Díaz, Reyes requested the $2,000 he had promised Laredo's chief of police on Sandoval's capture, and suggested that the chief be contracted again to capture Ignacio Martínez. Reyes further advised that they should hold off on executing the three revolutionists that they had captured in Mexico, at least until after Ruíz Sandoval and his men had been handed over to Mexican authorities.[97] Reluctant to turn over prisoners to the Mexicans if they knew that they would immediately be killed, prosecutors decided to try the would-be revolutionaries in U.S. courts.

Sandoval and eight of his followers were quickly brought to San Antonio where they stood trial on charges of violating neutrality laws. The *Laredo Times* remarked that the revolutionists, when marched into the courtroom, looked like a "woe-be-gone army of men and boys," hardly a force capable of invading and taking over Mexico. The throng of spectators who packed the courthouse in San Antonio to watch the trial demonstrated that there was great public interest in this aborted rebellion. The *Times* portrayed Sandoval in a positive light, describing him as a "stout built Mexican," with erect bearing and walking with "firm tread." His followers, on the other hand, were characterized as a "woe-be-gone set" gathered from the "plebeian class," and ranging in age from very young to very old.[98]

Even if the rebels were not impressive to this reporter, the financial support the rebels received from prominent men in Laredo suggested that the undertaking was a serious one. Ignacio Martínez raised $4,000 for bail and another $800 to $1,000 for legal expenses. According to a Mexican government informant, the accused had "a great deal of sympathy among Mexicans" which had even grown since their apprehension. Whereas Sandoval could not find anyone to lend him a peso before his arrest, he now found himself flush with money. Sandoval's bail bond was signed by seven of the most prominent politicians and businessmen of Laredo: Raymond Martin, Honore Ligarde, Romulo Zardeneta, Dr. Lino Villareal, Antonio Salinas, Tomás Villastrigo, and Crecencio Rodríguez. According to the consul's report, Martin, of French descent, was one of the wealthiest residents of Laredo, was a leader of the dominant Bota party, and had good relations with Mexicans. Ligarde, a member of the city council, was a propertied man with connections to Martin. Villareal, a mid-level doctor, served the poor Mexican community and was friends with Ignacio Martínez and Zardeneta. Villastrigo was also a member of the city council. The presence of such prominent men as signatories of this bond led the consul to conclude that politicians were using their support of Sandoval to show themselves as "protectors of the *raza mexicana*" for the upcoming elections.[99] By signing the bail bond, Consul Varrios surmised, these men had "bought" Sandoval so that he would campaign for the Bota party in the November election.[100] The other possibility that the consul did not entertain was that the rebels actually had widespread support, especially among people of Mexican or French descent, such as Raymond Martin who shared a "Latin" background. Of the seven signatories to the bail bond, none had an Anglo surname.[101]

Not long after being released on bail in San Antonio, Sandoval was arrested again in Laredo. Attorney Charles Pierce requested the arrest on the pretense that it would "conserve the peace." It was readily apparent to everyone familiar with border politics that Pierce was acting at the behest of the Mexican government. Justo Cárdenas, a lawyer who went into exile from Monterrey after Reyes declared a state of emergency in 1885, criticized the San Antonio consul for acting like all of the other consuls under the Tuxtepecano administration, which was to say, very badly. Cárdenas also blamed the complicity of U.S. officials, arguing that they had demanded a "ridiculous and anti-legal" bail of 1,000 pesos.[102] There is no direct proof that Laredo's attorney was taking orders from Mexico, but just a couple of weeks earlier, Reyes had written to Pierce offering him money for the capture of the oppositionists' arms and munitions.[103] Although he was unable to come through on that request, Pierce succeeded in incarcerating Sandoval on trumped-up charges, thereby satisfying his benefactor, Bernardo Reyes.

The proceedings at Sandoval's trial in San Antonio revealed the revolutionists' poor organization and lack of resources, as well as the presence of government spies within the ranks of the group. The prosecution had to prove not only intent to violate the neutrality law, but that Sandoval had prepared a "military expedition" on Texas soil and then invaded Mexico. In spite of having been caught in their still-soaking-wet underwear after having crossed the river back to Texas, the high burden of proof made it difficult to prove culpability, especially in front of a jury drawn from a generally anti-Díaz public.

The testimony elicited from the defendants and witnesses established that Sandoval had made inquiries about buying weapons and had crossed with several other men into Mexico, but the group that was arrested numbered no more than thirteen and it was unclear whether they had taken guns across the river with them. All of the witnesses corroborated the assertion that Sandoval had very little money and no resources. One man testified that Ignacio Martínez had filed a claim against Sandoval, but that he was unable to collect anything because all of Sandoval's possessions, a trunk and his wife's clothing, were still being held until he paid his rent. Thus, even though Martínez was owed money by Sandoval, and had gone to court to recover it, he was still willing to raise money for Sandoval's bail and legal defense.[104] The prosecution finally acceded that "the defendants were poor men and as far as they knew entirely without means."[105]

Much of the trial focused on the issue of whether Sandoval and his men carried weapons into Mexico, thereby implicating them in an aggressive military action. One of the defendants, Dario Sánchez, turned state's witness and claimed that they had brought weapons across to Mexico, and on Sandoval's orders had dumped them in the river on their way back to Texas. This damaging assertion, however, was less convincing when on cross-examination by Sandoval's lawyer, Sánchez admitted to being an undercover agent for Laredo's police chief, Eugene Iglesias, since June 22.[106] Police Chief Iglesias was at the time receiving money from the Mexican government for his efforts to suppress anti-Díaz movements in Texas.[107] Furthermore, Manuel Valádez, who had seen the "revolutionists" emerge half-naked from the river on their return from Mexico, provided credible evidence in his testimony that, at least on their return, the men were unarmed. The defense lawyer's questions comically undermined the believability of the prosecution's witness while making use of his testimony to exonerate the defendants:

BETHEL COOPWOOD (defense lawyer): Did Sandoval have on a short undershirt?
VALADEZ: Yes sir.

COOPWOOD: Did it reach down to his navel?

VALADEZ: I did not pay any attention.

COOPWOOD: If he had a Gatling gun under his undershorts do you think you would have seen it?

VALADEZ: I might not have.[108]

The court never determined just what Sandoval was hiding in his undershorts, but the defense was able to poke holes in the prosecution's case. While the grand jury found enough evidence to indict Sandoval and twelve of his followers, two of the state's witnesses changed their testimony at the December 1890 San Antonio trial. In July of that year, Reyes had suggested to San Antonio Consul Ornelas that "some financial support and some hope for the future" be offered to Zertuche and some of his "exploitable" comrades in exchange for their testifying against Sandoval.[109] Although this strategy may have worked initially, Rafael Zertuche and Salomé Arce, both indicted as part of Sandoval's raiding party, contradicted their earlier testimony, thereby exonerating themselves and Sandoval. Zertuche and Arce were jailed for perjury, but their refusal to testify against Sandoval made it very difficult for the prosecution to obtain a conviction.[110]

In their closing arguments, the prosecution claimed that Sandoval was not a common thief or robber but rather "a political man of revolution" who called himself general and whose purpose was to "raise a revolution and plunge the people of Mexico into a horrid war."[111] The defense, meanwhile, argued that the prosecution had not proved that Sandoval had organized a "military expedition." There was no evidence that people were trained in Texas or that they did harm to anyone in Mexico, or even that they were armed, except for one gun in the hands of the state's witness. The revolutionary proclamation found by the Mexican government was not even signed by Sandoval, and he argued that, even if it were, publishing a proclamation of revolution would not constitute a "military enterprise."[112]

On the morning that the jury handed down the not-guilty verdict, the prosecuting lawyers, McLeary and Flemming, wrote to Consul Ornelas to explain the outcome: "We believe that the insignificance of the parties and the ridiculous fiasco in which their expedition terminated went a great ways towards securing their acquittal. If they had burned a few houses and could have had the courage to shoot down some of the rural guards then we think there would have been no difficulty in securing the conviction."[113] Beyond the "insignificance" and lack of "courage" of these revolutionaries, the inability to convict Sandoval and his men demonstrated the widespread support that the anti-Díaz movement enjoyed in South Texas. Before the trial had even begun, Ornelas feared that a jury would acquit the revolutionists because "crimes such as these, are generally regarded by the masses, erroneously, as political, and consequently of little importance." Juries were therefore inclined to unconsciously reflect "certain public sentimentality that turns in favor of the accused when the offense has ceased to impress the public mind and the accused remains as an object of sympathy and commiseration."[114] Overlooking Ornelas's paternalistic attitude toward the "masses" that comprised juries, he recognized that a jury, unless made up of "superior men," would not view this revolution as a moral crime such as "a murder, robbery or rape."[115] There are "plenty of Mexicans along the frontier that have no love for President Díaz," as one Texas newspaper put it, but that was not grounds for prosecution.[116] Furthermore, the fact that Arce and Zertuche were willing to change their testimony, openly perjure themselves, and go to jail to exonerate Sandoval implies that community pressure worked in the revolutionists' favor.

The case posed a broader dilemma for Consul Ornelas, who wrote to the prosecution lawyers expressing his belief that the key to maintaining good relations between the two nations was "the proper use of the divisory line." The important issue here, therefore, was not that Sandoval represented a great threat but rather that the case could establish a "precedent calculated to prevent the occurrence of the same offense for all future time."[117] For Ornelas these movements, when successful, resulted in "bloodshed, murder, plunder, destruction of property, arrest of commerce, industry and trade, in which foreign capital, life and property are equally exposed." Even in the case of a failed insurrection, such as Sandoval's, it had "very materially injured the commercial condition of the border."[118] The real tragedy of the inability to convict Sandoval, therefore, was the effect it would have on outside capitalists who would be scared away from investing in the border region and in Mexico.

During the period that Sandoval waited in Laredo for his trial date, Reyes was busy devising a sophisticated plan with Colonel Luis Cerón to kidnap Sandoval and bring him to Mexico where he would be charged with fomenting rebellion. Reyes did not want to wait for the outcome of Sandoval's trial because he had little faith that a San Antonio jury would render justice. For the plan to succeed, it was crucial that the public be convinced that Sandoval had crossed the river with the intent of launching a revolution. Otherwise, Reyes explained, "the act would appear like a kidnapping in the United States by our agents and it would allow for serious international claims, that in addition to bringing demands against our government, would provoke a great scandal in the press of the two countries."[119]

This plan, including international kidnapping, planting of evidence, false declarations, and payoffs, was not the work of some rogue element of Mexican state security but was devised by General Bernardo Reyes with the personal knowledge and approval of President Díaz.[120] The careful attention to fabricating a "legal" case for Sandoval's capture and the sensitivity to U.S. public opinion and the press both illustrate that countervailing forces limited the brutality with which Reyes could act. Especially given the international context of the border, they could not just murder Sandoval. They first had to have "legal" proof of wrongdoing, whether real or fabricated, and then they could either incarcerate, or, depending on the nature of their evidence, kill him. Although it is evident that none of these plans succeeded in drawing Sandoval across the river, they do demonstrate the lengths to which the Mexican government was willing to go to silence oppositionists. Reyes had been plotting since April 1890 to bring Sandoval across to Mexico, and he would have attempted the same with Ignacio Martínez, but, as he lamented, Martínez was "very well informed and surrounded by precautions."[121] Understanding these kinds of covert government operations helps us to appreciate the fears that Garza expressed in his autobiography that Díaz agents would one day assassinate him. The existence of spies and infiltrators must also have contributed to divisions and suspicions among the oppositionists because many of them were clandestinely on the government's payroll.

Not having had access, as we do now, to the private papers of these officials, made it virtually impossible for revolutionists to prove government complicity in particular assassinations. Even with access to the official correspondence of important figures like Díaz, Reyes, and Matías Romero, other archives, like Mexico's Archivo de Defensa Nacional, have restricted access.[122] Given the multilayered nature of these conspiracies, where even consuls and lower-level military officials would be unwitting accessories to higher-level counterintelligence operations, it is difficult if not impossible to resolve particular issues, such as whether the opposition fractured on its own or mainly because of government manipulation. The irresolvable nature of these troubling and important particularities, does not, however, prevent a general understanding of how the Porfirian machine functioned.

Díaz was a master, not only of image control but also of the actual, material control of Mexico's population. Co-optation, patronage, and, when necessary, brutal violence were employed to "keep the peace." The insurrectionary attempts on the border, however, as well as less dramatic forms of resistance, demonstrate that Díaz's control was not absolute. Large sectors of the Mexican population along both sides of the border knew that the government was tyrannical and despotic and, given a chance, they vigorously and repeatedly opposed it. Therefore, exposing the mechanisms that "manufactured consent" and imposed silence helps to uncover the traces of alternative and at times resistant histories.[123]

"THE COMADRES ARE MAD AT EACH OTHER"

Given the Porfirian regime's elaborate counterintelligence operations on the border, it is often difficult to separate truth from fabrication. The Mexican government manipulated the press, spread false rumors, and even plotted assassinations, all to discredit and demobilize the opposition on the South Texas border. The first incursion by Sandoval in June 1890 inspired Reyes and the Mexican consuls in Texas to increase their spying activities and to devise clandestine plans to capture other revolutionists operating in Texas. Immediately following the incursion, Reyes suggested that Colonel Cerón and Consul Ornelas do everything they could to exploit the division between Ignacio Martínez and Ruíz Sandoval.[124] Within a few months, Reyes's plan succeeded in turning the border oppositionists against one another.

The oppositionists presented a united front around the time of Sandoval's revolt, with Ignacio Martínez securing Sandoval's bail bond and helping Paulino Martínez, another revolutionary journalist, to escape capture. Even by late July 1890, Ignacio Martínez and Sandoval seemed to be collaborating as they traveled together to meet with Catarino Garza and twenty other men at Palito Blanco ranch, near San Diego.[125] A few months later, the cooperation between these men disintegrated after Ignacio Martínez fell out of favor with his coconspirators. In early October, Justo Cárdenas, a former comrade of Dr. Martínez, had united with Ruíz Sandoval, and in an article entitled "Applaud or I'll Kill You," Cárdenas publicly rejected Martínez as the leader of the opposition in South Texas.[126] Eusebio García, who personally knew how Ignacio had helped secure Sandoval's release from jail, considered Sandoval a *desgraciado* (ungrateful wretch) for turning against the general. Don Ignacio had even requested that García loan his horse, a silver-inlaid saddle, a pistol, and five dollars to Paulino Martínez so that he could escape from Laredo and hide with their friends at San Diego.[127] Just when or how the split occurred, or whether it developed naturally or at the instigation of Reyes agents, cannot be definitively ascertained. One may suspect, however, that at the very least government counterintelligence operations exacerbated distrust and dissent among revolutionary leaders who were already prone to fear betrayal and jealously guard their leadership of the movement.

Even after Sandoval's revolt failed, Mexican exiles in Laredo continued to plot their revolution. Dr. Ignacio Martínez, who had been a principal organizer of previous insurrections, soon found himself the target of a campaign of harassment. Ever since his involvement with the rebellion in Tamaulipas in 1886, government officials watched Martínez's movements, suspecting that he would organize another revolution from Texas soil. Their concern led them to go beyond just surveillance, and over the next several years Reyes and Díaz oversaw a far-reaching effort to discredit Martínez and foment discord among his supporters. In February 1891, these schemes finally reached their ultimate conclusion when Dr. Ignacio Martínez was gunned down on the streets of Laredo.

To understand how Díaz managed to divide and foment conflict among the oppositionists on the border, it is important to analyze the primary means of mass communication, the newspapers. Manipulation of the press in South Texas was one of the most effective tactics employed by the Mexican government to combat its enemies. Newspapers were also one of the oppositionists' most dangerous weapons. As early as 1888, Bernardo Reyes wrote to Porfirio Díaz complaining about Martínez's publication, *El Mundo*, and suggesting ways to undermine him. Among other strategies, Reyes wanted to encourage opponents of Martínez to write negative articles about him.[128] Díaz approved of the plan, arguing that even if it required money it would be worthwhile if they were able to rid themselves of a few of these men.[129]

A few days after Sandoval's aborted invasion of Mexico in late June 1890, Reyes was already devising a plan to use the press to exacerbate frictions between Martínez and Sandoval: "It is important that the American newspapers speak of how badly Ignacio Martínez behaves toward Ruíz Sandoval and his accomplices, and with the rest who were in the conspiracy after he had inspired them to take action. These newspapers could still add that the men who had involved themselves, upon seeing the conduct of Martínez, naturally feel hurt by him. In this way, it is probable that we can remove the few sympathies that Martínez has and it is possible that they will even view him with antipathy. I spoke about this with Ornelas because he can bring about the desired publications."[130] Reyes thus wanted to use the U.S. newspapers to exploit the tensions between Martínez and Sandoval and thereby divide the anti-Díaz opposition. Within months Ignacio Martínez, Ruíz Sandoval, and Paulino Martínez were trading accusations of corruption and incompetence in the border press.

By September, Reyes's plan showed signs of success. Ignacio Martínez publicly attacked Sandoval in a letter to a U.S. newspaper, calling him a "nobody, who is neither a General, nor a Mexican."[131] Justo Cárdenas quickly joined Sandoval's camp and condemned Martínez in *La Colonia Mexicana*.[132] By January, the two factions were hurling personal insults at one another in their newspapers, while the progovernment Mexican press delighted in reprinting the exchange. In an article entitled "Se enojaron las comadres" (The comadres are mad at each other) Nuevo Laredo's *El Orden* sarcastically commented that "the patriots on the other side of the Bravo, jealous of we don't know what, because for the sensible society they are all the same, are telling some truths in the press that . . . show that a complete harmony reigns among them." Ignacio Martínez's *El Mundo* had called Paulino Martínez and Ruíz Sandoval "vagrant swindlers who want to live like parasites on the labor of others, covering themselves with the mask of patriots." Meanwhile, Paulino's *El Chinaco* derided Ignacio as "a scoundrel, a coward, assassin, villain, ambitious, false patriot and crazy."[133]

Reyes's mouthpiece, *La Voz de Nuevo León*, reprinted the full-length text of the exchange between *El Mundo*, *El Chinaco*, and *La Colonia Mexicana* under the headline "Los Revoltosos de allende el Rio Bravo pintados por si Mismos" (The Revolutionaries on the Other Side of the Rio Bravo Painted by Themselves). The mutual recrimination among these oppositionists was a propaganda boon for Reyes, and he saw to it that their dissension reached a wider audience. Martínez accused Ruíz Sandoval of belonging to a group of pseudo oppositionists who used the movement to line their pockets with money. "They have a little businessman who leads them and collects their checks, a little military man who represents the company, a little lawyer who defends them, a noisy press which exalts them and at the same time slanders those who do not allow them to rob." Martínez contended that because he had not lent his name to their operations, "they profess a deep hate for us, they insult us, and slander us." Their relations with Porfirian elites and their "continuous and calculated attacks" against him could only be explained, Martínez argued, if they were working for "*el bandido* Díaz." Finally, he affirmed his revolutionary principles, declaring that he was against substituting worse bandits for the ones in power. "I will neither protect nor tolerate these blackmailing and miserable rascals, who without valor, without gratitude, without honor, nor shame, insult like women and allow themselves to be slapped in the face like godmothers, wretches who pretend to be revolutionaries of Mexico to embezzle the product of honorable men's labor and soil with infamy and insult our Mexican community on this border."[134]

Not only had Martínez attacked their political integrity, but he questioned their masculine honor by claiming they acted like women, had no shame, and were too lazy to work. Martínez's critique continued in the next issue of *El Mundo*, personally insulting Ruíz Sandoval for being a vagrant and not working in an "honest" profession. The language Martínez employed to attack Sandoval echoed the northern Mexican developmentalist ethic; it was also the argument used by the Mexican government to discredit all exiled oppositionists: "We hope that he now dedicates himself to some work, because he has lived here for close to one year with everything and his family without earning three cents in any honest job, and taking large sums from this neighborhood by more or less astute means." And then, approving the Mexican government's deportation of Ruíz Sandoval for being a "pernicious foreigner," Martínez asserted that Sandoval "lived scandalously in the cantinas without capital and without any known honest means of subsistence."[135] The developmentalist ethic of honest work, fiscal discipline, moral probity, and manliness so heralded by Porfirian *científicos* (technocrats) was also invoked by anti-Porfirian exiles in Texas.

Paulino Martínez responded in *El Chinaco* that the insults by Ignacio should have been expected because "pigs never stop wallowing in the mud." Paulino stated further that he would unmask "the true Judas of the Mexicans: the hour of justice has arrived. I am the echo of the voice of justice. I come to shout to you what others have not had the valor to tell you. You are a wretch who bends down on your knees to clean the shoes of great men, and puts down the humble Mexicans who have no wealth or influence to put at your disposition." Paulino continued, accusing Ignacio of turning against Sandoval after he had secured his bail bond because a "cacique" had warned him not to get involved. Ignacio had allegedly told Sandoval's defense lawyer to abandon him because they had no money. Paulino asserted that Ignacio's rancor stemmed from his not having been named leader of the revolution. Finally, he criticized Ignacio's arrogant attitude ever since he moved to Laredo, which he characterized as "haughty with the humble, and humble with the haughty."[136] *La Colonia Mexicana* lamented the bitter insults that marked the debate between *El Mundo* and *El Chinaco*, arguing that "they only prove the impotence and hatred in he who lavishes others with them."[137] Meanwhile, Reyes gloated over the infighting between Ignacio and Paulino Martínez, reminding Colonel Cerón that "it would be good if the Nuevo Laredo press reproduced these paragraphs and fired up the spirits of one against the others."[138]

SHOT DOWN ON THE STREETS OF LAREDO

The war of words in newspaper columns soon turned to physical violence on the streets of Laredo. On a Sunday afternoon, Ignacio Martínez met Romulo Zardeneta in front of the office of the *Laredo Times*, and, believing him to be responsible for the insults in the newspaper, whipped him with his riding crop from atop his buggy. However, the whip missed its mark and fell on one of two Anglo businessmen who had accompanied Zardeneta. According to the version published by *El Mundo* (Martínez's newspaper), Deputy Sheriff Victor Morel refused to arrest Martínez, saying that he was a man of property and "gentleman enough to present himself at the first call by the authorities."[139] After Ignacio had whipped Zardeneta, he went to Paulino's house and challenged him to a fight, which Paulino refused. Later that same evening, General Martínez found Sandoval drinking in a bar, and after "abusing him roundly" he also dared him to fight. "Sandoval plucking from his pocket the undershirt in which he was captured last spring[,] exhibited it to the irate Dr. M as evidence of how much he had dared and suffered in the same cause with Dr. M, and declined to fight him."[140] Sandoval's waving of his undershirt in Martínez's face was meant to show that he had the courage to fight Díaz, and was thus honorable.

General Martínez was forced to defend his honor because Sandoval had days earlier questioned his courage in an interview published in *El Chinaco*. In that interview, Sandoval denied Martínez's claim that the general had fled Brownsville to escape Mexican government persecution. Rather, Sandoval insisted, Martínez escaped from Brownsville to avoid a duel with Eulalio Vela, who had challenged him to "settle the matter as men."[141] If Martínez's challenge to Sandoval could be interpreted as a defense of honor, Sandoval's refusing to fight Martínez could also be taken as a sign of honor in that he was able to stand up to him verbally while at the same time demonstrating his self-discipline and control. Sandoval's public accusation that Martínez had left Brownsville to avoid a duel was a stinging insult, and one that could have provoked the whole incident, because it showed Martínez as a coward who runs from his enemies. While there may have been political differences between these factions, honor was the currency by which each side measured itself, and in many cases it was a question of honor that ultimately provoked the violent conflicts.[142]

This episode could not have helped Martínez's tarnished reputation. Not only had the old doctor engaged in ad hominem attacks in his newspaper, but now he was riding around town using his riding crop to whip his enemies and generally wreaking havoc. Insulting a man's honor with words or whips had serious consequences, and everyone expected that Martínez would have to pay one way or another for his transgressions. One local newspaper suggested in an article titled "Adema's de loco, cobarde" (As Well as Crazy, a Coward) that Don Ignacio be straitjacketed and sent to the madhouse.[143] On Monday morning Don Ignacio declared himself guilty of "disturbing the peace" and agreed to pay the corresponding fine.[144]

Laredo waited in anticipation as news spread of the whipping incident. When shots were heard that night from the bank of the river, many people believed that Martínez was involved. As it turned out, he was not. What had happened was that another man, a bit drunk that night, shot his revolver in the air while on the international bridge. Two policemen from Nuevo Laredo returned the fire, killing the inebriated man after firing a volley of twenty-five bullets at him.[145] As *La Colonia Mexicana* put it, the events of Sunday and Monday caused a "great sensation" in Laredo and they "still await something serious."[146] On Wednesday night, Tomás Martínez's young daughter Estela opened the door to see if her father was returning from his job as cashier at the Mexican National Railway. Instead of her father, she was faced by a man dressed as a *pelado* (peasant), pointing a pistol at her face from half a yard away. Estela then screamed, and when her mother came to the door she saw the man release the hammer on the cocked pistol and run away toward the center of town. *El Mundo* theorized that the assassin was after Tomás because he had signed Ignacio's bail bond earlier on Monday along with Eusebio García.[147] However, it later became clear that the assassin had mistaken Tomás Martínez (Ignacio's brother-in-law) for Ignacio, and therefore almost killed the wrong man.

It would not be long before the assassin's bullet found its target. On Tuesday morning, February 3, 1891, Dr. Ignacio Martínez was gunned down in his buggy while conducting his normal rounds visiting patients. All of Laredo's newspapers expressed shock and anger that such a brutal murder could have been perpetrated in broad daylight in their town. The *Laredo Daily Times* declared that "when a citizen of Laredo, of whatever standing, rich or poor, popular or unpopular, is shot down in this city like a dog in broad daylight, it is time that the people of this section should raise their might and rid the country of a cowardly assassin."[148] Even *La Colonia Mexicana*, directed by Justo Cárdenas, which had severely criticized Don Ignacio days earlier, eulogized the general as "an old soldier of liberty": "We drape with mourning the columns of our newspaper in testimony to the pain of the heartfelt death of a Mexican who had occupied a respectable position for his patriotic services, for his scientific and literary knowledge, and for his unbreakable faith in politics." Notwithstanding his merits, however, Cárdenas also blamed Martínez's violent character for having prepared the ground for the killing.[149] Another local newspaper was not surprised at the turn of events, because "he was a man so frank and outspoken, so open in his enemies, so defiant in his manner and words, and so bitterly opposed to the Díaz administration of the Mexican government that a violent death was to have been anticipated or at least was probable." Martínez had even told his personal physician that he expected "personal or political enemies to kill him sooner or later."[150] If the Mexican government had been planning Martínez's death, then the public recriminations in Laredo among the oppositionist community gave them the perfect opportunity and excuse. Whoever ordered the assassination, Reyes and his diplomatic henchmen can be credited with having carefully prepared the ideological soil for just such a harvest.

The *Gate City* described the murder scene in great detail and in such a manner as to inspire sympathy for Martínez and his mourning wife. The overall effect of this poetic account elevated the murder of one individual to an attack against all of society: "In a few minutes after his death Mrs. Martínez came in one of the city carriages, in which someone had gone to notify her, and during all the long time of the confusion, the writing and the examinations she was in the room adjoining the parlor in agonized convulsion of hysterical grief, prevented by friends from entering the room where the corpse lay, the face stained with the blood issuing from the mouth and nose mingled with the dust of the street where he had fallen. Her screams rent the air, and her soul seemed turned out, in a very abandonment of grief, piercing into the very heart of the large crowd that stood outside the house, and solemnizing them with pity and sympathy."[151]

The image of Martínez's wife "in agonized convulsion of hysterical grief" added a personal element to what otherwise would have been dismissed as a political killing. The article continued with vivid detail: "Gen. M always dressed tastily, and as the corpse lay on the floor, the elegant clothing disarranged, the chest covered by the bloody shirts which had been cut off to find the wound, his glossy silk hat on the floor by his head, the striking contrast between his trivial surroundings of society life and the awful solemnity of sudden death was overwhelming."[152] The general's "elegant" and "tasteful" clothes symbolized a society that had been torn open and bloodied by the violent killing.

A biographical pamphlet published by *El Mundo* shortly after Martínez's assassination in 1891 described him as an "apostle" of modernity and liberal ideas in northeastern Mexico: "Martínez was the soul of the young border generation, the motor of modern principles in the states of Nuevo León, Coahuila and Tamaulipas. What others could not do with arms, he attempted and accomplished with the force of propaganda: each of his co-disciples was a new apostle, and every apostle formed innumerable believers in constitutional and reformist dogma."[153] The pamphlet's hagiographic description presented Martínez as the messiah for anticlerical liberals. It was also meant to contextualize his assassination on the streets of Laredo within this contentious history and, more important, give it a political meaning.

Martínez's assassination spawned many theories about the identity of the killers. The most common version held that Martínez had gone to Eusebio García's house between 9 and 10 A.M. for a medical visit. He had left the house and was heading toward the center of town in his buggy, armed with a pistol and a carbine, but unknown to him two well armed and mounted men awaited. While one of these men spoke to Martínez, the other passed from behind and shot Martínez in the back. The general fell immediately from the buggy, the horse took off for town, and the assassins escaped across to Mexico.[154] The *Gate City*, however, cited a witness to the murder who denied the version of two men shooting from the street, suggesting instead that the shooter must have been hidden in a nearby yard.[155] The difficulty in even establishing where the bullet came from and how many gunmen there were, combined with the fact that Martínez had so many enemies in Texas and Mexico, made it very difficult to identify and convict the guilty parties. The *Gate City*, however, on the day of the murder had identified the assassins as Manuel Aldrete and José Maria Martínez, both former allies of Don Ignacio. Aldrete, the newspaper contended, was an agent of the Porfirian regime.[156]

Although the *Gate City* noted that there was no evidence linking local enemies to the recent killing, they suggested that it would be "highly appropriate that Mssrs. Sandoval and Paulino Martínez . . . publicly deny and as far as possible disprove any connection on their part with this foul, cowardly, brutal, hateful crime." This public denial was all the more urgent because *El Duende* had just published an account that described Ignacio's efforts to engage both Paulino and Sandoval in a fight. The oppositionists continued to distrust each other. A few days after Don Ignacio's death, Paulino Martínez ran into Tomás Martínez (Ignacio's brother-in-law) and the encounter nearly ended in a shoot-out. Paulino drew his gun on Tomás and cocked it. Tomás shouted back, "Stop you coward, that is not the way to kill a man," and then pretended to pull a pistol from his own pocket. Paulino then backed into a store, claiming that Tomás had threatened his life.[157] Whoever was to blame, both men had to appear in county court on charges of carrying pistols.[158]

Reyes and Díaz must have felt satisfied that their goal of dividing the revolutionists had succeeded so well that the oppositionists now spent their energies pointing fingers and pistols at one another. Mexico's government-controlled press immediately began to blame oppositionists in Laredo for Martínez's death and to publish alibis for the Mexican officials who stood accused. Monterrey's *La Voz de Nuevo León* and Mexico City's *El Monitor Republicano* blamed Martínez's death on the polemic between *La Colonia Mexicano* and *El Mundo*.[159] Meanwhile, Nuevo Laredo's *El Duende* published a letter from friends of Manuel Aldrete, the government agent accused of Martínez's assassination, claiming that Aldrete was at a funeral in Monterrey the day of the killing: "Monterrey knows well that Manuel did not commit the crime."[160]

Not trusting the local police to conduct a thorough investigation, Martínez's family hired Sheriff Robert Bolton to find the killers. Bolton accused Hilario C. Silva, Nuevo Laredo's district attorney, of murder and arranged for his arrest. The only evidence, however, that Bolton presented before a district court judge at a preliminary hearing consisted of a letter that circuitously linked Silva, one of Reyes's most trusted aides, to the murder. The letter sent in December 1888 from Silva had been recently published in *El Mundo* as evidence of Reyes's role in the assassination.

The letter addressed to one of Martínez's enemies suggested "that if he confronts Martínez in a decided manner and performs an important service he could count on the protection of the authorities on the Mexican side."[161] That Reyes was behind this veiled threat against Martínez's life makes sense given that he had written to Díaz a few months earlier explaining his desires and plans to undermine Martínez. Justo Cárdenas and Romulo Zardeneta had obtained the letter during a visit by Silva to a brothel in Laredo. While Silva was otherwise occupied with a prostitute in another room, Cárdenas and Zardeneta rifled through his clothes and found the letter in a pocket. The letter, vague as it was, would not have proved anything conclusively, but Bolton did not even present the original letter in court and so the judge released Silva for lack of evidence.[162]

In spite of the absence of conclusive proof as to the identity of the assassins, many newspapers suggested that Díaz was either directly or indirectly responsible for Martínez's assassination. As *El Progreso*, a Spanish-language newspaper in New York stated, "If Don Porfirio Díaz can wash his hands like Pilate, he should do it as soon as possible because many will believe that they see blood-stains on them."[163] Whether they had concrete proof or not, Garza was convinced that the Mexican government directed Martínez's assassination. "Never had a better opportunity been presented to the official assassins of Mexico to wash their hands with their local enemies, supposing that these men had challenged the deceased Martínez at every moment, calling him a coward, villain and assassin." However, Garza emphatically stated that nobody would believe that the assassins had acted on their own. Directly accusing Díaz of the murder, Garza wrote that "these vile assassinations have completed the mission entrusted by the author of 'matalos en caliente' [kill them in cold blood], to who now can be attributed the new sentence 'kill them abroad, and I will protect you.'" They killed Martínez, proclaimed Garza, but his newspaper *El Mundo*, has "not yet died."[164]

CONCLUSION

In this chapter I have shown that Garza's 1891 rebellion was part of a longer insurrectionary movement on the border; that the Porfirian regime skillfully led a propaganda campaign against political dissidents; and that the dissidents themselves were often divided. The frequency of armed rebellions beginning with Martínez (1886) and continuing through Sandoval (1890) suggests that there was significant discontent with the Porfirian regime, at least in Mexico's North and in South Texas. However, the short duration of these attacks and the lack of popular support for these efforts also shows that in the 1880s the border opposition did not yet pose a serious threat to Díaz. The absence of enthusiasm for revolt can be attributed in part to Díaz's popularity for having provided stability and economic growth in a country that had undergone repeated foreign invasions and economic stagnation for most of the nineteenth century. Another plausible explanation for the inability of the revolutionaries to succeed has to do with the increasing effectiveness of Díaz and his pro-consul Reyes to sniff out and crush rebellions before they had a chance to obtain popular support. The advent of railroads and telegraph made suppressing revolts quicker and more efficient.

The longevity of the regime should not be attributed solely or even mainly to the ability of the military to squash rebellions once they had occurred. I have shown here how Reyes and Díaz led a propaganda war to win the hearts and minds of border Mexicans and to discredit their enemies. They manipulated the foreign press, used the courts to extradite political dissidents, fostered dissension among the Laredo oppositionists, and devised elaborate schemes to incarcerate or kill key leaders such as Martínez and Sandoval. These strategies proved to be very effective, but they did not prevent Garza from trying to organize his own revolution.

It would be wrong, however, to attribute all of the fighting among oppositionists to the skillful manipulation of the Porfirian regime. Indeed, individual ambitions to lead the revolution and personal rivalry were certainly present among would-be rebels and helped divide their supporters. The trading of public insults and challenges to honor that preceded Martínez's assassination illustrate the internal problems that plagued the anti-Díaz community on the border. These tensions played right into the hands of the regime, making it easier to portray them as a group of opportunistic and disgraceful mercenaries.

The anti-Díaz oppositionists were also hindered by having to fight two battles at once, one against Díaz and another against Anglo Texans. Journalists and political leaders like Garza and Ignacio Martínez engaged both of these struggles with equal fervor and resolve. As Sebree's attempted assassination of Garza shows, defending Mexicans in Texas could be a dangerous affair. However, even though these struggles were aimed at political change in two different countries, they were both motivated by the same liberal ideals, including the right to political participation, equality before the law, and freedom of expression. In spite of the failed rebellions from 1886 from 1891, the divisions in the dissident community, the difficulty of fighting a regime that had such an extensive spy network in Texas, and the energies that had to be devoted to protecting Mexicans in Texas, Catarino Garza was still convinced that Díaz could be overthrown. He also began to believe that he would be the one to do it.

3. REVOLUTION AND REPRESSION

For Catarino Garza, revolution began to seem not only possible but, increasingly, the only hope of achieving change in Mexico. Garza was intimately involved with both Martínez and Sandoval, and he was well aware that their revolts had failed miserably. Yet, after his near-death experience in 1888 in Rio Grande City and the killing of his political ally Ignacio Martínez in Laredo in 1891, there seemed to be an urgency to start the armed rebellion before he too was killed. Such experiences could have led him to turn away from politics and the impossible odds of toppling Díaz, but in actuality they had the opposite effect.

When Garza finally launched his revolt on September 15, 1891, it appeared to both the press and the Mexican government that it would be like the earlier cross-border insurrections that were crushed in a few days. Whether a result of better organizing or the experiences that Garza had gained from the other aborted revolts, his movement would last much longer and would pose a much greater threat to the Porfirian regime than did earlier efforts. The Mexican military responded with its full weight, carrying out a campaign of terror to eliminate support for the rebels in Mexico. The Texas Rangers and the U.S. military also became increasingly heavy-handed as they grew frustrated at their inability to find or capture the rebels. The Garzistas continued their cross-border incursions until late 1892, and the battles on the Texas side still flared up through 1893. In February 1892, Garza fled Texas with his rebellion in full swing, and hundreds of armed men continued to camp out in the chaparral of South Texas. This rebellion was the longest lasting and most serious threat to the Porfirian regime in its fifteen years of existence.

SOILING THE HONOR OF A LADY

While Garza later proclaimed Ignacio Martínez's assassination as the incident that convinced him to take up arms against Díaz, an article by Garza insulting Bernardo Reyes's mother was in many ways a public declaration of war before the official proclamation. Not only does this incident help to explain the timing of Garza's insurrection, but it also reveals the significance of honor in border society. Garza's bitter condemnation of President Díaz and governors Reyes and Garza Galán could not have pleased the Mexican government, but his insult to Reyes's mother was seen as having gone beyond the pale of decency. To maintain his honor, Reyes would have no choice but to declare war on Garza. This transgression of propriety and gender boundaries forecasted Garza's transgression of the border line.

In late July 1891 Garza published in *El Libre Pensador* a biography of Bernardo Reyes, in which he described the Mexican general as "the most furious, cowardly and insane of the uniformed assassins." However, the biography concentrated more on Reyes's parents and their sexual proclivities than on the man who ruled northern Mexico with an iron fist. Garza described Reyes's father as a "bandido" with "bestial instincts and a bloody spirit," but essentially chaste in his sexual affairs. In contrast, Garza characterized the mother in decidedly sexualized terms: in addition to being "voluptuous and of lymphatic temperament," he reported that she had in her youth "more lovers than fingers" and liked to "get drunk on strong tequila." Garza's account of Reyes's early life was as follows: one year after her husband was killed, Sra. Señora Ogazón de Reyes threw herself into the arms of a young man in Jalisco, and then quickly fell in love with another man, known as the Burro de Oro (golden ass). Unhappy with the new arrangement, the thirteen-year-old Bernardo allegedly stole jewelry from his stepfather and took off for Mexico City. On the way there, highway bandits attacked Bernardo and made him serve them as their trumpeter.[1] Garza's minibiography, replete with accusations of sexual promiscuity and drunkenness by the mother and impotence by the father, inspired widespread and hysterical condemnation by the Porfirista press throughout the region.

Criticism of Garza's article centered on his violation of the sacredness of private life, especially the "honor" of a lady. *El Cronista Mexicano*, from San Antonio, condemned *El Libre Pensador* in an article titled "Cowardly Action," stating that "we would never have imagined that a newspaper published in Castillian would offend the honor of a respectable and virtuous lady." Not only had Garza lied to discredit his enemies, he had even attempted to "soil the honor of a lady."[2] *El Heraldo* condemned Garza as "a cowardly defamer," and *El Duende*, of Laredo, criticized him because "he tore the always sacred veil of private life and approaching the monstrous, he stained with his viper tongue the honor of the wife, the husband and the son."[3] One Spanish-language San Antonio newspaper argued that although they were in favor of the freedom of the press and even "reasonable and decent opposition to some bad politicians in our patria; we protest energetically against the vulgar language used by this newspaper [*El Libre Pensador*]."[4]

The critique, therefore, was not so much about Garza's attack on Reyes, which he and others had been guilty of for years, or even the unflattering depiction of the father, but about "soiling the honor of a lady," and a mother at that. Laredo's *Gate City* made this point well, distinguishing between what was a "manly" and legitimate attack and what was cowardly. Even if the charges were true, the *Gate City* argued, "it was exceedingly out of place and in very bad taste to publish it as no gentleman ought to say aught, to hurt a political enemy, against a woman. A true man should confine his attacks on a political enemy to his record alone and not try to injure him by attacking the good name of the female members of his family." As he had transgressed the bounds of decency, bringing women into a political (read male) battle, they argued that he was neither "patriotic" nor "valiant," but simply an "agitator."[5]

THE VANISHING DAYS OF REVOLUTION

A letter to *El Cronista Mexicano* in mid-August stated that there was "great excitement" in Laredo because an arrest warrant had been issued for Garza for the "obscene biography" of Reyes published in *El Libre Pensador*.[6] Ranger Captain McNeel, together with nine of his men, had traveled to Laredo on August 7, and found at least one thousand Mexicans gathered at the train depot. Because they were unarmed and showed no hostility McNeel ignored them, but he expected trouble from the local Laredo officials who were "all at loggerheads." McNeel then spoke with Alejandro González, Garza's father-in-law, and came to an agreement that Garza would surrender to McNeel if he would protect him and not turn him over to the Mexican authorities.[7] However, before McNeel's plan could be initiated, a sheriff went to arrest Garza at Palito Blanco. Needless to say, Garza was nowhere to be found.[8] *El Cronista Mexicano* declared that "after having vomited his filthy venom he escapes like a reptile."[9] Portrayals of Garza as someone who had transgressed the bounds of civility served to delegitimize his political struggle. By painting his opposition to Díaz as solely a product of personal rancor, the mainstream press could ignore his larger political critique. Even when the major newspapers identified problematic aspects of the Porfirian regime, they could not bring themselves to support a revolution to unseat Díaz, or motherhood or womanly virtue.

Nonetheless, Díaz's image of a modernizing country clashed with news emanating from Mexico of revolts, banditry, and political instability. While U.S. newspapers wrote about the growing class divisions in Mexico and the dictatorial powers that Díaz exercised, the regime's ability to employ modern technology to crush opponents convinced most newspapers that the days of revolution were over. In early September 1891, an article in the *San Antonio Express* accused Díaz of colluding with foreign enterprises for personal gain, so that "while he has become a man of great wealth, people of the Republic have grown poorer and poorer." The article argued that Díaz's attack on the clerics had made him unpopular with the masses and predicted that their anger would soon manifest itself publicly.[10] The *Washington Post*, on the other hand, quickly dismissed the rumors of "volcanic fires" that would "sweep the great Díaz from power," pointing out that Díaz had just appointed a minister plenipotentiary to arrange a commercial treaty with the United States, that a wealthy English corporation was seriously considering investing $50 million in the Mexican and Northern Pacific railroad, and that "capitalists [were] gaining increased confidence in the financial stability of Mexico."[11] The two images of Mexico, one of a country of "smoldering volcanic fires" and seething masses, and the other of a stable nation where foreigners could invest and make money, were not necessarily incompatible.

In the same article in which the *Express* admitted that Díaz had dictatorial powers, it also argued that improved railways, telegraph lines, and troop mobility prevented revolution: "Railways have pierced the country in every direction. The army has been placed upon a much more substantial footing. Troops can be massed at any given point in a short time. The day when a handful of bandits could gather upon the frontier, purchase a lot of black-number muskets and terrorize the land has passed. The telegraph locates them, a handful of soldiers arrests them, the courts try them, the constabulary shoots them and the country laughs at them."[12]

Modernization, understood as the establishment of rail and telegraph networks, not only increased economic productivity but also augmented the government's ability to repress opposition. When county clerk Thad Smith returned from Mexico in mid-September 1891, he reassured *Express* readers that plenty of Americans were still making money there and that "the days of revolution, like our own Indian days, vanished with the advent of the iron horse."[13]

In addition to reports in local and national newspapers, rumors of a revolution being organized on the Texas border reached the Mexican government by other private channels. Robert Bolton, who had been hired by Ignacio Martínez's wife to investigate her husband's murder offered information to Laredo's Mexican consul about a revolution being organized in Texas. Bolton named Catarino Garza and Francisco Ruíz Sandoval as the two principal leaders and claimed that they had made inquiries about the price of weapons in the United States and were in constant communication with military leaders in Mexico. As well as gathering information about this revolt for $8 per day, a princely wage in those days, Bolton offered to stop working for Martínez's widow and to destroy the proofs and documents that they had collected. He apparently wanted to switch sides because Martínez's widow had not paid him for his investigations.[14] While he recognized the potential benefits of having such an insider act as a secret agent for the Mexican government, Reyes concluded that the talk of revolution was baseless and he advised against entering into any agreement with Bolton. From Reyes's perspective, the opposition in Texas had already been crushed.[15]

By the summer of 1891, Ignacio Martínez had been killed, the oppositionists were divided and fighting among themselves, and Garza was a fugitive from the law. So, when the governor of Tamaulipas, Alejandro Prieto, wrote to Reyes in mid-September warning him that Catarino Garza had left Duval County with a group of armed men and was heading toward Mexico, the general told President Díaz that "according to the news I have it cannot be true." Bernardo's friends in Texas had assured him that Garza was busy hiding from the law, and besides, Reyes was sure that if such a revolution were imminent his spies would have informed him.[16] A day after Reyes wrote to Díaz, Garza crossed the Rio Grande and declared his insurrection against the Porfirian regime. The revolution was on.

On the long journey down to the border from Palito Blanco Garza met up with some of his fellow revolutionists, and by the time they reached La Grulla, a small town on the Rio Grande, there were between sixteen and forty of them in the party. Although they borrowed arms, horses, and saddles from ranches they passed, Catarino's father-in-law, Alejandro González, supplied almost three-quarters of the horses for the entire expedition. Although González believed in the cause championed by his son-in-law, and the substantial wealth he had built up as a rancher allowed him to part with the horses, the insurance agent in him kept trying to figure the odds that such a revolution would actually succeed. Stealthily, they crossed the river and began their march. Another seventy men had pledged to go into Mexico at different points and meet up with Garza's band.[17]

At 2 A.M. the rebels ran across Mexican customs guards three miles below Camargo. Believing that they were bandits, the guards immediately opened fire on them. The revolutionists lost two horses in the battle, but the guards beat a hasty retreat when the Garzistas shot back. The Mexican guards were not the only ones to turn tail and run once the bullets started flying. Juan Garza, who had crossed in Catarino's group, hurried back to the Texas side as soon as he heard the shots. Even so, the first day of the revolution went as well as could be expected. They had reached their preordained rendezvous point thirty miles above Camargo on the San Juan River, where they were met by two other groups, bringing their numbers to about one hundred.

TERROR ON THE BORDER

Immediately following the first incursion, the Mexican Army fanned out along the border and began searching for the revolutionists. Bernardo Reyes's orders to General Lorenzo García at Camargo were straightforward: if they captured a *gavillero* (gang member) or even someone distributing their *proclamas*, they were to be "executed without a great display."[18] Within ten days this policy had claimed the lives of two U.S. citizens, Juan Bazan and José Angel Vera, who were killed by General García at Guardado de Arriba ranch on suspicion of being revolutionists. "Many families would cross to the Texas side if they had boats to cross in," one newspaper declared, "as the terror caused by the recent military assassinations [in Mexico] is very great."[19]

General García had a bad reputation along the border, so bad that many thought he was a cannibal. Some people even believed that García had "eaten the bones of all of those individuals" who he ordered to be executed.[20] Like Dr. Jeckyl and Mr. Hyde, García could be a gallant gentleman one moment and a brutal torturer the next. During a visit by

Captain Bourke, García demonstrated his gentlemanly side by graciously offering to send his band over to Fort Ringgold to serenade the troops.[21] However, García could also employ music for sinister purposes, like on the occasion when he ordered trumpets, drums, and church bells to make a "fearful racket" so as to drown the cries of a soldier he whipped to death.[22]

García's zealousness was a potential public relations disaster for the Mexican government, especially if U.S. citizens happened to fall victim to his terror. Four days after the killings of Bazan and Vera, Reyes warned Colonel Luis Cerón to be careful not to execute prisoners if they turned out to be U.S. citizens, and to strictly follow the law in those cases so as to avoid complaints by the U.S. government.[23] While some newspapers condemned the killing of U.S. citizens by a foreign government, other Texans supported this quick frontier justice. Several Starr County officials, including Judge James Nix, Clerk Everest Estarke, and Sheriff W. W. Sheley, even wrote a letter to the Mexican foreign ministry explaining that the men killed by García had bad reputations and arrest warrants in the United States for horse stealing.[24] The killing of a few Texas Mexican criminals did not seem to bother these men at all, even if they were U.S. citizens. Texas Mexicans, however, were incensed, and they complained to Mexico's consul in Rio Grande City about General García's repressive campaign on the other side of the river. They were so fearful that they even requested passports from the consul so that García would not confuse them with revolutionists when they crossed the river to visit their families.[25]

One month later, two more U.S. citizens of Mexican descent were murdered in Mexico, and all signs pointed toward the infamous General García. The bloated and disemboweled bodies of the victims were found floating in the Rio Grande. Their bodies had been so mangled by repeated stab wounds and decomposition that it was only after their mother arrived that a positive identification could be made. The victims, Severo and José Castillo, were living at Charco Escondido ranch, thirty miles south of Reynosa, when García drafted them into the Mexican Army to fight against Garza. It was a cruel coincidence, or perhaps not such a coincidence, that Severo Castillo, who was both a friend of Garza's and an apparent supporter of his cause, would be sent to the frontlines to attack Garza's army. There had been several public gestures that linked the Castillo brothers to Garza's movement, including an article in *El Libre Pensador* that noted the kind reception that Garza had received at Charco

Escondido the summer before the rebellion.[26] The Castillo brothers were also friendly with General Juan Cortina, an internationally known border raider and defender of Mexicans in Texas. When Cortina was arrested in Matamoros on suspicion that he sympathized with Garza, he gave power of attorney over his ranches to Severo Castillo. Most people on the border believed that General García was responsible for the Castillo brothers' deaths, even though the Mexican government insisted that it was smugglers with whom their father had feuded fifteen years earlier who had killed them.[27] A Mexican laborer at Fort Ringgold told Captain Bourke that García had killed and disemboweled the two young Mexicans, after they "couldn't tell where Garza was." The laborer said that "it is truly sad to know of the numbers of families on the Mexican side of the river, from which husbands and fathers, brothers and sons, have been taken upon the mere whim or caprice of a drunken military despot, and have disappeared never to return again."[28]

While these particular killings were carried out by this one maniacal "military despot," such murders occurred regularly with the knowledge and tacit approval of the highest-ranking Mexican government officials. In a couple of letters to President Díaz, Reyes named those who had been executed by the Mexican Army and the precise manner of killing, assuring him that all of those who were assassinated either belonged to the gavilla or came to distribute revolutionary manifestos. The casual tone with which eight of these murders were recounted to Díaz indicates that these sorts of killings were not surprising or shocking for Reyes or for the president. They often invented stories of attempted prisoner escapes to cover up cold-blooded executions. In his private correspondence with the president, Reyes even admitted that one man who was apprehended while attempting to pass to the U.S. side was "killed in a clandestine manner and made to look as if it had been done while he was escaping."[29] Reyes's campaign of terror forced his opponents into exile or the grave, but it also had the unintended effect of fomenting popular sympathy for the rebels.

The commander at Fort Ringgold, Captain Bourke, began hearing stories about the killings in Mexico shortly after Garza's rebellion erupted. In October, just a month after the revolt started, a "Mexican gentleman" traveling through Rio Grande City told Bourke that twenty-six suspected Garzistas were shot to death without trial by Mexican military officers. The gentleman also informed Bourke that within the last three years, three generals and thirteen colonels had been assassinated.[30] In November, an American drugstore owner in Mier, Mexico, told Bourke in hushed tones about "the fearful tyranny now prevailing all over Mexico." He noted, "General García had no less than (80) eighty persons put to death without trial since the Garza invasion began, and this between Reynosa and Mier alone." People were just disappeared from one day to the next, like the five men who were arrested one afternoon, judged on the second day, and killed on the third.[31] One might expect that the oppositionists would have reason to exaggerate the level of brutality in Mexico. However, the strikingly similar descriptions of extra-judicial killings from sources as different as a U.S. Army captain, a Mexican laborer, and Mexican and Anglo travelers, along with the Porfirian regime's own documentation of these murders, suggests that the terror they described was very real.

Although less frequent than the wanton executions on the Mexican side, Texas authorities were also quick to fire their weapons first and ask questions later. Within the first week of Garza's rebellion, two Rangers and a local constable shot down two Mexicans on the streets of Realitos, Texas. According to Ranger Captain McNeel's report, the Mexicans had "fired off their guns and pistols and yelled like Comanches and called on the Americans to send out their d——Rangers." The Mexicans, McNeel claimed, tried to draw their arms when confronted by the authorities; the constable, using a shotgun, and the Rangers, with their Winchester rifles, shot the two Mexicans, killing them instantly. While it is impossible to determine the veracity of the Rangers's story, McNeel justified the killing by asserting that the Mexicans who were killed "were the worst desperadoes on the Rio Grande and were leaders of gangs." Rather than expressing his sorrow over the killings performed by his men, Ranger McNeel went to the town afterward and told the inhabitants "that this business had to stop or some good Mexicans would visit the other world."[32]

It would not be long before a "good Mexican" found himself at the mercy of an angry Ranger. In mid-May 1892, Ranger Thomas decided to have some fun with Doroteo Gómez, a seventeen-year-old railroad agent at Realitos. According to the story related by Gómez's father, Ranger Thomas drew his pistol and demanded that Gómez dance or he would kill him. Gómez refused, and told Thomas that even though he had a pistol he was not afraid of him. Thomas then laughed, and Gómez made some retort. Angered by the disobedience of this young Mexican, who refused his orders and talked back to him, Thomas grabbed Gómez by the throat and began to choke him. Although he survived this brush with Ranger justice Gómez pleaded with his father to be taken away from Realitos, but his father wanted him to continue his promising career with the railroads.

Instead, his father wrote to Adjutant General Mabry, begging him to protect his son from the Rangers. The father made it clear to the adjutant general that as an American citizen who had lived in Texas for twenty-seven years, he deserved protection from the law. Called on to explain the Ranger's behavior, Captain Brooks simply stated that Thomas had been discharged at the end of May for "bad conduct while scouting." Brooks also claimed that Gómez had told him that he harbored no ill will toward the Rangers.[33]

This incident illustrates the type of relationship that existed between Rangers and Mexicans. Rangers demanded obedience, and when they did not receive it they were quick to resort to violence. However, even if the Rangers possessed disproportionate power in terms of weapons and their ability to legally use them, Mexicans were not at all defenseless or passive victims. Mexicans such as Gómez confronted Rangers by refusing to jump to their orders, even when they were faced with pistols and threats. The fact that Ranger Thomas was discharged and that Captain Brooks was forced to answer to the adjutant general also demonstrates the limits of the Rangers's power and the capacity of Mexicans to appeal to higher branches of government to defend themselves.

Although Texas Rangers were rarely tried, much less convicted, for their arbitrary execution of "justice," Ranger Rogers had to appear before the Bee County Grand Jury for killing two innocent Mexicans. According to George Schmitt, who was writing to the governor seeking an appointment as a Ranger Captain, Rogers and two of his men had falsely arrested two Mexicans on suspicion of stealing a mule. While the two young Mexicans lay undressed and asleep on their blankets, Rogers and his men shot and killed them. Rogers claimed that the Mexicans had reached for their weapons. The next day, the men who had actually stolen the mules were spotted in another part of Texas. In his letter, Schmitt warned the governor about the political cost of having Rogers promoted just after the killings. To the Mexicans, Schmitt explained, it looked as if "Rogers was promoted for killing Mexicans instead of being discharged."[34]

While some Anglo Texans worried about excessive force being used against Mexicans, others applauded the army's vigorous measures and even suggested more violent ones. In March 1892, John Dix wrote to Adjutant General Mabry, arguing that if the troops had "hung [the Garzistas] to the first tree and burnt their possessions long ago this matter would have ended harsh, hard and apparently cruel, but it would have saved lives to our country and money to our treasury." While Dix understood that these might seem like "unwarrantedly harsh measures," he argued that it was "the only way such people [meaning Mexicans] can be governed or managed."[35]

Understanding that lynching Mexicans in the United States could have caused legal problems, Dix suggested the more efficient method of sending them to their deaths in Mexico. Acknowledging that the "mode in Mexico is to shoot them first and try them after," Dix asked Mabry if "a few bands of vagrants could be rounded up, and allowed to escape into Mexico from this land of abused liberty." "It would have," Dix asserted, "a salutary effect upon this whole country, morally, financially and politically, and tend to the purification of the ballot." On some level Dix must have known that his suggestions were both illegal and immoral, leading him to distance himself from them by saying that they were written "half jestingly." But as Dix himself wrote, "there is often more truth than poetry in a jest."[36]

CAPTAIN BOURKE VISITS MEXICO

Texas Mexicans were in a difficult position no matter which side of the line they were on. Staying in Texas was not exactly safe with so many Rangers and U.S. Army troops roaming the countryside looking for "bandits." On the other hand, they could be killed if without the correct papers they ran into the Mexican Army on the other side of the river. Captain Bourke discovered that even he, an officer in the U.S. Army, was not safe from the Mexican military's harassment. On November 11, 1891, Bourke crossed into Mexico with U.S. Deputy Marshal John Jodon and a wagon driver to try and gather information on the Garzistas. Having failed to locate Colonel Nieves Hernández in Guerrero, who they were going to talk to about the rebellion, Bourke and Jodon made their way twenty-two miles southeast to Parras (fig. 4). There they had the misfortune to run into what Bourke described as "a drunken, mescal-soaked 'rural' who was very much swelled up with a sense of his own importance." Ironically, the drunk guard suspected that Bourke and Jodon were Garzistas. The U.S. Army men grew especially nervous when the driver overheard the guard saying in Spanish, "los tenemos: los chingamos" (we've got them: we'll kill them). In spite of Bourke's furious protestations and letters from customs agents in Guerrero and Carrizo attesting to their identities, the guard refused to release them. They finally convinced him to take them to a telegraph station at Cerralvo. On the way, they stopped at Aguasleguas

4. Captain John G. Bourke in the 1890s. This photograph may have been taken in 1893 when he was living
in Chicago on assignment at the Columbian Exposition.
(Nebraska State Historical Society Photograph
Collections, RG 2955-2)

where the mayor demanded that they turn over their weapons. It was at
this point that Bourke began to feel like a "prisoner of war." He wrote
down the names of his captors and made it clear that he was "determined
to have punishment visited upon each and every person guilty of dis-
respect towards [him], an Officer of the US Government."[37]

By the evening, the guard was beginning to sober up and tried to apolo-
gize to his prisoners. Bourke, however, would have nothing to do with him
and told him in no uncertain terms to "go to hell." Always the curious
folklorist, Bourke took advantage of his quasi-captivity in Mexico to
stroll through the streets, taking notes on the architecture and agriculture
and visiting some of the local sites. In Parras, Bourke saw the famous
church of La Purissima, home to the miraculous Madonna — "La Virgen
sudando" (the sweating virgin). According to local lore, the virgin would
begin sweating profusely whenever there was threat of a war; victory

depended on having the virgin in your possession. As the virgin was not perspiring at the time of Bourke's visit, he surmised that "the present Garza revolution was not much of a 'war' and would not last long." Bourke also learned that the faithful would make offerings of gold and silver to the Madonna in exchange for *milagros* (miracles). Once a large quantity of gold and silver had amassed, the priest would collect all of the precious metals and send them to Monterrey where they would be melted and cast into sacred vessels or sold to benefit the church.[38]

In addition to his anthropological observations, Bourke's journey through northeastern Mexico also allowed him to survey the Mexican military response to the Garza revolt and to gauge the sentiment of the populace. In Aguasleguas, he was surprised to find so many troops, including eighty-four cavalry, one hundred soldiers, and fifty-six infantry, guarding against an attack by Garza. However, Bourke doubted the effectiveness of these troops, given that half of the seventy-one men protecting Parras were auxiliaries, pressed into service by the government. Furthermore, whereas Garza's men paid for everything they took, the government soldiers, many of who were criminals drafted into service, "stole all they could lay their hands on." In addition to the fact that Garzistas did not steal, Bourke found that Garza had many sympathizers on that side of the border. "Indeed, it was whispered to us that Parras, Aguasleguas and Cerralvo were full of friends and 'parientes' (family) of Garza who would surely 'pronounce' if not held in check by a display of force."[39] His trip to Mexico turned out to be very enlightening. Not only did he hear positive portrayals of Garza, but also he found that the Mexican Army was filled with unscrupulous criminals. And, to top it all off, he was being held prisoner as a Garzista.

After finally arriving in Cerralvo one day into his captivity, Bourke attempted to leave on his own by hiring a carriage and four horses. The town's main administrator, however, had sent word not to let the Americans leave town. When Bourke tried to hire a carriage, all of the liverymen suddenly discovered that their horses were lame and could not be moved. His last resort was the telegraph station. Bourke dashed off several telegrams to U.S. and Mexican consuls along the border and to General Reyes in Monterrey. Reyes responded immediately to liberate the prisoners once the Mexican authorities were satisfied of their identities. Given that nobody there could vouch for Bourke and his driver, they remained in captivity until a telegram arrived from U.S. Consul Warner Sutton attesting to Bourke's identity. Although satisfied that he was indeed a U.S. Army captain, the main administrator told Bourke that he would have to wait until morning to leave. Undeterred, Bourke announced to his captors that he was not going to wait until morning but would leave immediately. "It wouldn't have been Mexico," Bourke explained, "if we all hadn't embraced and hugged like long-lost brothers. They, who a moment before would have shot us all like dogs, now wanted to do us all sorts of . . . kindness." Not wanting to test their luck, the U.S. officials made a beeline for the border. Bourke was only fifty miles away when he thought to himself, "what a great pity that we could not open up closer trade relations and learn to know each other better."[40]

The English- and Spanish-language press in the United States expressed great indignation over Captain Bourke's arrest. The *Omaha Bee* described the incident as an "outrage on an American officer," and even invented a story about Bourke being moments away from being shot when Reyes's telegram arrived. General García was supposedly so upset when he heard about Bourke's captivity that he issued orders to shoot the rural guards responsible for the arrest. While Bourke was not treated as a friend by the local authorities, he was neither handcuffed, placed in jail, nor shot as had been many other suspected Garzistas of Mexican descent. The coverage of the thirty-six hours of captivity was also a boon for Garza because it portrayed the Mexican authorities as arbitrary and cruel. As the *Bee* overstated, "Bourke left the United States in sympathy with the Mexican government, but he returned strongly in sympathy with the Garza movement."[41] It would not be long, however, before Bourke's sympathies for Garza waned.

REVOLUTIONARY PROCLAMAS

Even though the coverage of Bourke's arrest lent credence to the Garzista contention that Díaz was a brutal dictator who ruled by force, most of the press in both countries continued to discredit the Garzistas by portraying them as common bandits and criminals. While such characterizations may have convinced people far away in New York, the circulation of several Garzista manifestos and a better knowledge of Mexican politics on the border made it difficult to deny to a local audience the movement's political motivations and aims. In order to silence the Garzistas and prevent their case from being heard, Reyes cracked down on the dissemination of revolutionary literature in Mexico. The very act of distributing a revolutionary manifesto or proclama was, for Reyes, grounds for execution.

Handing out a manifesto would not get you killed in Texas but it would land you in jail, as Andres Moreno Nuñez found out when he was arrested in Rio Grande City for riding around in a buggy with a bottle of mescal and scattering Garza's revolutionary proclamations through the streets. Although the judge set a high bond of $1,000 he refused to extradite him, saying that he had no such authority.[42] Despite such repression on both sides of the border, the Laredo consul noted that the proclama had been "profusely" distributed in Nuevo Laredo.[43] Meanwhile Texas newspapers such as Rio Grande City's *El Cromo* and Laredo's *Gate City* reprinted the full text of the proclama, rendering futile efforts to suppress its circulation.[44]

El Cromo ridiculed Garza's plan, especially the manifesto's offer to make anyone a second captain if they presented themselves with twenty-five armed and mounted men. The article chided, because it did not cost anything, that Garza should have offered more: "For example, make whoever presents himself with a ham and two bottles of Tequila into a division general. A brigadier of those who bring a turkey molé and six shots of pulque. A Colonel of those who present themselves with a hen, their own or someone else's, and a sheep. A Lieutenant Colonel of those who bring hot tortillas and likewise promote to second Captain those who present themselves with a pair of eggs [balls]."[45]

The various Garzista revolutionary proclamations (fig. 5) follow the basic pattern and language of the "plan político" disseminated during the 1886 rebellion in Tamaulipas and Nuevo León, and the manifesto distributed by Francisco Ruíz Sandoval during his June 1890 raid into Mexico. The similarity of these documents and the involvement of the same individuals in all three attempts, most notably Ignacio Martínez's leading role, suggests that these insurrections were all moments in one longer liberal revolt in northeastern Mexico.

Although following the general guidelines of previous manifestos, many of the Garzista proclamations personalized the liberal struggle thereby highlighting Garza's role as protagonist. For instance, Garza's first "Proclama," disseminated after he crossed the Rio Grande on September 15, 1891, referred to himself directly: "The last of the independent journalists, the most humble of all, puts down today the pen to seize the sword in defense of the people's right."[46] Other proclamas, such as the one signed by Juan Antonio Flores in Nuevo León on January 1, 1892, and another from Coahuila, dated June 26, 1892, also explicitly recognized Garza as the leader and founder of the revolution.[47] The attachment of Garza's

PROCLAMA.

CONCIUDADANOS:

El vergonzoso estado de abyección á que nos han reducido los hombres del poder, tratándonos no como ciudadanos de una República independiente y federal, sino como á despreciables esclavos;

Los fuertes impuestos y contribuciones á que nos han sujetado, haciendo del todo imposible que podamos honradamente vivir de nuestro trabajo;

La humillante disposición del Gobierno de que compañías extranjeras vengan á practicar medidas y á servir de jueces en el deslinde de nuestras tierras, ó á obligar á los propietarios que paguen una fuerte suma, como "Contenta" para no ser molestados;

La corrupción espantosa que hace años existe en los titulados gobierno Federal y de los Estados, en que los hombres mas nulos que se prestan para dóciles instrumentos, los miserables que trafican con la honra de sus familias, y los traidores y criminales que han cometido espantosos hechos, son los de influencia, mando y valimiento;

El asesinato oficial que los Gobiernos de Chihuahua, Coahuila, Nuevo León, Tamaulipas, etc., etc., han establecido como recurso ordinario, para deshacerse de los hombres que pueden con el trascurso del tiempo protestar contra tanta infamia;

La impunidad absoluta é irritante de que gozan los ladrones oficiales que se han apropiado millones del tesoro público;

La ley últimamente expedida de "Suspensión de Garantías," con la que cualquier partida de fuerza armada, cualquier agrupamiento de gente pueden matar al que gusten, declarándolo bandido, siendo el hecho aprobado de antemano por el Gobierno: lo que nos coloca en peor condición que á esclavos ó animales domésticos, pues á unos y á otros sus dueños los cuidan y no los matan por no perder el capital en ellos invertido, mientras que á nosotros al asesinársenos nada pierde el Gobierno porque nada les hemos costado.

La entrega mal disimulada que se esta haciendo de nuestro territorio, dando á vil precio á negociantes norte-americanos inmensas fajas de terreno de nuestra frontera con los Estados Unidos;

El falseamiento de la Revolución de Tuxtepec y de nuestra Carta Constitucional de 1857, que tanta sangre costaron al país;

La Reelección vitalicia ó indefinida, que para mayor baldón de nuestros principios democráticos, han establecido como recurso desesperado para robar á mausalva y extorsionar á los pueblos;

La muerte completa de la libertad de la prensa y los asesinatos alevosos cometidos en muchos escritores dignos y liberales.

Y por último, la imposibilidad de remediar estos graves males de un modo pacífico, porque en la lucha electoral el Gobierno dispone siempre de poderosos medios de corrupción y de las bayonetas para hacer triunfar sus candidatos, cuyos nombres aparecen con muchos meses de anticipación en las hojas sucias que con el nombre de periódicos tiene á sueldo;

Haciendo uso del derecho de insurrección que nos asiste como á pueblo á quien sus gobernantes han traicionado, nos levantamos en armas en defensa de nuestras vidas, de la integridad de nuestro territorio, de la Constitución de 1857 y del decoro de la Nación Mexicana.

CONCIUDADANOS:

Levantaos en masa para derrocar en unos cuantos días á los tiranos que con el nombre de Gobierno Federal y de los Estados nos oprimen; y salvemos á nuestra querida Patria que está próxima á desaparecer, víctima de la esclavitud, del robo, del asesinato y de la miseria.

Levantaos en masa á nombre de la Libertad, de la Constitución de 1857 y de la conciencia pública.

El último de los periodistas independientes, el mas humilde de todos, abandona hoy su pluma para empuñar la espada en defensa de los derechos del pueblo.

¡Abajo los tiranos! ¡Viva el pueblo mexicano!

Vuestro compañero de sacrificios y de peligros.

C. E. GARZA.

Jurisdicción de Matamoros, Tamaulipas, Septiembre de 1891.

5. A Garzista manifesto signed by Garza; it was the first one issued when he crossed into Tamaulipas in September 1891. (Colección de Porfirio Díaz, Universidad Iberoamericana)

name to these manifestos, even ones he had not written or signed, helped to mark the entire movement in the local and international press as the "Garza revolution," and its followers as Garzistas.

The Garzista program for postrevolutionary Mexico, which circulated in various versions under the headings of "Plan Revolucionario," "Proclama," and "Manifiesto," united themes of nationalism, liberalism, and progress. However, while this program guaranteed many political freedoms and civil liberties, it gave few details on issues of economic and social equality. Garza's "Plan Revolucionario" did not propose a completely new social order, but the call to overthrow Díaz and restore the 1857 Constitution was revolutionary for its time.[48] Rodney Anderson explains how Mexican industrial workers at the beginning of the twentieth century also invoked the 1857 Constitution, not to call for a "new social order but a *restoration* of the rights granted them by the liberal reform movements of the nineteenth century."[49] Whether these workers, or the Garzistas, understood the technical details of the 1857 Constitution is beside the point. For them, it signified rights and freedoms that had been usurped.

The plan argued that Díaz should be considered a traitor to the liberal cause because he had taken away the most important privileges, namely, "the right to personal security, the right to individual liberty, and the right of property."[50] Article 10 of Garza's plan laid out more specific protections against corruption, including prohibiting reelection and forbidding any revolutionary leader from becoming president, at least for the first election. This article also guaranteed political and economic liberties, such as freedom for all political parties, free trade, and state and local sovereignty. Article 12 allowed all civil and military authorities who joined the revolution to keep their positions. Only Article 11 addressed economic inequality, promising that after the revolution triumphed "all vacant lands will be distributed to Mexicans who promise to cultivate them."[51] In other words, there would be no expropriation of large landholdings; indeed, the vague promise to distribute *terrenos baldíos* (vacant lands) might have even resulted in increased concentration of landholding in Mexico if large landowners had taken over those plots.

The language of these manifestos, including exhortations like "¡¡¡Viva la libertad!!!" (Long live liberty) and "¡¡¡Abajo los tiranos!!!" (down with tyrants), might have sounded militant, but the actual content of their program was somewhat moderate.[52] Although Garza's program opposed Díaz, given the spectrum of ideological orientations within the 1910 Mexican Revolution Garza's plan was not explicitly radical. His program was more akin to that of the liberal elite Francisco Madero's Plan de San Luis (1910) than it was like the radical peasant leader Emiliano Zapata's Plan de Ayala (1911) or the manifesto of the anarchist Ricardo Flores Magón's Partido Liberal Mexicano (1911). Zapata's Plan de Ayala goes farther than did Garza's in that it speaks specifically about expropriating land from "monopoly" owners, but Zapata, like Garza, also invoked the "immortal code of '57."[53] Garza's revolutionary plan promised liberal political freedoms and touched on popular liberal themes like the redistribution of land and the principle of no reelection. This language of liberty, progress, and patriotism allowed Garza to garner support from landless farmers and ranch hands without losing the aid of merchants, ranchers, and professionals.

Like other nineteenth-century liberal revolts, Garza's invocation of abstract concepts such as liberty, freedom, and democracy glossed over the issue of class. By appealing to universal principles, Garza was better able to forge the multiclass alliance he needed for his revolution. In order to inspire a popular uprising against Díaz, Garza's plan had to appeal to liberal merchants, ranchers, and landless farm workers, groups whose interests did not necessarily coincide and in fact often clashed. The lack of militancy in the manifestos does not mean that the revolt would necessarily have taken a conservative turn if it had succeeded. Garza's political life before the revolution indicates a serious commitment to workers' rights. Furthermore, radical demands and social change can follow from movements that seek limited reforms, either because those reforms fail and release pent-up anger or because they succeed and present opportunities for more profound and far-reaching struggle.[54] While it is difficult, if not impossible, to determine why landless ranchers joined Garza's movement, we should not assume that they would have been satisfied with a free press, free elections, and a new government.

Although Garza made no promise to expropriate private estates, a position that would certainly have alienated Mexican landowners, he criticized foreign ownership of land in Mexico. In his September 1891 "Proclama," Garza attacked the "humiliating disposition of the government that allowed foreign companies to measure and act as judges in the surveying of our lands, or forced the owners to pay a large sum as a 'gift' so as not to be harassed." This method of dispossessing Mexicans, Garza reasoned, gave "North American businessmen immense strips of land on our border with the United States."[55] While Garza pointed out that North

American companies were the ones buying this land, his critique was directed at the Mexican government for allowing such practices to occur. Garza even went so far as to argue that "we are put in a worse position than slaves or domestic animals, because the owners of both of these would care for them and would not kill them so as not to lose the capital that had been invested, while the government loses nothing in killing us as we have not cost them anything."[56] In his November 1891 "Manifesto," Garza called the people to arms to "dethrone these enemies of the Fatherland and corrupt liberticides."[57] This manifesto thus not only attacked Díaz for attempting to assassinate Garza, but also accused Díaz of killing liberty itself.

The Garzistas's logic that linked political and economic democracy enabled them to forge a multiclass alliance, or at least to turn attention away from differing class interests within this coalition. A manifesto signed by General Francisco Benavides of the Garzistas paints a vivid picture of the Díaz government as a "mob of false patriots that distributes the last remnants of our liberty like hungry cannibals.[58] Abstract concepts such as "liberty" could be interpreted in many different ways, thereby serving as a unifying standard for a broad range of classes with very different interests. For instance, Benavides's manifesto complained that "today, the little that the poor person has is taken away, the free thinker is assassinated, and the press is muzzled. All our liberties have disappeared."[59] By combining these diverse issues the class interest of the poor was rhetorically linked with the desire for political liberties. The final lines of Benavides's manifesto invoked the universalizing principles of patriotism, liberty, and even immortality to convince Mexicans to die for this cause: "Forward, Mexicans: Let us march to die for Liberty. Immortal glory for those who know how to die for her! Scorn and degradation for those who prefer to be slaves rather than patriots!"[60]

Referring to iconic figures in Mexican history helped to link their fairly localized revolt to a long and illustrious lineage that stretched back to the Aztecs and continued in the nineteenth century as a battle for independence, federalism, and liberalism. Some manifestos condemned Díaz as "another Santa Anna," while others invoked Cuauhtemoc, Morelos, and Juárez as guardian angels for their struggle.[61] As Karl Marx noted, people harken back to the past at the moment of revolutionary change: "Just when they seem engaged in revolutionizing themselves and things, in creating something that has never yet existed, precisely in such periods of revolutionary crisis they anxiously conjure up the spirits of the past to their service and borrow from them names, battle cries and costumes in order to present the new scene of world history in this time-honoured disguise and this borrowed language."[62] The Garzistas thus used this "borrowed language" of patriotism and liberalism to legitimize a revolt whose substantive issues were specifically pertinent to northern Mexicans. Garza's condemnation of official assassinations, for example, referred only to the northern border states of Chihuahua, Coahuila, Nuevo León, and Tamaulipas, with an "etc., etc." meant to include the rest of the states. Similarly, the border was the only region mentioned as having been threatened by the sale of land to foreigners.[63] One "Plan Revolucionario" exposed Díaz's plan to sell northern Baja California to the United States as proof that "another General Santa Anna" was governing the country.[64] Juan Antonio Flores's "Proclama" even invoked the mid-nineteenth-century hero Servando Canales, who fought for the "liberty and sovereignty" of Tamaulipas, as a precursor to Garza's movement.[65] The Garzista program, like the one issued in 1886, employed northern Mexican symbols of liberalism and patriotism and demanded state sovereignty and municipal independence. In many ways, the Garzista rebellion reenacted the mid-nineteenth-century federalist struggle against the centralizing power of Santa Anna. To achieve their goal of regional autonomy in the North, they would first have to depose the despotic ruler in the center.

"THE CATARINOS ON HORSEBACK"

Beyond the threat posed by the circulation of a revolutionary manifesto, there was the greater danger of a well-organized army willing to carry forward the plans laid out on paper. As a result, determining the size and strength of Garza's forces became a central concern for both the U.S. and Mexican governments. So many contradictory reports and sightings of the Garzistas makes it difficult to compose a definitive chronology of their movements, but a fairly good picture of their activities can nonetheless be pieced together by comparing numerous government reports and newspaper articles. Some maintained that Garza remained in Mexico after his initial incursion in mid-September. Adolf Osterveen, a Dutch schoolmaster in South Texas, told Captain Bourke that Garza had been disappointed by the paucity of followers who joined him during the September attack, and that Garza blamed his lack of success on the excessive rain. According to Osterveen, Garza stayed in Mexico following the September invasion, and then traveled to the San Carlos Mountains in southern Tamaulipas and from there went to Mexico City. While he sent his recruiting agents to both sides of the river, the Dutch schoolmaster claimed that Garza had remained in Mexico until at least mid-December.[66] Sheriff Sheley, on the other hand, told Bourke that Garza had crossed back to Texas on September 27, and after four days along the river he had returned to Palito Blanco.[67] Sheley's story jibed with what Bourke had heard from Colonel Hernández of the Mexican Army, who had told him at the end of September that Garza's father-in-law had sent a buggy down to the border to pick him up.[68]

It is unlikely that Garza stayed in Mexico after the initial battle, but in either case he and his recruiters continued their organizing efforts on both sides of the river. In early October, Reyes's agents reported that Garza's men were gathering at Uña de Gato, Texas, and two men had crossed into Mexico to recruit revolutionists.[69] With their forces regrouped one month later, a Garzista band of one hundred launched another offensive into Mexico on the night of November 7. They made it twenty miles into Mexico but, according to the Laredo consul's report, they could not remain in one place long enough even to eat two meals owing to the government forces' tenacious persecution. The Garzistas, unable to continue their incursion, were beating a hasty retreat to Texas on the afternoon of November 11, when Nuevo Laredo's police captain, Pedro Hernández, with a force of twenty-five men, engaged them in combat near Las Tortillas ranch, just five miles from the river. After several skirmishes claimed casualties on both sides, the Garzistas sneaked back across the river under the darkness of night. The consul reported that Hernández had routed the Garzistas, killing five of them, while the *San Antonio Express* version proclaimed a rebel victory, noting the death of three government soldiers.[70] It is unclear whether Garza planned these brief forays into Mexico as a public relations ploy or as part of a larger concerted invasion, but the U.S. press reported these guerrilla attacks as evidence of an imminent revolutionary upheaval in Mexico. The difficulty of reconciling the wide disparity between the different accounts of this battle can be attributed to the biases of the sources. The Mexican government tended to downplay their own losses and overstate their successes, while U.S. newspapers, eager for a sensational story, often exaggerated rebel victories.

Mexican officials grew extremely frustrated at the difficulty of apprehending the revolutionists who made guerrilla-style raids into Mexican territory and then withdrew to Texas before troops could engage them. Once in Texas, they would disperse themselves to ranches along the border and blend in with the local ranchers and farmers. As the exasperated consul noted: "You can see them and speak to them, but nobody knows anything, nor have they heard anything; and they wear so habitually their ruse and dissimulation, that even taking into account their whole lives as smugglers and professional thieves, they are so well versed in all kinds of audacity and tricks they make it difficult to believe that they are really the criminals for whom you look." The local police and the U.S. Army had little success in capturing the Garzistas because, according to the consul, the rebels "mixed them up and made fun of them at their whim."[71] As the journalist Richard Harding Davis commented, "it would be as easy to catch Jack the Ripper with a Lord-Mayor's procession as Garza with a detachment of Cavalry."[72]

A little more than one month after their previous raid, a group of ninety-two *pronunciados* (rebels) crossed into Mexico on December 20. After engaging government troops in combat at Las Tortillas ranch, three revolutionists lay dead and several more were injured, while government forces suffered roughly equivalent losses. On the morning of the 21st, Garzistas were attacked 18 miles outside of Vallecillo, losing one man, four horses, and two carbines. The battle at Las Tortillas was memorialized in a corrido, told from the perspective of Don Cristóbal, who defended the ranch against the pronunciados. The corrido refers to the Garzistas as "Los Catarinos," and it ends with a melancholy verse lamenting the killing of men and horses:

> "Los Catarinos" de a caballo
> y los rurales también
> y las balas tumbaban hombres
> y a veces caballos también.
>
> ("The Catarinos" on horseback
> and the Rangers too
> and the bullets felled men
> And sometimes horses as well.)[73]

While the bullets were flying at Las Tortillas, Captain Bourke received information that another band of pronunciados was gathering near La Grulla, on the Texas side of the river, and was about to invade Mexico. Deputy Marshal Manuel Bañados, who knew Garza from the time he worked in Brownsville as a clerk, learned of Garza's whereabouts from another deputy marshal who was in league with the Garzistas. Through

Texas Mexican spies such as Bañados, Bourke finally succeeded in penetrating the wall of silence that had protected the rebels for so long.[74] At La Grulla, Bourke arrested U.S. Deputy Marshal Tomás Garza, the one who had trusted Bañados with the information about the Garzistas. Having been discovered as a Garzista collaborator, Tomás agreed to help the army. He informed Bourke that the earlier attacks in Mexico had been planned decoys to draw Mexican troops away from Camargo. Furthermore, he added, on that very night, December 21, the third party led by Garza was planning to cross into Mexico at the rising of the moon and to lay siege to Camargo. At midnight, Bourke's nineteen-man troop came upon a camp of one hundred to two hundred Garzistas at Retamal Springs, an overgrown, half-dry swamp five miles from La Grulla; they were just where Tomás had said they would be. A firefight broke out between the two sides, and before the Garzistas dispersed, Corporal Edstrom of the Third Cavalry had been killed and Lieutenant Charles Hays of the Eighth Infantry was slightly wounded.[75]

In the international press the Mexican government attempted to downplay the seriousness of the rebellion, a job made more difficult by some embarrassing facts: three armed incursions within four months, combat casualties on both sides, executions in Mexico, and now the killing of U.S. troops in Texas. The fact that the Garzistas only remained in Mexican territory for a few days at a time suggests that they had less support among the population there than in South Texas. Testimony by those who had come into contact with the Garzistas during their incursion provides some indication of how the Garzistas were received on the Mexican side of the river. Witnesses described Garza's men as wearing hats with a tricolor band (presumably the colors of the Mexican flag), and explained how the revolutionists had forcibly taken their property, including corn and horses. One man at the Aguas Negras ranch asserted that when he asked to be paid for the corn the revolutionists had taken, he was told "don't ask who will pay for it *chingado* [asshole]." Meanwhile, another witness at the Lazos ranch provided a different view, contending that Garza had personally told him that he would pay the bill for everything that they had taken.[76] In terms of violence, one person testified that during a fight with government forces on December 20, the pronunciados killed three rurales, a woman from his ranch, and a prisoner who was shot by the revolutionists while he tried to escape.[77]

These statements, collected by Nuevo Laredo's district attorney, H. C. Silva, must be viewed skeptically because they form a part of the Mexican

6. A wartime receipt from Garza's Mexican Constitutional Army. (National Archives, Records of U.S. Army, RG 393)

government's case for extraditing Garzistas from Texas. Silva, it should be remembered, was a trusted aide of Reyes and had been accused of having a hand in Ignacio Martínez's assassination. While Silva's witnesses claimed that the Garzistas stole food and supplies from ranches in Mexico as well as engaged in combat when attacked, the revolutionists do not come across as particularly violent or mean-spirited. Unlike the Mexican Army, which regularly assassinated government enemies and even suspects, the Garzistas were only accused of having killed during combat, although one of those killed was a woman. Furthermore, Garza's offer to pay for everything they had taken, even if unrealistic, throws a positive light on him as willing to assume responsibility for the debts incurred by his army. Garza's Mexican Constitutional Army even issued formal receipts for goods they had requisitioned, which could be drawn on the Mexican treasury when the revolution had succeeded (fig. 6).

After each raid, Mexican and U.S. officials and the press would announce the definitive end of the rebellion; a few months later, another proclamation would surface or there would be another incursion into Mexico. The revolution had not been silenced. In May and June 1892, a series of raids in the lower Rio Grande Valley and another revolutionary manifesto issued in Coahuila gave new energy to the Garza rebellion. The most serious of these incursions occurred on the evening of May 10, when a band of about 175 men led by Garza's first lieutenant, Julian Flores, crossed into Mexico at Ramireño. Flores, who owned a ranch of several thousand acres in Starr County and was credited with having done most of the planning of Garza's movement, was killed in the raid. Although Mexican government troops emerged victorious after killing ten Garzistas

and three of their horses at La Mecca ranch, the ability of the revolutionists to mount such a large offensive after so many months in the field
demonstrated their tenacity.[78]

One month later General Lorenzo García reported that the Garzistas
had reorganized into small bands and were "marauding" around El Ebano
and El Talisman, below Rio Grande City.[79] When on June 30, the windows at the municipal palace in Villa Garza Galán (present-day Ciudad
Acuña) were broken and seven carbines stolen, it appeared as if the disturbances might spread upriver from the lower Rio Grande Valley. This robbery, in combination with the recent publication of a revolutionary manifesto by Mexicans who lived in Del Rio, just across the river from Villa
Garza Galán, gave weight to the notion that a new Garzista offensive was
being planned.[80]

The Porfirian regime had good reason to worry about the loyalties of
northern Mexicans because another armed rebellion had broken out in a
small village in Chihuahua in December 1891. Although this revolt in
Tomochic overlapped with Garza's rebellion, and although they both
came into armed conflict with the Porfirian regime, there is no evidence
directly linking the two efforts. The Tomochic rebellion came to an abrupt
and bloody end in October 1892, when the Mexican Army laid siege to
the town, killing sixty men, women, and children in combat and sum-
marily executing the remaining survivors. The Tomochic movement was
motivated by the spiritual guidance of a local folk saint, Teresa Urrea, who
explicitly denied the political content of her teachings.[81] Garza, in contrast, issued explicitly political manifestos that were devoid of references
to God or spirituality. Although Garza, a Mason, may have shared some
of Teresa's spiritualist ideas, his revolution was a very secular and worldly
affair. Historian Paul Vanderwood, in his vivid portrayal of the Tomochic
rebellion, notes that a newspaper editor in Chihuahua published accounts
of the border skirmishes and received packages from Garza. Newspapers
such as the *San Francisco Chronicle* also claimed that people in northern
Chihuahua sympathized with Garza and were ready to join his cause.[82]
Wherever the sympathies of the people of Chihuahua lay, they never
openly joined Garza's rebellion or fought with him against the Díaz regime.

While the Teresistas and Garzistas apparently never linked their struggles in 1891–1892, individuals from these two movements actively conspired against Díaz several years later. In March 1896, two of these men,
Lauro Aguirre, credited as Santa Teresa's political mentor, and Manuel

Flores Chapa, who had been involved in Garza's revolt, were arrested and accused of organizing from Arizona a revolution against Mexico. Aguirre and Chapa, along with Santa Teresa, who had gone into exile after the massacre in Tomochic, were reported to be meeting in Solomonville, Arizona, to discuss plans for a new revolutionary movement.[83] We know that both Chapa and Aguirre rented a printing press and published a revolutionary proclamation entitled "Plan Restaurador de la Constitución y Reformista," but while Chapa admitted that he opposed Díaz, he denied being involved in any armed movement. As he put it, "I advocate the democratic doctrine in Mexico. My business is justice."[84] The alliance between Chapa, a well-known Garzista, and Aguirre and Santa Teresa in 1896 suggests that the Garzista and Teresista rebellions in 1891 could potentially have fused into a single, more powerful movement. The inability to broaden and link each of these movements, therefore, might have had less to do with their ideological differences than with Díaz's ability to isolate, silence, and murder his opponents.

A GARZISTA IN THE MEXICAN ARMY

Although Mexican government officials publicly asserted that Garza's revolt found no support in Mexico, they privately worried about the movement's clandestine sympathizers, especially among army officers. As early as September 1890, Reyes had information that Colonel Nieves Hernández had received four carbines from Ruíz Sandoval, but he advised Colonel Cerón that "it is advantageous to not show displeasure because it is in our interest to have Hernández completely content."[85] Given Hernández's popularity on the border, it was important for Reyes to keep him loyal rather than force him into an open confrontation. Maintaining the appearance of loyalty was sometimes more effective than diligently punishing every act of covert dissent. Nonetheless, after evidence emerged that Hernández, who was in charge of the section of the border where the pronunciados had crossed, sympathized with and perhaps directly aided the revolutionists, Reyes dropped the co-optation strategy and recommended a direct attack. In a lengthy letter to President Díaz, Reyes explained that he had always doubted Hernández ever since the insurrectionary movement of 1886 in Tamaulipas. Reyes's suspicions grew when he realized that Garza had only crossed back to Texas after his own forces arrived on the scene, indicating that either Hernández lacked "diligence" or had turned a blind eye to the Garzistas because he sympathized with them.[86] An article in the *St. Louis Globe Democrat*, featuring an interview with a captured Garzista, also suggested that Hernández hesitated from engaging the revolutionists. According to this Garzista, "the two forces passed within 100 yards of each other and the leaders met in the middle of the intervening space where they conversed a long time." However, he attributed the gentlemanly agreement not to fight to the fact that Hernández was outnumbered by four to one, and that fighting just then would have been "an act of madness."[87]

Hernández's behavior during the Garzistas's second incursion in November 1891 finally convinced Reyes that some action had to be taken. Although Hernández had followed closely behind the pronunciados, Reyes argued that he had obstructed other troops from pursuing the rebels. At one point, Hernández sent fifty of his own cavalry ahead and they began firing while still a great distance from their ostensible targets. Reyes concluded that their actions were meant more as a warning to the revolutionists than as an attack on them. Another officer who joined Hernández's chase of the Garzistas also complained that he had slowed his pursuit. Reyes was still worried about driving Hernández into open rebellion, and so he proceeded carefully so as not to arouse his suspicions. After drawing Hernández to Mier under the pretense of discussing the increase of his command, he and those loyal to him were immediately arrested.[88]

On December 7, the *Laredo Times* claimed that Colonel Hernández, the popular leader of troops at Guerrero, had been "ruthlessly shot down" one hundred miles north of Monterrey while under military escort. The next day Laredo's Consul Díaz wrote a letter to the editor of the *Times* denying the reported killing and arguing that Hernández was "perfectly sound and safe" in Monterrey where he would be tried by a military court for complicity with the Garzistas.[89] The rumor of Hernández's killing spread throughout the United States, with one resident on the Texas border fabricating a detailed story of how soldiers shot Hernández in the back under the false pretense of an escape attempt.[90]

Confidential papers captured from Garzistas corroborate the assertion that Hernández actively aided the revolutionists. These documents listed Hernández as a voluntary contributor to their cause, indicating that he donated $250 in cash, three horses, and four loads of corn in September 1891.[91] The evidence thus suggests that Hernández sympathized and probably even colluded with the Garzistas, but Consul Díaz made him out to be a central leader, arguing emphatically that "with the imprisonment of Nieves Hernández and the bandits that accompanied him, the vandal incursions of these vagabonds are terminated."[92] The incursions did not stop, however, and the arrest of Hernández and twenty of his men had the unintended effect of publicly demonstrating the sympathy that Garza's cause had inspired, even within the ranks of the military. Such precipitous action by Reyes was double-edged; it showed his power and decisiveness on one side, and revealed his fears and weakness on the other.

On January 23, 1892, the war council in Monterrey sentenced Hernández to death for his collaboration with the Garzistas. Reyes spoke with the war council and attempted to have the punishment reduced because he felt that the execution would cause a stir within the military. In particular, he worried about the international visibility of the case and the possibility that it would tarnish the reputation of the military by showing that one of its leaders had collaborated with "bandits." However, given the wording and sentencing requirements of the relevant laws, Reyes felt that the war council had no other choice. The only hope was for the supreme court to reduce the punishment or for Díaz to commute the sentence.[93]

By early February, Reyes had changed his mind and wrote to Díaz that Hernández "deserved" his death sentence, and suggested that it be done before he had time to appeal to the supreme court. Reyes's change of heart occurred after he received a copy of the Garzistas's captured papers in early February. These papers, together with his own investigations, convinced him that Hernández had directly supplied and aided the revolution.[94] Even if Reyes was now calling for blood, Díaz still had to be concerned with his international image. Executing Hernández was made more difficult by positive portrayals of the colonel in the foreign press, such as a *San Francisco Examiner* article that called him "one of the most popular and widely known officers in the Mexican Army."[95] Laredoan Federico de los Santos appealed to Díaz for Hernández's life on the grounds that Hernández had been falsely accused by personal enemies. In addition to testifying on behalf of Hernández's patriotism, noting how he fought against the French invaders, Santos included an article from the *Laredo Times*, which had always been "a true admirer" of Díaz's government, to demonstrate the support that Hernández enjoyed among the border community.[96] The article reported a rumor that Hernández had been shot by the government, and as well as being overflowing in its praise for the popular colonel it was meant to show Díaz the potential negative consequences of his execution. The *Laredo Times* asserted that this "gallant" soldier had done more "to suppress crime along the border" than any other Mexican officer. "Brave, manly and honorable, he was loved and respected by all that knew him except a few enemies who feared his popularity with the people and it is these who sought his death." The article continued, claiming that Hernández had made a valiant effort to capture Garza, but that his failure to do so had been exploited by his enemies as an excuse for his arrest. And finally, this pro-Díaz newspaper concluded, "the death of Hernández will ever be a blot on the administration of Díaz."[97] Consciously or not, the *Times* misjudged Hernández's connections to the Garzistas. Nonetheless, this premature obituary for Hernández must have made Díaz realize that, whatever the truth of the charges, the execution would be viewed unfavorably and as politically motivated in the foreign press. In February 1893, one year after his arrest, Díaz commuted Hernández's death sentence and reduced it to twenty years in prison.[98] Colonel Nieves Hernández ended up dying in Mexico City's military prison at Tlatelolco.

A "BARBAROUS ASSAULT" ON SAN IGNACIO

Even after Hernández had been removed far from the border, the raids continued. Over a year after the first incursion, and after countless pronouncements by U.S. and Mexican government officials that Garza's revolt had come to an end, invasions of Mexican territory seemed to be gathering more strength. Although Garza fled Texas in spring 1892, his army kept carrying out raids and distributing Garzista manifestos. One particularly brutal attack in December 1892 on San Ignacio, Mexico, demonstrated that the Garzistas were still able to organize large groups and carry out guerrilla raids in Mexico without being captured (the town across the river in Texas was also called San Ignacio).

An hour before noon on December 10, Garzista rebels split into three groups and crossed into Mexico near Ramireño. Three army auxiliaries managed to escape to Guerrero and report the imminent attack before the assault on San Ignacio could begin. The rebel band of one hundred men led by Maximo Martínez, otherwise known as "bushy head," and Eustorgio Ramón greatly outnumbered the forty soldiers and three officers defending the Mexican military post (fig. 7). The surprise attack at noon caught offguard the soldiers, who were grooming their horses in the corral. The raiders set fire to the military post, making defense almost impossible. After three hours of heavy fighting, four Mexican soldiers and three officers, including the post commander, had been burned to death. Four other soldiers died from gunshot wounds. The rebel leader Maximo Martínez burned the body of the commanding Mexican Army captain, Rutilio Segura, after he had been killed. Incinerating Segura's dead body must have been meant more as a symbolic act of domination than as a practical war tactic; and that Martínez was a former servant of this army captain suggests that the cremation could also have been motivated by personal revenge against a former boss.[99] Whatever the motivation, the number of soldiers killed and the ways in which their bodies had been purposefully desecrated made this raid seem more brutal and violent than the others. Bourke would later refer to this incident as "the vilest outrage upon a friendly nation in the history of the nineteenth [century]."[100]

The Mexican government took advantage of this raid to paint the Garzistas as savages, and they even invoked images of Apache Indian attacks to drive home their point. One Mexican official told the *Galveston News* that "there was nothing in the annals of Indian Warfare more dastardly and cruel than the action of the Garza bandits in their raid upon the garrison of San Ignacio."[101] Meanwhile, Reyes's *La Voz de Nuevo León* ran a series of articles condemning the raid as a "barbarous assault" led by "bandits."[102] Concerned about the tendency of the U.S. press to disassociate the "barbaric" raid on San Ignacio from Garza's previous incursions, San Antonio's Consul Ornelas argued that even though Garza did not lead this latest attack, the two efforts were connected, "with the same leaders and for the same purpose."[103]

This rebel victory, over one year after Garza's first incursion, came as a blow to the Mexican Army. More devastating perhaps was the fact that the surviving soldiers had gone over to live among the pronunciados in San Ignacio, Texas, and refused to return to Mexico. According to Reyes, the surviving soldiers were apprehended by the rebels and brought to San Ignacio along with their horses.[104] Four days after the raid, Reyes asserted that the Mexican soldiers were still being held in San Ignacio, and that when they tried to return to Mexico, armed men had prevented them from leaving.[105] However, when a U.S. officer investigated the alleged imprisonment, the locals told him, that "these soldiers have repeatedly expressed their unwillingness to return to Mexico."[106] U.S. deputy Marshal Hall, together with three armed Mexican officers commanded by Captain Eduardo Zerna, led a search for the missing soldiers on December 21. According to several witnesses, when the town constable questioned Captain Zerna, who was leading the Mexican soldiers to the river, Zerna intimidated the soldiers into agreeing to return "voluntarily" to Mexico. The constable persisted after sensing fear in the Mexican soldiers, but when an

7. Maximo Martínez, aka "bushy head," led the attack on San Ignacio, Mexico, on December 10, 1892. (Photograph courtesy of Maximo's granddaughter, Janie Martínez)

armed Mexican rurale reached for his gun, the constable was forced to retreat and allowed the soldiers to return to Mexico.[107]

Even though the people of San Ignacio seemed to cooperate with the investigation, the officer in charge undermined their credibility by claiming that their story was a "tale." They were all pronunciados, he asserted, and "none of them have ever yet told me the truth." Nonetheless, he argued that presence of armed Mexican soldiers on U.S. soil demanded an explanation.[108] This international incident became a black eye for the Mexican government, which came off looking pretty badly. The Mexican ambassador could not have been pleased when the U.S. secretary of foreign relations, John W. Foster, told him that the Mexican soldiers had chosen to remain in Texas "because they prefer life in the United States and also because they are afraid to return to Mexico, fearing punishment."[109] The raid on San Ignacio, therefore, not only demonstrated the military strength of the insurrectionists, but also indicated that, if given half a chance, Mexican soldiers would desert their posts and their country.

The December 1892 attack on San Ignacio would prove to be the last major border incursion of the Garza revolution. The battles, however, continued to rage on the Texas side as U.S. authorities stepped-up their efforts to capture and arrest Garzistas. The war of words in the columns of newspapers and magazines continued as well. It was clear after a year and a half, however, that the Garzistas were not just a ragtag band of outlaws and that the combined might of the U.S. and Mexican armies had been unable to definitively crush the revolt. At the same time, the reports of brutality by the Mexican military made the Díaz regime, which desperately aspired to be modern and respectable, look like a backward authoritarian dictatorship. The border rebellion could not, in the end, be dismissed out of hand.

CONCLUSION

Garza's rebellion lasted from September 1891 into 1893. In that time there were five major incursions into Mexico, with hundreds of rebels engaging in active combat. This was not a paper revolution, as some newspapers later claimed. Rebel forces skirmished with army troops in the United States and in Mexico, leaving scores of casualties on both sides. The publicity that the terror campaign in Mexico received in the U.S. press helped to depict the Porfirian regime as dictatorial and brutal; it also helped the rebels gain some degree of sympathy from the U.S. public and the courts who repeatedly refused to extradite captured Garzistas to Mexico. The support that the rebels received in Mexico from popular military leaders like Colonel Nieves Hernández also revealed the cracks in the supposedly solid wall of support for Díaz. The caution with which Reyes proceeded against Hernández suggests that the top circles of the Porfirian government understood that these cracks could easily grow into holes that could bring down the entire regime. Díaz played his hand masterfully by imposing terror in the countryside and selectively punishing caudillos whose support for the rebels became public while co-opting others who had only covertly supported the rebels.

What were the Garzistas fighting for? They publicly declared that they opposed Díaz because he had betrayed the liberal principles of no-reelection and individual freedoms, and had begun to sell out the country to foreigners. Although they did not provide many details about the kind of society they wanted to construct once the regime was overthrown, they promised to distribute "vacant lands" to anyone who would cultivate them, to establish free trade, and to restore municipal and state sovereignty. The language of the manifestos as well as the historical references to the 1857 Constitution linked the revolution to a long history of popular liberalism in Mexico. Even though they did not propose a radically different social order, the critique of Porfirian liberalism was radical for its time. Nonetheless, the Garzistas invoked the same developmentalist ethic to defend their rebellion as their *científico* counterparts in Mexico did to condemn it. Ultimately both sides claimed to represent the same ideals: liberalism, progress, and honor.

Garza's caricature of Reyes's mother in his newspaper indicates the centrality of honor to the political battles on the border. Garza hoped his article would discredit Reyes, the strongman of the North. If Reyes's mother was oversexed and his father was emasculated, then what could one expect from the son? The personal, in this case, was political. Several newspapers, however, turned the tables on Garza, insisting that it was he who lacked honor by dragging a woman, Reyes's mother, into a political battle. While I am not suggesting that Garza's revolution was caused by an insult to Reyes's mother, honor was central to the revolt. War was, to twist Clausewitz's famous maxim, the continuation of the struggle for honor by other means.

4. BOOMS AND BUSTS

Capitalist development in the border region at the end of the 1800s led to a new ideological construction of the border. Developers, investors, and town boosters projected a new image of the border as a zone of economic and cultural modernity. The border had outgrown its "frontier" days of Indians, bandits, and economic stagnation; the border was poised, its proponents argued, to assume its position at the forefront of the emerging binational commerce. However, some border Mexicans like Garza questioned this narrative of progress and development. Although they remained modern liberals and echoed the rhetoric of the developmentalist ethic, they also recognized the tremendous costs of this "progress" for the Mexican community on the border. They were not against progress and free trade, but they were against the kind of progress and free trade that had been pursued by the Porfirian regime and Anglo capitalists. In both cases, wealthy outsiders, usually Anglos, displaced poor Mexicans; in Texas, the Tejano elite was also supplanted by newcomer Anglos. The Garza rebellion was thus part of a larger struggle over how to define the terms of capitalist modernization, as well as what image of the border would be projected to the outside world.

Landowners and merchants were doing well on the border at the end of the nineteenth century. The arrival of the railroad had increased property values and opened new possibilities for the commercial exploitation of mining and agriculture. Bankers were giddy at the prospect of buying up land and developing industries while it was still relatively cheap to do so. Government officials couldn't have been happier about the prospect of turning this troublesome zone of conflict and war into a stable region producing revenues for the national treasury. For those distant from the border, Garza's rebellion was a reminder of the earlier days of "bandit wars" and smuggling, along with the uneasy sense that the economic boom could go bust very quickly. Several large landowners and merchants on the border, however, saw Garza's revolution as an opportunity to expand their trade and influence at a moment when the Mexican government was imposing new duties and taxes on transactions that had previously been free. While some of the wealthiest men in south Texas supported Garza, the ranks of his army were filled with those small landowners and landless peons whose suffering was directly related to the commercialization of agriculture. It was a time of great economic change, changes that inspired many on the border to support Garza's revolt, as well as motivated others far from the border to do everything in their power to quell it.

AWAKENING THE BORDER

Eager to project an image of the border as a new zone of economic development, boosters constructed a narrative of progress, an awakening from a backward, sleepy past to a forward-looking, vibrant future. Commercial promoters and journalists wrote as if the border region had been in a deep sleep until the railroad whistle woke it up. While granting such vivifying powers to the "iron horse" is certainly an exaggeration, the railroad, more than any other single technology, changed the face and body of the border. Almost as soon as the railroad connected the United States and Mexico in Laredo in the early 1880s, land values and commercial ventures skyrocketed. At the time, Laredo was the most important border crossing point in Texas, and it functioned as an intellectual and economic center for the largely rural regions of South Texas and northeastern Mexico. San Antonio in Texas and Monterrey in Nuevo León were much larger cities, but located several hundred miles from the boundary line they were at the outer edges of what can be considered the border region.

Laredo's Mayor Atlee welcomed this new industrial era in an inaugural speech in the late 1880s. "The importance of Laredo is being recognized, as is evidenced by the influx of population and the large investments of capital. Our borders are being enlarged, and the cottages of new-comers are rapidly dotting the slopes. An era of prosperity has dawned upon our city."[1] Garza had arrived in Laredo just a few days after the railroad, and he quickly integrated himself into the town's extensive network of mutualistas, Spanish-language newspapers, and well-heeled merchants. It was in this bustling border town that Garza developed a base of political allies and financial backers for his insurrection.

The presence of a well-established Mexican elite in Laredo prevented or mitigated overt racial discrimination against Mexicans, but even as the Anglo promoters advertised the history of racial harmony, they encouraged "Americanization." While boosters heralded progress and development on both sides of the border, Anglos tended to racialize their analysis, casting the "sleepy" past as Mexican and portraying the "energetic" future as Anglo. Promotional pamphlets produced by the Laredo Immigration Society at the end of the 1880s provide insight into this racialized vision of the future, as well as illustrating the heady optimism of the era.[2] Along with the detailed descriptions of the various commercial opportunities available in Laredo, the pamphlets trumpeted the town's increasing Anglicization, decreasing Mexicanness, and its history of racial harmony. An 1888 pamphlet stressed that Laredo, "being an old Spanish town still retains much to remind the present citizens of the ancient manner and customs . . . that seem to characterize the Mexican people generally." It quickly pointed out, however, that although "very few Americans had made their homes so far from the 'States' [until the] advent of the railroads, . . . now they constitute fully one-third of the population."[3] The proportion of "Americans" (read Anglos) was probably smaller than one-third, but their overestimation served to entice fearful Anglos to a predominantly Mexican town. The 1889 Laredo directory celebrated the Spanish and Mexican early history of the town, but argued that "with the advent of the white people, the old Mexican customs and manner of government rapidly disappeared, and new ideas, American styles, and customs prevailed to a great extent."[4] In writing thus, the pamphlets' authors came to terms with Laredo's non-Anglo history by dismissing its continuing presence and by placing it in a distant past. In either case, the message was that "Americans" or "white people" would be welcomed and that Laredo was already becoming increasingly "American."

Anglos in Laredo, a town where Mexicans held substantial political and economic power, could not simply ignore or dominate Mexicans. Therefore, the Anglo and Mexican elite worked together to promote industrial development and encourage outside investment. These commercial pamphlets advertised the real and desired harmonious relations between the races as one of the factors, like access to water and transportation, that made Laredo a good investment opportunity. The "local government," the 1889 Laredo directory boasted, "is now administered by both Americans and Mexicans who live in peace and contentment, each striving his utmost to make Laredo the great international commerce center of the southwest."[5] Touting Laredo's multiculturalism, boosters proclaimed that "with a population representing every nation beneath the sun, her people live together peacefully and harmoniously."[6] They also emphasized the respectability of the new immigrants and the welcome they received by the Mexican residents. "The immigration induced by the advent of railroads has added many good citizens. Men, generally of the better class, with their families have made homes here and have always found a welcome among the old residents."[7] The pamphlets further served to assuage Anglo fears of domination by Mexicans by rendering the Mexicans in the safe image of hard-working people who shared "American" capitalist values and who awaited the arrival of Anglos with open arms. "Almost every citizen," including Laredo's Mexicans, they reassured, had "enterprise, pluck, and vigor."[8] This emphasis on hard work and cultural respectability echoes the developmentalist ethic so prevalent in northern Mexico. In Texas, however, this ethic had a slightly distinct racial and national tinge, being portrayed as paradigmatically "American." Laredo's Mexicans could be seen as respectable because they were of the "better class" and had adopted these "American" values.

The businessmen of Laredo bolstered the image of racial harmony between Anglos and Mexicans by focusing on a past of racial conflict between the "savages" (Indians) and the "civilized" (Spaniards, Mexicans, and Anglos). Thus, they constructed a triumphant pioneer narrative that joined Mexicans and Anglos in a common struggle at the same time that they located danger at a safe distance in the past. Nonetheless, promoters complained about the difficulty "to induce strangers, who have heard of the bloody border, as commonly represented, to believe this is an inviting field for capital."[9] Thus, when the Garza rebellion broke out it only added to the image of a "bloody border" scarred by violent racial strife and rampaging Mexican bandits: such stories circulating in the international press could not have been good for business.

Other towns along the Texas border, such as Brownsville and Rio Grande City, shared Laredo's optimism about commercial prospects in the region. However, the new era that dawned in Laredo in the early 1880s would only arrive in the lower Rio Grande Valley twenty years later, when a rail line to Brownsville was finally constructed in 1904. In the meantime, soldiers and developers laid the groundwork. Just as the Garzistas rebellion was subsiding in 1893, Lieutenant W. H. Chatfield, a U.S. Army officer stationed at Fort Brown, published a forty-three-page promotional booklet for the lower Rio Grande Valley. Like Laredo's Immigration Society publications, Chatfield wrote enthusiastically about large crop yields, tropical weather, and abundant land in order to entice outside investment and Anglo immigration to the region.

In addition to its geographical isolation, Chatfield blamed Brownsville's backwardness on the lethargy of the Mexican population. "The position of the city, on the farthest border of our territory and without means of rapid transit to and from the great centers of population, combined with half its inhabitants being foreigners who clung to the traditions and customs of their native country, are facts which have heretofore retarded its growth and nurtured procrastination in developing its natural advantages."[10] Thus, once the railroads made Brownsville accessible, "men with a little capital, brawny arms, clear brains, and 'Yankee grit,' . . . [would] benefit the section," and themselves as well, by developing the abundant "natural advantages."[11]

Like his counterparts in northern Mexico, Chatfield heralded the valley's awakening. The notion that the border stood at the edge of a dramatic transformation appeared in practically every description of the region at the end of the nineteenth century. Chatfield waxed poetic on this point, exclaiming that despite the vicissitudes of fortune in Brownsville up to that point, "the base metal will be transmuted into gold. Brownsville will pull off her sackcloth, and rise from her recumbent position to an exalted station in the bright galaxy of commercial cities that adorn our beloved land of the free."[12] The transmutation to gold, the taking off of the sackcloth and the rising to join the celestial galaxy of commercial cities all reinforced the idea that Brownsville and the region held something of extraordinary value that had been covered over and hidden from view. Chatfield's entire development plan for the lower Rio Grande Valley, however, depended on irrigation, and building irrigation depended on outside capitalist investment. Chatfield's interest in developing this part of Texas was not merely academic; he had organized the Chatfield Irrigation Company with an initial stock offering of one million dollars. As a non-Texas resident, the soldier and entrepreneur appealed to Governor Hogg in December 1892, begging him to make sure that pending legislation would not adversely affect "capital invested in Texas by non-residents." He also asked the governor to sign his name and formally endorse the irrigation company. With his help, he assured the governor, "there will be little difficulty in transforming this needy section into the most brilliant ray from any point of the Lone Star."[13]

Along with the technological evidence of the modern era — telephones, factories, and railroads — villages and towns in the region began to acquire a different human face as new arrivals swelled the population. This demographic explosion provided grist for the mill of progress. Immigration helped solve the perennial problem of labor shortages at the same time that it created a larger market for basic goods such as clothing, food, and housing. Europeans, Anglo Americans, and Mexicans moved to South Texas with increasing frequency as job opportunities in commerce, agriculture, and industry opened. A steady stream of migrants flowed northward from central Mexico to cities such as Monterrey and across the border to Texas. This *población flotante* (floating population) of agricultural workers, miners, and day laborers moved northward, pulled by the promise of higher wages and pushed by increasing pressures on their land. They provided the labor for the burgeoning industrial economy in Mexico's north and the southwestern United States, and they caused northern Mexico's cities to swell and swoon along with the booms and busts of the economy. While their labor was essential for industrial development, northern Mexico's sociedad culta scorned and feared this group of rootless workers, viewing them as vice ridden and dirty.[14] At the same time, as Mexican workers crossed into the United States, Anglo American and European skilled workers and capitalists moved to Mexico to take advantage of the industrial boom in the northeastern part of that country.

A precise picture of demographic change on the border is difficult to ascertain given the unreliability of the census and the difficulty of counting a population that continually moved back and forth across the border. Nonetheless, general trends, such as the boom in population after the railroads arrived, can be identified. Just before Garza's revolt, the combined population of both Laredos stood at approximately "15,000 souls," with two-thirds of those on the Texas side.[15] Historian Gilberto Hinojosa in his demographic study of Laredo finds that the city's population nearly tripled within a decade of the railroad's arrival. In contrast, in the two decades before the railroad, from 1850 until 1870, Laredo's population barely grew.[16]

Some of the newcomers who arrived in the wake of the railroads were Anglo Americans or Europeans, but Mexicans continued to come as well. The same pattern of migration that occurred in the period after 1850 appears to have continued after 1880 but at an accelerated rate. Therefore, poorer, less-skilled Mexican-born migrants swelled the city's population along with a sizable number of Anglo American and European professionals and merchants. In arguing that "there is sufficient unskilled labor [in Laredo] already," promoters particularly encouraged "such immigration as will bring intelligence and capital to employ and direct our cheap labor."[17] Hinojosa concludes that "in the process of rapid growth Laredo developed into two societies, one Anglo-American and one Mexican-American."[18] However, such a clear dichotomy between the two societies does not recognize the class cleavages and affiliations that divided Mexicans and united the Mexican and Anglo elite. Although the "cheap labor" in Laredo was almost exclusively Mexican, the fact that employers were Anglos, Europeans, and Mexicans undermines the notion of Laredo as two societies divided only or even primarily by race.

As mentioned earlier, Laredo's trajectory from a mainly agricultural frontier town to a center of manufacturing activity differed from the changes experienced in other border towns in the lower Rio Grande Valley. For instance, Brownsville and its Mexican counterpart, Matamoros, experienced dramatic economic and population growth during the U.S. Civil War because of its strategic location as the transshipment point for Confederate cotton.[19] By the end of the century, however, the boom had become a bust, and the estimated 20,000 who populated Matamoros at its height had decreased to about half that amount by 1893.[20] While Brownsville's populations did not experience a drastic decline, it barely grew between the Civil War period and the arrival of the railroad forty years later.[21] Brownsville's location near the mouth of the Rio Grande had from its founding until 1881 made it the primary transit point for trade between the United States and Mexico. However, once the railroad reached Laredo in 1881, that city quickly eclipsed Brownsville as the main gateway to and from Mexico. When a line finally linked Brownsville to the rest of the United States and Mexican system in 1904, the city and the entire lower Rio Grande Valley began to develop in roughly the same pattern as did Laredo.[22] By 1909, Brownsville boasted 10,000 inhabitants, and Cameron County's population, of which Brownsville was the seat, more than doubled from 1900 to 1909, suggesting a corresponding growth in the countryside.[23]

The population of South Texas grew throughout the nineteenth century, as did the proportion of Mexicans to Anglos. While numerically outnumbered by Mexicans in the cities and the countryside, Anglo influence grew as a result of their economic and political position. In their study of Texas demography, Arnoldo De León and Kenneth Stewart note a pattern in this period in which Tejanos tended to migrate to the countryside and Anglos to the cities.[24] Thus, in sheer numbers Anglos were becoming more of a minority in South Texas, but in the cities their absolute numbers increased as did their economic and political influence.

The increasing numbers of Mexicans in South Texas did not escape the notice of the Anglo press and may have prompted the plethora of immigration pamphlets designed to lure Anglos to the region in the 1880s and 1890s. An 1871 Texas almanac noted that in Starr County "there is constant intercourse with Mexico on the other side of the river, and many of the inhabitants of this county are Mexicans."[25] When over three decades later the racial balance of the county had not changed significantly, the almanac complained that "more than nine-tenths of the population of [Starr] county are Mexican, speaking mainly Spanish and addicted to the old ways of their people."[26] In the larger commercial cities like Brownsville and Laredo, the percentage of Anglos would have been greater than in the countryside. However, even the Laredo Immigration Society estimated Laredo's 1888 Anglo population at only one-third of the total, and that proportion was certainly overinflated to calm Anglo fears.[27]

Although the population data for Mexico are even scarcer than for South Texas, a general pattern of growth can be deduced from the existing sources. The state of Nuevo León and its capital Monterrey experienced dramatic population growth at the end of the nineteenth century due to an influx of foreigners and Mexicans from other states. As the principal city in the region, Monterrey received many of these new arrivals, especially during the U.S. Civil War and again after railroads linked the city to the rest of the country in the 1880s. In 1863, Monterrey's *Boletín oficial* took note of the city's "rapid development" in just one year, indicating that the population had "multiplied in astonishing proportions."[28] Growth continued throughout the century, and by 1895 over 56,000 people lived in Monterrey, up from only 12,000 in 1824.[29] The population of the whole state of Nuevo León also grew dramatically in the 1880s, but by the early twentieth century its growth had leveled off, and with the outbreak of the Mexican Revolution in 1910 it even declined slightly.[30]

While far from scientific, this data illustrates a general trend of increasing migration to the region from other parts of Mexico and the United States, especially after the introduction of railroads. Demographic change prompted new social and racial configurations. In South Texas, Anglo influence increased even as its percentage of the population declined. Similarly, Anglo American influence grew in northeastern cities like Monterrey as foreign capital flowed into the region. However, in spite of a growing physical and financial Anglo presence, the region continued culturally to be thoroughly Mexican. The desire to become a commercial center led modernizers on both sides of the river to try and distance themselves from earlier generations and to change the demographics of the region by encouraging white professionals and entrepreneurs to settle there. For many poor Mexicans, and even for some of the elite, this demographic, economic, social, and political modernization resulted in their disenfranchisement. The Garzistas thus rebelled to hold onto land, political power, and a sense of place in this rapidly changing society.

The immigration and investment pamphlets, city directories, and some newspapers successfully disseminated the image of the border as a site of thriving economic modernization. Nevertheless, alternative and critical views of this modernization project also made their way into print, including the manifestos of the rebellions of Martínez in 1886 and Garza's in 1891. The 1886 "Plan Restaurador del Orden Constitucional" (Restoration plan of the constitutional order) condemned the Díaz regime for the "privileges and monopolies that have been granted to the banks and other companies . . . [and] the dispossession of property on the pretext of surveying vacant lands."[31] The Plan also guaranteed the freedom of peons, promised restoration of all ill-gotten property and land, and declared null and void all the concessions and monopolies granted by the Díaz and González governments. Garza's 1891 "Proclama" also indicted Díaz's corruption, specifically condemning his act of selling huge tracts of land along the border to North American businessmen.[32] Even though both of these manifestos explicitly supported expanding free trade, and were not against modernization per se, they were critical of how the Porfirian "free trade" policies had made the foreign investors and a few cronies of the president extremely wealthy while the vast majority of Mexicans had been dispossessed. These revolutionary manifestos pointed to the dark underside of the Porfirian economic miracle that was being heralded in New York City, Mexico City, and London. Although they provided an alternative perspective to the Porfirian cheerleaders, the limited circulation of these tracts in small, Spanish-language border newspapers diminished their impact.

In addition to his critique of Porfirian modernization, Garza condemned the way Mexicans had been dispossessed and exploited in Texas. One article in his newspaper *El Comercio Mexicano* asked "where are the plots of land that Mexicans once had?," which was followed by the reply that they had been taken over by some lawyers and "aventureros Americanos" (American adventurers). Garza also pointed to the low pay given to Mexicans in contrast to that for Anglos and even blacks as evidence of the discrimination they faced in Texas.[33] More than two decades later many of the same problems still faced the Mexican community in Texas, and in some ways things had gotten worse. In 1911, the Primer Congreso Mexicanista was held in Laredo with the goal of organizing the Gran Liga Mexicanista, an association to defend the legal rights of Mexicans in U.S. courts and to prevent the exclusion of Mexican children from schools with Anglo students. While the Gran Liga apparently never functioned as an organization, and the speeches at the Primer Congreso Mexicanista did not directly address the issue of economic marginalization, the discriminatory practices they were organizing against suggests that the modernization trumpeted by Laredo's boosters had not resolved racial problems on the border, and it may even have exacerbated them.[34]

While the Primer Congreso Mexicanista focused on racial discrimination in the courts and schools, socialist unions targeted capitalism itself. During a 1905 strike at the Mexican National Railway Company machine shops in Laredo, Texas, the Federal Labor Union's (FLU) newspaper, *El Defensor del Obrero* (The worker's defender) articulately protested the discriminatory pay scale in which Mexicans, regardless of their position, earned $.75 for a ten-hour workday while Anglo machinists earned $3.50.[35] The union's militant rhetoric moved beyond merely asking for a pay increase to questioning the whole relationship between labor and capital. One of their recruiting pamphlets provocatively queried, "Do you want to continue to be a slave to the bourgeoisie?. . . . Do you want to ready the projectiles that you shall use tomorrow in the formidable struggle for existence?"[36] The FLU's strike against the railroad, the preeminent symbol of modernization, dramatized the class and racial conflict between the beneficiaries and the losers of this unprecedented period of economic growth.

By 1915, the commercialization of agriculture and the Anglo takeover of land in South Texas were well underway. As Jovita González wrote in her 1930 master's thesis, "Rude then, was the awakening of these border people when the development of the Rio Grande Valley brought hundreds of foreigners to their doors. This invasion of fortune-seeking Americans was a material as well as a spiritual blow to the Mexicans, particularly to the landed aristocracy."[37] The 1915 Plan de San Diego articulated the resentment of Mexicans who had been displaced by modernization and capitalist development in South Texas. The irredentist plan aimed to reclaim the southwestern United States (which was taken from Mexico during the 1846 Mexican-American War) for Latinos, Indians, African Americans, and Japanese. While the plan was discovered before it could be launched, cross-border raiding continued for two more years. The rebels attacked the prime symbols and vehicles of capitalist development in South Texas: irrigation pumping stations, railroads, and Anglos. A revised "Manifesto to the Oppressed Peoples of America" gave a more specifically anarchist bent to the movement, calling for "social revolution," the distribution and communal sharing of land among "proletarians," and the building of modern schools where all children could learn the norm of "universal love." The rhetorical and organizational links between the Plan de San Diego and the anarchist Flores Magón brothers and their Mexican Liberal Party also suggests that this was an attack on capitalism and not just a racially motivated revolt against Anglo discrimination.[38] Whereas Martínez, Garza, and the organizers of the Congreso Mexicanista fought against the pernicious effects of the particular type of capitalist development being implemented in the region, the railroad union in Laredo and the Plan de San Diego conspirators took on capitalism itself. All of these people, however, offered an alternative perspective on economic modernization, one that pointed to the high social costs of Porfirian and Anglo-led capitalist development.

VIRGIN FIELDS AND THE ZONA LIBRE

Although there were alternative visions of modernization and outright attacks on capitalist development on the border, national elites were unified in their desires to increase trade and investment in the region. By the 1890s, economic and social ties between Mexico and the United States had become more than just a local concern of border inhabitants. Trade policy and political relations between the two nations was debated at the centers of political and financial power in Washington, D.C., New York City, and Mexico City. As the significance and size of transnational trade grew, so too did the international importance of political stability on the border. The growing importance of the border as a zone of economic development helps to explain why Garza's rebellion quickly became a major international incident. President Harrison even commented on the Garza revolt in his 1892 address to Congress, touting the suppression of the "lawless foreign marauders" as an "opportunity to testify its [the U.S.

government's] good will for Mexico and its earnest purpose to fulfill the obligations of international friendship by pursuing and dispersing evildoers."[39]

The Mexican ambassador in the United States, Matías Romero, led his government's efforts to discredit the Garza movement. As well as forging closer ties between the two countries, the ambassador was responsible for boosting trade relations and selling Mexico as a safe and welcoming market for international investors. Denying the significance of Garza's insurrection was crucial because investors were not keen on putting their money into an unstable country in the midst of revolutionary upheaval.[40] At a dinner hosted by the Democratic Club of New York City in December 1891, Romero outlined the mutual benefits to be gained through binational trade. He underscored the importance of Mexico's openness to foreign investment, especially at a moment when the closing of the U.S. frontier made "it difficult to find a new field for profitable enterprise." In contrast to the diminishing potential in the United States, Mexico offered "a very large and profitable virgin field." Trade would also improve social relations between the two countries. Thus, he predicted, the "new bonds of cordiality, good will, and mutual profit between the citizens of these two great republics," would make them "lasting and true friends, and strengthening thus their position among the family of nations, each preserving, of course, its own nationality."[41] Sexual metaphors drove home the "family" relationship between different nations as Romero encouraged the capitalist men in New York City to take advantage of the open and "virgin" Mexico.

Fortifying the ties between the two nations also led to a reconsideration of the ad hoc trade relationships that had been cobbled together along the border for half a century. The *zona libre* (free trade zone) in Mexico was at the center of this discussion. In the years preceding Garza's revolution, the future of the zone hung in the balance as the United States and Mexican congresses debated its future. Ever since the Mexican-American War, a de facto free trade zone had existed in Tamaulipas, allowing residents to import goods for consumption without paying duties.[42] In 1861, the Mexican Congress finally ratified this practice, and by 1884 they expanded the zone to include the entire U.S.-Mexico border.

The extension of the free trade zone enabled goods to be imported into Mexico with a minimal 3 percent tax added, but the law stipulated that merchandise had to be consumed within the zone, which extended thirteen miles into Mexico and ran along the border from Brownsville to

Tijuana.[43] The binational trade in the zone had become important enough by 1890 that the Senate launched an investigation into its impact on the U.S. economy. Opposition to the zone had been building since 1884, as Texas merchants sought to protect themselves from Mexican competition. A petition signed by forty El Paso merchants, bankers, and politicians argued that the extension of the zone "greatly increased opportunities for smuggling and [led to] the utter demoralization of legitimate business." The petitioners urged their representatives to pressure the Mexican government to repeal the zone. Failing that, they demanded "the immediate establishment of a 'Free Zone' on our borders." While manufacturers benefited from an open Mexican market, the El Paso merchants argued that Mexican merchants imported foreign (mainly European) goods free of duties and then smuggled them back to the United States, thereby cutting into the sales and profits of U.S. businesses.[44] The Mexican ambassador tried to defuse the tension, explaining that the free trade zone was not intended to be an unfriendly gesture toward the United States, but rather originally was designed to equalize conditions on both sides of the border.[45]

The U.S. consul in Nuevo Laredo entered the debate in 1890, expressing his support for the free zone and hoping to convince the U.S. Senate not to take punitive measures against Mexico. Ending the free zone, he warned, would benefit the German, French, English, and Spanish interests in northern Mexico by making it more profitable to transport merchandise on their railways in Mexico, rather than through U.S. ports. After all, the consul noted, the representatives of foreign interests were the ones "who say most and speak oftenest" against the zone.[46] Although twin border towns such as Laredo and Nuevo Laredo were rivals, he contended that "they are also to a considerable extent mutually dependent on each other. The prosperity of one — crosses over to a greater or lesser degree and benefits the other." The estimated free zone trade of $2,000,000 per year would be cut in half, he predicted, if the zone were abolished. Moreover, because U.S. products accounted for three out of every four dollars imported to the zone, its abolition would hurt U.S. manufacturers the most.

Further, the consul felt that abolishing the zone would increase rather than decrease smuggling. To illustrate this point he recounted a story of a dinner he had in the Mexican border town Piedras Negras (across from Eagle Pass) before the free zone had been extended to that section. During the meal he discovered to his amazement that almost every item on the table came from Texas. Each day the cook went across the border to Texas and smuggled back provisions. Finally, the consul warned, like the present-day proponents of the North American Free Trade Agreement (NAFTA), the end of the free zone would spark massive migration of impoverished Mexicans to the United States.[47] The consul's remarks displayed the deep ambivalence that Anglo Americans had and continue to have about Mexico and Mexicans. They recognized the importance of Mexico as a trading partner and they needed cheap Mexican labor, but they constantly worried about being overrun by Mexicans. The free zone, the consul argued, benefited the United States economically and helped to stem the flow of Mexican migrants northward.

The zona libre was also hotly debated in northern Mexico where merchants in Monterrey, which lay outside of the zone, complained that border towns received an unfair advantage by being able to import goods free of duties. In a series of twelve editorials, a Matamoros newspaper defended the zone by responding point by point to a report by the Monterrey Chamber of Commerce that argued for its abolition. The Chamber of Commerce's report, published in a business newspaper, portrayed the zone as a "depopulated region with a miserable ranch here or there," and contended that "this sparse population is the focus of all of the illicit actions, of robbery, of murder, and of contraband, that are perpetrated on this border."[48] Furthermore, they argued that the zone's "most scandalous contraband trade" competed unfairly with established businesses that sold "legitimately imported merchandise."[49] The editor of the Matamoros newspaper replied with a detailed historical analysis of the origins of the zone, attributing the declining prosperity of border towns to the invasion by U.S. troops in 1846. The zone was not, he argued, responsible for the deterioration of border towns, but rather it allowed those towns to survive after having suffered great losses due to the U.S. invasion and occupation of South Texas.[50] He also argued that the best way to combat contraband "would be a prudent reduction of the [Mexican] tariffs," because "frankly speaking, it is against nature to pay 15 or 16 cents for a yard of cloth when 500 steps away you can get it for 6."[51] Rather than producing honest workers out of contrabandistas, as the Chamber of Commerce predicted, with the abolition of the free zone "the contrabandistas would count on a wider field for their operations" and a much larger market to supply.[52] His final argument played on nationalist sentiments, reasoning that as the first line of defense against attack by U.S. forces, it was imperative that the border towns remain strong. Therefore, the free zone, by helping border towns, benefited the whole nation.[53]

. The debate over the zone libre, within both Mexico and the United States, illustrates the variety of interests that were at stake in the lucrative binational trade. Ultimately, merchants on both sides of the border profited from free trade.[54] Businessmen in cities like Laredo, especially those with dry goods or grocery stores, stood to lose most from the abolition of the free zone. In Laredo, almost the entire economy had some link, directly or indirectly, to the Mexican side. For instance, Nuevo Laredo's water, electric, telephone, and electric streetcar services were all operated from the Texas side.[55] Also, as the U.S. consul argued, the location on the Texas side of industries such as the Mexican National Rail shops and the Mexican smelter had led to "a considerable share of the present prosperity of Laredo."[56] Therefore, given the border merchants' interests, it makes sense that they would support an effort to protect and expand free trade with Mexico. Although Garza never referred directly to the free zone in his manifestos, it is perhaps not just a coincidence that he proclaimed his revolution in the very month that the import tax within the free zone was raised from 3 to 10 percent.[57] Increasing this duty was just the kind of policy that border merchants were against. The timing of the increase helps to explain the merchants' decision to support Garza, who promised free trade. Ultimately, however, national concerns in Mexico and the United States about unfair advantages enjoyed by the border region won out over local interests, and the zona libre officially ended in 1905.

MINING AND COMMERCIAL AGRICULTURE

Expanding mining and smelting operations in the region also brought border trade policy to the fore at the national level. As railroads extended into the mineral-rich regions of Coahuila, lead-ore and coal mines multiplied. If railroads fertilized the ground for industry, mining was their first major crop. Northern Mexican newspapers advertised new mining ventures, encouraged capital investment, and even helped recruit laborers.[58] In 1910, one coal mining company in Rosita, Coahuila, announced that they needed five hundred laborers to expand their operations, emphasizing that they would pay wages daily and in cash.[59] Meanwhile promotional pamphlets touted the boom in Sierra Mojada mining, reporting that the yearly output of metals for Coahuila exceeded $10 million in 1893.[60]

In 1902, Coahuila received nearly 10 percent of all U.S. investment in Mexico.[61] Much of this mineral wealth was shipped to smelters in the U.S. Southwest. Two companies alone, the Kansas City Consolidated and Guggenheim's Philadelphia Company, imported to their smelters in the U.S. Southwest eight thousand tons of mineral ore per month from the Sierra Mojada district in Coahuila.[62] As historian John Hart shows, by 1907 the Guggenheims had established a virtual monopoly over smelting in north-central and northeast Mexico.[63]

Soon after mechanization transformed mining and smelting in northern Mexico, a similar process began to revolutionize agricultural production and labor relations in the countryside. U.S. planners viewed the asymmetrical cross-border relationship as the key to commercializing agriculture. In the case of mining, minerals were to be extracted in Mexico and smelted in the United States, so that Mexico exported natural resources and imported manufactured goods. Meanwhile, the U.S. would export capital, farm machinery, and irrigation equipment to Mexico while importing Mexico's crops and her main natural resource: cheap labor.

The commercialization of agriculture followed quickly on the heels of urban industrialization on both sides of the border. Railroads, irrigation, and farm machines revolutionized agriculture, stock raising, and labor relations. These changes manifested themselves concretely in the value and concentration of landholdings. In general, the value of land increased as its productivity grew, resulting in highly skewed land tenure where a few owners controlled most of the land and the vast majority subsisted on small plots or worked for wages.

Anglo promoters of the lower Rio Grande Valley stressed the fertility of the soil, the potential for irrigation, and the inability of the local Mexican population to exploit its natural resources. One such booster, Lieutenant Chatfield, declared that the lands of the valley were "unsurpassed in fertility" and that "no finer body of lands is to be found in the limits of the United States."[64] This "unsurpassed fertility" remained barren, he argued, because the Mexican population had not been capable of developing it. As he put it, "nature has endowed this Land with all things to assist in man's endeavor, but a majority of the present population will never rise to the urgency of her demands; other hands will till the soil and disclose to those 'to the manor born' the mine of wealth over which they have heedlessly trod for years."[65] The absurd image of border inhabitants as lazy aristocrats was meant to justify the appropriation and commercialization of land, just as today's image of the "welfare queen" justifies cutting funding to the poorest members of society.

At the end of the nineteenth century, stock raising remained the primary commercial pursuit in Cameron County, with few crops being grown on a large scale. The 1890 county assessor's rolls indicate that at $828,432 the total value of livestock, primarily consisting of cattle, sheep, horses, and mules, vastly outweighed the value of crops, $15,420, comprised mainly of bananas and melons.[66] Although farming remained a marginal activity, promoters pointed to potential profits from agriculture, especially after irrigation had been introduced. Lieutenant Chatfield even reprinted sections from a report commissioned by the Texas legislature in 1891 that provided specific statistics on every climactic condition imaginable for Brownsville, including average monthly temperatures, degree of cloudiness and sunshine, amount of rainfall, and velocity of wind.[67] Such scientific data, as well as the fantastic descriptions about the ease with which sugar cane, vegetables, fruits, and cotton could be grown in the region, was designed to lure prospective settlers.

While the natural fertility of the soil and the sunny climate made for auspicious conditions, commercial agriculture required irrigation. Droughts like the one that had devastated South Texas in the early 1890s, along with the lack of rail connections to the lower Rio Grande Valley, presented obstacles to development, but water was seen as the solution. As Chatfield confidently predicted, "let capital put water upon any portion of this land and before a year elapsed there would be such a rush for privileges that the system of irrigation would have to be extended to accommodate the applicants. By the time the first crops were ready for market there would be one or two railroads bidding for the business of transporting them."[68] The agricultural revolution in the "Magic Valley," predicted and planned in the 1890s, began in earnest at the beginning of the twentieth century, resulting in an influx of newcomers, an increase in the number of farms, and a corresponding decline in the average size of those farms. The cattle industry shrunk as agriculture grew, with the number of cattle almost halving in Starr, Hidalgo, and Cameron counties between 1910 and 1920.[69] A new era had indeed dawned.

By the end of the nineteenth century, before the economy had shifted from cattle to agriculture, the Texas legislature appeared to be moving to facilitate the transfer of land from Mexican to Anglo hands. A law passed by the legislature in 1891, just half a year before Garza's revolt, stated that "no alien or a person who is not a citizen of the United States, shall acquire title to or own any interests in the lands within the State of Texas." The law, however, allowed foreigners who expressed an intention to become naturalized citizens to purchase land so long as they actually became citizens within six years.[70] Although illegal seizures and market forces resulted in the dispossession of Mexican land, this law was erroneously blamed as the cause.

Mexicans understood the implementation in Texas of these "alien land laws" as an attack on their right to hold property. While such laws were common in other parts of the United States, Mexicans had owned the land prior to the arrival of Anglo Americans and had special protections as a result of the treaty that ended the war between the United States and Mexico. A Spanish-language San Antonio newspaper published several articles and editorials condemning the law as a violation of Article 8 of the Treaty of Guadalupe Hidalgo and a negation of the protocol agreement on Article 10. Article 8 of the treaty guaranteed that property rights of Mexicans in the ceded territory would be "inviolably respected." While the U.S. government had refused to accept Article 10, which granted legal status to Mexican land grants, they did sign a separate protocol agreeing to respect those land grants.[71] In addition to attacking the alien land law, Luis Bossero of the Mexican Liberal Party lambasted the Texas Congress, which had, he argued, managed to examine only 150 land titles and to confirm just 71 of those in the forty-two years since the treaty was signed.[72] He also took aim at the process of surveying lands to perfect a title, complaining that owners were required to pay half of the costs up front, and that the "measuring and surveying operations will be done in the interest of the U.S. Treasury, not in the interest of the legitimate owners of the land."[73] The law forced Mexicans, many of whom had lived and owned land in Texas for years without legally changing their nationality, to become U.S. citizens or risk losing their land. Legislators thus further eroded the middle ground occupied by border Mexicans, by either expropriating the land for the state or forcing "aliens" to become U.S. citizens.

A study by Armando Alonzo of land-grant adjudication in South Texas disputes the claim made by Brossero and many others that Mexicans were discriminated against in this process. "Contrary to popular history," Alonzo claims, "the adjudicatory process concerning land grants in the Trans-Nueces was generally quick and it favored Mexican land tenure."[74] While this land-grant adjudication may have favored Mexicans, as Alonzo asserts, we can understand Brossero's claims as an attempt, albeit mistaken, to explain the loss of Mexican land that was happening before their very eyes. While legal maneuvering and illegal seizures only accounted for a small amount of land transfers, market forces dispossessed capital-poor Mexicans of the bulk of the land. In either case, the result was the same: wealthy Anglos took control of the land base from Mexicans.

Nowhere was this tendency toward Anglo control and land concentration more pronounced than in Cameron County in the southeast corner of Texas. Lieutenant Chatfield's examination of this county's 1892 tax rolls revealed that only 115 owners controlled over 1.5 million acres, accounting for approximately 97 percent of the total land held by individuals. And even of those 115, only a small handful (21) owned almost 80 percent of that land (1.228 million acres).[75] Using this same data, historian David Montejano has also demonstrated how even though Anglos owned a smaller absolute number of large ranches than did Mexicans (forty-six versus sixty-nine), those ranches were much bigger, comprising 80 percent of the land in parcels of 1,000 acres or greater. He therefore shows the extent to which land had been concentrated in the hands of relatively few Anglo Americans in the half century since U.S. annexation. "By 1892, forty-six non-Spanish-surnamed owners owned over 1.2 million acres of land, nearly four times as much as the acreage owned by Spanish-surnamed owners." In addition, "all recorded transactions in the 1848–1900 period occurred between Spanish-surnamed and non-Spanish-surnamed individuals, and in all cases the land passed from the former to the latter."[76] Arnoldo De León's analysis of the class structure in South and West Texas in the latter half of the nineteenth century demonstrates a similar trend. After U.S. annexation, the proportion of Texas Mexican ranch and farm owners and skilled laborers declined and the percentage of manual laborers grew. At the same time, the percentage of Anglo ranch and farm owners rose.[77]

Alonzo's exhaustive study of land tenure in South Texas provides a more detailed picture of how and when Anglos became the majority landholders in the region. In *Tejano Legacy*, he shows that the displacement of Mexicans along the coastal counties of Cameron and Nueces proceeded at a much faster rate than it did in the interior counties of Starr, Zapata, Webb, and Duval.[78] The location of Cameron and Nueces counties at the edge of the Gulf of Mexico and the relatively early rail service in Corpus Christi may help explain why the land in those areas was the first to be taken over by Anglos.[79]

Based on land adjudication and tax records, Alonzo also questions the thesis that there was a steady process of land grabbing and usurpation by Anglos ever since the Mexican-American War in mid-century. Instead, he shows that most Mexican ranchers lost their land during the 1880s and 1890s as a result of the market. While he recognizes that some Anglos manipulated the U.S. legal system to illegally take Mexican land, he concludes that it was the bust of the ranching economy and the transition to commercial agriculture that accounted for the bulk of land loss by Mexicans. By the time a worldwide economic depression hit South Texas in the early 1890s, many of the large Mexican landholdings had already been broken up into smaller parcels through inheritance. Small landholders, comprising almost all of the Mexican holdings, did not have access to enough credit to ride out the economic crisis and ended up losing their land to Anglos who did.[80] Alejandro González, Garza's father-in-law, for example, was forced to sell several thousands of acres to the King ranch in the early 1890s, as a result of both the drought and the cost of financing his son-in-law's rebellion.[81] There were, however, some notable exceptions to this general rule. Manuel Guerra, for example, one of Garza's financial backers, managed to secure large loans during the crisis and maintain his wealth and political power.[82] Although a few Tejanos managed to hold out during the depression and make the transition to commercial agriculture, most Mexicans had been dispossessed by 1900.

Leaving aside Alonzo's distinction between the "illegal" taking of land and the "legal" displacement through the market, his periodization of land loss in South Texas coincides exactly with Garza's revolt in the early 1890s. The general economic depression was exacerbated by a four-year-long drought in the region, virtually putting an end to the ranching economy and speeding up the transfer of land away from the Mexicans. In the midst of this desperate situation, Garza proposed a plan to open up vast amounts of land for colonization in Mexico. Access to land formed part of the border community's sense of what rightfully belonged to them; indeed, along with *decencia* (propriety) and liberalism, it composed their moral economy, the violation of which led them to paint Díaz as a tyrant who had to be overthrown.[83]

"A PANORAMA OF STARVATION"

In the early 1890s, the threat to Mexican ranchers and vaqueros came not only from rapacious Anglo lawyers and impersonal market forces but also from nature. Border people had to contend with natural cycles, including droughts and hurricanes, before full integration into international markets, but ironically it was capitalism, which was supposed to liberate people from nature, that rendered those on the periphery even more vulnerable to the capriciousness of the weather. As border inhabitants grew increasingly dependent on the international market in the late nineteenth century, they also became susceptible to the violent "boom" and "bust" cycles of capitalism. The new era that was so heralded on the border had, by 1892, turned into a season of despair as the crops withered and the cows died on the scorched wasteland that had offered such promise.

While a wide range of opinions existed about the seriousness and military strength of the Garzistas, all parties agreed that a four-year drought in South Texas and northern Mexico had caused severe destruction and hardship. Desperation and starvation, combined with rising expectations for a boom that had been dashed by a prolonged bust, may have helped to motivate the poorest sectors on the border to join a rebellion that offered them food, money, and an opportunity to acquire land. Similarly, some of the large landowners whose estates were being slowly eroded in the 1880s and early 1890s became some of Garza's greatest financial backers.

Mexico's consul in Laredo certainly blamed the revolt on the prolonged drought of four years and the failure of numerous businesses. "All of this makes it so the men who do manual labor remain idle and without bread and that they look as if to a redeemer to the one who promises them a peso each day and other great deals for joining them in their revolutionary jaunts."[84] According to the consul, the drought and the decline of other businesses had thus created a veritable reserve army that Garza could readily employ for one peso a day plus food. While Garza sometimes paid for supplies and horses with scrip money drawn on Mexico's treasury, apparently he paid real money to his soldiers. More than just gaining the support of his soldiers, Garza also earned the "adoration" of their families who appreciated the sustenance that he provided. As Laredo's Mexican consul said, "the families, through these men, see the heavens open from this perspective and Catarino Garza becomes for them an object of adoration, and he seems to the general eyes that do not study the causes of these phenomena, with such a halo of sympathy and prestige that he could very well be taken for a hero."[85] These descriptions served to discredit Garza's followers as blind and starving hero worshippers.

By 1892, the devastation of the four-year drought prompted citizens of Starr County to make an urgent appeal to the governor for aid. "Our stock are dying by the thousands," they proclaimed, and "if it does not rain in two months our stock will all be gone." Given the economic crisis, even the stock that survived the scorching sun could not be sold at any price. The signatories, including Sheriff Sheley, Judge Monroe, Manuel Guerra, and T. W. Kennedy, were the same ones who had written several weeks earlier to complain about Captain Bourke's heavy-handed methods in his campaign against Garza.[86] After their requests for assistance from the state government went unheeded, they appealed directly to the people of Texas for help. The appeal published in the local newspapers noted that the counties of Starr, Hidalgo, and portions of Zapata and Duval "have been subjected to a drought of such severity as to render the production of the necessaries of life impossible."[87] The planting season had already passed for that year and unless they received rain in June they would not even be able to count on a light fall crop. The failure of crops and dying of cattle rippled through the economy wreaking disaster on the entire region: "The loss of stock, the depreciation in values of all kinds of property, the inability of ranchmen to procure money for payment of taxes, a depleted county treasury, the prevalence of small pox through a section extending from San Ignacio in Zapata County to Rio Grande City in Starr County and the baleful effects of the Garza revolution, all combined to have produced a destitution hitherto unknown." Rather than viewing Garza's revolt as a response to the economic crisis, they blamed the insurrection as part of the problem. "The famine district," as they called it, contained an estimated fifteen to twenty thousand people, one-fifth of whom required assistance; the remainder had just enough food to maintain themselves and their families. In graphic detail the reports explained, "some of the people are using the flesh of the cattle which have died from disease or starvation and others are drying the meat for future use."[88]

Laredo's Mexican consul believed that the appeal was a cynical attempt by former Garza supporters to replenish with public charity the money they had spent on the revolt. "It is strange," the consul quipped, "that after having . . . fomented the Garzista agitation, the lower Rio Grande counties show up to clean out public charity."[89] His analysis, however, would imply that those directly involved in the appeal for money were former Garzistas. Yet the committee, presided over by the Honorable T. W. Kennedy, while ethnically mixed with slightly more Anglo than Spanish-surnamed members, was not comprised of well-known Garza supporters.[90] Furthermore, the authors of this appeal did not invent the destruction and suffering wrought by the drought.

One *Chicago Herald* reporter described his travels through the lower

Rio Grande Valley in January 1892, providing vivid testimony of the misery caused by the drought. In addition to his racist assessment of Mexicans as "lazy" and "natural thieves," the journalist was struck by the image of starved cattle lining the railroad between San Antonio and Laredo: "There are supposed to be bands of cattle in this jungle, but the few that were to be now and then seen from the car windows were either dead or dying. As far as the eye could penetrate the cactus waste there could be seen not a vestige of pasture. What the poor brutes have to live on nobody knows. In fact they do not live very enthusiastically. Carcasses of starved creatures could be seen on either side of the railway for miles, and here and there little bunches of those just ready to drop, and with not enough to be scared away by the locomotive, lined the ditches beside the track. It is a pitiful spectacle this panorama of starvation." The journalist further mused that it was "no wonder that they are ripe for revolution or anything else," given the "deplorable" condition of the people and the annihilation of their only means of livelihood, cattle and sheep.[91]

Reports from points as far away from the border as Durango, Mexico, indicated that people were starving because of the drought. One article argued that immiseration in Durango would lead to revolt, implying that Garza's insurrection could possibly extend to Mexico's interior. Referring to the desperate situation in Durango, the author of the article warned that "if the government continues deaf to the cry of the sufferers a rising of the people may be expected. To use the words of a man of influence among the common people: 'I prefer to die fighting rather than from hunger.' "[92] A Mexican consul even recognized the connection between hunger and the revolution in a report about a Garzista attack on La Mecca ranch in May 1892. As the consul so eloquently put it, "hunger, that bad advisor, instigated everyone in this last craziness."[93] Whatever other benefits could be derived from Garza's rebellion, Garzistas and their families could count on being fed, at least in the early stages of the revolt. While Garza's liberal ideals may have sated their political souls, the food he provided his troops satisfied a very real and immediate need for sustenance in this "panorama of starvation."[94]

In the decade prior to Garza's revolt, the socioeconomic foundation of the border began shifting, resulting in a boom in some sectors of the economy and a bust in others. Mining, smelting, and other commercial enterprises grew at unprecedented levels, especially benefiting the border towns that had railway connections. While livestock and wool production remained the mainstays of the South Texas economy, the prices of these commodities plummeted in the 1890s. Cattle that cost $10 per head in Texas in 1870 could be purchased in the lower valley in 1891–1892 for just $4 per head. The price of sheep saw a similar drop from $3 in 1878 to $1 in 1893.[95] The rapid decline in market prices combined with a series of severe droughts devastated these industries. The weight of this economic downturn fell heaviest on small Mexican landowners who, without access to credit, were forced to sell their land at bargain rates.[96] This season of despair began what would become the nearly wholesale dispossession of Mexican landowners by Anglos over the next thirty years. A similar process of land concentration, particularly though not exclusively in the hands of Anglo Americans, led to immiseration and desperation in northern Mexico as well.[97] It was at the beginning of this long downward spiral that Garza came along, offering the people a chance for bread, land, and freedom, a chance to set the world straight again.

5 · THE GARZISTAS

Se presentó bien en la palestra, tenía

dinero, pagaba con regularidad sugente. (He

made himself look good in the palestra, he had

money, he paid his people regularly.)

— Mexican consul in Laredo

What was it that motivated Manuel Guerra, a wealthy Texas Mexican merchant, to support financially Garza's revolt? Why would a poor, landless ranch hand put his life on the line by joining Garza's army? Why would an Anglo sheriff like John Buckley risk his livelihood to protect Texas Mexican outlaws? And finally, why would a popular Mexican Army colonel like Nieves Hernández risk the wrath of Díaz to support a rebellion with slim chances of success? Each person in this diverse group stood to gain in some way from the revolution. Analyzing Garzista manifestos and the newspaper debates helps to elucidate the overt demands of the revolt, but to understand the full range of underlying motivations one must move beyond these documents. Poor Mexican peons, rich merchants and ranchers, Anglo elected officials, and Mexican Army officers may have aided Garza because they agreed with his liberal ideals, including no reelection, a free press, and civil liberties, but they were also fighting for something much less abstract. The usurpation of their land and the infringement on their regional autonomy by outsiders violated their sense of dignity, honor, and what was rightfully theirs.

In a seminal 1971 essay E. P. Thompson outlines a theory of the moral economy of the crowd to explain food riots in eighteenth-century England. Thompson's moral economy approach rejected the "spasmodic" explanation of peasant rebellion and "mob riots" that reduced complex responses, rooted in customs and traditions, to "rebellions of the belly." Thompson recognized that "riots were triggered off by soaring prices, by malpractices among dealers, or by hunger," but he also showed how these grievances operated within a "popular consensus of what were legitimate and illegitimate practices."[1] While Thompson's moral economy focused on why the poor engaged in "riots," his theory can be extended to understand why a multiclass coalition would rebel in a more overtly "political" revolution. Thus I argue here that it was not only the conditions of hunger and economic deprivation that motivated the Garzistas, but their perception that their customs and traditions of honor, patriotism, regional autonomy, and liberalism had been violated both in Mexico and in South Texas.

Although one could argue that sectors of the local elite, both Anglo and Mexican, supported Garza's movement because it was in their economic interest to do so, one could just as easily argue that jumping on the bandwagon of Porfirian capitalist development would also have benefited them. Therefore, economic interest cannot by itself explain the support of the elite for the revolt. Railroad connections through Eagle Pass and Laredo increased the Anglo presence on the border after the 1880s, but Texas Mexicans still maintained a fair degree of control over local political and financial institutions. Thus, numerically, politically, and culturally, Mexicans still dominated along the border despite a disproportionate amount of Anglo control in towns like Brownsville and Laredo. Anglos who arrived in border towns in the 1850s and 1860s became Mexicanized and entered into a power sharing alliance with the local Mexican elite.[2] Even at the end of the nineteenth century, it was impossible for Anglos to completely ignore or spurn Garza, whose movement was so popular among virtually the entire Texas Mexican community. Border businessmen relied on trade with Mexico as a market for manufactured goods and as a place from which to extract natural resources. Local landowners also depended on the Mexican market to sell their produce and their livestock and as a source of cheap farm labor. Therefore, it might have made good economic as well as political sense for landowners and merchants to support Garza, especially given his ideological orientation in favor of industrial development and free trade. However, it would have also made just as much sense for border businessmen to support the Díaz regime that favored free trade, and whose policies had made many of them wealthy.

In Laredo, where Garza found much of his support, the economy depended almost exclusively on trade with Mexico. With the advent of railroads linking the United States to Mexico, Laredo businessmen saw a new era of progress dawning on their city. So why did they not support Díaz, a leader who had overseen the phenomenal growth in railroads and the modernization of the economy? Rather than Díaz's overall economic program, it was the perception that his stranglehold on power violated liberal ideals and held Mexico back that turned these former supporters into enemies. In particular, they protested his violation of the no-reelection pledge, his betrayal of the 1857 Constitution, and his imposition of political appointees in northern Mexico. The liberal revolution that they proposed would sweep away the "feudal" elements of the Porfiriato and usher in an era of modern industrial capitalism. Their location at the crossroads between the U.S. and Mexican markets would put them in a prime position to reap the rewards of economic liberalization. Therefore, border businessmen could expect to do well under Garza, just as they had done well with Díaz in the presidency.

Beyond economic considerations, border businessmen were politically motivated to support Garza's revolution, having themselves fled Díaz's repression in northern Mexico. More important, their ability to maintain local political power in South Texas depended on their being responsive to the desires of the voting masses of poorer Mexicans. In this way elites were forced to recognize and, in some instances, accede to the expectations and desires of the mass of poor Mexicans. Non-Mexicans who held elected or political positions, such as Duval County's Sheriff Buckley and Laredo's District Attorney Hicks, also had to worry about the Mexican voters who sympathized with Garza. In 1892, the wealthy Italian businessman Antonio Bruni began his political career as Webb County commissioner in the midst of Garza's revolution. A few years after the revolt he was elected treasurer, a post to which he was reelected eighteen times until his death in 1931. Although Bruni was convicted in federal court for his support of Garza, this record appears not to have hindered his political aspirations, and if anything it may have helped his popularity with voters.[3] Manuel Guerra, a Starr County merchant who had supplied Garza with food and ammunition, went on to become one of the county's biggest power brokers.[4] Recognizing the power that they held over local politicians, U.S. Army Captain Bourke warned that Garza's Mexican supporters were "a dangerous class of citizen" because they could vote, and that "the civil authorities if they desire to hold office cannot afford to offend them."[5]

Supporting Garza in Mexico, on the other hand, would not be a factor in winning political office or greater business opportunities. Given that the revolt was aimed at the Porfirian regime, supporting it carried a much greater risk in Mexico. As a result, the public expressions of sympathy for Garza that can be easily found in the U.S. press are absent in the Mexican press. Nonetheless, coded letters and other documents captured by the U.S. Army indicate that the Garzistas received significant supplies and financial support from several people within Mexico, including important northern military and political leaders. While there is no direct testimony from these leaders explaining their position, it is reasonable to surmise that they saw the Garza rebellion as an opportunity to overthrow a regime that was draining their power. Furthermore, these liberals would have been convinced by the time of Díaz's third term in office (1891) that the old man would never respect one of the central tenets of liberal ideology: no reelection. These ideological and personal motivations help to explain why these men would risk their comfortable positions to throw in their hat with a rebel leader from across the river. The fact that they kept their support secretive and never openly joined the rebellion allowed them to benefit if Garza had succeeded and to save their lives if he failed.

Although Garza's support in Texas came from a multiclass and to some extent a multiethnic coalition, there were some who opposed the violent tactics of the revolution, or condemned the entire enterprise. Just three days after Garza proclaimed his revolution, *El Correo de Laredo* announced that although it sympathized with the anti-Díaz cause it did not support Garza's armed revolt. They warned their readers that "this revolutionary attempt can neither count on our sympathies, nor that of the Mexican people, who having been taken advantage of a thousand times by professional revolutionaries, have lost faith in these free redeemers, and only look to peace and work for their personal happiness and that of their country."[6] Another newspaper published a few miles from Garza's camp at Palito Blanco insisted that the idea of prompting a revolution in Mexico "was a dream of madmen, of bums, and of people without a profession." Their conservative message could not have been clearer: "The true revolution is work. . . . Long Live Work! Death to the Revolution!"[7] Although *El Correo de Laredo* continued to blame the Garzistas for stirring up trouble along the border, they also criticized the U.S. Army for its ineptitude and inability to put an end to the disturbances.

Some political bosses like James B. Wells opposed the revolt and even went around recruiting men for the anti-Garza fight.[8] A group of like-minded wealthy ranchers and merchants from Duval County finally petitioned the governor for protection. The recent killing by the rebels of "one of the best citizens" of their county while he was acting as a guide for the federal troops had incensed the ranchers.[9] Richard Harding Davis, a *Harper's Weekly* reporter who happened to be on the border when Rufus Glover was killed, was stunned by the intensity of the reaction to the "killing of one man in an almost uninhabited territory." For someone so familiar with murders in New York City, it must have been a surprise to see that the killing of one relatively undistinguished person could cause such a scandal. Reporters from throughout Texas swooped in and people held mass meetings in towns as far away as Laredo to sign on to the petition. The "East should reconstruct a new Wild West for itself," David quipped, "in which a single murder sends two committees of indignant citizens to the State capital to ask the Governor what he intends to do about it."[10] What Davis failed to understand is that Glover's killing was a symbol to Anglo Texans of their worst fear: being killed by a Mexican. Their paranoia was understandable given the pain and suffering they had caused Mexicans.

The Duval County petitioners urged the governor to "augment the State forces sufficiently to ensure the immediate suppression of the present lawless condition of affairs."[11] Of the twenty-six signatures, only one, M. L. Valverde, had a Spanish surname. These petitioners were "the most prominent citizens of Duval County," including N. G. Collins, who was one of the "wealthiest" and "most intelligent men in southern Texas," owning one million dollars in property, 250,000 acres, and "great herds of stock." Another signatory, F. Gueydan, was reportedly "the wealthiest merchant on the line of the RR, between El Paso and Corpus Christi (not including San Antonio)." For wealthy ranchers and merchants like Collins and Gueydan, "the Garza men and their sympathizers [were] ruining this section, keeping away immigration, [and] reducing travel."[12] These "prominent citizens" understood that they were outnumbered, and in fact they requested a bigger Ranger force "on account of the sympathy either active or passive exhibited by the great majority of the inhabitants of said area."[13] Not everybody supported Garza, but even his most bitter opponents recognized that the "great majority" did.

SUPPORT IN THE MEXICAN ARMY

U.S. Army officers might have had reason to inflate the amount of support for Garza's revolution in order to justify their inability to squelch the movement. However, Garza's own records, captured from rebel Colonel Pablo Muñoz, also indicate a high level of active support.[14] The forty-page booklet and folder includes an outline of the organizational structure of the rebel army, the monthy expenses for October 1891, a list of voluntary donations, and some correspondence and secret codes. According to these papers, by the end of 1891 Garza's Mexican Constitutional Army had 1,043 soldiers, 186 officers, and 63 commanders.[15] The army was divided into eight battalions of approximately 150 soldiers, each with its own snappy name: Libres Fronterizos, Libres de Zaragoza, Guerrilleros de Coahuila, Tiradores de Chihuahua, Carabineros de Guerrero, etc. At least on paper, Garza's band resembled a highly organized army and not the disorganized band of "outlaws" that they were often accused of being (fig. 8). Just one month after the start of the revolution, the rebels had received donations of horses, guns, ammunition, food, and cash amounting to $25,556.[16] The donations came from individuals and groups of people throughout northern Mexico, and one large sum of $3,500 came from a New York individual. In another section, unnamed "Americanos" (probably meaning Anglos) were listed as having donated $2,940. One can conclude from the substantial size of the army, and from the level and geographical breadth of donations, that Garza received a considerable amount of active support, mostly from Mexicans and Texas Mexicans but also from several "Americanos."

The extent of Garza's support in Mexico is more difficult to measure given the repressive nature of the government. Although the rebels had extensive contacts in northeastern Mexico, Díaz was ultimately able to maintain the loyalty of his army and prevent a mass uprising. Nonetheless, the captured Garzista papers indicate that key Mexican military leaders, including generals Sóstenes Rocha (Mexico City), Francisco Naranjo (Nuevo León), Sebastián Villareal (Tamaulipas), Luis Terrazas (Chihuahua) and Luis E. Torres (Sonora), were in cahoots and communication with the rebels.

Only fragments of their correspondence remain because they were supposed to be destroyed just after they had been read, but I found in Bernardo Reyes's archive codes for sending these secret missives as well as eight short messages. The letters addressed to the generals mentioned above were all dated between February and March 1892, and all were signed either with the pseudonym J. J. North or Juan Villa.[17] The letters asked these generals to join the Garza movement, and indicated that even though their plans had been thwarted, they would have "better resources"

EJERCITO CONSTITUCIONAL MEXICANO.

En atención al mérito y servicios del ciudadano *Eugenio Hinojosa* se le confiere el empleo de *Capitán 1º de Cª* con el caracter de provisional, interin el Supremo Gobierno de la Nación se sirve expedir la patente respectiva

La Oficina de Hacienda a quien tocare, tomará razón de este empleo, haciendo el abono del sueldo que le corresponde.

Libertad y Constitución *Estado de Tamaulipas,* *Dic. 12 de 1891,*

POR EL DIRECTORIO:

CATARINO E. GARZA

El Jefe del Ejercito Constitucional Mexicano

8. An official wartime commission naming Eugenio Hinojosa as first captain of cavalry in Garza's Constitutional Mexican Army. Such documents show that Garza's army was not just a ragtag gang of bandits and that Garza believed that he would succeed in toppling Díaz. The commission was made on behalf of the "provisional interim Supreme Government of the Nation" (Colección de Porfirio Díaz, Universidad Iberoamericana)

and a thousand men under arms by March or April. The notes to General Silvestre Ruiz and Colonel Nieves Hernández also spoke of paying for arms, food, and horses that they had provided to the rebels.[18] The letter to General Luis Terrazas in Chihuahua reads as follows: "If we gather one thousand men by this March, can we count on you to rise up in Chihuahua?" While these letters were requests for help from Garzistas, the informality of the language and the openness with which they shared information about the planned rebellion suggests that they expected these generals to be sympathetic to their cause. One of the other Garzista documents, a list of coded messages that had been deciphered, corroborates that supposition. It lists letters that had been received and/or replied to, showing that Garza had been communicating with Villareal, Terrazas, and Rocha as early as November and December 1891. Furthermore, the brief notes next to the list show that these generals were not only talking to the Garzistas but had accepted their proposition: "Dec. 6/91 General Luis Terrazas accepted agreeable proposition. = Dec. 9/91 General Sóstenes Rocha responded favorably to the proposal letter." Using the secret codes that were discovered with the cache of documents, I was able to decipher the coded messages and confirm that they indicated what the notes suggested.[19] This was not an insignificant group of discontented junior officers, but rather the strongmen of Mexico's North. The fact that Garza was secretly communicating with them, and that he had apparently received their approval, indicates that he had support from powerful dissident sectors within the Porfirian state.

Although these Mexican generals ended up benefiting under Díaz, with a few amassing obscene fortunes as state governors, their loyalty was not so assured in the early 1890s. It makes sense that these generals might join an anti-Díaz conspiracy given that some of them, such as Terrazas and Rocha, had longstanding enmity toward Díaz dating back to the early 1870s.[20] During the Garza insurrection, Terrazas was also secretly supporting the Chihuahuan Tomochic rebellion in the hopes of discrediting a local political rival.[21] While they were offered the chance to benefit materially as part of the Porfirian regime, Díaz made sure to severely curtail the northern caudillos' political autonomy. It is curious that these men remained in Díaz's innermost circle after their betrayal had been uncovered.[22] When Don Porfirio received the incriminating documents and saw that generals Torres and Villareal were listed as Garza's supporters, he wrote to Reyes that "it gives us the right to doubt everything else."[23] Perhaps Díaz could not believe that his most trusted generals were contemplating betraying him even after being faced with the damning evidence. He sent copies of the documents to Bernardo Reyes, asking him to investigate further, but without letting people know too much. Díaz's strategy of co-optation rather than open confrontation managed to head off the rebellion before it grew, and to reign in the maverick military caudillos of the North.

SUPPORT IN SOUTH TEXAS

Although Garza never garnered the support of a U.S. Army general, he was surprisingly successful in recruiting Texas sheriffs, deputy marshals, and judges. The voluminous newspaper articles and the evidence the U.S. military gathered through spies, informants, and interrogations provide a fairly complete picture of Garza's supporters in Texas. After reading through all of the army investigations, it is clear that Garza's supporters came from a wide range of classes. Individual officers, however, returned time and again to characterize and thereby dismiss Garza's movement as the work of poor Mexican farm workers and vaqueros. The Garzistas were, according to Captain Bourke, nothing "more nor less than outcasts and outlaws."[24] Denigrating Garza's followers helped army officers to justify their suppression of the rebellion.

In April 1892, Bourke remarked that only the "worst elements" of Garza's band remained: "Now these people dress just as do the common Mexicans of this country and when pushed hard on a trail you find the ranches you pass full of *vaqueros* all just in to see their cousins and their aunts, unarmed and perfectly innocent."[25] Although it is likely that Bourke confused many innocent vaqueros for Garzistas, the guerrillas also took advantage of their ability to blend in with the local population. Whether the rebels were real or merely disguised *vaqueros* is impossible to determine from the available sources. However, the willingness of *vaqueros* and poor Mexican farmers to hide, feed, and protect them suggests that they enjoyed a significant level of support among the Mexican rural poor.

The panic about the rebellion expressed by many U.S. newspapers reflected a latent Anglo fear of a widespread Mexican peasant uprising to reclaim the land taken from them during and after the U.S.-Mexican war. One San Francisco newspaper declared: "That Garza is aided by the Mexican peasants there is no question, for they see in him a possible liberator. Then again, wild as the idea may seem, some of these people look forward to regaining of the territory that was taken from them during the war with the United States."[26] While none of the Garzista manifestos, proclamas, or public statements indicated a desire or plan to retake South Texas from the United States, one scout reported that Garza made such a claim in a speech to his men. According to this scout, Garza proclaimed that "this time the movement would be completely successful and then he would insist on the Yankees falling back behind the Sabine," referring to the river in northeastern Texas that was the boundary line between the United States and Mexico prior to Texas's declaration of independence in 1836 and the subsequent U.S. annexation of Texas in 1845. The informant continued, explaining that Garza had "also told his people that if they can't get supplies anywhere else they can take Fort Ringgold and find plenty."[27] Garza's comments were probably hyperbolic, perhaps even meant as a bit of comic relief for his battle-weary men. Bourke, who commanded Fort Ringgold, dryly noted in his telegram, "when he takes this post I'll let you know." While there is little evidence that the Garzistas really planned on storming Fort Ringgold, not to mention retaking South Texas, such an assertion exacerbated smoldering Anglo-Mexican racial tensions. Several years after the revolt, Captain Bourke even claimed that Garza had exhorted his followers to drive the "last Gringo north of the Nueces [river]."[28] Invoking the Nueces would have reminded Texas Mexicans of the 1846 Mexican-American War, which was provoked because of a dispute over the strip of territory between the Nueces and the Rio Grande.

As I show in chapter 4, data on the shifts in land tenure in South Texas during the mid- to late nineteenth century illustrate an overall trend of Anglo dispossession of Texas Mexican landowners. Garza's plan, which included promises of land and opportunity in Mexico, would have been attractive to Texas Mexicans who had lost their land and economic security to newcomer Anglos. Even those few Texas Mexicans who had managed to hold onto their land in Texas would have benefited from lowering taxes on cross-border trade and from greater opportunities to buy new land in Mexico. However, to attribute support for the rebellion simply to the miserable economic conditions in the border region was a way of downplaying its political seriousness. Consul Ornelas in San Antonio dismissed the sympathy of businessmen and hacendados as only a momentary and illusory phenomenon, yet at the same time he attributed the support for the revolt by poor agricultural workers purely to the economic crisis: "One circumstance which favors much of the propaganda among the Mexicans of the Texas border is the lamentable state of misery which afflicts them because most of them come from the states of Tamaulipas and Coahuila that are in a truly alarming state of decay and lack of resources for the laboring class." Ornelas explained how agricultural workers who migrated in search of work and better pay often found that Texas had also "suffered shortages because of the drought and decline of the cattle industry."[29]

Rather than admitting that Garza's revolution legitimately responded to the problems and interests of these migrant farm workers, Ornelas viewed them as vulnerable and easily swayed by a charismatic leader. These workers were, in his estimation, "material ready to be seduced by Garza's promises." Ornelas's paternalistic reference placed the workers in the role of women who are easily "seduced" by a charismatic man. Nonetheless, at least he situated the rebellion within the context of economic deprivation on both sides of the border, and denied the rumors that blamed Garza's revolt on foreign speculators. While still unable to view Garza as anything other than a "criminal adventurer," the consul went deeper than most others by explaining some of the material factors that inspired sympathy for Garza among migrant Mexican vaqueros and agricultural workers.[30]

The Mexican consul in Laredo, Lameda Díaz, also seemed to appreciate the particularities of the local economy and the climatic conditions that would predispose the population to support a revolution. Although he recognized that Garza enjoyed a certain amount of idolatry among the "lower class," especially among the women, he claimed that Garza lacked personal valor. Again, portraying Garza's supporters as women was a way of discrediting the entire movement. "Circumstances" had forced Garza into his leadership role, "obliging him to be some sort of hero by force and decidedly favoring his performance of his role." The "circumstances" to which Consul Díaz referred were the presence of many fugitive Mexicans in Texas, some of whom were escaping political persecution but most of whom had fled Mexico for personal reasons, he argued, thereby attaching a political meaning to their activities only post facto. The well-educated exiles used their newspapers, the consul complained, to portray themselves as "victims" and to turn the Mexican masses against Mexico.[31]

The way in which the consul described the ephemeral yet dangerous nature of these newspapers made them sound like tactical guerrilla raids: "They are suspended, they appear again, each time continuing with greater falsehoods, more bald faced slander, more atrocious lies; each curse surprises; the government is an infamous tyrant; it beats the public writers in the grim dungeons, it assassinates them and degrades them; the most well known people in this situation are shameless thieves, and blood-thirsty traitors." These "ignorant" Texas Mexicans, in the consul's estimation, supported Garza simply because he presented himself as the head of the movement, "without determining if this Garza could realize his promises."[32]

In addition to the gullibility of Texas Mexicans, Consul Díaz blamed the entire population's reliance on smuggling as one of the main reasons for their support of Garza. "Poor and rich, foreign and national, of Mexican origin and others, everyone makes a fortune for the simple reason that they expand smuggling, which is the big business here." Texans of all classes and ethnicities encouraged the rebellion, according to this view, simply because Garza brought an economic boom to the region. Such a perspective discredited the rebels as smugglers and cattle rustlers and denied their political motivations. The poor masses supported Garza, the consul contended, because "he made himself look good, he had money, he paid his people regularly, [and] he demonstrated that he was well connected and had great resources."[33]

Outside financing, according to the consul, allowed Garza to pay his soldiers regularly and to keep the revolution popular. The money was supposed to have come from clerics in league with the Hapsburg Prince Iturbide, foreign "gamblers" in the stock market, and even the English-language press, all of whom, following the logic of the conspiracy theory, had a lot to gain from Garza's revolt.[34] Here the consul is merely repeating the baseless rumors that sought to discredit the rebels. While all of these groups had contributed to the "boom," he admitted that most of them probably participated "unconsciously." "Now, after the crash nobody here remembers Garza, unless to recriminate him and judge him as he is; a harebrained idiot, without valor, without intelligence who inspires only ridicule and scorn." When the war resulted in deaths and losses of cattle in Texas, his support dwindled. "The same ranchers of the lower Rio Grande, such sympathizers and supporters of Garza until only yesterday, are the first to ask that they remove from their midst this plague of criminals with an open cause who still remain hidden over there in the back country."[35] The crash to which the consul refers was due to a series of severe droughts that destroyed the cattle industry, to a withering of tourism and investment during the rebellion, and to a growing U.S. national economic crisis that would reach full pitch in 1893. If Garza had lost support from the rich ranchers and merchants who may have bet on his revolution opening opportunities for their businesses, he still, even after the "crash," had sympathy from certain poorer sectors of the population. Even the consul agreed that "Garza does not lack some degree of enthusiasm among the low people, especially the women in this contemptible condition who lack civilization and self respect."[36]

The consul thus employed the rhetoric of the northern Mexican developmentalist ethic to dismiss Garza's supporters as low class and women who lacked respect and civilization. One can argue that rich ranchers and merchants initially supported the revolt as an opportunity to enrich themselves, but they quickly withdrew their support when it became clear that the rebellion also damaged their businesses in Texas. Another theory for why border merchants were so quick to turn against Garza is that they had incited the trouble in the first place just to profit by supplying the federal troops that were brought in to squash the revolt. The most elaborate conspiracies were concocted in the consul's imagination, all in an effort to deny credit to Texas Mexicans for a hugely popular political movement. While there may be some truth to the economic interest argument, the initial support by this multiclass coalition makes sense given the perception that Díaz had violated longstanding traditions of liberalism, autonomy, and honor.

Whether any of these explanations is plausible or not, one can imagine that wealthy ranchers might not have been too comfortable with the idea of their ranch hands roaming the countryside with guns and hatbands proclaiming themselves *libres fronterizos* (free bordermen). After having already risked their lives for Garza's revolution, and with little hope for improving their lot, poor Mexican workers may have clung to the idea that revolutionary change in Mexico would afford them greater opportunities; certainly they had fewer options than Garza's elite backers. At the very least, Garza was known to pay his men well and regularly. Regarding women, one can only surmise that they were particularly prone to sympathize with Garza because they felt more intensely the weight of economic hardship on their families. Or perhaps the Porfirian consuls told these stories of women being "seduced" by Garza simply to discredit the movement and dismiss its political importance.

SUPPORT BY WEALTHY RANCHERS AND MERCHANTS

Like Consul Díaz, Captain Bourke had a hard time explaining why Garza had such widespread and multiclass support. While Bourke painted a picture of Garza's followers as lower-class criminals, he believed the revolution's key supporters and leaders came from the upper classes, specifically ranchers. He advised the army to put pressure on Garza's wealthy backers rather than only attacking the lower-class followers, asserting that "if the government of the United States pursues nobody but ignorant peons and lets some half dozen rich ranch-men go free, it will have this Garza business on its hands for a long time to come; but let an example be made of a few prominent inciters and abettors and the whole thing will at once collapse."[37] Bourke's apparently contradictory statements reveal his frustration at not understanding who supported Garza's revolution. At times he portrayed the revolution as the work of the lower classes, "outlaws," and "desperadoes," and at other times he portrayed it as being orchestrated by the upper class, a few "rich ranch-men." He connected these two different explanations by contending that "the intelligent people of the Valley are almost to a man arrayed against the present government of Mexico . . . and they influence the minds of the ignorant" through their periodicals, such as *El Libre Pensador* published by Garza at Palito Blanco.[38] While he described the Garzistas as "criminals," "professional bandits," and cutthroats," the "honest, ignorant peons" were viewed as victims of their circumstances and of the drought. The "shadowy . . . shop keepers of Rio Grande city, Roma and Laredo," had fomented rebellion, Bourke concluded, only to increase their sales of cartridges and saddles.[39] This argument thus absolved the poor masses for their involvement and placed the blame on the educated and wealthy elite.

Another U.S. Army officer, Captain Chase, agreed that "some of the most prominent ranch-men and influential citizens of Zapata County were implicated directly or would not help authorities." Therefore, garnering the assistance of "prominent land and stock holders in the infested district" was the only way to defeat the rebels. In a meeting of stockmen at the San Pedro ranch in January 1893, Chase attempted to convince these wealthy men that Garza's revolution was a lost cause. He explained to the stockmen that because the Garzistas would be prevented from entering Mexico, they would have to "feed and support about two hundred and fifty of the worst kind of bandits indefinitely."[40] Many of these "prominent Mexican citizens" agreed to cooperate with the U.S. forces, ultimately resulting in the capture of several Garzista leaders.

Through the interrogation of captured Garzistas and the examination of evidence obtained during raids on their camps, officers learned the names of particular merchants who had helped supply the revolutionists.

9. Portrait of Bernardo de la Garza. (Courtesy
of Bernardo de la Garza, great-grandson
of the first Bernardo)

One such Laredo businessman was the Italian immigrant Antonio Bruni,
who ranked among the wealthiest merchants and largest landowners in
South Texas. Bruni supplied the revolutionists with arms and ammunition, and he even gave Garza a personal gift of a carved-ivory-handled
pistol.[41] Meanwhile, three prominent Texas Mexican ranchers and merchants, Manuel Guerra, Alejandro González, and Bernardo de la Garza,
provided Garza with money, horses, and hideouts (fig. 9).

Manuel Guerra, whose family in Starr County owned large tracts of
land dating back to Spanish grants, and who would become the de facto
"boss" of the county's Democratic Party, provided food and ammunition
to Garza.[42] In a raid on the Garzista camp at Abra de los Federales, troops
found sacks of corn marked "M. G." and eight thousand metallic cartridges, "with all evidence pointing to Manuel Guerra of Rio Grande City
as the source of supply."[43] Bourke was particularly peeved because Guerra
had been one of the signers of the latter complaining about him to the
governor. Guerra skillfully played both sides, secretly supporting the reb-

els at the same time that he curried favor with his political benefactor James Wells who was working to put down the insurrection.[44] Bernardo de la Garza, owner of Randado ranch and other holdings totaling eighty thousand acres, also admitted to providing safe haven for the revolutionists. Finally, Alejandro González, Garza's father-in-law, who reportedly owned thousands of acres of land and up to ten thousand head of cattle and who was frequently described as one of the most prominent and wealthy ranchers of Nueces County, was complicit with the revolt. González not only allowed Garza to publish his newspaper and operate his armed uprising from his ranch, but he also donated horses to the rebels and posted thousands of dollars in bonds to bail Garzistas out of jail.[45] Needless to say, fighting legal battles and outfitting Garza's army, combined with a severe drought, had by the end of 1892 taxed all of González's available resources. He mortgaged his property for $26,000 to continue financing the revolt, but once he had paid off his debts and settled his legal and hotel bills González had no money left for the revolution.[46]

Landless and poor Mexicans filled the ranks of Garza's army, but the rancheros and merchants provided the resources to feed, arm, and outfit hundreds of combatants. According to a Garza "sympathizer" who Bourke interviewed, the rebels offered "each man a good horse, Winchester and ammunition, and also the support of his family during his absence." Based on this information, Bourke reasoned that Garza's main support came "from rancheros who can spare horses, and merchants who during the present troubles wish to find a better market for their goods than smuggling them across the river."[47] Garza's own accounts listed several people who voluntarily donated horses, guns, food, and large sums of cash, in some cases over $1,000.[48] Obviously these supporters had to be extremely wealthy to be able to afford to make such generous donations. At the same time that Garza was receiving donations of arms, food, and supplies from local ranchers and merchants, the Rangers were, according to Special Ranger S. A. Brito, being charged exorbitant prices for their "fodder, corn and provisions." While high prices could be expected as a result of the scarcity of food due to a long drought, Brito felt that Garza sympathizers were gouging the Rangers.[49] Chase was emphatic on this point: "There is no doubt left in my mind that there is a large number of wealthy Mexicans who are deeply interested in Garza's success."[50] But it was not only a war by and for rich people. Garza's revolution was a multiclass movement led by urban professionals, men like Dr. Ignacio Martínez and Garza, and supported in the countryside by both the wealthy ranchers and their poor vaqueros.

Supplying the rebels while at the same time avoiding detection by the authorities required an extensive network of merchants, ranchers, store owners, and vaqueros all working in concert. Sisto Longoria, a captured Garzista, revealed how they surreptitiously moved supplies from Rio Grande City and Laredo. As well as carrying small quantities of extra cartridges wrapped in rawhide boxes, vaqueros would travel with three or four horses, and instead of one rifle they would each carry two so that they could leave the surplus with the revolutionists.[51] In addition to the help of the vaqueros, Garza's father-in-law arranged elaborate schemes by which to have ammunition and guns transported to Palito Blanco. One contrast required arms to be delivered from Houston to Corpus Christi, from there to Alice, and then to Gómez's Saloon where they would be transferred to a box marked "hardware" and finally shipped to González's ranch at Palito Blanco.[52] Merchants, ranchers, vaqueros, and bar owners were all part of a complex supply network, providing Garza with the horses, guns, ammunition, and food necessary to carry out the revolution.

THE ENEMY WITHIN THE STATE

Active support for Garza's movement came not only from a multiclass base of private citizens but even from South Texas government officials. Captain Bourke believed that these state and federal officials sympathized with the revolution "either because they [were] anxious to get the votes of the Garza men, . . . or because they [had] raised Mexican families, or [were] themselves of mixed blood."[53] Racial mixing through intermarriage often surfaced in these reports as a primary explanation for Garza's popularity, even among those with Anglo surnames. Bourke complained specifically about U.S. Marshall Paul Fricke who had deputized a Mexican by the name of Peñas; aside from not speaking English, Bourke was "sickened" by the fact that Peñas had several warrants out for his arrest for supplying the revolutionists with twenty-four horses. Bourke had stopped Peñas with a large supply of ammunition, presumably for the Garzistas, but he had to release him when Peñas showed him that he was a deputy marshal.[54]

Other officers also expressed anger at local and federal officials for undermining their efforts to defeat the Garzistas. When Captain Chase raided a rebel camp on February 18, 1892, he discovered in Garza's bedding a copy of *El Internacional*, a newspaper published at Palito Blanco, the Texas ranch owned by Garza's father-in-law.[55] The newspaper cited Marshal Fricke's positive comments about the level of popular support for Garza as evidence that some high U.S. government officials recognized the significance and legitimacy of the revolution. Fricke had publicly expressed his conviction that the "voice of liberty of Garza and his supporters would soon find echo in the Mexican Army."[56] Referring to this article, Bourke noted that the "incautious remarks attributed to US Marshal Paul Fricke have given great buoyancy to the hopes of Garza's sympathizers."[57] More than simply making positive comments about the revolt, the U.S. marshal even dissuaded his deputies from pursuing the Garzistas.[58] The evidence against Fricke was so damning that the attorney general eventually charged him for abandoning the court when he was most needed, for publishing favorable interviews about Garza, and for failing to pursue the revolutionists.[59]

While the marshal's positive comments about Garza and his refusal to chase the Garzistas certainly did not help the U.S. troops, the intimate involvement of certain politicians and law enforcement officers rendered their efforts nearly impossible. According to Pablo Longoria, a former Garzista soldier, Sheriff John Buckley of Duval County aided Garza "in every way possible."[60] Buckley was eventually indicted for assisting Garza's movement, but local support for men such as Buckley astounded U.S. officers. Chase noted that in the last Duval County election "Garza was employed by the party now in power . . . to make speeches in order to control the Mexican vote."[61] In a letter to the governor of Texas, Laredo's city marshal even argued that it was Garza's influence that helped Buckley win election as county sheriff.[62] Although Buckley vigorously denied such allegations, several former Garzistas informed army officers that Buckley had met with Garza at Peña just after Christmas 1891, at the height of the rebellion.[63] By 1893, Chase "became thoroughly convinced that the county officials of Duval County were exercising their authority to intimidate the people of the country and prevent their working for or rendering assistance to the United States Government." However, this picture of local government coercing the population to support Garza does not fit with the observable popularity of these local officials. In fact, Chase acknowledged that the revolution's popularity "might have been expected in a county that would unanimously elect a Sheriff [Buckley] who at the time of his election was under a $2,000.00 bond for violating the laws of the United States."[64]

Sheriff Buckley was not the only sheriff suspected of being a Garza supporter. Captain Bourke also believed that Sheriff Washington W. Sheley of Starr County had protected the revolutionaries (fig. 10) Bourke held a grudge against Sheley because he had signed a letter sent to the governor complaining about Bourke's heavy-handed measures in pursuing the Garzistas; such enmity may have influenced Bourke's decision to label Sheley as a rebel sympathizer. Nevertheless, Bourke presented compelling evidence to suggest that Sheley, if not an all-out revolutionary supporter, had permitted the movement to flourish through negligence. For example, he implied that Sheley turned a blind eye to the revolution by remaining almost entirely in the southwestern part of the county when Garza's camp was in the northeast section. Furthermore, when Bernardo de la Garza notified Sheley of the presence of revolutionaries in his pasture, he took no action. De la Garza, who stood accused of aiding the rebels, received no response until a letter from Sheley arrived over a month later stating that Ranger Captain McNeel had been notified and that he would send three Rangers up to his ranch to investigate. McNeel denied that he had ever made such a statement, thus implicating that Sheley had lied to protect the Garzistas.[65]

U.S. Army Lieutenant Stephen O'Conner also suspected both Sheley brothers, one of whom was a ranger (Joe) and the other a sheriff (Wash), of protecting their revolutionary friends and relatives and only pursuing their personal enemies. O'Conner complained angrily about the Sheley brothers, who were "content to leave well enough alone and not arrest the Garzistas." He concluded that the Sheleys' lack of zeal was a result of their being "Mexican half-breeds, and the southern portion of Starr County filled with their relatives, many of them whom were engaged in the late revolution on the border."[66] In his own racist way, O'Conner hit on one of the primary factors to explain the almost unanimous sympathy for the Garzistas, even among government officials: kinship connections. Many of these sheriffs, deputy marshals, and judges most likely had relatives who were either active revolutionaries or supporters. For example, the deputy sheriff of Starr County, Paul Nix, was seen meeting with several indicted Garzistas at a ball at Salineño ranch. Nix, as it turned out, was Sheriff Sheley's brother-in-law, and probably related to Starr County Judge James Nix, who was also accused of being a Garza sympathizer.[67] Even people with Anglo surnames, like Sheley, were products of inter-

10. Company F, Frontier Battalion, 1882: 1–J.W. Buck; 2–Pete Edwards; 3–Capt.
Joe Sheely; 4–George Farrer; 5–Brack Morris; 6–Charlie Norris; 7–Wash Sheely;
8–Tom Mabry; 9–Bob Crowder; 10–Cecilio Charo. The Texas Rangers loved to
have themselves photographed with their guns. (N. H. Rose Collection, University
of Oklahoma, no. 1409)

racial families, or "half-breeds" as O'Conner so infelicitously put it. It
would therefore be reasonable to expect some degree of understanding, if
not agreement, with a movement in which family members took part.

Captain Chase, contrary to both Bourke's and O'Conner's estimations,
credited the Sheley brothers for their instrumental help in arranging the
surrender and capture of Garzistas. Chase understood that their efforts
would not have been successful if they had not had the assistance of the
local population, and he singled out the Sheley brothers for their extraordinary efforts. He wrote: "[The Sheleys] have been untiring in their efforts
to serve the General Government. They have ridden day and night since
January 1, 1893, among the people of the border, bringing to us the
assistance of the leading men of the country, arresting Bandits wherever
found, inducing their surrender whenever possible and enforcing orders
even to the killing of the most treacherous bandit on the border."[68]

How can we reconcile these diametrically opposed characterizations?
Did the Sheleys lie to protect their revolutionary family and friends, as

Bourke and O'Conner suggested? Or were they "untiring in their efforts to serve the General Government," as Chase stated? Most likely both estimations were accurate. Having revolutionary family members and friends probably helped the Sheleys to understand and perhaps even sympathize with the Garza cause. Thus, early on, they probably either ignored the presence of Garzistas or even colluded with them to prevent their capture by the army, which was viewed by practically everyone as an outside and meddlesome force. However, by 1893, it had become clear that Garza's revolution could not succeed. The U.S. Army had intensified its campaign after several soldiers and scouts had been killed, and the Garzistas were scattered in groups of three or four men. Recognizing the damage that would be caused by a protracted war between U.S. Army troops and the revolutionaries, the Sheleys convinced their friends and relatives to stop providing safe havens for the revolutionists, and they induced the insurrectionists themselves to surrender and face trial for violation of neutrality laws. Thus, when Chase noted the Sheleys' success at arranging the surrender and capture of Garzistas in 1893, their success may have been precisely due to their previous protection of and friendship with the revolutionaries. On another occasion, Sheriff Robert A. Haynes of Zapata County persuaded U.S. Army Captain Harding to let him handle the rebels peacefully. Haynes arranged a meeting with a group of Garzistas with whom he was friendly, and he convinced them to surrender and face trial in San Antonio.[69]

THE GARZISTAS ON TRIAL

The battle over jurisdiction between federal troops and local officials heated up as army officers began a more aggressive campaign to capture the Garzistas. In December 1891, Deputy Collector John Jodon, supposedly at the direction of Marshal Fricke, took control over all of the deputy marshals and would not allow them to arrest anyone without first getting a warrant. According to Bourke, Jodon "threatened to have the head cut off from any Deputy Marshal who didn't obey his orders." It later turned out that Fricke had sent no such instructions, and that Jodon had illegally usurped control over the marshals.[70] A few months later, Bourke discovered that "Jodon Sr. had been acting as the financial agent of Catarino Garza for Starr County." Even worse, Deputy Marshal Tomas Garza, a Garzista who had escaped from U.S. troops during one of their clashes, had hidden in Jodon's house just after Corporal Edstrom was killed. And while hiding a Garzista fugitive, "Jodon was going about on the streets of Rio Grande City telling Mexicans that [Bourke] had murdered Garza."[71] John Jodon was the same man who had accompanied Bourke on his ill-fated journey to Mexico in the first months of the rebellion. By February 1892, Bourke ordered the troops at Fort Ringgold to not recognize the civic authority of Jodon for the duration of the Garza war. Facing his own investigation for complicity with the Garzistas, Fricke was finally forced to relieve Deputy John Jodon of his duty in August after a letter surfaced tying Jodon to the Garzista lawyers.[72]

In November 1892, newspapers throughout the country reported Bourke's untimely death. According to the stories, Bourke was testifying in court against the Garzistas and at the moment when he referred to Marshal Fricke's " 'lack of duty' . . . the marshal drew his pistol, and in the presence of the judge, jury and spectators shot him dead."[73] Bourke blamed Florent Jodon, John's son, for starting the rumor, and later concluded that such stories were circulated to scare potential witnesses from testifying against the Garzistas.[74] Bourke and Florent Jodon squared off with each other several times in the courtroom, hurling insults and calling witnesses to destroy the other's credibility.[75] On one of these occasions, Bourke was testifying in court when Jodon dramatically asked, "Did you not say during the recess of the court that if I came to Fort Ringgold, you would kill me?" Bourke responded defiantly, "I said during a recess of the Court to Commissioner Downs that you were in d——d good luck that you haven't tried to play such a roarback as that on me, because I'd have blown your d——d head off."[76] These courtroom theatrics where government officials lobbed insults and threatened one another illustrates the divisiveness that existed within the government. In general, local politicians and elected officials supported Garza while federal and state authorities did not.

The Garzistas had influence over county courts, judges, and sheriffs, but once their cases reached the level of the federal courts they were less successful. A federal grand jury was convened in Brownsville in winter 1891 to examine whether the Garzistas had violated neutrality laws prohibiting the organizing of armed forces on U.S. soil with the purpose of disturbing a friendly nation. In its report, the jury emphatically stated that they were "convinced that an aggravated breach of our Neutrality Laws has been committed by citizens of Mexico and of Mexican extraction." The jurors reserved their harshest condemnation for the "inefficiency and possible criminal culpability of the State officers in whose counties the revolutionists organized without hindrance, and some Federal officers who connived at his crossing with his followers without giving timely information to our authorities." However, while they charged the state and some federal officers with "dereliction of duty," they profusely praised the army troops stationed along the border. The government was responsible, they contended, for "the defenseless condition of this frontier" because the forty or fifty soldiers stationed at forts Brown and Ringgold were far too few to "successfully cope with treble the number recruited from probably the most daring and reckless characters." The jurors also blamed the small number of indictments on the Mexicans who shielded the rebels and refused to testify against them, and on the marshals who failed to pursue them. Specifically, the jurors condemned "the practice of appointing deputy marshals, or other Federal employees, who are unable to read, write and speak the English language."[77] Ultimately, even though the federal grand jury sympathized with the government's case against the Garzistas, they could not offer many indictments without the help of local officials and the general public. By focusing on the inability of some South Texas officials to read or write English, the jurors implied that the local state institutions had been taken over by foreigners.

By 1892, over a hundred Garzistas had been indicted and were facing trial in federal court in San Antonio. Excitement ran high in the city and spectators packed the courtroom. The *San Antonio Express*, which had been covering the story closely from the beginning, devoted space to a daily account of the courtroom scene. The trial of Pablo Muñoz, a colonel in Garza's army, illustrates some of the arguments forwarded by each side. The prosecutor had to prove two things to convict Muñoz; first, that Garza had organized a revolution against Mexico on Texas soil, and second, that Muñoz had participated in the revolt. There was plenty of evidence to prove that Garza had launched a revolution, including manifestos and combat and casualties on both sides of the border. The most damning piece of evidence, however, was a commission signed by Garza appointing Muñoz as colonel in his Mexican Constitutional Army. At the time of his arrest, this document was in Muñoz's possession, along with other incriminating papers including a letter of introduction from Garza for a young recruit. Meanwhile, Muñoz's defense lawyer presented affidavits to show that there was a state of terror along the border caused by the U.S. Army. When Muñoz ran at the sight of the federal and military authorities, he argued, it was not a sign of his guilt but rather a normal reaction under the circumstances. The defense also undermined the credibility of the state's case, calling people to the stand who testified that their witnesses were "not to be believed" or had a "bad reputation" in their community.[78]

The prosecution's final arguments painted a scenario of a turbulent race war and called on the jury to put an end to it by making an example of Muñoz and convicting him: "All of you people know the horrors of war. That is what these people are trying to do. Their cry was 'Kill the d——d Gringoes.' That was their war cry." If the images of Mexicans rampaging through the chaparral with guns and threatening to kill gringos had not convinced the jury, then invoking patriotism was supposed to do the trick. The prosecutor continued: "If [the Garzistas] are not restrained and punished they will continue to set on foot those movements and what will be the result? It will involve the United States in a war with Mexico."[79]

In his closing arguments, the defense lawyer said that it was "nonsense" to believe that the Garza revolt could drag the United States and Mexico into a war. He also drew the analogy between the Irish Americans who gave assistance to the anti-British movement in Ireland and the efforts of Mexican Americans to overthrow the Díaz government. The facts of the case were not in dispute. Rather, it was a question of whether Muñoz should be convicted for such an offense. The jury decided that he should. Muñoz, who was in his late fifties at the time, could have received up to three years in prison, but the judge reduced the sentence by one half on account of his age, and fined him $3,000. It also came out during the trial that although Muñoz had spent the past thirty-four years in the United States, and the last eight of those in Texas, he was not a U.S. citizen. Like almost all of the Garzistas, he had lived in the United States for most of his life but he maintained his Mexican citizenship.[80]

Although rich and poor Garzistas alike were indicted, the outcomes of their trials differed according to their class status. The ability to post thousands of dollars in bonds and hire competent lawyers to represent them, along with the nature of their involvement, resulted in reduced prison sentences for wealthy Garzistas. The less-well-to-do Garzistas were not as lucky, and many of them spent long periods in jail. By February 1893, around 150 men had been indicted in federal court for violation of neutrality laws. Many of them had not yet been captured and arrested, but the final sentences for 73 of the cases provides a good picture of how different levels of Garzista supporters fared in the courts. Sentences ranged from one day to three years in jail, with fines from $1 to $1,600. Although I do not have an economic profile for everyone involved, the very wealthy ranchers and merchants seem to have received less jail time and paid higher fines than the others. For instance, Alejandro González, Garza's wealthy father-in-law, was fined the highest amount, $1,600, and received the smallest jail sentence, one day. Maximo Martínez, who had been a servant in Mexico, received the longest jail time, thirty-six months, and had to pay the small fine of $1.[81] The average jail time for a convicted Garzista was between five and six months. Most served their time in Bexar or Nueces County jails, but ten of those with sentences between one and three years did their time at the state penitentiary.[82]

Even though the Garzistas fared less well in federal courts than in local ones, wealthy Mexican ranchers were still able to manipulate the legal proceedings to their advantage, as is clear from the light sentences they received. By analyzing Garza's father-in-law's trial, for example, we can see how ingeniously they thwarted the government's prosecution. In December 1892, González and 129 others were to stand trial in federal court on charges of violating neutrality laws. González petitioned the court for a continuance until May, claiming sickness as the reason. Three prominent doctors testified that he could not stand trial "without endangering his life." The varying medical excuses given by the doctors, including a brain tumor, epileptic fits, convulsions, and heart disease raises questions about their credibility. Bourke believed, probably correctly, that the real reason behind the delay was González's hope that a newly elected administration would appoint another district attorney who would be unfamiliar with the cases.[83] The judge finally agreed to postpone González's trial, and because the other defendants were secondary the prosecutor decided to delay all of the trials until the spring term of the court. González and the other Garzistas were eventually convicted, but such legal maneuvering demonstrates that they were not helpless, even when navigating the complexities of the U.S. federal court system.

"OPEN DEFIANCE AGAINST U.S. AUTHORITY"

The delaying tactics and intergovernment agency tensions that frustrated efforts to prosecute Garzistas in the courtroom was compounded by confusion and division in the campaign to capture Garzistas in the field. With rangers, county sheriffs, federal marshals, and army troops all out in the backcountry searching for Garzistas, it was difficult to determine through the thickets and dense chaparral whether any particular group of armed men were revolutionists or not. One cold and foggy morning in January

1892, a detachment of U.S. Cavalry soldiers, believing they had discovered a rebel camp, rushed in and surrounded a troop of Special Rangers. Special Ranger Brito ordered his men not to fire and managed to convince the soldiers of their identity, thereby thwarting any firefight between the heavily armed and nervous men.[84] While this incident was just a misunderstanding, other instances of support for Garzistas made U.S. Army officers feel like they were working at cross-purposes with local and state authorities.

The situation had become so surreal that by 1892 local officials with ties to the Garzistas were even arresting scouts working for the federal government. On one occasion, U.S. Army Captain Chase was away on a reconnaissance mission when he received a telegram saying that one of his trusted scouts, Lino Cuellar, had been arrested in San Diego on an old murder charge. The circumstances of Cuellar's arrest led Chase to believe that there had been "some underhand[ed] work in this case." It was while he was leading a prisoner through the streets that Cuellar was himself arrested on an old murder charge. The murder charge dated back three years to an incident in which a "smuggler" had been killed "while resisting arrest" by a posse of U.S. marshals. Cuellar had been one of the posse, but after three grand juries in Duval County heard the case, nobody had been indicted. Arresting a U.S. marshal and turning his prisoner loose, Chase complained, constituted "open defiance against U.S. authority."[85]

This Kafkaesque drama had yet to reach its climax. In January 1893, prompted by the advice of Captain Brooks of the state Rangers (figs. 11 and 12), Chase took his whole troop on an extensive scouting expedition. After traversing thirty miles, they finally arrived at the supposed location of the revolutionists' camp and found no signs of the rebels. Chase thought nothing more of the failed effort until he received a telegram a month later saying that one of his best scouts, the ex-Garzista Pablo Longoria, had been arrested by Brooks on charges of horse stealing. Similar to the case a year earlier, the charge against the army scout dated back to November 1891, and a warrant had been issued in December 1892. Furthermore, the officers who arrested Longoria had had the warrant for two and a half months, but they waited until Chase had left camp before they arrested him. Even more ridiculous, the man who arrested Longoria, José Angel Hinojosa Peña, had been instrumental in furnishing arms to Garza. In fact, at the time of Longoria's activity as a Garzista, he had picked up a supply of arms from Hinojosa Peña's house and transported them to Garza's camp.[86] He was also the one sprung free the year earlier after

11. Captain Brooks Co. of the Texas Rangers, stationed at Rio Grande, Texas, during the "Garza War." This photograph was made into a postcard and presumably reached a wide audience. (Wright [E. A. "Doagie"] Papers, Center for American History, University of Texas, Austin, CN 11574)

12. Company E, Frontier Battalion at Alice, Texas, 1892: 1–Capt. J.S. McNeel; 2–D. S. Robinson; 3–John Cameron; 4–Charles Johnson; 5–Luke Dowe; 6–P. J. McNeel (not a ranger); 7–Rigdon "Fat" Terrell; 8–Forest Townsley; 9–J. S. McNeel Jr.; 10–Everett E. Townsend; 11–Richard Flowers (not a ranger); 12–Charles Premont; 13–Bud Rader; 14–Louis Pauli; 15–Rut Evans; 16–Bob Townsley. Captain J. S. McNeel was one of the most active Rangers in the pursuit of Garza. Alice is only a few miles from Garza's headquarters at Palito Blanco. (N. H. Rose Collection, University of Oklahoma, no. 1481)

having been arrested by a government scout. In other words, Ranger Brooks had knowingly sent Chase on an arduous, but purposeless trek throughout the countryside and then waited until he had left camp to arrest Longoria.

Captain Chase was betrayed by his own men and probably felt that his worst enemies were within his own camp. It is hard to determine whether Brooks and Hinojosa Peña actually acted as double agents for Garza, as Chase seems to suggest, or merely had a personal gripe with Chase. However, many officers expressed the paranoid feeling that everyone seemed to be a Garza supporter. In utter exasperation, Chase decried how District Attorney Hicks of Laredo, apparently also sympathetic to the revolution, prosecuted the case that ended up sending Longoria to the "penitentiary for eight years for stealing horses."[87] In the end, however, Longoria was quickly pardoned by the governor and released from jail.[88] The Honorable James O. Luby of San Diego confirmed that the actions against Longoria and Cuellar were politically motivated. According to Judge Luby, "the Garza men had adopted new tactics and would now put charges of some kind or another against every officer, scout or witness concerned in the suppression of the 'pronunciados.' "[89] To Chase it appeared that everyone was a Garzista sympathizer; after all, it looked like they had infiltrated the rangers, the U.S. marshals, the sheriffs, the scouts, and even the U.S. legal system.

After receiving so little cooperation from local and state officials, Chase went directly to Governor Hogg with his plea. In that meeting, Chase requested that Texas "co-operate with US Authorities in suppressing the Garza movement." The governor responded "that he could not get an appropriation through the Texas Legislature for the State Rangers if they were to be used in doing duty for the US Government." He therefore had issued orders to the Rangers "not to interfere with the Garza men."[90] In other words, Hogg reasoned that because the Garzistas were charged with violating U.S. neutrality laws, the onus of capturing them was on the federal government and not the state of Texas. Chase, however, believed that Hogg's withdrawal of support for the anti-Garza effort had political motivations, especially because it came around the time of the state elections of fall 1892. Although Chase did not explain why, one can surmise that politicians courting the Mexican vote did not want to be seen at the forefront of a campaign against a movement that had aroused popular sympathies. Referring to this abrupt change of heart, Chase commented that whereas the Rangers had "done all in their power against the Garza

Revolutionists" in 1891–1892, by 1893 they "were watching for a chance to arrest our scouts."[91]

"TEN MILES FROM THE NEAREST WHITE MAN"

U.S. Army officers were not the only ones requesting more aggressive action by the governor. Even a few miles from Garza's headquarters, there were some vocal opponents who badgered the governor for more Rangers to protect them. By the end of March 1892, U.S. troops had been removed from the field after accusations that Captain Bourke had illegally arrested and terrorized suspected Garzistas. Upset at the recent killing during a fight with Garzistas, Judge Luby called a mass meeting in San Diego to discuss the Garza revolt and its impact on Duval County. A few days earlier, Robert Doughty was killed by the Garzistas while out on a scout with Captain McNeel of the Rangers. They decided to send a petition to the governor requesting more state Rangers because, they argued, the "force now in the field is grossly inadequate to suppress lawlessness and furnish protection to life and property." In their petition, which they contended had been "signed by nearly every American citizen in the county," they explained the difficulty of snuffing out the rebellion given that the "majority of the Mexican population between the Nueces and Rio Grande are in active sympathy with the element which has rallied to Garza." They demanded protection as "citizens of the state and tax-payers," and having twice made similar appeals, this latest request expressed extreme concern and sense of urgency. If the governor could not pass the necessary appropriations through the legislature, they wanted him to authorize the organization of a "volunteer force." The petition ended in an emotional pitch, urgently requesting help against "these lawless bands now roaming the country and murdering American citizens." What can a sheriff or a few deputies do against "numberless bands of cut-throats," they asked rhetorically. Their patience had run out. "Our people cannot stand everything and the wail of anguish from a grief stricken wife and cry of fatherless children for the husband and father who has been murdered by red-handed assassins, pierces their very souls. Something must be done, and done quickly, for the patience is now worn out and ceases to longer be a virtue."[92]

As the Garza rebellion progressed, requests to Governor Hogg for protection by state Rangers came streaming in from ranching associations, town meetings, and individuals throughout South Texas.[93] Prominent Anglos were almost always the signatories to such petitions; names such as N. G. Collins (wealthy rancher), John J. Dix (judge), E. A. McLane (Laredo's mayor), and Archie Parr (political boss of Duval County), were meant to capture the governor's attention and prod him to action. Individuals who requested appointments as Special Rangers used this situation to their advantage, referring frequently to what they perceived to be the tenuous position of "whites" in South Texas. In his request for a Ranger commission, Nicholas Dunn explained that he lived "17 miles from Alice and 10 miles from the nearest white man." While he expected no monetary reward, becoming a Special Ranger would give Dunn the legal right to carry a gun on and off of his property, as well as making him an agent of the state.[94] In a letter of recommendation for the appointment of E. R. Johnson as a Special Ranger, Captain McNeel explained that Johnson lived "alone on the [Seeligson] ranch among Mexicans."[95] The use of this recurring image of the isolated white man living amidst Mexicans as cause for a Ranger commission illustrates how the Rangers saw themselves as agents of "white" control over Mexicans. At times, Anglo demands for Ranger protection verged on the hysterical. The Anglo editor of the *Cotulla Ledger* wrote to the governor asking if the rumors were true that the Rangers were going to be moved out of La Salle County. The editor wanted to have a few days notice, because if the Rangers left, he and several other families threatened to abandon the county. Governor Hogg reassured the editor that the company would not be removed.[96]

The governor did not grant every request for a Ranger detachment or a commission. In one case, Captain Frank Jones advised against stationing Rangers at Polvo, a town on the Rio Grande in West Texas. His reasoning for this decision is instructive: "There are only two white men," Jones explained, "and they both have Mexican women."[97] The purpose of the Rangers could not have been made any clearer; they were there to protect whites from Mexicans. On another occasion, a group of stockraisers and farmers of Hidalgo County petitioned the governor to have Victoriano Reyna appointed as a Special Ranger to detect and punish "all offenders and depradators on our Stock interests of this frontier country." Of the one hundred signatures that followed, only two McAllen and Young, had Anglo surnames, the rest had Spanish surnames.[98] Reyna's chances for becoming a Ranger ended, however, when Hidalgo County Judge William Dougherty wrote to General Mabry about Reyna's "dubious character." As Dougherty explained, Reyna "is a Mexican, does not understand English and consequently was unfit to hold such an office."[99] While there were a few exceptions, the Rangers were almost exclusively Anglos.

Even though Governor Hogg had not committed the state's resources to the campaign, he had not been completely insensitive to the complaints and petitions coming to him from South Texas. In late February 1892, he issued a proclamation "warning citizens not to aid or assist Garza." The proclamation, published in English and Spanish in the *San Antonio Express*, called on all "citizens of Texas to abstain from giving aid, comfort or moral support to such unlawful movement on foot in the state." The governor also made a special appeal to the "citizens of Texas of Mexican birth, who have the honor and prosperity of the state at heart to uphold and support her laws and the laws of their adopted country." The governor insisted that as "citizens of Texas," their interests lay with U.S. laws and not with the Garzistas. To those who had already joined "this lawless movement," Hogg urged, "withdraw from it at once and return quietly to their homes and peaceful avocations."[100]

Captain Bourke used the governor's proclamation to frighten Mexicans who may have been aiding Garzistas. According to one account, Bourke rounded up Mexican suspects, placed them in a line, and with "an air of great importance read the document to the awe stricken Mexicans in Spanish." After he finished reading the proclamation, "he [brought] into play his vocabulary of forcible words and [informed] the affrighted suspicious characters that he will return to that place within three days and if he finds that they have not dispersed as the proclamation commands he will cause every one of them to be thrown into the juzgado." The *Express* applauded Bourke's actions, exclaiming, "the plan works splendidly."[101] They failed to mention, however, that nowhere in the governor's proclamation was there any prohibition of gatherings. The circumstances of Bourke's dramatic reading of the proclamation, with the suspects lined up facing the armed soldiers, made it clear who was in charge.

Frederic Remington's drawings of Third Cavalry Troopers searching "suspected revolutionists" were published in *Harper's Weekly*, thus bringing the "hunt for Garza" to living rooms across the country (fig. 13). These images of a Mexican with a wide-brimmed sombrero being searched by U.S. Army officers created a criminal profile that could be attached to many rural Mexicans. The persistence of such stereotypes of Mexicans as outlaw "bandidos" testifies to the power of these and other images (fig. 14).

One can find plenty of evidence of pro- and anti-Garza sentiments in

13. Frederic Remington's illustrations appeared in *Harper's Weekly* along with Richard Harding Davis's article "The West from a Car-Window." This Remington illustration depicts a Mexican vaquero being closely searched by U.S. troops. The caption underneath reads: "Third Cavalry Troopers—Searching a Suspected Revolutionist." (*Harper's Weekly*, March 26, 1892, p. 296; courtesy of the Rare Book, Manuscript, and Special Collections Library, Duke University)

local newspapers, but the vast majority of the population probably fit somewhere in the middle. These people might have agreed with Garza's revolutionary plan, but they may not have been so convinced as to risk their lives and property. Nonetheless, the harassment suffered by many innocent Mexicans at the hands of the U.S. Army may have made some fence-sitters go over to Garza's side. Because they were seen as Garzistas

14. This Frederic Remington illustration depicts a Mexican tracker. The caption underneath reads: "The Mexican Guide." (*Harper's Weekly*, March 26, 1892, p. 296; courtesy of the Rare Book, Manuscript, and Special Collections Library, Duke University)

anyway, and the U.S. Army did not trust them, what could they lose by helping Garza? Chase even admitted that some of the troops went too far by arresting everyone, breaking into houses, and threatening to kill and hang people by the neck. The result of the heavy-handed measures "was to excite hatred on the part of the people for the troops and to increase their efforts to assist the Garza men."[102] In a pamphlet condemning Bourke, the publisher of *El Bien Público* argued: "The harassment of our citizens by the military and other employees, whose duty was preventing the invasion of Mexico, came to such a point that they should be punished."[103] Even though he claimed that he did not support the idea of revolution in Mexico, once the U.S. troops began attacking Mexicans in Texas he felt obliged to defend their cause. Ironically, Bourke's policy of terrorizing the local population by burning their houses, seizing their weapons and property, and arresting them without cause, probably ended up pushing many Mexicans over to Garza's camp.

U.S. military officers had a contradictory view of the Garzistas. On the one hand, they wanted to portray them as common criminals and bandits, but on the other hand they had to recognize the strength of their adversary to explain their inability to crush the revolution. The colonial mindset could not imagine the possibility of natives launching a serious liberation movement, and any attempt at revolt had to be put down as the work of criminals or opportunists.[104] While officers discussed the tremendous level of popular support for the revolution in their internal reports, they requested that their reports and information about arrests not be given to the press.[105] Their desire to convince others of the weakness of Garza's revolution and of Garza himself ultimately led to self-deception.

At the beginning of January 1892, Lieutenant Langhorne stated confidently that "Garza's revolution is practically over" and that his dissatisfied men had reached the conclusion that "he is no General."[106] Following each new engagement with the Garzistas, a host of officers and politicians would pronounce the revolution dead, but Garza remained in Texas until spring 1892, and the armed disturbances continued into 1893. Even Captain Chase, who so eloquently expressed the strength of Garza's movement, felt obliged to belittle Garza as a leader. In his final report, Chase commented that "Garza was a man of no force of character. He was poorly educated and possessed of no ability to lead men other than as a talker."[107] Instead of giving Garza credit for his ability to elude capture, they often blamed bad weather or the "dense chaparral."[108] Bourke left no room for doubt, accusing Garza of every fault he could dream up, and thus labeled him "the wife-beater, defaulting sewing-machine agent, blackmailing editor, and hater of the Gringos, who suffered under the hallucination that the people of northern Mexico were eager to salute him as their president."[109]

CONCLUSION

The Garzista revolt was a multiclass movement, made up of wealthy merchants and landowners, lower-middle-class professionals, poor farmers, and landless ranchers. The vast majority of Garzistas were either Mexican or Texas Mexican, although a few supporters were of Anglo or Italian heritage or had a mixed Anglo Mexican background. Most of the active members of Garza's army lived in Texas, although there were also important contacts with people on the other side of the border. Of greatest importance were the northern Mexican military leaders, who communicated clandestinely with Garza and who had also apparently approved of the rebellion. While Garza's supporters spanned the spectrum of classes, the wealthier ones provided supplies and financial backing while the poorer ones filled the ranks of the army. Garza's Mexican Constitutional Army aspired to have over one thousand men under arms, but the evidence suggests that even at its height he was only able to gather several hundred together at any one time. Still, for the late nineteenth century this was a formidable force, one that a decade earlier would have stood a much better chance of toppling the Mexican government.

As in any revolution, this heterogeneous group had diverse motivations to join the rebellion. The economic crisis together with a severe drought in the early 1890s provided "objective conditions" that may have led desperately poor people to rebel for the chance to make some money, eat some food, and have hope for a brighter future. However, economic deprivation alone does not explain why poor Mexicans chose to rebel, nor does it explain why wealthier sectors of the community also supported the revolution. The moral economy approach, however, allows us to consider how the economic crisis itself was understood according to cultural traditions and customs. Ultimately, poor Mexicans on the border felt that their traditional rights to land and dignity were being usurped, both in Mexico and in South Texas. Furthermore, they felt that their tradition of liberalism, meaning regional autonomy, free trade, and civil liberties, had been betrayed by President Díaz. Wealthier Mexicans shared these liberal ideals, and also worried about the deterioration of their economic position in

South Texas, especially in comparison to newcomer Anglos. This common sense of tradition and custom served to unite virtually the entire South Texas community to directly or indirectly support Garza. At some point in early 1893, this support waned, especially among the wealthier backers, and over one hundred Garzistas were arrested and put on trial in San Antonio. There were multiple causes for the disintegration of the movement, including Garza's departure from Texas in spring 1892, the absence of an uprising in Mexico, and the terror caused by the U.S. Army. What is striking, however, is not that the movement eventually fell apart but that it was able to survive for so long in spite of the combined efforts of the U.S. and Mexican governments to crush it.

This chapter has shown how local government officials, including sheriffs, judges, deputy marshals, and scouts, thwarted the best efforts of the U.S. Army. The ability of Mexicans to manipulate the courts and the sympathy that most jury members had for the Garzistas made it difficult to legally prosecute the rebels. Support for the rebels, even among the scouts and marshals who were supposed to be helping the army, also rendered futile their anti-Garza campaign. The army only succeeded in capturing Garzistas and bringing them to trial after they had secured the cooperation of some of the local ranch owners. It was less the perseverance of the military than a shift in the local sentiment that led to the end of the rebellion. By early 1893 — with Garza in exile, the army busting into Mexican homes and threatening to hang the inhabitants, and investors skittish about putting money into a war zone — the wealthier backers pulled their support and negotiated a peaceful end to the rebellion. While the Garza revolt ended, the accumulated grievances of the Mexican community had not been resolved. Even if they did not take up arms in the ensuing years, the sense that their traditions and customs were being violated motivated other, less dramatic forms of protest. The most prudent among them, the ones with the most to lose, realized that they would have to wait for a more opportune moment for revolution.

6. THE IDEOLOGICAL BATTLE

I know the place newspapers

hold in public affairs. — Catarino Garza,

interview in the *New York Times*

On January 30, 1892, the *St. Louis Globe Democrat* reported that "There is the greatest excitement along the whole Rio Grande border, and there seems to be no question but that the movement inaugurated by Garza, which has been drifting along so slowly, is going to develop into a bloody war."[1] Ten days later the *San Antonio Express* called the entire revolt "a myth — an imaginary creation of sensational reporters."[2] The chasm of difference between these two accounts makes it difficult to evaluate using newspapers as sources the seriousness of the rebellion. This quandary is multiplied when we consider that even individual newspapers vacillated in their coverage of the Garzistas, one day calling them courageous revolutionaries and the next day deriding them as opportunistic bandits. Nonetheless, the divergence in accounts illustrates the importance of newspapers and magazines as partisan players on the ideological battlefield.

Garza's revolution and the campaign to stop it were conducted in the ideological realm as much as on the military field. Pitched battles were fought and soldiers on both sides died, but the way the insurrection was covered in the press had a longer-lasting impact on the way the border was perceived by outsiders. The Garzistas needed many more soldiers than they actually had, and so they counted on masses of people flocking to their cause once the revolt began. However, to convince the populace that an uprising could succeed, they had to exaggerate the strength and popularity of their forces. The Mexican government, on the other hand, had to downplay the significance of the revolt to boost investor confidence in the regime's stability and prevent a more general uprising. As a friend of the Díaz regime, the U.S. government had an interest in undermining Garza's legitimacy, while local officials tended to favor a movement so popular with voters. Press stories about the rebellion often diverged wildly, responding to these different and conflicting interests. Even though the Mexican and U.S. governments were in a better position to influence major daily newspapers and popular magazines, Garza's position as a journalist and his contacts in the profession allowed him to wage a very effective propaganda campaign of his own.

On a very mundane level, the propagandistic battle in the newspapers was about facts. Did such a battle occur? How many men were in Garza's army? And, was so-and-so killed? These individual facts, however, merely served a larger narrative that either characterized Garza as a criminal and a bandit or as an educated and charismatic leader. Not all articles fell neatly into such diametrically opposed views. Some admitted to the popularity of the movement but disagreed with the notion of armed revolution, while others argued that although Garza's intentions were honorable, he was being manipulated by outside agitators identified in various theories as foreign financial speculators, Mexico's clerics, or even the young Hapsburg Prince Iturbide.

The Spanish-language penny press along the border was a key actor in the rebellion. Dozens of small Spanish-language newspapers began publishing along the border beginning in the 1870s. The existence of relatively inexpensive printing presses made this boom possible, but it was the emergence of a reading public in the expanding towns that provided the demand. Most of these newspapers were four to eight pages in length and appeared weekly or biweekly. They reported on local cultural events and politics, but some newspapers, like Ignacio Martínez's *El Mundo*, were explicitly dedicated to opposing Díaz's regime in Mexico. There were at least five Spanish-language exile opposition newspapers along the South Texas border between 1885 and 1890.[3] Other newspapers, such as the one cofounded by Garza in Brownsville, *El Bien Público*, were official organs of mutualistas. While the circulation numbers of these newspapers is hard to determine, the short duration of many of them suggests that they had a fairly localized readership and an unstable source of financing. Nonetheless, these newspapers reprinted and commented on each other's articles, thus creating a broader discursive community along the entire South Texas border. The Texas border periodicals also reprinted articles from and responded to Mexican newspapers, thus forging a transnational community of readers. It is clear from the vigorous reaction of the Mexican government to these opposition newspapers that they were being read and taken seriously.

These newspapers not only created a Spanish-language community of readers but they also were in dialogue with the English-language readers as well. Articles were occasionally translated and reprinted, especially when the article had caused a controversy or was perceived as having slighted either the Anglo or the Mexican community. Garza's writings frequently got him in trouble with angry Anglo Texans and Porfirian officials, who charged him with libel on several occasions. These controversies suggest that there existed some degree of cross-border and cross-language communication. This interchange, however, did not necessarily result in better understanding between Anglos and Mexicans, because both the Spanish- and English-language press had very different perspectives on questions such as Garza's rebellion. Nonetheless, the Spanish-language press was also divided ideologically over many issues including Garza's revolt, especially after the Mexican government made a concerted effort to influence their coverage. While these small border newspapers had an important role during the rebellion, they were not successful in changing the dominant national narratives, especially those that appeared after the events. Indeed, because most of these newspapers were not preserved, and because historians and others relied on national newspapers and magazines to tell Garza's story, these alternative perspectives on the rebellion have been silenced.

MAKING A GOOD STORY BETTER

Right from the outset Garza's revolution was written in the popular press as a western frontier story. All of the necessary elements were present; a mysterious Mexican revolutionary/bandit, an exotic locale on the Rio Grande, a young and beautiful love interest, a brave Indian-fighting army captain, and lots of combat. With such material it is no wonder that reporters fixated on the Garza revolt, even embellishing the rich story with their creative talents, and rumors about the revolution spread quickly through the U.S. press. One Washington, D.C., newspaper invented a dramatic story saying that Garza's head was in a noose about to be hanged, when out of nowhere his men galloped in to save their leader from imminent death.[4] A Philadelphia newspaper picked up the story, editorializing that "there are a few more bandits that should be treated to the same length of rope assigned to guerrilla Garza." Unabashedly, the paper clamored for more blood and lynchings as a preventative measure: "If a half a dozen or so of these out of date filibusters could be strung up by the neck, on general principles as it were, the Rio Grande would be well rid of them."[5] Journalists liberally wove fact with fiction, cutting and pasting from rumors and reports to construct engaging and suspense-filled narratives.

The boldness and carelessness with which the press invented their stories undermined the movement's credibility, preparing the ground for the ultimate revisionist account that denied the existence of the revolution altogether. A Buffalo newspaper complained that so much misinformation abounded that nobody could even agree on such facts as Garza's physical appearance, his economic status, and the revolution's aims: "One New York paper paints him as a stalwart man, six foot three inches tall with a fine military carriage; another asserts that he is a person of slight physique and bad horsemanship, who relies more on his pen than aught else for his leadership, while the St. Louis *Republic* . . . says he is five feet ten in his shoes, slim and lithe, with a cat-like tread. In view of this disagreement in regard to so simple a matter as his looks, is it not wonderful that the estimates of his character don't disagree more widely."[6] This dissonance between Garza's image as an impoverished, "unscrupulous adventurer" with a "slight physique" and a "cat-like tread" or a "six foot three inches tall" "stalwart," wealthy, and "courageous" man, derived from two opposing visions of the revolution. Each, in its own way, exaggerated or diminished the physical stature and character of Garza as a means to defend or denigrate the movement in general.

Although many Mexican government officials believed the reports of Garza's revolution to be exaggerated or completely fabricated, they also considered him a public relations genius. The Mexican consul in Laredo hypothesized that all of the telegrams supporting Garza were being sent by one person in New York. While he derided Garza's conduct as being "of the stupidest and most disgraceful in the world," he also allowed that Garza must have an intelligent plan and lots of money to be able to get the newspaper to write about the revolution as they had: "President Harrison could not, with all of his resources, move the press with the dexterity, uniformity and timing which has been agitated by this vagabondage of Garza."[7] Even Captain Bourke grudgingly admitted the importance and impact of the Spanish-language newspapers, but he attributed their influence to the malleable minds of the "ignorant and dissolute classes."[8]

Granting Garza credit for manipulating the media, however, enabled the consul to discredit the actual movement. By February 1892, it became possible for the *San Antonio Express*, which had been accused by many Mexican and U.S. officials as having sensationalized their coverage of the rebellion, to turn around and claim that the movement had never existed. More than that, the *Express* contended that they had from the beginning held the position that "the so-called revolution was a complete failure, that Garza, having at no time as many as one hundred men together, had failed to find the Mexican people disposed to revolution and that the so-called Garza war would amount to nothing more than the pursuit of a few Garza adherents through the chaparral of southwestern Texas." Having promoted sales of their newspaper by publishing false and exaggerated reports, the newspaper now took the moral high ground and condemned such practices. As quickly as the *Express* had built up Garza's army, it tried to make it disappear, declaring that "the 'Garza army' was a myth — an imaginary creation of sensational reporters."[9]

Depending on their political sympathies, local newspapers portrayed the revolutionists either as hugely popular or as an isolated group of loony bandits. A San Antonio newspaper published by Garza's former colleague León Obregón, and financed by General Reyes, described the revolution as a "ridiculous attempt" and derided Garza and Ruíz Sandoval as "desperadoes of the decadent Carnaval who want to resuscitate themselves with their grotesque clowning."[10] Meanwhile, Laredo's *Gate City* reprinted Garza's newspaper's explanation of why Garza laid down his pen and took up the sword to liberate his country from Díaz. The *Gate City* also rejected the characterization by the *San Antonio Express* of Garza as a "famous bandit" and "well known border ruffian," arguing instead that he was "an intelligent and highly educated man, of a fine physique and commanding carriage and has every appearance as a gentleman."[11]

Some newspapers went beyond the saint or devil polarity and attempted to situate the revolt within its social and economic context. For instance, *El Correo de Laredo* argued that the revolt had been generally received badly in Laredo because "the businessmen reprove of any movement that will obstruct mercantile traffic; the men of politics tend to favor the Mexican government." Although the article portrayed the revolution negatively, it also condemned the American men who had attempted to deliver Sandoval to the Mexican authorities, "without due process, without law, with nothing, like the lynching justice."[12] The *Laredo Times* condemned Garza in more unequivocal terms, claiming that he had "made himself obnoxious to all the more intelligent class of Mexicans by his libelous and vulgar assaults on Governor Reyes." The *Times* did, however, admit that Garza had some followers among the lower classes, who saw him as the "Moses of the Mexican Republic." There was no such sympathy among Mexicans in Laredo, however, who they contended were all "strong believers in President Díaz and heartily endorse his administration."[13]

Spanish-language newspapers on the border engaged in a lively and at times vituperative debate over the merits of the revolt and the veracity of each other's reporting. On one occasion, Rio Grande City's *El Cromo* criticized Laredo's *El Mundo* for publishing a false report that Garza had taken over the town of Cerralvo in Mexico. Arguing that Garza's revolution was not a political movement, *El Cromo* portrayed those who joined the rebellion as dupes of the leaders: "Because many wretches have given space to the stories and promises of these imbeciles, they have paid and are perhaps paying for the faults of others. Do not leave your home, do not abandon your family and honorable work to follow a shameful cause."[14] Their message thus posited the developmentalist ethic of home, family, and honorable work against Garza's "shameful cause." *El Cromo* wanted "to prevent, as much as our poor forces allow, the ruin, the dishonor, the death perhaps of men who by only focusing a bit of attention on public opinion can still be useful and honored by the country which we all have an obligation to consecrate."[15] This type of negative reporting formed part of a concerted campaign to sway public opinion toward the Mexican government and "legality," and save Garza's followers from ruin, dishonor, and death.

Like other newspapers, *El Cromo* saw itself as a partisan player in a political game. The director of *El Cromo* even recommended his paper to the Mexican ambassador as a useful tool in exchange for some help dealing with a difficult postmaster. The postmaster in Rio Grande City had prohibited *El Cromo* from circulating in the mail, citing the newspaper's announcement of a raffle as an illegal lottery. The editor warned that if the postmaster succeeded in stopping his newspaper, the consequences "would resound against the Mexican citizens who were loyal to public powers, of the authorities on the other side of the river, who count on this newspaper to repel the aggression of other newspapers and of the military chiefs, who from the beginning of this [Garza] campaign have found this publication to be significant factor and a useful ally, sincerely loyal and impartial."[16] In an effort to solicit the Mexican ambassador's help, the editor thus cast his newspaper as an important ideological weapon in the battle against Garza and the "aggression" of pro-Garza newspapers.

The Mexican ambassador, Matías Romero, directed his own propaganda campaign by publishing a detailed essay about the revolt in the prominent national journal *North American Review*. In his article, titled "The Garza Raid and Its Lessons," he denied the existence of outside backers as evidence of the weakness and isolation of Garza's movement. One by one, Romero dismissed the theories that Garza had been backed by the clergy, by a financial syndicate, by U.S. citizens with property in Mexico, and finally by the young Prince Iturbide, who claimed to be the legitimate heir to Mexico's monarchy. Instead, Romero asserted that, of Garza's donors, "there is not one who could even be suspected as representing any combination of any standing whether civil, political, or military character." He thus concluded that Garza's movement was "unimportant, even insignificant."[17] Thus, rather than blaming outside speculators or clerics for Garza's revolution, Romero transferred to the U.S. press the responsibility and credit for the importance given to the insurrection. It was the U.S. press's "exaggerating and magnifying of the importance of that chimerical attempt [that] has produced serious and far-reaching injuries."[18] While theories changed as to who were the "outside agitators" who could be blamed for the "serious and far-reaching injuries" caused by the Garza revolution, Mexican government officials would never publicly recognize and credit border Mexicans for organizing, financing, and risking their lives for this cause.

The ambassador's views became the official assessment of Garza's movement. Newspapers such as the *San Antonio Express*, which had initially published favorable articles about Garza and the causes for the rebellion, would come to adopt the ambassador's viewpoint. Spanish-language border newspapers like *El Cromo* (Rio Grande City) and *El Correo de Laredo* also played an important role in discrediting the movement, and sought to curry favor with the Mexican government for their services. While sorting out "the truth" in this episode is a sticky business, it is clear that the consuls, Governor Reyes, and President Díaz purposefully misinformed the press, devised elaborate espionage operations to lure Garzistas to Mexico, and plotted assassinations in Texas.

GOVERNMENT PROPAGANDA

Lying became such a habitual response for the Mexican government that they resorted to it even when the truth would have not been so damaging. One incident involving a press story fabricated by Minister Romero and

President Díaz illustrates the larger modus operandi of the Porfirian regime. At the end of 1891, Porfirio Díaz telegraphed Minister Romero complaining that the U.S. troops were not persecuting the Garzistas with enough zeal. Romero reprinted this telegram in the *Washington Post*, thereby causing a negative reaction by the U.S. government, which felt that it was inappropriate for Díaz to criticize the U.S. Army's efforts. Sensing that he had committed an indiscretion in publishing Díaz's telegram, Romero offered to tell the press that the message had been improperly decoded.

A few days later an article titled "Minister Romero Makes a Correction" appeared in the *Washington Post*, dutifully printing the lie that Romero had concocted to save Díaz from embarrassment. The article reported that the content of the original message was altered due to problems with "transmission" or "deciphering," but that the "copy now does not contain any allusion to any want of the proper zeal on the part of respective officers of the US government on the frontier in the execution of the neutrality laws in that case."[19] While admittedly a small matter, the proof of a premeditated effort to manipulate the press illustrates the extent to which the Mexican government would go to win the ideological battle. And it is all the more significant that this blatant lie came directly from the man who so self-righteously and publicly condemned the U.S. press for publishing falsehoods about the Garza revolution.

Although many government lies made their way onto the pages of respected newspapers, the attempted manipulation of the press was occasionally unmasked. A letter appearing in the *San Francisco Chronicle* exposed the Mexican government's efforts to suppress news of Garza's revolt and predicted that "the movement has taken formidable proportions and threatens to extend." The Mexican consul at Laredo, the letter revealed, "has received orders from the government to doctor all reports passing through his hands and destined for the US."[20] While the revolt never extended much beyond the border region, as this letter prophesied, it correctly pointed to the Mexican government's fears of revolution and to their "doctoring" of information.

The highest levels of the Mexican government allowed rumors to spread, and they even helped to circulate them to discredit Garza. In January 1892, Governor Reyes informed Ambassador Romero that he had "let run . . . and would even favor [the rumors that foreign speculators had financed the revolution to lower Mexican bond prices] because they make those who have formed the [Garza] *gavilla* look like sell-outs against the interests of their country."[21] Reyes continued by stating that because the press had not always been favorable to Mexico, he had not denied the notion that the newspapers were also serving the "interests of the enemies of our country's credit."[22]

Reyes fed these false rumors not just to newspapers but even to lower-level officials in his own government. When the Laredo consul sent a *San Antonio Express* article to Reyes that claimed that clerics had financed Garza, Reyes shot back that this was a "very malicious" rumor that should categorically be denied. The *Express* was probably backed by foreign speculators, Reyes asserted, and they had accused the clerics in order to draw attention away from the financial syndicate that had organized the revolution.[23] Reyes must have felt that it would be more damaging to the Garzistas to have people believe that a foreign syndicate had organized the rebellion than that Garza had the support of the clerics within Mexico. Or perhaps Reyes understood that few people would be gullible enough to believe that clerics would support an anticlerical liberal revolutionary who believed fervently in secular government.

The San Antonio consul had conducted his own investigation in March 1892 and determined that Garza was not being backed by either a foreign financial syndicate or the clerical party. After analyzing a list of donors found among the captured rebel papers, the consul concluded that "there is nobody who can be suspected of representing a political band, religious faction, bank or financial association, in sum a serious organization by any means protected by the stock market, by the clergy or by any other important social body." Instead, he believed that the donations came from military men, politicians, speculators, and businessmen who financed the insurrection with the hope of gaining some profit, "but in any case," he argued, "these meager resources did not come from far away but originated from the same Texas Mexico border." The consul categorically rejected the specific rumor that foreign speculators had backed the revolt after he received credible information from personal contacts in the European financial community. A San Antonio banker assured him that no such conspiracy existed and showed him a telegram he had just received from his European financial agent that read: "Boom in all Mexican securities if Díaz peaceably elected."[24] Nevertheless, the rumors of this conspiracy, encouraged by Reyes and Romero, had already done damage to Garza's image.

A few months later, the rumors of foreign speculators financing the revolution to lower the value of Mexican bonds were still being printed in the U.S. press. One Washington newspaper even suggested that President Díaz had been part of the syndicate, and that he and his partners had made "several millions by the deal."[25] Like many others, this newspaper believed that the Porfirian regime was so omnipotent that it even controlled the opposition. True resistance was literally unimaginable.[26]

Mexico's consul in Boston finally issued a public denial of the rumors that a syndicate had funded the rebellion. He showed that the price of Mexican bonds had only risen since February, thus demonstrating that the reports of alarmed stockholders flooding the markets was a "silly falsehood because if they had done so the price would have fallen."[27] Meanwhile, the *Chicago Times* had its own theory that credited North American capitalists with masterminding the revolution. According to the *Times*, Alexander "Boss" Shepard, owner of the huge Batopilas mining complex in Copper Canyon, had organized Garza's revolution with the ultimate goal of capturing Baja California, Sonora, Chihuahua, Coahuila, Nuevo León, and San Luis Potosí. The article asserted that Shepard had planned the revolution in association with a Texas syndicate that owned large tracts of land in northern Mexico and a half-dozen Mexican railroad promoters, so that their property values would increase after annexation to the United States.[28] One St. Louis newspaper combined the two theories, reporting that Ruíz Sandoval had been sent by the rebels to New Orleans to arrange a $100,000 loan from a London firm, while also asserting that corrupt Mexican clerics who gambled, ran bull rings, and maintained mistresses were behind the Garza revolt.[29] Rather than credit border Mexicans, newspapers devised elaborate theories blaming the revolt on lascivious Mexican clerics, London and Wall Street financiers, North American mine owners, and even President Díaz. From the extensive documentation now available, including the rebels' captured papers, it is abundantly clear that none of these rumors had the slightest truth to them. That Garza received money from wealthy backers there is no doubt, but there is no evidence that these supporters controlled or started the revolt for financial gain.

Time and again, and most recently with the uprising in Chiapas, the Mexican government has blamed internal social conflict on outside forces. In this case at least, the lies were concocted at the very top of Mexico's hierarchy, between Minister Romero, Governor Reyes, and President Díaz, and then spread through their own bureaucracy and to the outside media. If anyone was responsible for feeding false rumors to the U.S. press, about which Romero so vituperatively whined, it was the Mexican government, and, ironically enough, with the direct knowledge and participation of Ambassador Romero.

BUYING JOURNALISTS

While the Mexican government conducted a successful public relations campaign in the established press, they always looked for a more direct way to influence public opinion, especially in South Texas. To achieve this end they bought off journalists like Garza's former colleague, León Obregón, who received $278 from Reyes to buy a printing press and publish *El Cronista Mexicano* in San Antonio. With an eye on making the propaganda more subtle and effective, Reyes recommended that Obregón "not praise personalities from this country, so that dressed with an impartial character, he could defend with greater success the interests of the Government."[30]

Meanwhile, San Antonio's consul had a plan to distribute progovernment newspapers on the border as well as to expand the spy network. Beyond merely obstructing insurrectionary movements, he desired "to convert into sympathizers that force which is now so bitterly antagonistic to the interests of our country and of our government." By distributing *El Universal* and *El Partido Liberal* for free for the first six months under the guise of a business promotion, they could build their audience on the Texas border. After two or three years, the consul predicted that such propaganda would provide a counterweight to the "multitude of *periodiquillos* [small newspapers] published on this side of the Rio Grande . . . achieving to a large degree the alienation from them of the sympathies of the remote Texas border."[31] If all else failed, the consul planned to pay "when necessary" the *San Antonio Express* and other newspapers to publish information favorable to the government.[32] Unfortunately, few issues of the periodiquillos to which the consul referred have survived. Nonetheless, the few scattered issues that were preserved in U.S. and Mexican archives, along with our knowledge of the campaign to counteract their influence, indicate that there was a thriving counterdiscourse on the border.

In addition to the explicit bribing of journalists, Mexican government officials attempted to sway the press by constantly feeding them false information. Laredo's consul boasted that he had succeeded in manipulating the local press by holding conferences with journalists every afternoon. They had come over to his way of thinking so much, he argued, that they even published his articles in their newspapers.[33] One such article appearing in the *Laredo Weekly Times* hailed Mexico as a bastion of liberty, specifically pointing to the existence of the *Monitor Republicano* and *Diaro del Hogar* of the liberal party and the *Tiempo* and *Voz de México* of the clerical and conservative party as clear proof that "there were no restrictions upon the press in Mexico."[34] While the government could point to the existence of ideologically diverse newspapers, those that openly criticized the Díaz regime were quickly shut down.

Even more convincing, however, than articles by Mexican consuls or even known loyal Porfiristas, such as León Obregón, was the subtle support for the government by well-known oppositionists. The case of Justo Cárdenas, an oppositionist journalist and lawyer who went into exile from Monterrey in 1885 after Reyes declared martial law, illustrates how dissidents could be won over. In October 1891, just after Garza made his first incursion into Mexico, Cárdenas wrote directly to Porfirio Díaz, explaining in a fawning letter how circumstances had in the past "obliged" him to oppose his government. And then in a remarkable about-face, Cárdenas argued "I have always been one of the writers in Nuevo León who supported your candidacy for President . . . [and] I have never been the enemy of your government which has brought so much wealth to the country." Cárdenas then offered the services of his newspaper, *El Correo de Laredo*, to the president, hinting that more money would help him get the government's position across more effectively. Having had seven years of experience on the border, along with knowledge of the Mexican community in rural villages, made Cárdenas, a self-described "old supporter" of Díaz, particularly useful.[35]

This rapprochement, Cárdenas must have understood, could not be achieved with promises alone, and so his newspaper, which had previously supported revolution in Mexico, abruptly changed its tune in summer 1891. *El Cronista Mexicano*, Obregón's San Antonio mouthpiece for Díaz, reprinted an article from Cárdenas's newspaper to demonstrate that "the old comrade of the exiled oppositionists" had broken with them. *El Chinaco*, published by the Garzista Paulino Martínez, criticized Cárdenas for this change in sentiment, accusing him of selling out. In a defensive tone, Cárdenas responded that "we have always had the aim to separate ourselves from certain people who dishonor us, and we have proposed to no longer be the toys of captains of industry, and therefore we have retired from the oppositionist camp." He added, "we don't need to sell ourselves to live," arguing that they had always been successful and that "our independence is assured by our own resources and it will not be hunger that puts us on the edge of the abyss, nor the stomach that will determine our writing." Two months later, however, Cárdenas's letter to Díaz specifically asked for money so that he could better serve the government. While money appears to be one of the causes of Cárdenas's change of heart, there were other contentious issues that divided the oppositionists. Without elaborating on what he meant, Cárdenas accused Paulino Martínez of having dirty laundry that was so smelly as to "cause nausea."[36]

Not only did Cárdenas criticize Garza in his newspaper, but he even provided the Porfiristas with information about Garza's whereabouts and offered intelligence on a daily basis.[37] By February 1892, Reyes confirmed that Cárdenas had changed his attitude and that his newspaper had shown itself loyal to authorities, but he still refused to recommend Cárdenas for the job as consul in Laredo.[38] One month later, one of Díaz's cabinet members, Manuel Romero Rubio, wrote to Reyes about an "arrangement" he had made with Cárdenas, "so that his publication would follow a different direction than the one it had." More than merely ceasing his attacks on Reyes, Cárdenas would have to publicly support Reyes. Romero Rubio had entered into this agreement, not only to help Reyes rid himself of a critic, but to avoid the possibility that the publication be turned into "an element of hostility."[39] Reyes thanked him for his efforts, explaining that he had succeeded in changing Cárdenas's conduct, and that his "newspaper not only has an impartial character but has even attacked the papers that propagate subversive ideas on the other side of the Bravo."[40]

In spite of this arrangement with Cárdenas, Reyes could not always dictate *El Correo de Laredo*'s political opinions. In one instance, Cárdenas's newspaper supported a candidate for Nuevo Laredo's city council who was not the one chosen by the governor of Tamaulipas. Reyes asked Laredo's consul to make it clear to Cárdenas "that the Center will not appreciate hostility toward the government of a state."[41] Cárdenas went ahead anyway and supported the opposition candidate, who, not surprisingly, lost the election.[42]

THE ANTI-DÍAZ PRESS

While the Mexican government had some success with the English-language press on the border, the Spanish-language press continued to be almost universally anti-Porfirista. Laredo's consul complained that he could only publish his articles in English because the Spanish-language newspapers were all hostile except for Cárdenas's paper, a biweekly with a very small circulation. In 1892, the consul gleefully announced that two Spanish-language opposition newspapers, *El Mundo* and *El Mexicano*, would cease operations in Laredo because Ignacio Martínez's widow had packed up the printing press and was moving to San Antonio.[43] However, even in 1896, long after the Garza revolution had ended, Rio Grande City's consul described a similar oppositionist monopoly over the press. At that point, the only Spanish-language periodicals in Rio Grande City were published by former Garzista Paulino Martínez, director of *El Chinaco* and *La Estrella del Sur*, the organ of Starr County's Democratic Party, and Jesus T. Recío, the editor of *El Bien Público*.[44]

Such unanimity of anti-Porfirian sentiment among Mexican journalists was not only limited to South Texas but was present along the entire border. As the *Los Angeles Herald* boldly argued in an article titled "Garza a Patriot, Not a Bandit," the conditions inside Mexico could be better understood "from the Spanish-American papers published on this side of the Rio Grande than from anything we can learn from the Mexican papers." These Spanish American newspapers affirmed that Garza was a patriot and Díaz a despot. The *Herald* translated an article from *El Hispano-Americano*, published in Socorro, New Mexico, summing up the prorevolutionary and anti-Porfirian feeling among Mexicans in the U.S.: "Díaz ... has wiped out the liberties of the people and assumed autocratical powers. He has centralized the whole government in himself, and until he is overthrown there will always exist a reason for spasmodic uprisings, especially in the departments remote from the seat of government."[45]

Opposition newspapers in South Texas continued their own propaganda war, responding to government misinformation and attempting to sway public opinion in their favor. In 1886, *El Mundo* reported that there were thirteen Spanish-language newspapers along the U.S.-Mexico border.[46] A more recent bibliography lists eleven Spanish-language newspapers in Laredo alone, and dozens more in other border towns.[47] Unfortunately, most of these newspapers did not survive the repression and only a few clippings remain scattered in Mexican and U.S. archives. Nevertheless, the tenacity with which the Mexican government attempted to squelch these periodicals testifies to their perceived importance. The most dangerous newspapers from the standpoint of the Mexican government were the ones edited by the revolutionaries themselves. Ignacio Martínez published *El Mundo* and *El Mexicano* in Laredo and Brownsville; Catarino

Garza published *El Comercio Mexicano* in Eagle Pass, Corpus Christi, and San Diego and *El Libre Pensador* in Palito Blanco; and Paulino Martínez published *El Chinaco* in Laredo and San Angelo and *La Estrella del Sur* in Rio Grande City. The Mexican government continually charged the opposition press with libel, but having little success in the courts they relied on other methods to silence those presses.

In 1889, Coahuila's governor, Garza Galán, asked Reyes for help in preventing the circulation of *El Mundo* in northern Mexico. Reyes responded confidently that, at least in his state of Nuevo León, *El Mundo* had no distributors and that it very rarely arrived in the post.[48] By placing loyal clerks in Nuevo Laredo's post office, Reyes had prevented the newspapers of Ignacio Martínez, Justo Cárdenas, and Paulino Martínez from entering Mexico. When an official in the post office complained about the policy of opening and censoring the mail, Reyes had him replaced.[49]

In spite of the Mexican government's best efforts to suppress opposition newspapers from reaching Mexico, as well as their work to silence journalists on the Texas side of the border who refused to cooperate, criticism of the Díaz regime also made its way to the U.S. English-language press. One such article in the *Journal* in Milwaukee exposed the dictatorial powers of Díaz in Mexico, especially his manipulation of the press. The *Journal* contended that the outside world did not realize that despite having a progressive constitution, "Mexico is in fact a monarchy, more absolute a despotism, more terrible than that of Russia, as disguised are always more powerful than declared forces." The article contended that foreign correspondents in Mexico rarely knew Spanish well, nor did they have good relations with the people. Those who were well informed, it stated, were "subsidized to write such statements as are acceptable to the administration."[50]

GARZA'S PROPAGANDA CAMPAIGN

Given the repressive conditions and lack of space for an opposition press in Porfirian Mexico, Garza focused his attentions on local Texas and U.S. national newspapers. Even while running from the authorities Garza managed to continue the publication of *El Internacional*, and he granted interviews to national newspapers such as the *New York Times*. In spite of both governments' privileged access to the media, Garza succeeded in having his point of view broadcast to a wide audience. While *El Internacional* (Palito Blanco) and *El Mundo* (Laredo) probably had extremely small circulations, their articles were translated into English and reprinted in newspapers with much wider readerships, such as the *San Antonio Express* and the *San Francisco Examiner*.

One such article translated and reprinted from *El Internacional* in the *San Antonio Express* in January 1892 made the case that Garza's revolution was only finishing the work that Díaz had begun and therefore was "nothing to be scandalized about." Although *El Internacional* was published by a Cuban, F. S. Mendoza, Garza ran the operation behind the scenes. The article legitimated Garza's revolt by comparing it to Díaz's, which had raised "the same cry and the same proclamation . . . : 'No re-elections, no revenue stamps, and free suffrage.'" *El Internacional* compared the rancheros' "devotion" to Garza's cause to Díaz's soldiers' lack of loyalty, arguing that Díaz's army would quickly desert him in the event of a civil war. As well as demonstrating the popularity of the cause, the article dismissed the characterization of the Garzistas as bandits. While Garza conspired against the Mexican government, the author argued that "he does not deserve the name of 'wicked bandit' and many other such terms that are applied to him. . . . The fact that they committed no depredation, no robbery and no offense to peaceable citizens is proof that they are not bandits. They pay for everything and do not steal."[51] The insistence on this point shows that Garza was sensitive to being portrayed as a petty criminal, and it similarly demonstrates his desire to have his actions viewed politically.

Belying their own bias, the *Express* described *El Internacional*'s article as "rabid and incendiary," noting that "it is likely that an effort will be made to suppress [the newspaper]."[52] While it may be presumed that the *Express* reprinted Garzista proclamas and *El Internacional*'s articles in order to sell newspapers or to show the movement as "rabid and incendiary," the fact that Garza's perspective was published at all opened the possibility for a sympathetic reading, especially among the Mexican population. The *Express* could editorialize about Garza's words, but it could not control or prevent positive interpretations of these documents.[53]

An interview with *El Internacional*'s publisher, F. S. Mendoza, helped to further disseminate Garza's views, especially after the *San Francisco Examiner* translated and reprinted the interview. In this interview, Mendoza asserted that Garza decided to revolt after Mexico's fraudulent election in June 1891. Denying the rumor that Garza's support came from a financial syndicate, Mendoza argued that Garza found plenty of Mexican backers "who are rich both in money and patriotism." With these resources Garza organized an army of four hundred men in Texas, and he counted on a "passive and unknown army of many thousands in Mexico, which," according to Mendoza, "will spring up like mushrooms when Garza gives the signal."[54]

Given that Mendoza had to have close contacts with Garza, the former editor of *El Internacional*, and with Alejandro González, on whose ranch the newspaper was published, it is likely that Garza ran his own public relations campaign through *El Internacional* and Mendoza. Mendoza claimed that Generals Geronimo Treviño and Manuel González, both important caudillos in northeastern Mexico, would not participate in the revolution, but this statement was most likely designed to protect the generals from recriminations in Mexico. Similarly, Mendoza's assertion that Alejandro González "has no interest in the revolution and does not care what becomes of Garza" does not jibe with the fact that Don Alejandro spent large sums of money outfitting the revolutionists and bailing them out of jail.[55] It seems as though González subscribed to the same principles as Garza, but even if he had not, Garza was still part of his family.

In addition to using friendly newspapers such as *El Internacional* and *El Mundo* to communicate the reasons for his revolt, Garza granted interviews to English-language periodicals to explain his revolution directly to the U.S. public. One interview in early January 1892 was published on the front page of the *New York Times* and in the *Omaha Bee*. "I have been a newspaper man nearly all my life," Garza began. "I know the place newspapers hold in public affairs, and, in seeing you, I simply gratify the desire to have myself placed rightly before the people of the United States."[56] He thus claimed credit for agreeing to the interview, openly using it as an opportunity to set the record straight and influence public opinion. Garza's ability to shape the interview came across in his self-confident and well-prepared statement of the revolution's causes and goals, his refusal to answer sensitive questions, and his abrupt exit when he had decided the interview should be ended.

When asked whether the clerical party was behind his revolt, Garza responded that "for the present this is a Catarino Garza movement, or revolution, as you please," with the reporter adding, "said the bandit with a smile."[57] The disjunction between the two clauses of this sentence reveals a wider disjunction between the interests of the reporter and Garza. Garza allowed the reporter to choose between calling his insurrection a "movement or revolution," but the reporter, disregarding the hint, immediately labeled Garza a bandit. While Garza set the terms of the interview, such as not allowing his location to be disclosed and responding selectively to questions, the reporter chose the words and adjectives to define Garza. The reporter commented on Garza's appearances, noting that he "looks more like an American than a Mexican, but his complexion is very dark, and his hair and mustache are black." Apparently the interview was conducted in English, prompting the reporter to remark that Garza "speaks very good English."[58]

At the outset of the interview, Garza categorically denied the notion that he and his followers were "simply an organized band of border ruffians, seeking only to gratify personal ends." His critique centered on Díaz, blaming his authoritarian rule, intolerance of all opposition, and ill-gotten wealth for the growing discontent in Mexico. Explaining how Díaz had "grown immensely wealthy" since he became president, Garza exclaimed that "the price of a monopoly in Mexico is a block of stock in the enterprise, made out in either Díaz's name or that of a trusted lieutenant." He also criticized Díaz's "system of religious persecution which," he argued, "has gained him the cordial hatred of every good churchman and priest." Garza would not specify whether the church supported him, but it is highly unlikely that clerics would back a liberal who believed so strongly in the separation of church and state. In addition to suggesting that he had plenty of money and backers, Garza also hinted that a portion of Díaz's "half-starved soldiery" would join the revolution once it gained momentum.[59]

In this interview, aimed at a U.S. audience, Garza steered far away from his attacks on foreign land ownership in Mexico, focusing entirely on the despotic and corrupt Díaz as the cause of Mexico's problems. Arguing that he had "too wholesome a fear and regard for the Government at Washington to do anything which might bear the semblance of treason," Garza assured the U.S. readership that his movement was "aimed at the head of Díaz." When pushed on just how he would accomplish his goals, Garza responded evasively, stating that he didn't know himself and that even if he did he would not reveal them. Before mounting his mustang and disappearing behind a clump of bushes, Garza left these parting words: "We mean to succeed. That much you may say for me. Adiós."[60]

7. COLONIZING THE LOWER RIO GRANDE VALLEY

The conquest of the earth, which mostly means

the taking it away from those who have a slightly different

complexion or slightly flatter noses than ourselves, is not a pretty

thing when you look at it too much. What redeems it is the idea only.

An idea is at the back of it; not a sentimental presence but an idea;

and an unselfish belief in the idea — something you can set up,

and bow down before, and offer a sacrifice to.

— Joseph Conrad, *Heart of Darkness*

If Garza destroys Uncle Sam's army, Texas will

rise up hot as a hornet and stamp the revolutionary

greaser out of existence. — *Galveston Tribune*

The stories that a few U.S. Army officers told about the border in the process of prosecuting the campaign against the Garzistas helped to make the region known to the outside world and facilitated its incorporation into the nation. These narratives reached a variety of reading publics through mass-distribution newspapers, national magazines, and scholarly journals. The basic story portrayed the border as a zone of unsurpassed economic potential that had been left to rot under the management of lazy Mexicans. The publications enticed potential settlers and investors with images of an agricultural paradise populated by an exotic, friendly, and welcoming Mexican community. The "bad" Mexicans, the "bandits" and "outlaws," were quickly vanishing, they assured. At the same time, the persistence of the "bad" Mexicans helped both to justify the heavy-handed measures that the Texas Rangers employed to capture Garzistas and also to legitimate the massive transfer of land from Mexican to Anglo hands. The military activities and the narratives told about the border also helped the central government to incorporate the frontier region by physically mapping the terrain and ethnographically mapping the people. The war against the Garzistas thus served a broader nationalist and capitalist project that far surpassed the importance of quelling a border rebellion. This project was intimately linked to a nineteenth-century global culture of imperialism.

Although there are important differences between U.S. imperialism within its own boundaries and European colonialism, there are striking similarities in the narrative tropes used to describe each. By the late nineteenth century, the lower Rio Grande Valley had been legally incorporated into the United States for half a century. Even though it was contiguous with the mainland it remained distant, both physically removed from metropolitan centers of trade and power and psychologically isolated in the imaginary of those not from the region. When U.S. officers charged with capturing Garzistas and imposing order on a rebellious population arrived in this strange and distant land, they quite easily invoked the discourses and methodologies employed by Europeans and Anglo Americans in their imperial endeavors in Africa, Asia, and the Americas.

The campaign to capture the pronunciados for violation of neutrality laws became on several different levels a war of imperial conquest for the U.S. troops. The fact that they fought on U.S. soil did not diminish the geographical and psychological distance between the troops and the people of this region. To apprehend the Garzistas and more generally control, rule, and impose order, they had to map the land, not only by locating ranches, cities, and rivers on a two-dimensional grid but also by identifying social networks and classifying economic activities. Reports to the assistant adjutant general often contained mind-numbing detail about the physical terrain, distances covered, and routes taken on the innumerable scouting expeditions. Officers understood that the military mapping of the valley was a necessary first step to wipe out the Garzistas but was insufficient as a means of long-term control. The more astute officers recognized that they had to do more than just capture "bandits" and arrest criminals, and they saw themselves as principal managers of the development and "opening" of the valley to Anglo entrepreneurs and industry. Indeed, there was a distinct racial aspect to their vision of economic modernization for the valley.

To fully grasp the broader significance both military and literary of these officers' work, we must consider that their reports and descriptions circulated widely throughout the United States and even in Europe. Therefore, not only did the army officers squash a struggle for liberalism on the border and inflict terror on Mexicans in the process, but they contributed to a culture of imperialism that justified Anglo domination in the Rio Grande Valley specifically and in the U.S. West in general. Since the founding of the British colonies in North America, this culture of imperialism was intimately linked to notions of race.[1] This racial logic, what Conrad in *Heart of Darkness* refers to as the "idea" that justified the "conquest of the earth" had to be continually rearticulated to make the uglier side of imperialism palatable. The "idea" thus glossed over the violence and dispossession by making it seem both inevitable and, more important, morally necessary for human progress. Army officers, anthropologists, missionaries, travel writers, and explorers were at the forefront of the journey to these "unknown" exotic regions. As well as making these areas "knowable" to the dominant Anglo American society, their accounts justified colonization. Their literary and scientific portraits of the border circulated in newspapers and magazines, either in the form of their direct reports or as primary source material for diplomats and politicians who offered their opinions about Garza's revolution. Given that very little was known about South Texas by the outside world, the coverage of the border that this event inspired took on paramount significance in defining the region.

Although Garzistas mainly operated in the lower Rio Grande Valley, an area that had not yet been pierced by railroads, the proximity of the disturbances to major international trade routes threatened the new commercial partnership between Mexico and the United States. The image projected in the national media was of a region poised for economic and social transformation. Potential investors, however, had to be assured that there was money to be made and that political instability would not threaten their investments. News of an armed Mexican revolutionary force roaming through South Texas calling for the overthrow of Díaz did not, to say the least, put capitalists at ease. The Army thus had several tasks: squash the Garza revolution; devise a strategy to prevent further outbreaks; convince the national media that peace and stability reigned on the border; and propagate the ideological justification for exploiting the natural and human resources on the border.

At the same time as Anglo army officers and investors were writing about the border, Mexicans articulated counternarratives in Spanish-language border newspapers and in travel narratives, autobiographies, and corridos. The Garza rebellion became a moment when some of those counternarratives briefly surfaced in the English-language press, either in papers like the *San Antonio Express* or in national newspapers in New York and San Francisco. Over the long term, however, the dominant narratives about the border, told mainly by outsiders, trumped the local stories. It is quite likely that Spanish-speaking border people never accepted the outsider view of the border, and they even tried to contest the dominant narrative by attempting to disseminate their own stories to a wider English-reading public; ultimately, the outsiders' perspective won out. While in most of this chapter I explore the Anglo army officers' perspectives, I also analyze the border Mexican views about Garza's rebellion and the role of the army in the lower Rio Grande Valley. The interpretation of Garza's revolution and the border was contested frequently and vigorously. Unfortunately, the process of silencing has been so effective that many of the traces of the Mexican counterdiscourse have simply disappeared.[2]

AN OFFICER AND AN ANTHROPOLOGIST

Captain John Gregory Bourke did not seek out service on the border, and he was not happy when he heard about the possibility of being removed from his scholarly duties in Washington, D.C., in 1890. At the time of his reassignment he was working on a book about the Apache, and after his strenuous frontier duty fighting Indians in Arizona and capturing Geronimo, he felt that he deserved time to devote to his intellectual pursuits. In the seven years he spent in the capital between 1886 and 1891 he worked at a feverish pace, organizing his massive fifteen-year accumulation of field notes and publishing numerous journal articles and three books. This intense work regimen gave him insomnia, and the physically and psychologically exhausted Bourke verged on the edge of a nervous breakdown. However, in spite of complicated efforts to reverse his reassignment, including doctor-prescribed medical leaves and the intervention of several U.S. senators, the army dispatched Bourke to Texas in April 1891. In denying Bourke's request for a leave of absence, the acting secretary of war suggested that military duty on the border would relieve his "mental strain." Within a month, Bourke assumed command of the Third Cavalry at Fort Ringgold in Rio Grande City.[3] It was an unexpected and even unwanted assignment, but it put the officer and anthropologist once again at the center of a well-publicized frontier war.

Bourke's journey out to the U.S. western frontier to fight Indians and Mexicans mirrors the travels by Catarino Garza to Texas and St. Louis. Like Garza, Bourke used writing as a way both to make sense of his experiences and to publicize his "discoveries" to a wider audience. Compared to Garza, however, Bourke had much greater access to an academic and general audience because he wrote in English and could claim dual authority as an experienced military man and an anthropologist. Bourke's most popular book, *On the Border with Crook*, recounted his participation in the suppression of Apaches in Arizona and the capture of their leader Geronimo. Bourke also penned numerous scholarly articles on the customs and folk practices of Apaches and one dense academic treatise that enumerated hundreds of medicinal and ritualistic uses of human and animal excrement. These publications and his membership in several prestigious scientific societies, including being named to the board of the Anthropological Society of Washington, lent weight to his observations about the border. When Bourke talked about the Rio Grande Valley he spoke with the authority of an expert. As his good friend, the archaeologist Dr. J. H. Porter, commented after reading Bourke's article about the border, "An American Congo," "nobody but a fool could read this paper and not see that its author spoke ex cathedra."[4]

From 1872 until his death in 1896, Bourke faithfully recorded in his diary the minute details of his daily life along with grander anthropological observations. Of the 124 volumes of his diary 10 cover the period when he was living in the lower Rio Grande Valley and pursuing Garzistas. Along with a running account of his military strategies to squelch the revolt, Bourke described theatrical performances, marriage rituals, folk remedies, and other cultural practices he encountered in the region. Thus, in addition to helping us understand the campaign against Garza from the U.S. Army officer's perspective, Bourke's diary helps us to see inside the mind of the ethnographer and soldier who played such a key military and public relations role in suppressing and discrediting the Garzistas.

MAPPING THE VALLEY

None of the U.S. Army officers and troops sent to the valley was from the area. The complete foreignness of the region meant that officers could not make fine distinctions, or perhaps any distinctions at all; "they all looked alike," as the saying and attitude went. "The language, dress, customs, weights and measures, money used—everything about them," Captain Bourke claimed, "may be put down as Spanish; therefore, it is almost an impossibility to separate a 'revolutionist' from one of the ordinary inhabitants."[5] More had to be known about this population to be able to categorize them and distinguish an "ordinary" Mexican from a "bandit."

For this local knowledge, officers relied heavily on deputy marshals, scouts, and trackers to lead them through unfamiliar territory and identify people. They were especially dependent on the local scouts because the army maps were often inaccurate or incomplete. When Bourke arrived on the border in 1891, he found an utter lack of military preparedness: "There was not one single guide or interpreter on the pay rolls, or a map or chart of any portion of that immense district."[6] Thus he began the tedious process of plotting the topography and the various ranches in the region by sketching preliminary maps in his diary and reports. Lieutenant Stephen O'Conner, who took over the anti-Garza campaign from Bourke in 1893, felt similarly lost. O'Conner complained that when searching for rebels he had to rely on a scout "who lived and labored in that country for some years and who is thoroughly conversant with the roads and the location of Ranches, many of which are not noted on the map."[7] Until they could accurately map the region the army depended on locals, and such dependency proved to be a paramount weakness for the troops, who were often led astray by Garza supporters and their own scouts.

Mapping the valley, however, implied more than just locating ranches on a Cartesian grid, it also meant constructing a new communication network. During the insurrection, troops discovered that the rebels used a system of signal lights to communicate the precise movements of government troops, thus allowing them plenty of time to disperse and hide.[8] While the rebels always seemed to know the whereabouts of the army, government soldiers were rarely able to pinpoint the location of the Garzistas. They thus suffered a double disadvantage because local communication networks served the revolutionists well while at the same time worked against the U.S. troops. The revolutionary troubles would be short lived, the officers predicted, if they had access to a better information and a more extensive communication system. Their solution was to build railroads and telegraph and telephone lines through the "disturbed" regions.

In 1891, two rail lines passed through South Texas: the Texas-Mexican ran from Corpus Christi to Laredo, and the International Great and Northern railroads linked San Antonio and Laredo. A good portion of the valley, however, still lay beyond easy reach of the Texas-Mexican line. The Mexican side of the river was similarly isolated, with only one main line extending from Laredo to Monterrey, and on to Mexico City. Bourke was convinced that "if the Mexican government could possibly have the Matamoros Railroad extended the short distance from San Miguel to Monterrey, revolutions in Mexico, or attempts at fomenting revolution from this side, would be an impossibility."[9] However, the railroad that was supposed to link Matamoros to the main Mexican National line was perennially plagued with construction delays and stoppages.

Most directly, railroads allowed troops to be deployed rapidly to a trouble spot. Railroads also strengthened long-term social control by increasing economic and political ties to federal and state governments. These links to government institutions would ostensibly prevent discontent from exploding violently by channeling complaints through bureaucratic structures. Bourke's notion that the Mexican railroad line would have made revolutions an "impossibility" is clearly hyperbole, but the link between railroads and civilization was so strong that their very presence seemed incompatible with bandits or rebellions. As Bourke put it, once the connections are made to American lines, "this valley, instead of being a source of annoyance and expense to both nations would bloom like a flower garden."[10]

Colonel Anson Mills, who a few years later led the Water Boundary Commission that surveyed the entire U.S.-Mexico border, had an even more elaborate plan. Mills called for the establishment of eight border posts with communication links to their Mexican counterparts. Telegraph or telephone wires would be strung across the river to link Mexican and U.S. military posts, and these posts would be provided with "educated, discreet and reliable interpreters . . . who not only are perfectly proficient in both languages, but who know the habits and characteristics of both peoples."[11] The officers would be required to build mutual relationships of trust with the Mexicans, make frequent visits to the other side, and exchange news on a daily basis. The U.S. Department of Justice would furnish lists of wanted criminals to both armies, and a permanent telegraph along the Rio Grande would allow them to transmit information about "individual outlaws" using the "secret service code."[12] Having so few friends on the U.S. side of the river, even among local authorities, forced the U.S. Army to seek allies among the Mexican military. Therefore, Mills proposed that the joint mission of "civilizing" the border be directed by the U.S. and Mexican armies employing the most modern technology available: the railroad, the telegraph, and the telephone.

Facilitating free and intelligent communication between the two armies would, Mills argued, build trust and allow them to act in concert more effectively against the destabilizing forces on the border. In 1884, and again in 1896, the U.S. and Mexican governments even signed agreements allowing their troops to cross the Rio Grande in pursuit of criminals.[13] This type of military cooperation was especially necessary because, as Mills complained, the federal and state authorities could not always be trusted to come to an agreement on how to proceed. Such ineffective civil authority, combined with the fear that "a great portion of the Mexican population on both sides are born revolutionists, and many American Texans have more or less sympathy with them," led Mills to conclude that the military was the only institution capable of governing this region.[14] And then in a contradictory but very revealing statement, Mills asserted that because of the inferiority of Mexico as a nation and a race, the United States had to take the lead in such matters: "I know the Mexican Character pretty well, and their officials are a better people than they generally get credit for with us, but being a weaker race and nation, with equal pride, they by the laws of nature look to us for advances in all that is mutual and reciprocal."[15] Mills thus credited Mexican officials with being better than most people believed, but still held them to be racially and nationally inferior. Despite their "equal pride," the "laws of nature" led them to look to their superiors in the United States for guidance. The ideology of racial hierarchy was so deeply ingrained in Mills's mind that even "all that is mutual and reciprocal" had to be initiated by Anglos in the United States.

Captain Bourke also had a detailed plan for how the army should proceed in the field to squash the rebellion and prevent further eruptions. On the technological side, he called for small sailing vessels to be outfitted with electric searchlights so that they could patrol the Rio Grande. Like Mills, he advocated the construction of a telegraph and railroad line along the river. However, Bourke went further than Mills by advising that pro-rebel printing presses be closed and that "domiciled aliens" not be allowed to plead in the courts against their arresting officers until after their own cases had been tried.[16] In addition to a system of surveillance, Bourke recommended the suspension of civil liberties.

In prosecuting the war against Garza, U.S. Army officers had to become familiar with the social conditions in South Texas and learn about the local culture. In short, they had to become gun-toting anthropologists. Their detailed reports from the field included testimony from their "informants" and spies, as well as their own commentary on agriculture, geography, customs, and kinship networks. These reports are thus rich sources with which to reconstruct the officers' views of the social composition of the lower Rio Grande Valley. Because they were meant to be confidential correspondence and took the form of field notes, reports often included important details that were later suppressed when published in newspapers and magazines.

In order to fulfill their mission of apprehending the Garzistas, officers had first to understand the social and material base of their support. It would be reasonable to suspect that officers skewed their reports to make themselves look better to their superiors. Yet despite such a bias, they still admitted incredible impotence and lack of success in obtaining information and capturing and prosecuting rebels. The officers' analyses of the rebellion varied according to their linguistic ability, relationship to the local population, and their particular personalities. They did not, in other words, all view the situation in exactly the same way, nor did they propose the same measures for dealing with the revolution. Nonetheless, they all shared certain assumptions about Anglo superiority and Mexican inferiority, which gave coherence to their writings. Ultimately, these reports provide an in-depth look into the perspective of outsiders, armed representatives of the U.S. federal government who were struggling to understand the Rio Grande Valley, if only to subjugate its people.

SMALLPOX AND SCATOLOGY

More than most other officers, Bourke saw his mission as a commercial promoter heralding the natural resources of the valley to Anglo entrepreneurs. His reports thus assumed the style of a prospectus for potential investors. San Antonio's Mexican consul was so impressed with Bourke's reports that he even suggested that together they organize a company to develop the commercial potential of the lower Rio Grande Valley.[17] The ease with which Bourke's narrative flowed back and forth between information about the Garzistas and the economic potential of the region illustrates the close connection between the two; ridding the valley of rebellious Mexicans and developing Anglo industries were seen as interdependent goals.

Bourke's dual military and commercial roles meant painstaking yeoman labor plotting maps, interviewing inhabitants and taking detailed notes on everything from political participation to ethnic identity to the flora and fauna of the area. One such scouting mission took him to La Grulla ranch, two miles from the river just southeast of Rio Grande City, because it had figured prominently in Garza's raid and was, from his perspective, "so out of the way."[18]

Bourke conducted a full demographic survey of the ranch, "visited every habitation and ascertained the name and occupation and whereabouts of all grown persons."[19] He discovered that eighty-five men voted as American citizens and that many more Mexicans had not been naturalized. Only eight or ten pupils were in attendance at the school run by a "native" Anglo American Texan, while there were more than thirty students at a private school in which instruction was given in Spanish.[20] Not only does this observation demonstrate the popularity of Spanish-language schools, it also indicates a marked preference for this type of institution over the English-language public schools. Given that schools were often the only regular presence of the state in isolated rural areas, such a rejection of state-sponsored education can also be seen in part as a rejection of the state.[21]

One of Garza's principal supporters, Cayetano Garza Elizondo, owned a store at La Grulla and many relatives of the Garzistas lived at this ranch, but after a thorough search Bourke found no trace of the revolutionists or of any arms.[22] Up until this point in his description, Bourke characterized the ranch and its people positively. He seemed genuinely happy that the people offered "no resistance or even objection to our presence"; the locals even offered them a breakfast of tortillas and black coffee.[23] And then, as if an afterthought, Bourke added that "we could see nothing unusual, excepting a maniac, old woman" who was chained by the leg to a stock post in the middle of a room in one of the houses. The woman had gone crazy after her son died of cancer, and would occasionally "tear off her clothing and run wild and naked through the chaparral."[24]

This image of madness and bondage must have stirred thoughts in Bourke's mind, because he followed it with an outpouring of disgust about the lack of hygiene in the community: "The shocking disregard for every hygienic consideration shown by some of the people living in 'La Grulla' deserves notice. They are filthy beyond description. We saw children whose scabby heads hadn't been washed for six weeks, and others suffering from catarrh, whose faces could be cleaned by nothing but a stream of water from a fire engine. There were adults who were not much better off and yet they were living amid the bloom of beautiful roses, morning glories, honeysuckles, Balsanes and Oleandero."[25] The comparison between people "filthy beyond description" and the "bloom of beautiful" flowers contrasted the potential of the Rio Grande Valley's natural resources (the flowers) and the lack of the right kind of people (Europeans, for instance) to develop those resources. "It is impossible," wrote Bourke, "to repress an emotion of regret that this great Valley has been neglected by two governments instead of being systematically cultivated and turned into a garden of fruits and flowers."[26] For now the captain focused his attention on the filth and disease, which he conspicuously noticed among the rural Mexican folk.

Bourke worried that during the winter places like La Grulla would become breeding grounds for smallpox, and he suggested a quarantine system to prevent the infection from spreading to military posts along the border. His concern about a smallpox epidemic extended less to the local population living there, however, than to the health and safety of the U.S. troops. Rather cryptically, Bourke commented that he had read somewhere "that the Plague and Cholera can be stamped out only by employing vigorous measures towards the pilgrims to Mecca and other shrines where all the rules of decency are violated."[27] These unnamed "vigorous measures" should, he proposed, be put "in practice here upon this river."[28] The fight would not be so much against the conditions that allowed smallpox or the plague to spread, but against those people who violated the "rules of decency." Given Bourke's previous commentary about the "disregard for hygiene" in La Grulla, it would not be too hard to predict who would bear the brunt of Bourke's "vigorous measures" to stamp out smallpox.

Bourke's offhanded quip that "he had read somewhere" about the theory of how to eradicate the plague and cholera by imposing cleanliness on the pilgrims to Mecca and other shrines illustrates the centrality of "stories" and "narrative" to late-nineteenth-century imperialist thinking.[29] A technique of control in the Middle East could quickly be appropriated for use along the Rio Grande. Military, economic, and health-related knowledge about how to control the colonized circulated regularly in scientific as well as popular journals. While cholera epidemics had also ravaged the United States in the mid-nineteenth century, Bourke tellingly refers to the "violation of decency" among the pilgrims to Mecca, thereby rhetorically linking Arabs, Africans, and Mexicans. Theories of racial hierarchy had become so prevalent by the end of the nineteenth century that notions of filth and disease could be easily and interchangeably attached to Arabs, Africans, Asians, and Mexicans. Imperial racial discourse crossed borders more easily than capital.

The obsession with cleanliness and hygiene was a serious academic interest for Bourke. He even published a dense scholarly book entitled *Scatalogic Rites of All Nations* (1891) which compiled his personal observations, field notes, and historical research from every corner of the globe. The book received international notoriety, and Sigmund Freud eventually wrote a foreword to the book, praising Bourke for his "courageous . . . [and] valuable undertaking."[30] In *Scatalogic Rites*, Bourke explained the religious significance of ceremonies in which participants consumed human and animal urine and excrement, as well as imbibed narcotics to engage in sexual orgies. Much of this book, however, merely compiles in empiricist zeal citation after citation of evidence from around the world of diverse sexual practices and the positions and sites in which men and women of different cultures urinate and defecate. He also provides examples of people in Germany, France, and the United States who ate their own excrement in order to show that such "primitive" customs still left traces even at the core of civilized society.[31] Although Bourke admitted that he was "thoroughly disgusted" by such practices, he felt "constrained to reproduce all that he ha[d] seen and read" in the interest of scientific knowledge.[32] The point of collecting these "disgusting practices" in a volume, Bourke argued, was to demonstrate modern society's distance in 1891 from such primitive behavior and thus measure "the precise extent of advancement in all that we call civilization."[33] Bourke's simultaneous repulsion and fascination with these "dark" and "dirty" subjects echoes his ambivalent attraction and disgust with American Indian ceremonies and Texas Mexican culture. By wearing the authoritative mask of a scientist, he allowed himself to observe and participate in the orgiastic and hedonistic rituals that he and his Caucasian "civilized" society condemned so vigorously.[34]

In his article "An American Congo," published in the widely circulated national magazine *Scribner's*, Bourke once again focused on the dirtiness of the people in the Rio Grande Valley. He first corrected the "popular fallacy that these people never use soap," arguing that they had no need for soap because they had various kinds of saponaceous roots. Then he contended that they bathed only once a year. "These Mexicans will sleep on the earthen floors of their hovels arrayed in the garments of the day, and these are changed only once a year, at Saint John's Day, in June, when whole villages may be seen on the river-bank taking the annual bath."[35] Thus Bourke the scientist explodes the myth about "these people" never using soap at the same time that he constructs other myths about Mexicans changing their clothes "only once a year."

At certain moments, Bourke's description of the people, habits, folklore, and landscape of the Rio Grande Valley illustrates great understanding and even sympathy for their plight. At other moments, within the same text, Bourke distances himself, categorically rejecting the people and culture of the valley as dark, dirty, and backward. In an Army report in late 1891 that would serve as the basis for his "American Congo" essay, Bourke made the case for increasing the size of Fort Ringgold. Drawn from observations from the previous eight or nine months he had lived in the valley, Bourke described the landscape, resources, and the people of the border through analogies to locations in Africa, first to Egypt and then to the Congo. "Of the population of this part of the Rio Grande Valley not much can be said. There are some few people of education and refinement, but the mass of the inhabitants are saturated with ignorance and superstition which have no parallel this side of the Congo."[36] This "mass" of people could not be counted on to develop the resources of the valley, in Bourke's estimation, because they belonged to a backward, superstitious, and "darker" era. As he noted, they were "firm believers in the Evil Eye, Witchcraft, Cures by Magic, Nouer l'aguilette, Sorcery, Incantation, and all other ideas of the same kind which prevailed in Europe from the time of the crusades until the French Revolution."[37] More than just preventing rebellions and stopping smugglers, Bourke proposed a cultural project to enlighten the "ignorant and superstitious" masses. He bemoaned the false rumors that neighbors spread about each other and quipped, "as in Ireland in its Dark days, so on the Rio Grande."[38] There were "thriving intelligent communities" within this "dark Belt," but they "exert about as much influence upon the indigenes around them as did the Saxon or Danish invaders upon the Celts of Ireland."[39] His linking the Celts of Ireland to backwardness is particularly revealing given his Irish ancestry. The images and cultural referents that he invoked set Ireland and Africa against England, France, and the United States, the former representing superstition, backwardness, darkness, and colonial territories and the latter symbolizing rationality, progress, enlightenment, and, most importantly, empire.

The "successful" development that occurred in the U.S. West following the Mexican-American War and the opening of transcontinental communication stood, in Bourke's eyes, in stark contrast to the "failure" to develop the lower Rio Grande Valley. In the U.S. West, "the wild tribes at the head of the Rio Grande were subdued and placed upon reservations, and the mineral and arable wealth of a great empire made available to the commerce of the world."[40] Here Bourke explained the particularly U.S. form of imperialism in North America, different from the British, French, or Spanish colonial schemes that required the labor of the natives. In the "great [U.S.] empire" the "wild tribes" were simply killed or removed, Bourke argued, and natural resources were exploited by colonists from the metropolitan center. The contribution of imported African slave labor is noticeably absent from Bourke's account of U.S. development. Bourke lamented, however, that "no such good fortune smiled upon the lower part of the Rio Grande Valley, which remains today, as it has been for more than forty years, a sealed book, a *terra incognita* to the rest of the United States."[41] Bourke sought to map this terra incognita, to discover it, to make it known to the rest of the United States, and to "make it available to the commerce of the world." Thus articles such as "An American Congo" carefully charted and categorized the land, resources, and people in such a way as to justify the dispossession of those already there. The anthropological and geographical study of the region was an integral part of the colonizing mission.

"An American Congo" also included a few success stories of men in the valley who had commercialized agriculture and cattle, thus proving that abundant natural resources existed. Monsieur Brulé, we are told, produced over 600,000 pounds of sugar on two hundred acres near the mouth of the Rio Grande. The King family's Santa Gertrudis ranch with 750,000 acres, the Collins ranch with 500,000 acres, and the Young-MacAllan ranch were all trotted out as examples of what could be accomplished by "intelligent men with moderate capital."[42] Not surprisingly, all of Bourke's examples of intelligent men had non-Spanish surnames. "It goes without saying that these people live in a manner far different from that of the native-born smugglers and bandits, who are content to exist, while quietly waiting for the moment when a small lot of goods can be slipped through the '*resguardo*' (custom-house officers, their enemies to the death)."[43] Thus, in contrast to the energetic, intelligent, and entrepreneurial Euro-Americans, the "lazy natives," refusing to produce on the "rich soil," waited around to receive contraband merchandise. The only impact that "American ideas and improvements has made . . . upon these Rio Grande Mexicans," Bourke declared, was that "the sewing-machine has forced its way into the most squalid ranchos," and that the coal-oil lamp, American locks, carbines, revolvers, saddles, and cotton goods had followed suit.[44] It was possible for Rio Grande Mexicans to be changed by American "ideas and improvements," but like the sewing machine's entry into the "squalid ranchos," the process would require a fair amount of force.

The seeds of progress therefore already existed in the valley, but they had, according to Bourke, been suffocated by the "degraded, turbulent, ignorant, and superstitious population" (read Mexicans), who earned their livelihood through smuggling rather than developing agriculture. Bourke refers to two periods when the valley had the chance to develop, but he blames the "Mexican element" for missing these opportunities and returning to its old ways. The first of these "ethnic storms," as Bourke called them, came with General Zachary Taylor's army, resulting in the United States taking over the valley and what would become the U.S. West. After "the tempest abated," Bourke lamented, "the Mexican population placidly resumed its control of affairs and returned to its former habits of life as if the North American had never existed."[45] The second "wave of North American Aggression" refers to the period during the U.S. Civil War when the Confederacy turned the port at the mouth of the Rio Grande into a major shipping point for cotton. However, as he does regarding the first period, Bourke argues that after the "tempest abated" commercial energy dwindled and the people reverted to "old-time apathy."[46]

In an excellent chapter in his book *Dancing with the Devil*, José Limón hypothesizes that Bourke's ambivalence toward Mexicans derived from his own ambivalence about being Irish American. Limón points out that many of the same stereotypes used to characterize Celts in the mid-nineteenth century as "undisciplinable, anarchical, and turbulent by nature," were the same ones Bourke used to stigmatize Mexicans.[47] In the passage where Bourke recalled the two "North American Aggressions" in South Texas, Limón finds him "coping with his own repudiated and projected self-ambivalencies. For even as he thought of Mexicans as degraded, he seems at least subconsciously and critically aware that they, like his Irish forbears, also were victims of an unjust conquest and domination."[48] This analysis explains well the contradictory testimony provided throughout Bourke's published and unpublished writings. His "thick description" of the valley and interest in Mexican border culture indicates some degree of respect and admiration. However, another voice within him always covers his praise with a blanket condemnation of the "degraded and turbulent" Mexican masses.

While perhaps internally ambivalent, Bourke's propositions for the Rio Grande Valley were very straightforward and unambiguous: "My proposition is to Americanize the Valley, and let the people see that the government is determined to reward all who defend its interests, as well as protect them against their evil-disposed neighbors."[49] How would this "Americanization" happen? Bourke contended that the only way to succeed in the long run was to have the army reward by employment those who had helped crush the Garza movement. While the departments of state, treasury, post, justice, and agriculture should be equally interested "in suppressing disorder and in opening up that Great Valley, the War Department," Bourke argued, "was the best qualified to superintend the task."[50] His proposal to have the War Department manage the Americanization of the valley did not, however, mean just a military occupation by U.S. federal troops. Such crude social management had failed in the past because, he stated, "no matter how many troops may be sent into the Valley of the Rio Grande, the character of the population will remain unchanged and, upon withdrawal of the garrisons, the old-time bandit element will resume ascendancy."[51] After all, if "the great armies of General Zachary Taylor, 1846–47 and of General Herron (Brownsville, 1863–65, 10,000 to 15,000 men) left scarcely any impression upon the general tone of thought, the manners or customs of the population," a strictly military policy could never work.[52] Instead, Bourke recommended that thirteen people, some of them ex-Garzistas who "know the Valley thoroughly and know its population," be employed by the army.[53] These Spanish-speaking authorities would police the Mexican population and thereby "let the people see that the Government is determined to reward all who defend its interests." Coercive force alone could not forge hegemony; rather, they needed to convince Mexicans in the valley that their interests lay with the U.S. government and not with their "evil-disposed neighbors." Like the successful creation of the Indian Civil Service, whereby Indians, under their British superiors, micromanaged the colony, Bourke intended to superintend the valley through loyal Mexican civil and military servants.

In an interview in a Brownsville newspaper, which subsequently was reprinted throughout the country, Bourke elaborated on his social engineering proposal. Based on the regiments of "negroes" and Indians, he sketched out a plan to make a "battalion of carefully selected young Mexicans." As an incentive to "Americanize" these young recruits, he advised giving only half pay to those who did not speak English and full pay to "those who can and will speak it." Feminizing the valley and masculinizing the occupying force naturalized the Anglo colonization. After a half a century of "so called occupancy by the American element," Bourke complained, "[the valley] looks more like a poor 'widdy' woman's farm than anything else." The army captain's solution for his young Mexican recruits was to "try and make men out of them instead of having them run about in the chaparral like coyotes and wild hogs."[54]

Bourke was not alone in comparing border Mexicans to undomesticated animals such as "coyotes and wild hogs."[55] The *San Antonio Express* rhetorically linked the Garzistas to both animals and Indians by arguing that "these cutthroats are neither Mexicans nor Americans—they are simply coyotes and a premium of $100 a piece should be offered for their scalps."[56] The *Gazette* in Fort Worth exclaimed that the revolutionists were "entitled to no more consideration than the wolves that prey upon the cattle there." Such references desensitized the public to the plight and humanity of Mexicans who were being shot like dangerous wild animals by the U.S. Army and the Texas Rangers. These comparisons paved the way for the *Gazette* to proclaim that "the only effectual crusade against them is a warfare of extermination."[57] Although Bourke was not the only one to dehumanize Mexicans by portraying them as coyotes, his words had a greater impact because they were reproduced in newspapers throughout the country.

"THE CHEAPEST THING TO DO IS
TO SHOOT THEM DOWN"

At the outset of his mission, Captain Bourke kept his soldiers on a short leash to prevent them from overstepping their authority or making unjustified arrests. Believing that people were falsely accusing their personal enemies of being rebel sympathizers, Bourke left the job of arresting suspects to the deputy marshals. As he said, "I do not intend to allow the troops of my post to be made the instruments of oppression for innocent parties."[58] Bourke compared his prudent and respectful attitude to that of the Mexican officers "who have martial law of the stringent kind on the other side of the river, and who arrest every man or women on the merest suspicion." "I am certain," Bourke boasted, "that I am acting according to the spirit of our own Constitution."[59] He thus extolled his own restraint and glorified the U.S. Constitution that compelled him to respect the presumption of innocence until he found proof to the contrary. Furthermore, while denying any inappropriate behavior, he shifted the responsibility for his troops acting as "instruments of oppression" across the river to malicious Mexicans informing on their neighbors. A short while later, Bourke modified his orders, instructing soldiers to arrest only armed men "against whom a reasonable suspicion might attach, but to be careful not to harass innocent parties in violation of the 4th amendment of the Constitution."[60] He added that he always "insisted upon the presence of US deputy marshals with proper warrants for the apprehension of 'suspects.' "[61]

Bourke's prudent and restrained attitude began to change after one of his own men died in a shootout with the rebels. On December 22, 1891, Corporal Charles Edstrom was killed in a particularly bloody and grueling battle against Garza's forces near Retamal, Texas. He was shot twice through the head and once through the leg. Two other soldiers were slightly wounded, but the killing of Edstrom, whom Bourke called "a most excellent soldier," made a deep impression. The fact that Edstrom's "face was powder burned" proved to Bourke's satisfaction that not only was he killed in combat but he was ruthlessly shot point-blank after he had fallen.[62] In his diary entry, Bourke painted Edstrom's final moments in courageous brushstrokes: "Edstrom fell with his face to the foe, but before he went down, one of the enemy felt the force of his carbine and the trueness of his aim."[63] The fact that the soldiers wore a full uniform and were "plainly seen" by the Garzistas suggested that they knew they were shooting at U.S. troops. Just after Edstrom fell, the troops pushed ahead in hot pursuit. As they gave chase, according to Bourke, they heard the Garzistas shouting in English and Spanish, "Kill the d——d Gringoes!" "Matenlos-Gringos cabrones!"[64]

Perhaps it was the brutality of Edstrom's death, shot twice in the head and at close range, or the rebel yell "kill the damned gringos," but Bourke now demanded vigorous action: "So long as the American government dilly dallies with these people, they will continue to plan and combine against Mexico, while at the same time they hate the very sight of the Damned gringos."[65] And then, in a separate paragraph, as if a new thought had occurred to him, Bourke blurted out: "The cheapest thing to do is to shoot them down whenever [they are] found skulking about with arms in their hands, and to burn down some of the ranchos which give them shelter."[66] A year earlier in his diary Bourke had penned a similar phrase of sarcastic condemnation of the massacre of Sioux Indians at Wounded Knee: "The cheapest thing for our Government to do now will be to shoot down every man, woman, and child wherever found."[67] This time, however, the sarcastic criticism became a declarative proclamation. Less than a month after refusing to have his troops used as "instruments of oppression," Bourke had decided to direct the oppression himself. The death of his comrade and the sense that the Garzistas "hated the very sight of the Damned Gringos" weighed heavily on his mind, the Constitution and the assumption of innocence be damned. While initially he had been careful to avoid violating people's legal rights, he now had a different modus operandi. In a memorandum to the War Department, Bourke advised shooting on sight any nonuniformed men who fought soldiers.[68] As he put it, "technicalities should be brushed aside like cobwebs and the only principle of action be that enunciated by Gen. Sheridan — 'hit 'em again and hit 'em hard.' "[69]

Corporal Charles H. Edstrom received a full military burial in Rio Grande City. The soldier's corpse became a patriotic symbol, literally shrouded in the stars and stripes of the U.S. flag. After Edstrom's casket was borne through the town to its final resting place on the banks of the Rio Grande, Bourke read the service for the dead from the Book of Common Prayer. The *Express* waxed poetic about "the last sad honor" Edstrom received as his comrades turned their weapons south and shot volleys that "died out in a sound in far off Mexico." As the sun set over the Rio Grande, the bugle played "taps" and "all eyes were moist as the sad notes stirred the hearts of the listeners."[70] Edstrom's life and death, captured so vividly in the *Express*, cried out for revenge.

"THE GREATEST LIARS ON THE FACE OF THE EARTH"

The troops' feelings of danger and insecurity were exacerbated by their lack of knowledge of the Rio Grande Valley. First, they were outsiders who had little or no prior understanding of the physical or social geography of the area. Second, few of them spoke Spanish and thus they could not communicate effectively with the rural population. Finally, the memory of U.S. soldiers invading this area and starting the Mexican-American War had not faded. Officers seemed perplexed by Garza's popularity among the Mexican population, but they were positively indignant about the sympathy that he enjoyed among Anglos and local authorities.

After learning nothing about the fugitives in his first extensive scouting mission at the La Grulla ranch, Bourke concluded that "the apprehension of fugitives had best be left to the US Deputy Marshals who know the population."[71] The military's role would be limited to checking the ranches occasionally "to let the people know that they are watched by the Army, for whom they have both fear and respect."[72] The deputy marshals, many of who were Spanish-speaking Mexicans, would have an easier time gaining the trust of locals and obtaining information about the Garzistas. Captain Francis Hardie also employed Mexican deputy sheriffs to accompany him on his scouting missions because, he argued, "it was utterly impossible for me wearing the uniform of the United States Army to gain any information as to the whereabouts of Garza and his band."[73] The problem was not only Mexicans but that the Anglos also sympathized with Garza. Exasperated, Hardie claimed that "the people along the river, Whites and Mexicans, seem all favorable to his cause, with the humble exception of Mr. Robert W. Haynes, the sheriff of Zapata County, and Mr. McConnel, the collector of Customs at Carrizo, Texas."[74] While clearly an exaggeration, that he could only think of two people along the whole border who did not sympathize with Garza illustrates the rebel's popularity among both Anglos and Mexicans.

Border people resisted the army with what political scientist James Scott calls the "weapons of the weak."[75] These tactics of lying, feigned ignorance, slander, deception, and dissimulation thwarted the troops' efforts and allowed Garza to escape capture, and all of this could occur without them ever having to openly confront the army. While army officers eventually figured out that they were being lied to and led astray, it was virtually impossible for them to respond to such pervasive and subtle forms of resistance. It is important to emphasize the symbiotic relationship between the subtle forms of resistance and open confrontation. Without the help provided by thousands of common folk who undermined the army's mission, the armed insurgents would quickly have been discovered and arrested. The fact that the insurgency ultimately failed and that many rebels were arrested should not be surprising given the imbalance of resources (arms, money, communication, and transport) favoring the government. What is truly remarkable is that the rebellion survived as long as it did. To understand this success we have to look at the vast network behind the men who took up arms.

A large network equipped the Garzistas with arms, munitions, and food, provided safe haven for them, and supplied the men to fill the ranks of Garza's Mexican Constitutional Army. U.S. Army Captain Chase estimated that nine-tenths of the population was either "active in their support of the Revolution (assisting it in various ways by contributing supplies, furnishing information, etc. etc.) or they were prevented by fear or other reasons for taking active part against the Revolutionists."[76] He concluded that "they are all just alike—Mexicans in favor of Garza and the Revolution."[77] Judging from the abundant supplies found at one rebel camp, including "120-159 Winchester Carbine cartridges to the man, . . . saddle bags loaded with coffee, sugar, fresh beef, and wheat biscuits made with baking powder," the rebels seemed "well equipped." Captain Bourke complained that "the Rio Grande valley is practically unanimous in support of Garza whose followers buy all the ammunition they want and all their necessaries."[78] Newspapers such as the *San Francisco Examiner* came to the same conclusion, stating bluntly, "a census of Garza's sympathizers in Nueces and Duval counties, Texas, meant and still means simply a census of people living there who bear Mexican names. The same is said to be true of all the counties of Lower Texas."[79] Although it would be difficult if the troops were confronted by an openly hostile population, at least they would know who the enemy was. The problem in this case was that they could not even identify their foes because those who claimed to be "friends of the United States and enemies of Garza . . . secretly sympathize with his cause."[80]

While officers recognized that their inability to obtain accurate information demonstrated Garza's popularity, it also confirmed their belief that Mexicans were congenitally disposed to lie. Mexicans would "lie about [Garza] when it suits their convenience" Captain Hunter complained, "or tell the truth when they consider that the best policy."[81] Army Captain Hardie lamented that "when a man was hauled up, a wrong name was sure to be given and Mexicans can stick to a lie in the face of anything better than any known race." "Mexicans of this border," he insisted, "are the greatest liars on the face of the earth."[82] The message was clear: "they" were never to be trusted.

The evidence suggests that Garza's sympathizers engaged in a willful and highly successful effort to undermine the army by misleading them or simply feigning ignorance. When officers received a tip as to Garza's whereabouts, they would invariably spend days getting there to find nothing or to discover that they had been led astray. "A great deal of harm has been done by these jawbone friends of Garza," who, Bourke protested, "have been reporting Garza and his confederates in so many places that the troops have been worn out running each lie to earth."[83] More frustrating perhaps was the foot dragging and deception by Mexican guides and trackers. While more subtle forms of sabotage probably went unnoticed by officers, on at least one occasion this form of resistance became so obvious that Lieutenant Hedekin felt compelled to pen a report condemning Mexican guides.

Hedekin and his men were out in the countryside searching for the rebels when the lieutenant sent his Mexican guide, Martiano Arce, to investigate the source of some smoke emanating from the pasture of wealthy Laredo businessman and rancher Antonio Bruni. The guide returned, declaring that it was just a campfire of some of Bruni's cowboys. Hedekin later discovered that the men identified as Bruni's cowboys were actually some forty Garzistas who were camped just a short distance from him. Undeterred, Hedekin insisted that the guides find the Garzista trail. Finally, after much urging, the guides discovered a trail leading southward. As their superior the lieutenant had some power over his guides, but his comments reveal that his control was severely limited by their resistance: "I found it impossible to get them to move quickly. The guides then declared that they could go no farther although the night was the clearest moonlight, and I was therefore compelled to camp, probably within a few miles of the outlaws."[84] Not only does this show a willful desire on the part of the guides to mislead and undermine the troops, for whom they were allegedly working, it also demonstrates that they could be extremely successful. The lieutenant, despite being their boss and military commander, found it "*impossible* to get them to move quickly" and was "*compelled* to camp," even though almost within reach of the Garzistas.

Hedekin believed that "all of the poorer class along this border," even his own guides and scouts, "belong to or sympathize with these outlaws." He especially suspected one Mexican scout, Martiano Arce: "In the first place [Arce] persuades me not to go down the river where outlaws intended to cross. He leads me aimlessly through the brush for two days. Then he takes me to a camp three days old. He prevents me from attacking a camp in Bruni's pasture and then he has the effrontery to tell me that he cannot follow a large trail by bright moonlight. This trail led to a camp near Lopeña from which the bandits crossed the next day into Mexico."[85] Thus, not only did his scout not pursue the Garzistas with zeal, but apparently he knew where they would cross and led Hedekin in the opposite direction. Bring in either Arizona Apache or American cowboy scouts, the lieutenant recommended, because they were "better trailers than any Mexican and neither will play one false."[86] The lack of cooperation by

15. Scout Billy July, date unknown. July participated in what was probably the unit's last armed conflict in 1893, fighting the remaining Garzistas in South Texas. His granddaughter, Ethel July, is currently one of the leading black Seminoles in the Brackettville–Del Rio area. (Courtesy of William "Dub" Warrior)

Texas Mexicans finally forced the army to hire undercover Mexican military spies to infiltrate the rebels.[87]

By late summer 1892, U.S. military authorities had ceased their persecution of the "bandits" due to a scarcity of scouts and the government prohibition on using Mexican Army guides in Texas. "A company of blacks and Indians" who were excellent backcountry trackers were sent to the border to fill the void.[88] In early October, this group of over twenty black Seminole Indian scouts were moved from Fort Clark in West Texas to Fort Ringgold in Rio Grande City and were put to work pursuing the rebels (fig. 15). In fact, the very last battle that the detachment of black Seminole Indian scouts fought occurred during the campaign to capture Garzistas on February 23, 1893. The Seminoles performed so well on the Rio Grande that Brigadier General Frank Wheaton praised them as "intelligent, brave and reliable trailers," and claimed that "little or nothing was accomplished until they were utilized."[89] However, as discussed above the army officers also recognized the need to use local Mexican guides, and thus they found themselves caught in a catch-22 situation: even though the Seminole scouts performed well, without the local Mexican guides they obtained no information and yet with the local guides they were continuously led astray.

One of the subterfuges employed by Mexicans to sabotage the army's persecution of the Garzistas was even memorialized in a corrido about Ranger Captain Hall.

> El diez y seis de diciembre
> salió Hall de San Ignacio
> a seguir los pronunciados, ay
> pero salió muy despacio
>
> En el rancho de Don Proceso
> se dió el primer agarrón
> con un costillar de vaca, ay
> lo hicieron con bonito jalón
>
> (On the sixteenth of December
> Hall left from San Ignacio
> to follow the pronunciados, ay
> but he left very slowly
>
> In Don Proceso's ranch
> he got his first tug
> with a cow's rib, ay
> they gave him a good jab)[90]

The corrido begins with Hall chasing the pronunciados from San Ignacio on December 16, and the song mocks by stating "pero salió muy despacio" (but he left very slowly). We find out in the next stanza that he had his first "tug with a cow's rib," referring to Hall's indigestion after eating barbecued ribs at Don Proceso's ranch. In 1954, folklorist Américo Paredes recorded several corridos about the pronunciados sung by Don Proceso's son, Mercurio Martínez. In this interview and in a book he cowrote, Martínez explained how his father gave Captain Hall such a big portion of barbequed ribs that he fell asleep and missed the opportunity to chase the Garzistas.[91] The corrido thus gloats about the ways in which Mexicans obstructed the Rangers without directly confronting them. Given the un-equal power relations, with the biggest guns in the hands of the Rangers, along with the legal authority to use them, border Mexicans had to be-come creative in their resistance. Stuffing the Rangers with food to cause indigestion could be a powerful weapon against men who had to spend many bumpy hours riding their horses through the chaparral.

As in the case of the corridos, the struggle between Mexican and U.S. Army troops occurred in the cultural realm as much as on the battlefield. Theater was one of these sites of struggle. In the main border towns like Nuevo Laredo and Brownsville, performances and theater stages were more formal than they were in smaller outposts like Rio Grande City. In the latter town, a big corral behind the Garza supporter Manuel Guerra's dry goods store served as a makeshift theater. The Pastorelas, or Miracle Play of the Shepherds, recounting the birth of Jesus Christ, grabbed Bourke's attention because it provided evidence to link the border to the Middle Ages. By showing that border Mexicans lagged behind Europeans and Anglo Americans on an evolutionary cultural scale, Bourke confirmed his racial theories as well as justifyed his civilizing mission. Bourke wit-nessed rehearsals and full performances of the Pastorelas, and he even copied the full libretto into his diary. The play was a thinly veiled moral lesson about the struggle between good and evil.[92]

What is especially interesting here is the way that Mexicans on the border incorporated Bourke into the narrative. The managers of the Pas-torelas play wanted "to have the Devil represented as a cavalry officer." When Bourke, clad in a cavalry uniform, offered them the use of an infan-try uniform, they refused; it had to be a cavalry uniform.[93] Theatrical performances were safe cultural spaces that allowed border Mexicans to represent and work through the moral quandaries they faced in this time of great social upheaval. That a cavalry officer like Captain Bourke should be portrayed by Mexicans as the devil should not be surprising given the role that he was performing in his real life.

While Mexicans were busy dressing up Lucifer as a cavalry officer, Bourke's analysis of border theater and culture exoticized Mexicans by placing them beyond the bounds of the U.S. nation and of modern civiliza-tion. In this study of the Pastorelas in South Texas, anthropologist Richard Flores argues that Bourke's writings were part of an "American nationalist modernism" that "required the displacement of indigenous peoples, Mexi-cans included, so as to reconstitute them not as active agents of American-ism, but as relics of a bygone era."[94] However, even in the push to marginalize them, not all Mexicans were equally displaced. Some Mexicans would become the agents of modernization on the border while others would have to be "purged."

Bourke's task was finding out which sectors of society, and even which individuals, would be best suited as colonial agents. He emphasized this point in an interview with a Washington newspaper about the rebellion. There were two kinds of Mexicans in Texas, he argued, "those who reside in towns — such places as Laredo, Brownsville, Matamoros, Corpus Christi and San Diego are in the main very decent people and of course have nothing to do with these troubles." On the other side was "the belligerent class . . . made up of the worst elements that ever stood in the way of civilization. . . . Their character is utterly devoid of principle and in all their utterances there is no semblance of patriotism. . . . They live from hand to mouth and are altogether extremely undesirable people to have any dealings with." In addition to being criminals, Bourke accused these "bad Mexicans" of being lazy and of making no effort to raise crops. The Rio Grande Valley would prosper, he argued, "but before such a desirable condition is possible we must purge ourselves of the detestable class that now prevents civilization from putting its foot in the valley of the Rio Grande."[95] For Bourke, the Garzistas were part of the "belligerent class," and his job was to "purge" them.

"KILL THOSE GREASERS": THE WHITE MAN'S BURDEN ON THE TEXAS BORDER

Whether the weapon was a big barbecued rib, a miracle play, or a Winchester rifle, there was a low-level race war underway on the Texas-Mexico border. Although some Anglos supported Garza and some Mexicans fought against him, race played a crucial role in determining alliances among pro- and anti-Garza forces in Texas. Images of an impending race war kept Anglos on edge as the Garza revolt stretched into its sixth month. In February 1892, the wealthy Duval County rancher N. G. Collins wrote a private letter to Governor Hogg insisting that if the "Garza men are not hunted down soon . . . this matter will drift into Brigandage and a Race war which you know means the ruin of this whole section of country."[96] John J. Dix sent a letter that same month to General Mabry, predicting a "War of Races" and asserting that "Garza was imported to cause 'race feelings and contests.' "[97] Contrary to these Anglo fantasies of a race war, Garza welcomed and received Anglo aid in the form of ammunition and supplies. Nonetheless, almost all of his soldiers were Mexicans or of Mexican descent. Of the 130 men charged with violating the neutrality laws in connection with the revolution, only three did not have Spanish surnames.[98] Given the highly charged racial situation in South Texas, it would make sense that the Garzistas would view the U.S. Army and Texas Rangers in racial terms and vice versa. When the rebels yelled, "Kill the damned gringoes!" they were expressing a collective resentment toward the Anglo Americans who had come as guests but ended up taking over their houses and expelling the hosts.[99]

The Garzistas's use of racial epithets like "gringo" and "Yankee" to describe Anglo troops was matched, if not surpassed, by the virulent racism expressed by the U.S. press throughout the country. For example, an article by the *Galveston Tribune*, reprinted in the *San Antonio Express*, proclaimed that "if Garza destroys Uncle Sam's Army, Texas will rise up hot as a hornet and stamp the revolutionary greaser out of existence."[100] The *Chicago Post* ran an article entitled "Kill Those Greasers" in which they advocated a violent solution to the disturbances on the border. The article stated that the military "should shoot all the 'revolutionists' on sight without parley. These wretches are the scum of a disorderly population and know no law but that of the rifle. They may or may not have rights, but our troops should not therefore hesitate. The sooner the war is removed from the Texas border to Washington, the sooner the 'Greasers' will learn to respect a nation which they have always treated with contumely."[101] Thus the "Garza affair" provided Anglos with an opportunity to vent and hone their racist attitudes about Mexicans. The very presence of Mexicans in the United States instilled fear in Anglos who worried incessantly about the day when the "disorderly" Mexicans would rise up and reclaim their land.

Although Anglos worried about a Mexican takeover of the U.S. Southwest, it was the Anglos who invaded and occupied this Mexican territory fifty years earlier. Backed by notions of manifest destiny, these Anglos projected onto Mexicans living in the United States their own imperialist desires to invade Mexico. Beyond the issue of land, Anglos worried about the pernicious effect of racial mixing. Even those who favored the annexation of Mexico by the United States felt that it would be detrimental to the racial purity of the nation. In 1892, an Indiana newspaper adopted this perspective, pointing to the biological problem of annexing Mexico: "If we could get the territory without the population it would be a good thing. But hybrid races are very undesirable acquisitions, especially when of

Spanish and Indian origin. The 'greaser' as a citizen is eminently objectionable."[102] A New Jersey newspaper in 1893 explained that because Mexico was not able to handle its own problems it will, by "manifest destiny," become part of the United States. The article spun out the scenario that "Mexico will be annexed; the peons and half breeds would not be consulted. It would make no difference to them, so long as they could lie in the sun and only work when they felt like it. They would be fit only as servants, as hewers of wood and drawers of water."[103]

These crude racist sentiments were backed by the scientific discourse of Social Darwinian and eugenic theories that had gained popularity throughout the United States and Europe at the end of the nineteenth century.[104] As well as justifying the obscene wealth of industrial magnates, Social Darwinism had a racist component that served to legitimize U.S. intervention in Cuba, Panama, Puerto Rico, and the Philippines. Similar arguments justified English and French imperialism in Asia, Africa, and the Caribbean. As one newspaper put it, because "the Latin races appear to lack the qualities to adapt themselves to a republican form of government," Anglo Americans would have to assume the "white man's burden" and run their countries for them.[105] Years after the rebellion, a small Laredo newspaper even reprinted a stanza from Rudyard Kipling's poem "The White Man's Burden." This widely circulated poem, written by a racially mixed Anglo Indian, poignantly expressed the racist justification for imperialism: "Take up the White Man's burden and spread Civilization."[106]

FRONTIER MASCULINITY

Spreading civilization was a common theme in easterners' journeys out to the West. Equally important, however, was the masculinizing effect that the "wild" West could have on the eastern man. Popular nineteenth-century writers from the eastern states such as Ralph Waldo Emerson and Walt Whitman worried that industrialization was emasculating men, leaving them alienated both from themselves and from nature. For these poet-philosophers, the debilitation of the self-reliant male individual endangered the American character and thus eroded the foundation of the nation itself. It was not only the militant working classes who threatened middle-class men, but also the increasing assertiveness of the nonwhite races. In 1898, the trumpeting of middle-class masculinity, white racial supremacy, and U.S. empire came together dramatically in the media-friendly image of Theodore Roosevelt's Rough Riders bringing "civilization" to Cuba on Roosevelt's charge up San Juan Hill.[107] Reporters and illustrators covering the campaign against Garza provided images of brawny rangers and soldiers displaying their muscles in the harsh Texas sun. It was a feast for a country hungry for displays of "primitive" frontier masculinity.

Harper's reporter Richard Harding Davis devoted a whole chapter of his book *The West from a Car-Window* to a glowing description of the bravery and self-reliance of the Texas Rangers and U.S. troops who pursued the Garzistas. This chapter, originally published in *Harper's Weekly*, used the Garza episode as a mere backdrop for exhibiting the strong bodies and vigorous action of the soldiers and Rangers. While the text portrays the soldiers' heroism and bravery, the illustrations that accompanied both the article and the chapter provide an even more dramatic and sexualized rendering. Frederic Remington, the famous illustrator at *Harper's*, drew the soldiers in erect poses in full uniform with knee-high riding boots, hats tipped at cocky angles, and long pistols hanging from their waists. In addition to the portraits, there was an illustration of soldiers "searching a suspected revolutionist" (see figs. 13 and 14). The Mexican revolutionist is standing shoeless next to his horse while two soldiers pat him down, presumably for weapons. The one soldier standing directly behind the revolutionist has his hands on the suspect's waist while his long rifle protrudes from the soldier's pelvis to the suspect's rear.[108] The overall effect of these visual clues is to render the shoeless Mexican as subordinate and passive next to the dominant and active soldiers.

Davis's description of the Garza affair does with words what Remington did with images: depicting the soldiers as active agents and the Garzistas as passive subordinates. The *Harper's* reporter summed up the entire revolt as follows: "It is only of interest to the Eastern man to know that a Mexican ranch-owner and sometime desperado and politician living in south-west Texas proclaimed a revolution against the Government of Mexico, . . . and that followers of this Garcia [sic] should not be allowed to cross through Texas on their way to Mexico." It was not uncommon for journalists to mistakenly refer to Garza as Garcia or even to switch willy-nilly between the two names. The lack of precision about something as basic as Garza's name was symptomatic of an utter lack of interest in understanding the revolution, and it reflected a genuine inability to make a distinction among Mexicans. Remington visually reinforced the notion that all Mexicans were alike by drawing the soldiers' Mexican guide in an almost identical manner as he depicted the "suspected revolutionist" (figs.

16 and 17). In his article Davis studiously avoided an explanation of the revolutionaries' goals or demands, and instead used the revolt as a screen on which to project his homoeroticized fantasies about this remote border. It was an opportunity to show Anglo men in the field displaying their muscles and raw masculinity. "The Garza campaign is only of interest here," Davis admitted, "as it shows the work of the United States troops who were engaged in it."[109]

It was not only about displaying U.S. soldiers in action, but these bodies had to be set in rugged, dangerous, and exotic landscape. When Davis described the region as the "darkest Texas," an unmistakable analogy to the popular nineteenth-century phrase "darkest Africa," he was highlighting its foreignness and distance from the "civilized" East Coast. Captain Bourke would further develop this comparison between the Rio Grande Valley and Africa in his "An American Congo" article.[110] While Davis's stated purpose was to correct some of the fanciful images of the West as portrayed in Buffalo Bill's Wild West Show, his book actually reinforced such myths. Writing in the third person from the perspective of the "Eastern man," he rendered his travels "across the prairie of cactus and chaparral" from San Antonio to Laredo to Corpus Christi in a highly romanticized manner. The eastern man, Davis wrote, would feel "assured that at least he is done with parlor-cars and civilization; that he is about to see the picturesque and lawless side of the Texan existence, and that he has taken his life in his hands." The journalist was not disappointed as he quickly found the exotic and cartoonlike border that he had imagined. Right in front of him, on the train to Corpus Christi, Davis witnessed a "young man with the broad shoulders and sun-browned face and wide sombrero" shooting at the telegraph poles as they went by. The rugged young man was, we are told, "Will Scheely [Sheley]," a Deputy Sheriff who was one of the leaders of the anti-Garza campaign.[111] By writing the story as a third-person description, Davis universalized his experiences and created border character types: the rugged Ranger; the cool, yet untamed sheriff; the cowboy; and of course, the "Mexican bandit."

The Texas border was the "backyard of the world" for Davis, the most inhospitable place to live on the planet. To underline the point, he quoted General Sheridan's infamous words that "if he owned both places, he would rent Texas and live in hell." It was a fight over this strip of land between the Nueces and the Rio Grande that led to the Mexican-American War, and Davis joked that given the "utter desolateness of the land . . . we should go to war with Mexico again, and force her to take it back."

16. The caption for this Frederic Remington illustration reads: "U.S. Cavalry Hunting for Garza on the Rio Grande." (*Harper's Weekly*, March 5, 1892, p. 220; courtesy of the Rare Book, Manuscript, and Special Collections Library, Duke University)

17. The caption for this full-page Frederic Remington illustration reads: "Garza Revolutionists in the Texas Chaparral." The original drawing was done in color. (*Harper's Weekly*, January 30, 1892, p. 113; courtesy of the Rare Book, Manuscript, and Special Collections Library, Duke University)

The landscape could not have been painted as more bleak: "It is a country where there are no roses, but where everything that grows has a thorn. . . . It is a country where the sun blinds and scorches at noon, and where the dew falls like a cold rain at night." More than just a harsh and desolate climate, this was a land that was thoroughly Mexican, where "no white men, or so few that they are not as common as century-plants, live in it."[112] The exaggerated picture of the harsh conditions highlighted the feats of the Anglo American soldiers who were on a mission to tame this "wilderness" of thorns, blinding sun, and Mexicans.

Nature and animals were the oft-employed metaphors used to represent the essence of masculine power, but like nature and wild beasts masculinity had to be harnessed and civilized. Davis admired that the Anglo soldiers were "living as near to nature and . . . to the beasts of the field, as men often come." He also praised the "wonderful powers" of an exconvict Mexican scout because the "picturesque ruffian" had the "gift of second-sight cultivated to a super-natural degree."[113] The scout's ability to know how many horses had passed along a trail hours earlier and his joy in charging after a camp of revolutionists made him seem more animal than human. While the Anglo soldier's bravery was tempered and controlled by the laws of society, the Mexican scout was depicted as a wild and uncontrollable force of nature. Remington's illustration of the mounted guide showed him as a virtual extension of his horse (see fig. 14). The whip attached to the guide's wrist echoes the movement of the horse's tail, and the energy captured by freezing the movement, display the synchronicity between horse and man. In creating these vivid and colorful portraits of the border, both Remington and Davis played on one of the most popular themes of nineteenth-century ideology: the struggle between civilization and barbarism. Articles and illustrations such as these justified the expansion of the military presence on the border by raising the counterinsurgency operations to the level of a battle for the nation and for civilization itself.

"ANOTHER SPIRIT IS NEEDED"

Spreading civilization and looting the colonies of their natural resources required a good transportation network. Up until the railroad arrived, rivers served as the main vehicle for colonization. For those explorers searching for the source of the Nile in the mid-nineteenth century it was as if traveling up the rivers or arteries would lead them to the heart of Africa and thereby open up the "dark continent" for colonization and commercial development. Given the lack of an adequate road and rail system, rivers provided the only efficient means to travel through and transport goods from Africa's interior. A similar absence of roads and railroads, especially in the lower Rio Grande Valley, made the Rio Grande a major artery for transportation in spite of its tortuous curves. Beyond its utilitarian purposes, the river also represented for Captain Bourke the channel by which civilization could be brought to remote sections of the border. Domingo Sarmiento, a nineteenth-century Argentine politician, went so far as to attribute the "barbarism" of his country's interior to the lack of navigable rivers. It was not just the absence of appropriate rivers that was to blame however, but also the lack of racial ardor among the Argentines, who had not transformed their rivers into conduits for European civilization and commerce as had the North Americans. "Another spirit is needed," he wrote in the 1840s, "to stir these arteries in which a nation's lifeblood now lies stagnant."[114]

For Bourke, the Rio Grande was just such a major artery that had been left to stagnate. On his journeys up and down the Rio Grande, Bourke commented repeatedly on the poverty and lack of beauty of the natural scenery. "There is nothing picturesque about the lower Rio Grande: the channel is tortuous, the water turbid, the current variable, now rushing swiftly against the soft sandy-clay banks and biting off piece after piece, now languidly trickling over sand bars, or caressing a snag torn away from its home in the mountains of Colorado. There is no vegetation but a thick matting of 'jarral' close to the bank and behind it, scattered about, a few mesquite or ebony bushes." The bleak description of the land and riverscape was only matched by a dreary review of the people and their homes: "There are few habitations and not one of any pretentions to comfort and decency. One cannot fill notebooks with descriptions of half-clad, open-mouthed boys and girls standing on a bluff, half-starved cows gazing out upon us from the brush, an occasional detachment of Mexican soldiers moving up or down the Valley, the shooting of a few ducks or geese — or the soaring away of an indignant hawk from its nest in the tree-top." If the flora, fauna, landscape, and people could not inspire note-books full of writing, Bourke was duly impressed with the blue sky, the "glorious burst of invigorating sunshine," and the potential for commercial agriculture. The view from the river provided the necessary disgust at the absence of "civilization" and wealth, and at the same time it allowed for the possibility of colonization. As Bourke wrote, "the field is open for enterprise, intelligence and money."[115] They only lacked the "spirit," that "lifeblood of the nation" to which Sarmiento had alluded so elliptically.

Bourke's writings were designed to encourage that "spirit" necessary to develop the valley. Even when not published under his name, journalists often used Bourke's reports as background source material. This recirculation of Bourke's impressions by various authors and newspapers led to an artificial manufacturing of consensus. Rather than competing portrayals or at least diverse perspectives on the Mexicans in the Rio Grande Valley, the vast majority of these articles came to the same conclusions and employed the same adjectives and metaphors. The astonishing homogeneity was not a coincidence; the information all came from the same reports by Bourke and other army officers.

A detailed analysis of one article about Garza's revolt illustrates how this process of "manufacturing consent" worked.[116] A *Herald* reporter in Chicago opened his article on "Garza's Revolution" with a poetic description of the landscape of this "terra-incognito [*sic*]," comparing it unfavorably to the "bad-lands of Dakota, the arid plains of Wyoming, the sage brush deserts of Nevada, and the chalk and sandstone coast range of California." The Rio Grande Valley was simply the "worst," according to this reporter. "Of all the hopelessly barren and God-forsaken regions that ever lay outdoors, that section of country extending from Laredo to Brownsville along the Rio Grande and north as far as the Nueces is the worst." The author combined descriptions of the "dismal" geography and starving livestock with an equally depressing account of the Mexican inhabitants of the region. While admitting the difficulties posed by natural obstacles, the journalist made sure to attribute the degradation and poverty he witnessed to the laziness of the natives. "When a Mexican ranchero is not too lazy — which is very seldom — he will feed prickly pear to his starving animals, but for the most part they must shift for themselves. The prickly pear plant is prepared for feeding by burning off the millions of little thorns, but as this required first the cutting of the plant, that means more work than most Mexicans will ever consent to do."[117] Did this journalist observe this laziness from his railroad car, or did he merely add this ethnographic note based on reports he had heard?

The *Herald* reporter's firsthand description of the devastation wrought by a four-year drought in the region helped him explain why people might have been "ripe for revolution": namely, material deprivation. However, rather than draw a conclusion from this observation, the reporter retreated to a racial explanation that he gleaned from another source. "It must be remembered," he implored, "that the desolate region of the Rio Grande is occupied by a very motley throng of humanity. All are of Mexican and Indian ancestry. Occasionally are found the descendants of some American outlaw, or some fugitive fleeing from a pursuing Sheriff, but for the greater part the population is made up of the ignorant Mexican peasantry. Though nominally Americans, they are apparently unconscious of the fact that they live within our boundaries and under our laws." Although the reporter recognized that many of "them" were legally "Americans," "they" (read Mexicans and Indians) still remained the "other," unwilling to conform to "our" (read Anglo) boundaries and laws. Then, by directly invoking the colonial comparison, drawn I might add from Bourke's own fascination with the conquest of the Congo, the article continued: "It is doubtful if Stanley in Africa ever found a much more benighted people. In thought, habit, speech, and dress they are as thoroughly un-American as they can be. In respect for law or race or government they are just as anti-Mexican. They are 'agin the government-' 'agin every government.' They hate Díaz as cordially as they detest 'Los Gringos.' "[118]

While changing a few words and slightly altering the references, the *Herald* reporter clearly lifted his description from Bourke's December 10, 1891, report in which he compared the population of the Rio Grande Valley to the Congo. The similarity becomes obvious when Bourke's earlier report is compared to the newspaper article. For example, Bourke stated: "In thought, habit, speech and dress they are essentially anti-American, but they are also anti-Mexican. They have no sympathy with either government."[119] Whole phrases like "in thought, habit, speech and dress" were plagiarized, as were Bourke's ideas and observations. To see how this reporter summarized Bourke's observations, compare the following excerpts:

Herald: Their superstitions border on the grotesque. They have little confidence or faith in priests, but they believe in weird incantations, cures by magic, "evil eye," and all forms of sorcery and witchcraft, some of which have been handed down from the middle ages.[120]

Bourke: To maker clear how thoroughly superstitious these people are . . . I noted down all their superstitions and weird remedies, and found that they were firm believers in the Evil Eye, Witchcraft, Cures by Magic, Nouer l'aiguilette, Sorcery, Incantation and all other ideas of the same kind which prevailed in Europe from the time of the crusades until the French revolution. They still have the miracle plays of the middle ages.[121]

From the comparison of the Rio Grande to the Nile to the comparison of the fertile Rio Grande as a potential "garden spot" (*Herald*) or "garden of fruit and flowers" (Bourke), the reporter simply adopted Bourke's insights without citing him as the source. In the most blatant example of this plagiarism, the journalist copied a whole paragraph directly from Bourke's report. In fact, it looks as if the reporter had access to Bourke's original report, in which he placed quotation marks around the paragraph he plagiarized. This paragraph argued that building railroad lines through the Rio Grande Valley would forestall future revolts, and the valley, "instead of being a source of annoyance and expense to both nations, would bloom like a flower garden."[122]

The point here is not just that this reporter plagiarized or lifted ideas from Bourke, a common practice of shoddy journalists, but that articles such as this disseminated Bourke's observations and metaphors to a wider audience. Moreover, when several different authors began to use the same adjectives, describing Mexicans as "lazy" and "superstitious," such labels achieved legitimacy and currency. While the process of forming the cultural and racial stereotype for Mexicans in South Texas cannot be credited solely to Bourke and surely predates him, key intellectual figures play fundamental roles in articulating those stereotypes as graphic images and poetic metaphors. Captain Bourke was just such a figure whose literary skill, not to mention his military prowess, helped him to colonize the lower Rio Grande Valley for Anglo capital. The image of the "lazy" and "dirty" Mexican was both the prerequisite and the byproduct of this process.

THE MYTH OF SILENT NATIVES

Imperial domination has always been predicated on the myth of silent natives and unpopulated territory. Colonizers filled in blank spaces on pieces of paper as a way of feeding the fantasy that they had created the colonized from nothing and nowhere. Quite literally, the empire placed the colony and the colonial subject on the map. In spite of evidence to the contrary in their own reports, officers in pursuit of Garzistas continually cast Mexicans as illiterate and mute. If "they" could not speak, then "we" would have to speak for them, to describe their habits, customs, and history. Such was the logic that compelled Bourke to describe this "terra incognita" in such great detail, while at the same time systematically dismissing and silencing Mexican narratives.

Several Spanish-language newspapers existed in the Rio Grande Valley at the end of the nineteenth century, with Laredo alone boasting at least three of them. While each probably had a small circulation, they were all influential enough to compel President Díaz and General Reyes to sue Garza for libel on several occasions and to maintain other newspapers to counterbalance the opposition press. Bourke, for instance, blamed Garza's newspaper *El Libre Pensador* for "influencing the minds of the ignorant" and turning them against the government.[123] This newspaper and others he found in the valley were, he noted, "filled with denunciations of President Díaz, calling him 'traitor,' 'liar,' 'scoundrel,' 'thief,' 'assassin,' 'culprit,' 'rascal,' 'outlaw,' and other epithets."[124] Bourke was thus fully aware that these Spanish-language newspapers offered a counternarrative to the effusive praise for President Díaz found in most of the English-language press. This counternarrative was especially dangerous because, according to Bourke, the mass of "ignorant" Mexicans believed it.

A few years later Bourke denied the existence, not to mention the impact, of this Spanish-language press, and he claimed to have found high levels of illiteracy among the Mexican population. "Newspapers are never seen," he asserted, "and the number of books in the whole region from Piedras Negras to the Laguna Madre and from the Nueces to the Rio Grande, excluding the American ranchos and the large towns and some school-books now in the hands of children, will not foot up one hundred."[125] While he exaggerated claims about Mexican illiteracy in popular magazines such as *Scribner's*, his scholarly publications told a different story. In the *Journal of American Folk-Lore*, Bourke referred to the widespread presence of books in the region, commenting that "it is a mighty poor family in the Rio Grande valley that do not own and keep for constant consultation an 'oracle' or dream book."[126] Scholars could be trusted with the truth. For the general public, on the other hand, he had to prove the "ignorance" of Mexicans to justify their subjugation, even if it required shading the truth.

In his description of La Grulla ranch, Bourke carefully noted that the private Spanish-language school there had three times as many students as the public school. Here was strong evidence that rural Mexicans valued education, and even preferred to pay for their own school rather than send their children to the public one. What Bourke could admit in his private field report had to be excised in the more public magazine article that served a broader function of justifying the government's intervention in the valley. "The State of Texas, like the Republic of Mexico," Bourke asserted, was "making heroic efforts to break down the barriers of ignorance and superstition, and schools are springing up on every side and in every hamlet, which in another generation will be telling their own story."[127] He knew that at that very moment they were "telling their own story," but that story had to be erased from historical memory because it clashed with the narrative of a "heroic" government enlightening an ignorant population.[128]

WAR AGAINST PEACE, OR A NEW ATTILA

The propaganda efforts of Bourke, Matías Romero, and others succeeded, for the most part, in discrediting Garza's movement. It was only by silencing the Mexicans on the border that Bourke could have portrayed Garza's supporters as outlaws and bandits. It was not the case, however, that Mexicans had no voice; it was just that very few people were listening. In 1895 a Rio Grande City newspaper, *El Bien Público*, published a pamphlet titled *War against Peace, or a New Attila* (La guerra contra la paz ó un nuevo atila) attacking Captain Bourke as a "new Attila." The cases that were brought against Bourke in the courts had long since been dropped and the bullets had ceased flying almost two years before. So, why should *El Bien Público* have gone through such an effort to print this condemnation? They did it not for specific practical reasons but because they understood the importance of representing their side of the story. They could not allow Bourke's "insulting" portrayal of the border in his article "An American Congo" to go unanswered. So they translated Bourke's entire article into Spanish and then carefully argued their case: "Sr. Captain John G. Bourke instead of bringing peace to these regions, only came to make war on defenseless and peaceful citizens, and his campaign was accompanied by cruelty and devastation, identifying him with that famous Atilla, that is the scourge of God." As editor Jesus T. Récio put it in the prologue, they were incensed not only by Bourke's negative characterization of the border inhabitants, but by his "calumny . . . against the whole *raza Mexicana.*"[129]

In a four-page introduction, Récio criticized *Scribner's* for allowing Bourke to represent himself as an "innocent traveler," rather than as an army captain with a mission. Given that Bourke was able to present his side of the story, he demanded that *Scribner's* publish their commentary as well to give their readers the chance to judge the two stories for themselves. *Scribner's* never accepted the challenge, and Récio's story was never translated into English. Bourke, he asserted, "sowed terror among the peaceful inhabitants and scaring with threats and insults the elderly, women and children or defenseless neighbors, [he created] such disorders and outrages that even his own soldiers who accompanied him looked on with indignation and reproached his conduct."[130] The charges leveled against the army captain included burning the ranches of suspected Garzistas, threatening to hang them, entering their houses without warrants, and stealing guns, private papers, and horses. These accusations had already been formally submitted to the army, the district attorney, the attorney general, the governor of Texas, President Harrison, and the highest authorities in Mexico. However, as *El Bien Público* complained, even after formal complaints had been issued and the testimony of the aggrieved parties was published in the San Antonio *Daily Express*, none of these officials had condemned Bourke's actions.

The pamphlet reads like a legal brief, reprinting earlier articles from the *San Antonio Express* and *El Bien Público* and publishing letters that substantiated the case against Bourke. One petition, sent to Governor James Hogg on February 18, 1892, by employees and citizens of Starr County, suggested that Bourke had illegally acted as if the country was under martial law. Their protest made it clear that they had no complaints against any other U.S. Army official, only Bourke. They also emphasized that they had no personal vendettas against Bourke; in fact, they wrote that "socially we respect him as a refined and cultured gentleman."[131] *El Bien Público*'s rhetorical strategy of limiting their complaints to Bourke, and only to his official actions, underlined their loyalty to the U.S. Army and undermined Bourke's charges that they were only motivated by a personal vendetta against him.

The petitioners also rhetorically positioned themselves as defenders of the United States against Mexican corruption and illegality. They complained, for example, that Mexican General Garcia had sent over agents to provide false testimony in court cases against suspected Garzistas. Defending the sanctity of the truth, they declared: "We protest energetically against the introduction in American territory of such vicious and corrupt methods." Taking on the role as protectors of the border, they argued that American values were being threatened by the manner in which the war against Garza was being prosecuted. And, finally, they flatly condemned Garza's revolt at the same time that they argued equally strenuously against Bourke's actions: "While we condemn in the most energetic terms the disorderly movement of Garza and consider that it has occasioned in this area of our State grave and long-lasting harm, and while we are ready with all of the means that are available to us to help to suppress it, we consider that the acts for which there have been complaint (by those who should be the guardians rather than the oppressors of the people) are no less subversive of our civil rights."[132] The petitioners thus argued that they were on the side of law and order, and that Bourke was, like Garza, causing disorder and undermining U.S. civil rights. In this way, they appropriated the discourse of order and protection of America as a weapon against Captain Bourke.

On July 3, 1892, *El Bien Público* published an article titled "The Glorious Fourth," in which they waxed poetic about the U.S. Declaration of Independence and compared the destruction wrought by the king of England's troops in the American colonies to that of Bourke's troops on the border. " 'We hold these truths to be self evident,' " they quoted, " 'that all men are created equal; that they are endowed by their Creator with certain unalienable rights: that among these are life, liberty and the pursuit of happiness.' "[133] In another article, a week later, they specifically cited Bourke for violating the U.S. Constitution's Second and Fourth amendments guaranteeing the right to bear arms and protecting against arbitrary search and seizure. Bourke's campaign against the Garzistas was, for them, akin to the French Revolution's reign of terror. All of the peaceful citizens, they asserted, had been disarmed by the army, leaving the Garzistas as the only ones left with weapons.[134] By shrewdly basing their case on the nation's foundational texts, they undermined Bourke's effort to exoticize Texas Mexicans on the border and portray them as outsiders. Given that the pamphlet was published in Spanish, and presumably intended for a Texas Mexican audience, the decision to base their defense on the U.S. Declaration of Independence and the Constitution cannot simply be dismissed as an opportunistic attempt to appeal to Anglo American sensibilities. Rather, they chose these uniquely U.S. cultural references because they were beginning to see themselves as U.S. citizens and to assert their rights as such. When they said "*our* ancestors freed themselves" (my emphasis) referring to the U.S. Declaration of Independence, they were clearly claiming a genealogical connection to the United States.[135] They were Americans, but of Mexican origin.

The pamphlet *War against Peace* is written almost as a dialogue with Bourke. It is the kind of exchange that rarely if ever occurred because of the social distance between the U.S. troops and the Mexican population on the border. *El Bien Público* understood well the message behind Bourke's comparison of the border to Africa, and it countered with its own insults: "We hope that the Captain is not angry that we call him the new Atilla, but first he compared the Rio Grande to the Nile and later with the Congo. We are sure that tomorrow or the day after he will compare it to the Rhine, the Seine or Manzanares and we will be justified to compare him to Hannibal, Alexander the Great and Napoleon the First."[136] In other words, if you paint us as Africans we will portray you badly as well, but if you see us as European (like Germans, French, or Spanish) we will compare you to great military leaders. Although *El Bien Público* questioned Bourke's attempt to exoticize the border, it did not challenge his portrayal of Africa as backward and negative. In fact, it seemed to share Bourke's assumptions: Africa was bad, Europe was good.

In "An American Congo" Bourke painted border Mexicans as racially inferior to their European counterparts. *El Bien Público*'s response, however, illustrated its own thinly veiled racism towards blacks. After recounting how Bourke had refused to let ranchers use their own water, they stated that "even if one of the black soldiers he brought had been the commander, he would not have committed such barbarous actions." And then, throwing the association with Africa back upon Bourke, they suggested that he had made the comparison with the Congo because "a portion of his troops were of the African race and surely he *dreamed* of Africa."[137] They derided Bourke for depicting the Mexicans of the lower Rio Grande Valley as degraded and ignorant, and they asked sarcastically, "Well, Señor capitan, are you *enmarihuanado* (a pot-head) . . . ?" This was not idle speculation; Bourke's ethnographic investigations had led him to collect specimens of marijuana that he sent back to Washington for analysis.[138] Further, rather than the Mexicans being degraded, they contended that the most destitute people lived northeast of San Antonio, and that "these people . . . were not Mexican, but Americans of the white race, born and bred in Texas." The whole point was to turn the tables on Bourke by claiming that he was obsessed by Africa, was worse than a black soldier, and that white Texans were lazier and more degraded than Mexicans. They also defended the history of miscegenation on the border by declaring, "The children of these, upon reading in these pages where their parents are insulted and called degraded people, cannot but, filled with indignation, curse the author of these calumnies."[139]

El Bien Público, however, went beyond the racial argument, and countered each of Bourke's negative assertions about Mexican cleanliness, as well as about their motivation for emigrating. To Bourke's charge that Mexicans wore ratty clothes, they rebutted that certain workers required such clothes but when these workers went to the city they dressed up. Instead of Bourke's claim that they bathed once a year, the pamphlet claimed that Mexicans bathed almost every day in the summer. Finally, in response to the assertion that Mexicans who came to Texas were thieves and assassins, they contended that Mexicans crossed the border because they were "tired of fighting to establish an administration in their towns that banishes nepotism and monopolies," and they desired to be in a country where everyone was equal before the law. And then, metaphorically wrapping themselves in the American flag, *El Bien Público* explained that Mexicans, "not being able to realize their goals [in Mexico] they have emigrated to this country that covers with its mantle all honorable and peaceful citizens who come and shields them under the flag of the stars."[140]

In order to prove their respectability, and to respond to Bourke's assertion that he could find few books or newspapers in the lower Rio Grande Valley, *El Bien Público* reproduced a five-page exchange between Starr County Judge John Kelsey and the superintendent of public instruction in Texas. Although Kelsey noted that few children in the area knew English, he had a plan to instruct them bilingually in both Spanish and English. This letter thus showed that the authorities in the lower Rio Grande Valley were actively seeking to educate the populace, and especially to teach them English. As to Bourke's claim that everyone rejected medical doctors and instead relied on *curanderos* (Mexican folk healers), they responded that there were few curanderos and fewer people who believed in them. And, the curanderos who existed, they argued, were less pernicious than the astrologers and charlatans who advertised in U.S. newspapers. To Bourke's charge that border Mexicans were superstitious, they claimed journalistic objectivity and affirmed their belief in freedom of religious expression. Bourke, they concluded, must have been motivated by a "certain hate for the inhabitants of this region" to portray them as he did in "An American Congo."[141] *El Bien Público* thus challenged the accuracy of Bourke's account, and claimed cultural respectability for Lower Rio Grande Mexicans. In short, they declared Mexicans in Texas were educated and modern citizens who wanted to learn English and participate fully in their society.

The pamphlet *War against Peace* proves that border Mexicans were very capable of explaining their predicament and articulating a response to the negative portrayals being published in national magazines and newspapers. "We have seized the pen to say something in favor of our brothers," they wrote, "because it seemed to us that leaving in silence such gross and gratuitous insults by the famous captain, would be like confirming them."[142] The only problem, and this is crucial, is that Bourke's version received much greater exposure, especially outside of the border region, than did *El Bien Público*'s response. Although they asked *Scribner's* to give them equal space to refute Bourke's assertions, their story was never translated and never reached a national audience. Indeed, only scattered copies of the dozens of late-nineteenth-century Spanish-language newspapers on the border have been preserved, making it difficult to reconstruct alternative narratives. In the war of words, it was not the quality of the argument that counted so much as the ability to reach a mass audience and the institutional structure to insure long-term preservation.

STANLEY, KURTZ, AND BOURKE

As an ethnologist and intellectual, Bourke was well versed in the widely publicized explorations that set off the "scramble for Africa" in the 1870s. The references to the Congo and Nile in Bourke's reports and articles, as well as the citations in the bibliography of *Scatalogic Rites*, indicates that he was familiar with the African exploits of Henry Morton Stanley.[143] Stanley's "discovery" of Livingston in 1871, his explorations of the source of the Nile, and his subsequent work in the 1880s as a colonial administrator for the Belgian monarch Leopold made him one of the most famous and most controversial figures of his day. His brutal methods fell under increasing attack after he led a mission to Bumbire in the mid-1870s to punish the native inhabitants for earlier attacks on Europeans. Both the British Anti-Slavery Society and the Aborigines Protection Society publicly condemned Stanley's "act of blind and ruthless vengeance" and urged the British government to return Stanley to the scene of the massacre and hang him.[144]

The character of Kurtz in Joseph Conrad's *Heart of Darkness* was in part based on Stanley's life in Africa, and one senses a kindred spirit between Stanley, the fictional Kurtz, and Captain Bourke. Stanley and Bourke both came from subjugated parts of the British empire, the former being born in Wales and emigrating to the United States when he was sixteen years old, and the latter having Irish parentage. Both distanced themselves from their heritage; Stanley even denied his past and spoke with a heavy American accent. Both took part in the colonizing of the U.S.

Western frontier in the mid-nineteenth century. Further, both fought in the U.S. Civil War, with Stanley starting on the Confederate side and switching, after being made prisoner, to the Union cause; and with Bourke fighting for the North. Both traveled through the western frontier and lived in Omaha, Nebraska. Although they apparently never met, these two men had similar family backgrounds, had lived in the same frontier locales, and traveled in complementary intellectual circles. Significantly, it was Stanley's experience on the western frontier that prepared him for his exploratory and colonial pursuits in Africa, and not vice versa.[145] The link that Bourke and others made between South Texas and the Congo was thus not as far-fetched as it may sound. Both were "frontiers" from the Anglo American and European perspective, both were inhabited by "darker" people, and both provided the stage for ambitious and enterprising young men to make themselves famous.

Although Bourke never achieved the international notoriety of H. M. Stanley, he attracted a great deal of attention on the border, and most of it was not positive. Bourke may have been winning the public relations war in the national and international press, but he was being outflanked on the border, in the courts, the pages of the local press, and in the field of battle. It was Bourke's heavy-handed pursuit of the Garzistas, including illegally breaking into houses of suspects, violently threatening families, and arresting the men, all without warrants, that finally came back to haunt the army captain. Individuals who had suffered the brazen attacks by Bourke, together with local officials, protested to the governor of Texas and even went so far as to bring charges against Bourke in the courts. In one contrast with Africa, then, in South Texas not only were the "natives" not silent, they were fairly well connected.

LEGIS BASCILLUS AND OTHER VERMIN

The court battles between Bourke and the well-to-do Garzistas began when Garza's father-in-law, Alejandro González, traveled to San Antonio in February 1892 to meet with General Stanley, commander of the Department of Texas, to issue a complaint against Bourke. Before he could arrange the meeting, however, Bourke had González arrested by U.S. marshals on charges of "aiding and abetting Garza in furnishing subsistence and horses with which to carry on the movement."[146] In spite of Bourke's best efforts to jail his accusers, Governor Hogg referred charges to Brigadier General Stanley in March 1892, accusing the army captain of "exceeding [his] authority in entering without warrants the houses of Garza sympathizers and arresting the inmates."[147] The accusations originated with a complaint signed by J. R. Monroe (Starr County judge), Henry Hord (lawyer), Manuel Guerra (merchant), W. W. Sheley (Starr County sheriff), Ignacio Ramírez, Jesus Maria Ramírez, Wenceslas Hinojosa, and T. W. Kennedy. The fact that the complaint was signed by a multiethnic group, including one of south Texas's wealthiest Texas Mexican merchants, a lawyer, a sheriff, and a judge, demonstrates just how many sectors of society Bourke had managed to alienate with his tactics.

The petition detailed abuses by Bourke such as threatening William C. Chamberlain that if he harbored revolutionists Bourke would "burn [his] ranch . . . over the heads of his wife and children." He was also accused of entering José Ramírez Arce's ranch, arresting him without warrant, and announcing to his family that he had orders from his commanding general to kill them and burn their ranch. The accusations went on and on for three typewritten pages, recounting the numerous times that Bourke, without any legal authority, had broken into houses, threatened the inhabitants, and stolen or burned their property. The last part of the complaint focused on the ill effects on the U.S. legal system of using spies from the Mexican government to testify against Garzistas. Two of these "spies" had already been arrested for perjury, and they argued that the continued use of such witnesses would "undermine the safety of the citizens and residents of this frontier." While they condemned Garza's revolution and vowed to help suppress it, they considered the army's behavior "as no less oppressive of our civil rights."[148]

Bourke dismissed the charges as being politically motivated, noting that Monroe and Hord were lawyers for the Garzistas and that, with two exceptions, the rest of the signers were either "under indictment or to be indicted for complicity in the Garza movement." Sheriff Sheley, he argued, had signed the protest because "he was clinging to the Mexican vote for reelection, and Kennedy, a poor, broken down, drunken druggist . . . did not, in all probability know what he was signing."[149] It is noteworthy that of the eight signatories four had Anglo surnames: although Bourke directed his harassment primarily at Mexicans, Anglos publicly joined Mexicans in their condemnation of the U.S. Army.

Not wanting to wait for military justice to deal with Bourke, Laredo's District Attorney Hicks announced that he would bring criminal charges against the army captain in county court. In a letter to a Texas representative in the U.S. Congress, Hicks made it clear that "Bourke and his men" were the targets of his complaint, and not the other U.S. soldiers: "Their actions have been shameful, and if perpetrated against Americans instead of citizens of Mexican birth, would probably have met with armed resistance. He has subjected to arrest without warrant residents of that locality against whom no accusation was ever uttered and subjected them to such ill treatment afterwards that the people actually are afraid to venture out of their homes upon their own land. They frequently come to me for passes to go short distances on legitimate business so that they may not be turned back or made prisoners when they meet the soldiers. Think of that in the United States!"[150] This picture of harassment was dramatized by focusing on an incident where Bourke and his troops had broken through a door and invaded a house in the middle of the night after having been refused entrance. "The senseless arrests and gross ill-treatment of other innocent persons" had caused a general "terror" and compelled residents to let their cattle starve to death rather than risk traveling long distances with them to find food and water.[151] The many court cases against the Garzistas also gave Mexicans an opportunity to speak out against the army's harassment. Manuel Flores, whose nephew's house had been ransacked and robbed by Bourke's troops, testified that "we all feared on account of the violence of this Captain that they would be fired upon and badly treated by him."[152]

After his arrest in San Antonio, González, Garza's father-in-law, had his attorney come to Palito Blanco to take the affidavits of several people in the area who had suffered harassment by Bourke in mid-February 1892. The *San Antonio Express* ran a sympathetic article that represented González as a "highly respected" and "wealthy" rancher who, even though he never became a naturalized citizen, had lived near San Diego for twenty years. In the newspaper, González's attorney recounted the accusations against Bourke by asking a few questions of the reporter:

First, what would you think if the officer in command who, after arresting a man in person, would slap the prisoner in the face and curse and abuse him until stopped by his brother officer? Second, who after placing a prisoner under arrest, not only cursed him but choked and abused him, drawing a pistol, putting it up to the prisoner's head and demanding of him which way he wanted to die, by being shot or hung? Third, forcibly entering a man's premises at the dead hour of night and smashing down his door? Fourth, entering houses and making searches without any warrant or authority from a civil or military court? Fifth, prohibiting a man from using water from his own well for either his family or his friends. Sixth, marching armed forces into the private enclosures of a man and taking possession of same.[153]

These were not only abuses of power but gross violations of constitutionally protected rights of privacy and property. By highlighting the lawlessness of the troops, they were able to turn the discourse about "outlaws" on its head. González's attorney even convinced the *Express* to publish the affidavits from four witnesses who gave detailed accounts of Bourke's threats and harassment.[154]

Shortly after all of this publicity, District Attorney A. J. Evans gave Bourke new instructions to avoid pursuing the Garzistas because they had already been broken up into small parties. The district attorney insisted that Marshal Fricke and his deputies should be the ones pursuing and arresting the rebels. Bourke was supposed to provide assistance only to Fricke, and then only when he applied in person and gave the name, locality, and offense of the wanted person.[155] These new procedures were designed to keep Bourke away from the police duties that had gotten him into such trouble. Thus, the next time Deputy Marshal Bañados asked for some of Bourke's soldiers to go with him to Palito Blanco where Garzistas had been spotted, Bourke flatly refused. Citing Evans's instructions, Bourke told Bañados that "it was against the law to send troops until civil authorities had exhausted all powers, and Deputy Marshals had made attack, and been killed, wounded or driven back." The very next day, after receiving a report from the Rangers that they had located a camp of two hundred Garzistas, Bourke gave his troops their marching orders.[156] He was in a difficult position. If he sent his troops after the Garzistas, he could be accused of overstepping his authority, but if he refused to pursue them, he would be guilty of dereliction of duty. In Bourke's estimation, the whole mess could have been avoided and the Garzistas squashed if Texas had only been "placed under martial law at the outset of the revolution by an order from President Harrison."[157]

Even though General Schoefield submitted the case against Bourke to the secretary of war, he recommended that no action be taken by the military until after the civil cases in the matter had been concluded.[158] Meanwhile, Texas Representative Crain was called before the House military committee to give evidence in the case against Bourke. Crain explained that he had no such evidence but had only acted at the behest of a

San Antonio attorney who represented the people claiming to have been injured by the army captain. The committee declined to hear the case and referred it to the military.[159] Even though Bourke had his share of enemies, he also had his supporters along the Rio Grande. In the midst of his court battles Captain Kelley, a major steamship operator in the region, told him that "many of the old, respectable and prominent citizens of Rio Grande City . . . wished to send a paper to the President repudiating any sympathy with the Garza movement, or with the action of certain shyster lawyers in casting slurs upon officers of the US Army."[160] The Nueces County grand jury that heard the case against Bourke and his troops also found "no just grounds for such complaints." The grand jury explained that none of the witnesses "could or would testify to any fact reflecting upon the course or conduct of any officer of the United States Army," and those who had accused Bourke in the newspapers had not shown up in court.[161] With the exoneration from the grand jury in Corpus Christi and the refusal of the House Committee to hear the case, Bourke felt confident that he had put an end to the legal attacks by "shyster lawyers" in Texas.[162]

It would not be the end of Bourke's court battles, however. The embattled army captain spent the better part of the following year testifying against Garzistas in San Antonio. Even though the rebels proved adept at using the legal system to their advantage, the federal judge's rulings suggest that he tipped the balance to favor Bourke and the U.S. government's case. One particularly egregious example of bias was Judge Maxey's use of Bourke as the Spanish interpreter for the court. Given that many of the documents were written in Spanish and many of the defendants spoke only Spanish, having a partisan interpreter clearly posed a conflict of interest. However, when one of the defense attorneys declined to recognize Bourke as a "competent Spanish interpreter," Judge Maxey stated his trust in Bourke's abilities and offered to have him sworn in as the court's official interpreter.[163] While Bourke was apparently fairly proficient in Spanish, one can only imagine what could have been lost or added as the army captain interpreted the words of the same people he had arrested and terrorized.

Bourke showed particular contempt for the Garzista defense lawyers, whom he referred to in one article as "Legis Bascillus" and "vermin." The government's lack of success in the courts was, according to Bourke, a result of the wanton intimidation of witnesses by the Garzistas. He mentioned several cases where government witnesses were either kidnapped, held under house arrest, or taken across the river and shot to prevent their testimony in court. In one case, Bernardo de la Garza, who had supported the Garzistas and then turned against them, received a threatening letter that instructed him to bury $3,000 in a certain location or else "his 'friends' would attend to his case with due promptness."[164] In another instance, a former rebel was branded a lunatic by his friends after he began cooperating with the government. The former rebel, Manuel Cadena Canales, who was Garza's uncle by marriage, was, according to Bourke's account, almost forcibly shipped out of the area to prevent his collaboration with the army. Bourke implored the government to protect its witnesses if they ever hoped to put an end to the turbulence and prevent violations of the neutrality laws. Given the dangers of testifying for the government, he concluded that it was "a most extraordinary thing that the courts were able to extract any information."[165]

THE STRANGER

In spite of earlier statements indicating that Bourke would adopt a less active and aggressive posture in the persecution of Garzistas, he continued to play hardball and consequently continued to inspire the ire of border people. In March 1893, Sheriff W. W. Sheley arrested Captain Bourke on eighteen counts of false imprisonment and harassment (figs. 19 and 20). The charges stemmed from Bourke's arrest of eighteen Mexicans in Starr County on the suspicion that they had violated neutrality laws. The arrests were made without warrants and the men were held for one week before they were brought to court. Worse than the illegality of the arrests, however, were the accusations of torture. According to the arrested men, Bourke had tied ropes around their necks and threatened to hang them in order to extract a confession. Others said that Bourke threatened to shoot them if they did not give him information about other Garzistas.[166] While such charges were never proved one way or the other, there is evidence that Bourke was at least thinking about the justification for such harsh punishments at about this time. At the end of January, he quoted *Wharton's Digest of International Law* in his diary to prove, to himself perhaps, that "un-uniformed predatory guerilla bands are regarded as outlaws and may be punished by a belligerent as outlaws and murderers."[167] At the end of his diary entry for February 25, just a day after he was arrested, Bourke pasted in a three-line clipping from an article in the *Journal of American Folk-Lore*. It read, "The ancient Welsh laws authorize the killing of three classes of men on sight, — the outlaw, the madman, and *the stranger*."[168]

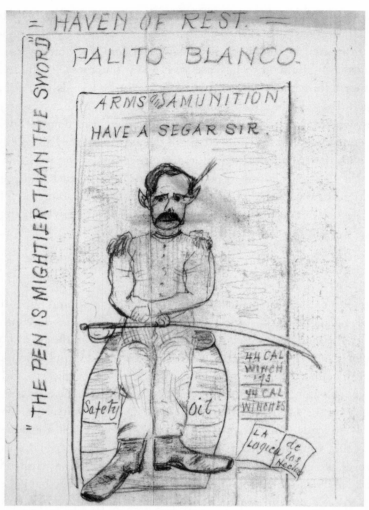

18. Drawing of Catarino Garza by Captain John G. Bourke in his diary. Bourke's depiction of Garza with horns coming out of his head indicates that he viewed him as a devil. He also appears to have a noose around his neck. The quote on the side, "The pen is mightier than the sword," foreshadows Garza's later explanation of how he "put down the pen to pick up the sword." Note also the depiction in the lower-right-hand corner of Garza's autobiography, "La lógica de los hechos," which Bourke captured in a raid on Palito Blanco. The overlarge feet, the sword, and the epaulets on Garza's uniform make him look like a clown more than a revolutionary. (Diary of John G. Bourke, United States Military Academy, West Point, New York)

19. Drawing by Captain John G. Bourke in his diary. The depiction of a sheriff saying "I would take C. Garza — but I must remember the next election" demonstrates Bourke's frustration at the lack of cooperation by elected officials in South Texas. In the background, Bourke portrayed one of the U.S. Cavalry's field camps with a U.S. flag flying overhead. (Diary of John G. Bourke, United States Military Academy, West Point, New York)

Could this have been Bourke trying to justify his recent attack against Garzista "outlaws" and "strangers"? Ironically, it was Bourke who was acting outside of the law and who was a stranger in the valley.

Like the *San Antonio Express*, many newspapers reacted with disbelief to the charges against Bourke. He was, in their words, one of the "most fearless and ablest officer in the United States Army," and they trusted that he would do what was necessary under the circumstances. The *Express* admitted that Bourke "is a terror to the neutrality law violators on the lower Rio Grande border," but they explained that such actions, "severe as they may seem, meet with general approval in military circles and among those thoroughly familiar with the situation in the lower frontier country."[169] Therefore, even if the allegations were true the situation required such brutality. Rather than hold Bourke accountable for his actions, the newspaper editorialized about the "horde of little jackleg law-yers whose mission is to breed litigation and stir up strife." These lawyers were, they argued, "the bacilli of the body politic, the bile of the social organism — useless as parrots, aggravating as sand flies, unclean as the lice on the head of a lazar [leper]."[170]

The day after Bourke was arrested, Ramón Paz, a former Garzista who had been helping the troops, showed up at the fort and demanded that his carbine be returned. Paz's carbine was taken from him when he was cap-tured and had admitted to being an active rebel soldier. Although he had helped the U.S. troops pursue the rebels, he had recently switched his testimony in court and thereby undermined the government's case. When Paz demanded his weapon, Bourke refused, proclaiming that he "did not propose — law or no law, to put a gun back in his hands wherewith to kill more of my soldiers." He did, however, allow Paz to see his weapon, which was in storage at the troops' quarters. When Paz went to the storage area he became involved in a dispute over his carbine and called the troops "*cabrones*" (bastards), not suspecting that they understood Spanish. Un-fortunately for Paz, they understood at least that much Spanish, and they proceeded to beat him with their fists until he was able to break away.[171] Needless to say, even after U.S. Commissioner Walter Downs wrote a letter asking for Paz's carbine, Bourke refused to turn it over.[172] Tensions between the townspeople at Rio Grande City and the soldiers at Fort Ringgold were growing more intense with each passing day.

Bourke didn't wait around to face his accusers or to resolve the issue of Paz's gun. Sheriff Sheley released Bourke without bail on the condition that he return to court later in March to stand trial. On March 1, just one week after his arrest, Bourke received orders from General Wheaton transferring him for duty in Chicago at the upcoming World's Columbian Exposition. Two days later, Bourke bid his troops farewell. He was es-corted out of Rio Grande City flanked by a half dozen of his soldiers.

When the news spread that Bourke was going to leave town, a Mexican who represented himself as a deputy sheriff turned up at Fort Ringgold saying that Bourke had only given bond for one of the charges against him. According to Bourke, Sheriff Sheley had only written out one piece of paper for the bond, but it included all eighteen counts. It did not really matter anyway whether or not Bourke was in compliance with the law. Bourke's troops had long since made it clear that they would not recognize the authority of local officials. This last-ditch effort to bring Bourke to jus-tice on the Rio Grande failed. Starr County's attorney, James H. Edwards, appealed to the governor of Texas in the name of the "majesty of law" to use his influence to have the military commander in Texas order Bourke back to the border to face the charges. Relations between the army and the townsfolk had broken down so completely that even this complaint had to be sent by mail to a nearby town, Peña, and then telegraphed to Austin because the army would not allow it to be transmitted from Fort Ringgold.[173] In the end, however, Captain Bourke never returned to Texas.[174]

"KILL THEM ON SIGHT"

The ideal imperial relationship involves a particular type of exchange in which the colonizers bring their "superior culture" and the "natives" surrender their natural resources. There are moments in this process when the colonizer is forced to confront himself or herself and reflect critically on the metropolis and its role in the colony. The moment of self-realization is traumatic and it brings unforeseen and unpredictable consequences for the colonizer. In literature and travelers' accounts, the journey up the river often serves as the symbol for discovery of self and others. It is unclear exactly when and where Bourke and some of the other officers began to realize that the barbarism they were seeking to stamp out was actually within themselves. The colonial mission was taking its toll on the troops just as it did on those they persecuted. After being in the field for a long time, Bourke's high-minded principles gave way to a scorched-earth policy, including orders to shoot Garzistas on sight. This moment of recognition and mental breakdown occurred most dramatically with Lieutenant Stephen O'Conner, who took charge of the campaign to stamp out the rebellion after Bourke had been forced out of South Texas. The longer O'Conner remained in the field amidst the thick chaparral, the more he began to realize that the "darkness" and "horror" was within him as well.[175] The road that he took from aggressive soldiering to pathological violence illustrates the psychological difficulty of the task that the soldiers were being ordered to perform.

By summer 1893, with Garza in Costa Rica and hundreds of Garzistas in jail, only scattered rebel bands remained. In the course of his investigations, O'Conner had identified ten or twelve "smugglers, bandits, and revolutionists" based in San Ignacio, Texas, who were delivering contraband liquor to Texas ranches. "There can be but one view as to what should be done to rid the country of these desperate criminals, namely: to pursue them until they either surrender, are killed, or leave the country."[176] With this in mind, he proposed in late July to withdraw his troops from San Ignacio and begin periodical midnight raids. According to the plan, he would encircle the entire ranch at midnight and arrest anyone who left before daylight on the assumption that they were smugglers.[177] Occupying the ranch would not work, O'Conner contended, because "every man, woman and child at the place is practically a spy in the interest of the criminals named."[178] By early August, they were conducting early-morning raids on the families of suspected smugglers and establishing nightly blockades on all roads leading into San Ignacio. Convinced that "activity should be the rule," O'Conner suggested, at a minimum, that biweekly patrols should be done of the ranches between Lopeña and Salineña, and that such patrols not "simply pass by the ranches but . . . go into them and look around the houses, the main object being to keep the criminals on the jump, to make life miserable for them, keep the troops in exercise and the horses on their feed."[179]

After reading reports from the field, Colonel J. P. Martin realized that O'Conner's sense of desperation had driven him to the edge of a nervous breakdown, which had led him to take illegal and overzealous actions. As Martin wrote to the assistant adjutant general: "Lieut. O'Conner's action in raiding ranches, searching houses by day and night, and making arrests without warrants and in the absence of civil officers of the state or general government, picketing roads and interfering with travel on the public highways, is going far beyond any authority he can possibly have and . . . its continuance will lead to conflict with the civil authorities." Martin insisted that O'Conner was "not a safe man to be trusted in command" and recommended that he be relieved of his post at once.[180] O'Conner had become a liability and, much like Conrad's Kurtz, he had to be removed. However, Colonel Martin's decision to relieve O'Conner of his duty did not mean that he questioned the validity of the colonial project but rather only the effectiveness of his "unsound methods."[181]

By September, O'Conner still had not been relieved of his post, and in what looks like his final report he summarized his observations of the previous ten months of duty. In this report O'Conner paints a picture of the troops' extreme isolation in the valley, where virtually everyone actively obstructed the troops and supported the "bandits." O'Conner was particularly upset at the lack of racial solidarity among Anglos, finding that the "white" folk also sided with the "outlaws." "Of all of the white men, whom I have met on the border," he lamented, "I know of but one who is not heartily in sympathy with the scoundrels, who infest Zapata and Starr Counties." The white schoolteachers of Zapata County, the local officials, and the two mounted customs inspectors at Carrizo all supported the "criminals." Such a network gave the "smugglers" a means of communicating troop movements which, O'Conner argued, "seems well nigh impossible to overcome."[182] Given that O'Conner had already begun to see the "scoundrels" as a disease that "infested" the counties, a program to exterminate them followed logically.

O'Conner seized on the deleterious effects of racial mixing and kinship networks to explain the unanimity of support for the rebels. The customs inspectors he mentions were, he chided, "married to Mexican women and industriously engaged in raising half-breed families." These women were in turn connected through family ties with the "revolutionists, smugglers, and bandits."[183] This oft-repeated phrase in his reports, "revolutionists, bandits, and smugglers," indicates O'Conner's confusion about the nature of his enemies' illicit activities, or perhaps he understood that these labels could be applied interchangeably regardless of the alleged transgressions.[184] In his estimation, the postmaster of Carrizo, the postmaster's brother, a school-teacher at Ramireño ranch, and all of the deputy sheriffs throughout the county were "practically one family, one blood through intermarriage."[185] From his besieged perspective, everyone was against him in a tightly linked criminal network, bonded together by blood and marriage. The only possible way "to correct this evil," he maintained, would be a declaration of martial law and to prosecute under English common law all those who harbored criminals as criminals themselves. Being of Irish descent, O'Conner must have had a healthy respect for the British methods of controlling colonial populations. If the owners of the Ramireño ranch were indicted by a grand jury and punished, he suggested, "it would strike terror into the land and Ranch owners of the border, and open a road to the final settlement of the troubles, now agitating the border counties."[186]

O'Conner's complaints continued: "Local civil authorities should be entirely ignored in this matter," he railed, because "to employ one of them would be . . . simply employing a spy, working at all times in the interest of the criminals."[187] He remembered the letter he had sent to the military authorities in Mexico informing them that a well-known bandit was living with his grandmother in a ranch above Mier. This letter, posted at Carrizo, never arrived at its destination because the postmaster, "an active sympathizer with the criminals of the border," had intercepted it.[188] While Mexicans were not to be trusted, O'Conner also blamed white politicians and large landowners for the troublesome situation, arguing that "no

Mexican can be prosecuted for, much less convicted of a crime, if he happens to be under the protection of a local land magnate, or one who is able to control votes in the interests of the local officeholders, who are generally white men." The Irish American lieutenant concluded that "civil law is practically dead in this region."[189]

One has to appreciate the isolation and the frustration that O'Conner must have felt as he was continually foiled in what he saw as righteous efforts to capture criminals. He could not understand the language spoken by most people in the valley, and even his white brethren had disappointed him by siding with the enemy. Civil law was, in his estimation, "practically dead," so how was he to proceed? O'Conner answers that question in what must have been a fit of rage and, perhaps, a moment of brutal honesty: "There may be policy in this condition of affairs, but from my standpoint there are only two ways of dealing with such people. Viz.: to arrest them quietly and peaceably if possible, if this cannot be done, kill them on sight, and pursue the rest until the last of them is dead or in confinement. A settlement of this kind would be sufficient for all time to come. And when one considers the class of people one has to deal with, it is the only safe method to pursue."[190] In Conrad's story at the end of his "altruistic" and "eloquent" report to the International Society for the Suppression of Savage Customs, Kurtz, in a fit of passion, "scrawled" in an "unsteady hand" the unwritten orders of imperial power: "Exterminate all the brutes!"[191] A few years before Conrad penned those memorable words, and a few years after Stanley had enacted them, O'Conner, overcome with emotion, inscribed his own realization of horror: "Kill them on sight and pursue the rest until the last of them is dead."

"THE SOONER THE KILLING BEGAN THE BETTER"

Like Lieutenant O'Conner, Captain Bourke's frustration during the Garza campaign led him increasingly to turn to violence. Even after he had left the border, the bitterness of being chased out of South Texas by rebel supporters seemed to stay with him. Immediately after his travails in Texas, Bourke served as curator for the exhibition La Rabida, which was featured at the 1893 World's Columbian Exposition in Chicago. La Rabida displayed documents, maps, and art artifacts relating to the European conquest of the Americas. It was somehow appropriate to have a man so intimately connected to the late-nineteenth-century conquest and colonization of the U.S. West as the curator of a show about the origins of that process. One year later Captain Bourke was again back in Chicago. This time he came not as a curator but as an officer with Troop C of the Third Cavalry to help put down a national strike by the American Railway Union against railroad magnate George Pullman. In fact, four Third Cavalry officers who figured prominently in the suppression of Garza's rebellion accompanied Bourke to Chicago.[192] Their experiences fighting Indians and their frustrated attempts to capture Garza had not, however, prepared them to face this new enemy: organized industrial labor. While Bourke had developed a benevolent paternalism toward the Indian groups that he had helped to capture and imprison, he demonstrated no sympathy toward the militant and vocal strikers.

The 1894 Pullman strike came in the wake of the official closing of the frontier. The same soldiers who massacred Lakota Indians at Pine Ridge during the Wounded Knee battle and pursued Garza's men through the chaparral faced off with the new "savages," industrial laborers. Just as with Indians and Mexicans in South Texas, Anglo American soldiers did not understand the languages or cultures of the predominantly immigrant workforce and they conceived and treated them like subhumans. And, as he had done earlier with his drawings of Garza's revolt, Frederic Remington popularized this negative view of the Pullman strikers through his vivid drawings and articles in national magazines.

The Pullman strike drew out the darker side of the gentleman and scholar Bourke. In a report to General Miles, Bourke suggested shooting and killing the strikers and their supporters as the most efficient means of resolving this labor dispute. "The way to put down a mob was to put it down," Bourke advised, "the sooner the killing began the better. . . . Men who threw anything at soldiers should be shot down as should all discovered uncoupling cars, destroying property, [and] intimidating or cajoling employees."[193] In his personal diary, where he exclaimed that the army should "smash up the turbulent mob of strikers and their sympathizers," and in his official military correspondence with his superiors, Bourke advocated wanton violence.[194] Bourke and Remington's portrayal of Pullman strikers, Mexican revolutionaries, and "others" as corrupt "foreign elements" within the nation's body justified and even encouraged the brutal violence against them. While Remington painted pictures and wrote articles, Bourke issued military orders. The ideological and military battles were, however, just two interrelated parts of the same struggle to maintain order and racial purity in the nation.

Although Bourke's efforts to develop and "Americanize" the border would succeed a few decades later, his brief tenure on the Rio Grande illustrates the limits to the power of the U.S. federal government. The South Texas border was still not fully incorporated into the United States at the end of the nineteenth century, despite half a century of Anglo settlement, commercial investment, and military occupation. Bourke and others could see that it would not be long before all of the necessary elements were in place—railroads, Anglos, and commercialization—but for all of the promise the region continued to remain "unknown" and remote in the U.S. popular imaginary. Bourke's central task, along with the military pursuit of Garza, was to render legible what seemed foreign and to fill in the vast blank spaces on a map. Stories and narratives about the border and its availability for enterprising Americans to make a profit was central to this mapping process. Although Mexicans published counternarratives and directly took on Bourke's depiction of the border as an "American Congo," their vision of the border never reached a national audience. In the war of words, it was Bourke's version of history that ultimately won.

After experiencing frustrations in the field, including long horseback rides, extreme temperatures, and constant misinformation, O'Conner, Bourke, and other officers began to advocate harassment, terror, and even murder. Ironically, Bourke's new manner of dealing with "suspects" became very much like the martial law he had criticized the Mexican authorities for employing. We should not assume that these men's personalities fated them to act illegally or even brutally and thus dismiss their initial statements about respecting people's rights as completely self-serving. Rather, it seems that the experience of colonial rule transformed them. The logic of the situation required them to give up their lofty ideals. And they did. Furthermore, for Bourke at least, his past duties fighting Indians and his frustration at the corruption and ineffectiveness of the government's Indian policies probably contributed to his quick conversion from an apostle of enlightenment to an advocate of violence. Much like Kurtz, the promising and intelligent company man in Conrad's *Heart of Darkness*, these officers went to the jungle to pacify the "natives" and ended up going a little mad themselves, thereby exacerbating the anger of the "natives" in the process.

The U.S. Army played a crucial role in the process of colonizing the lower Rio Grande Valley. From the moment when General Taylor led his troops across the Nueces River in 1846 and continuing on through the beginning of the twentieth century, the military was on hand to enforce control over a region inhabited mainly by Mexicans. Not only did the troops put down the occasional revolt and riot, but they served as front-line social engineers. The army thus helped to foster a local power structure capable of controlling a growing and heterogeneous population being displaced by commercialization and industrialization. Although the army eventually accomplished its goals of establishing U.S. and Anglo hegemony in South Texas and of transforming the economy, local resistance continually frustrated its efforts. As a target of a local campaign to end his reign of terror, Captain Bourke was permanently forced out of South Texas. Lieutenant O'Conner ended his tour of duty in frustration and near madness, with his superiors questioning his sanity and reliability. Individual officers could be spared along the way, but the colonization of the region continued. Richard Harding Davis, the astute observer of the West from his car window, put it eloquently in 1892: "The course of empire will eventually Westward take its way."[195]

8. EXILE, DEATH, AND RESURRECTION

IN THE CARIBBEAN

No pierdes la fé ni la esperanza, pronto nos veremos

tal vez para no volvernos a seperar nunca. (Don't lose faith

nor hope, soon we will see each other and perhaps never again

separate.) — Catarino Garza to his wife, Concepción

González de Garza, January 1, 1895

As early as November 1891, rumors circulated about Garza's escape to Central America; such information, however, routinely turned out to be false.[1] Similarly misleading articles in newspapers reported sightings of Garza in South Texas, months after he had fled the country.[2] While Garza's precise movements during the first few months of the rebellion remain vague, a good picture of his years in exile can be pieced together from the letters that he wrote back home as well as newspaper articles and consular reports. Even as Garza grew frustrated by the separation from his wife and child, and bitter about the seeming abandonment by his former comrades, he maintained faith in the liberal revolution. With no money, family, or friends Garza struggled just to survive, but his exile, which separated him from his home and family, may have helped him to identify more closely with Latin America as a whole. After defending Mexicans in Texas and fighting against a dictatorship in Mexico, Garza finally took on the much weightier task of struggling for liberalism and self-determination throughout the entire American continent.

The Garzista rebellion continued into 1893, but its leader fled Texas barely half a year after the revolt began. The transcription of Ranger McNeel's interrogation of one of the men who helped Garza and his

20. Portrait of Concepción (Chonita) González, Catarino Garza's wife. (Courtesy of the Pérez and Tijerina families)

brother escape from Texas, along with Garza's own letters, provide a detailed and credible account of Garza's route to freedom. Two Mexicans from the Carrilo ranch near Realitos, Texas, helped the Garza brothers, Catarino and Encarnación, to escape in February 1892. The fugitive brothers made their way up to Cuero on horseback, and then, assuming the pseudonym Martín Ortíz, Encarnación traveled by train to Houston. Meanwhile, Catarino, wearing a white cowboy hat, a ducking jacket, jeans, and green goggles, journeyed to Houston on a buggy under the pseudonym Concepción Tobar. Only 24 miles outside of Cuero his buggy broke down, forcing him to buy a two-wheel sulky to carry him the rest of the way. The Garza brothers met in Houston and continued by train to New Orleans, and from there traveled to a small nearby island. Catarino maintained an almost daily correspondence with his wife, Concepción, trying repeatedly to persuade her to meet him in New Orleans (fig. 20). Upset about the trouble caused by his revolt, Garza's father-in-law blocked his daughter from joining her husband.[3]

Exile, Death, and Resurrection 269

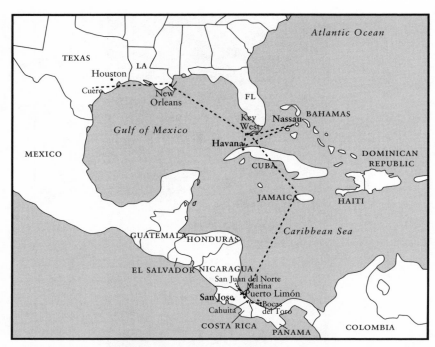

MAP 3. Garza's journey in exile from Texas through the Caribbean to his death in Bocas del Toro, Panama. The order of his travels is as follows: Cuero, New Orleans, Key West, Havana, Nassan, return to Key West, Jamaica, Puerto Limón, San Juan del Norte, Cahuita, Bocas del Toro.

Taking a steamer from New Orleans, the Garza brothers traveled to Florida and down through Key West, where Encarnación remained, and Catarino continued on to Havana, Cuba (map 3).[4] On the same day that Catarino arrived in Havana he wrote to Concepción, complaining about the constant threat from spies in Houston, New Orleans, and even on the steamship. To avoid detection, he was forced to journey by land, by horse, by buggy, and finally by sea. At last he had reached a country where nobody knew him, thus allowing him to remain incognito. It had been exactly a month since he had last seen his wife, and he begged her to come to be at his side. He could live happily in Cuba, he felt, "but with you at my side, because without you, I wouldn't be happy, not even in paradise itself."[5]

In this and in many subsequent letters Garza left detailed instructions for his wife's travel arrangements, giving the train and steamship routes for each leg of the journey and even leaving his brother Encarnación in

21. Portrait of Amelia Garza González, Catarino Garza's daughter. (Courtesy of the Pérez and Tijerina families)

Key West to meet her when she arrived. From Garza's letters it is clear that his wife corresponded with him, though not as frequently as he would have liked. He implored his wife, whom he referred to affectionately as Chonita, to ask her father, Alejandro González, for the money to travel to Havana. He was also desperately anxious to be with his daughter, Amelia, who was born on April 26, 1891, just a few months before his insurrection erupted (fig. 21). "If he [Alejandro] denies the biggest favor I have asked, it would be the same as killing my morale, because I don't think that I can live happily in exile without you, my wife. With you at my side, it will not be exile for me, because seeing you at my side I will remember all of my hopes about my Patria."[6]

Garza also wrote directly to Chonita's father, addressing him as "papa" and pleading for him to give his daughter the $500 that she needed to travel to Havana. The requests to have his wife and his baby daughter join him would adorn almost every letter he wrote, yet ultimately to no avail. In addition to the money for his family's travel expenses, Garza also requested that his father-in-law send more funds so that they could move to Central or South America where he felt it would be easier to remain incognito.[7] To keep his identity hidden, Garza adopted the alias Erasmo Betancourt, one of many he would employ in the coming years.[8]

INCOGNITO IN HAVANA, NASSAU, AND KEY WEST

Even though nobody personally knew Garza in Cuba, remaining incognito would be difficult because he had developed an international reputation as a result of his revolt. In the letter to his father-in-law, Garza described how he "with great satisfaction" saw a large portrait of himself in a Havana bookstore window, with the following inscription underneath: "The Mexican revolutionary. Antagonist of Gen. Don. Porfirio Díaz. Only 32 years of age." This moment of self-reflection, where Garza literally sees his revolutionary persona staring back at him through the bookstore window, helped to convince him of his importance; his recounting of the episode was perhaps also intended to convince his father-in-law of this fact (fig. 22). "I went closer to the store window and almost immobile I stayed in front of the portrait of my riddled persona. I felt proud to see myself distinguished by all of the social classes. We will see the future that awaits us."[9] The "us" could either refer to the broader movement, or it could suggest that Garza had begun to differentiate between his personal and political personas. In either case, he was overly optimistic about what that future would bring. "I never lose the hope," he wrote to his wife, "of seeing myself distinguished and appreciated in my country."[10]

In spite of the reputation that he had apparently achieved in Cuba and in other parts of Latin America, Garza had overestimated his own significance. One day he overheard a doctor in Havana saying, "if we had a man of the stature of the insurgent Mexican Garza, we would already be independent [from Spain]. Garza — the doctor said — has challenged the anger of two governments, the betrayal of many of his comrades, and still he has fought with the heroism of the Spartans." Hearing such comments, along with seeing his portrait venerated in store windows, convinced Garza that if the Cubans knew his name he would be "elevated to distinguished social positions."[11] Of course, he had good reason to speak highly of himself in his letters because he was still trying to convince his wife to join him. If her father was going to allow her to meet him, and if he was going to continue to finance this failed revolutionary, then Alejandro would also have to be persuaded of Garza's future.

Catarina Garza,
Mexican Revolutionist,
1 8 9 4.

22. Portrait of Catarino Garza, Mexican revolutionist, dated 1894 but probably taken earlier; by
1894 Garza was in exile in Costa Rica. (Courtesy
of the Daughters of the Republic of Texas
Library, Rose Collection, CN 96.801)

Garza had spent only five days in Havana before his fear that the
Mexican consul had blown his cover drove him to depart suddenly on the
afternoon of March 20. He returned to Key West and then immediately set
sail for the Caribbean island of Nassau. As his small boat launched into
the sea, Garza waved his hat in a farewell to his brother Encarnación, who
stood on the dock. The captain and crew on the boat treated Garza well
after he told them that he was writing a book about his voyage and would
include them in it. Sailing through the Caribbean for six days allowed
Garza time to reflect on his time in Cuba and on the prospect of living in
Nassau, an English colony.

While Garza had shown great admiration for Spaniards and Spanish
culture when he was living in St. Louis, his experience in Cuba, still a
Spanish colony in the early 1890s, left him with an entirely different, and
negative, view of Spanish culture. The uneducated Spaniard was, accord-

ing to Garza, "grotesque, abrupt, uncordial, and sometimes even vulgar." Garza was especially turned off by the way in which the monarchical Spanish government "considers its subjects like obedient slaves and not free men." In contrast, Garza had nothing but praise for the English, who, he noted, held popular elections in their colonial possessions.[12] En route to Nassau, the beleaguered revolutionary tried to put the best face on his future and to keep his spirits high as he fled from island to island trying to keep one step ahead of his enemies.

Garza arrived in Nassau on March 27, which he described as "poetic, romantic and precious," as well as being one of the "most beautiful [places] that I have known." He immediately became friendly with two Cubans who owned tobacco factories in Key West. After they expressed their admiration for and desire to meet the "Insurrectionist Chief" Garza, he decided to let them know his true identity. Garza then became fast friends with these Cubans, who offered him a job in a bookstore if he returned to Key West with them. They assured him that should the necessity arise, he "will count on the whole Cuban worker and Mason population, and also on the influence of various capitalists."[13] The support of the Cuban community, including five Masonic lodges and three worker societies with nine hundred members, would allow him to stay in Key West and remain hidden from his enemies, and thus allow him to continue his writing. The Cubans even offered to raise funds so that he could begin publishing a commercial and literary newspaper.[14] Garza took up the offer, in part because he was unable to find any decent work in Nassau. "It is an Island," he noted, "with an agglomeration of many black people who will work for two pesos a month."[15] So, just three days after he arrived in "one of the most beautiful small towns" he had known, he was off again, on his way back to Key West.[16]

Once in Key West, Garza's appeals to Alejandro González became more desperate. Garza demanded to know immediately if his family was coming, and then he insisted that his father-in-law should at least explain why they were being kept from him. While Garza was not explicit about his plans, he implied that if his family were not going to join him then he would begin another political campaign. As he said, "between being deprived of seeing my family in exile and being that way in a campaign, I prefer to be in a campaign and not in exile." Aside from seeing his family, Garza announced that he had arrived in Key West "without even a penny," and he reiterated his request for the $500 which would pay for his family's transport and allow them to establish themselves in Key West.[17] Garza did not even have enough money to leave to the nearby islands, but if he had some money, he suggested in one letter, he would have gone directly to Madrid and enlisted the Mexican General Vicente Riva Palacio in his cause. Riva Palacio was also "a great friend" of Garza's assassinated co-conspirator Dr. Ignacio Martínez.[18] Even though his influential Cuban friends promised to protect Garza, he was too embarrassed to ask them for money after all they had done for him. Garza emphasized his poverty to his family back in Texas in the hopes that perhaps they would take pity on him and send him money. On one occasion, he told his wife that he had almost turned down a dinner engagement because he was too ashamed to wear his cheap suit, the only one he had.[19]

The Key West Cuban Masonic community opened their arms to Garza, an eighteen-degree Mason; they invited him as an honored guest to festivities in their lodges and provided moral support for his political cause. The two Cubans he met in Nassau who helped him return to Key West were also Masons, as was a Cuban factory owner, Leon Agustín López, who provided assistance once Garza had arrived in Key West.[20] Not being able to leave, Garza had to do the best he could in Key West to keep a low profile and escape detection. As a result, he rarely even left his room at the boardinghouse where he was staying, and only crossed the street at night to drink coffee.[21]

At some point between May and October, Garza's enemies caught up with him in Key West. Garza had been staying at the "chaotic" hotel of Martín Herrera, but with Mexican and U.S. agents hot on his trail a hotel was too public a place for his safety. Fellow Mason Gerardo Castellanos y Lleonart, a prominent Cuban war hero and founder of the foremost exile organization in Key West, offered to hide Garza on the second-floor attic in his house. Providing safe haven was risky for Castellanos, as Garza was considered a "dangerous international criminal."[22]

Castellanos described Garza as a tall, thin man of military carriage who was hugely popular, cultivated, and a good talker. He was impressed with Garza's work as a fluent poet and a writer, as well as with the Mexican's marksmanship. Castellanos also remembered that Garza received large amounts of money from his family. From Garza's letters we know that this was definitely not the case, but Garza may have told his host that he was receiving money from his family so as not to appear like a desperate charity case. Throughout his exile, Garza expressed bitterness over his poverty and the lack of financial support from the "revolutionary" Mexicans. It would be difficult to live up to his reputation as an important revolutionary, he mused in his letters, if he could not even count on his family and supporters to provide the basics for his survival.

Catarino spent his last days in Key West holed up in Castellanos's attic. Armed with a Winchester rifle; several pistols, two of which he wore on a holster; and a ton of explosives, he waited for the inevitable knock on the door. In spite of his preparedness, or perhaps because of it, Garza paced the floor like a "caged lion." He even slept with his head propped up on an arm so as not to block his ears from hearing the approach of an enemy. One day, while staring out of the second floor window, Garza spotted a few assassins whom he recognized. He opened his boxes of bullets and prepared for a gunfight, but the enemy agents disappeared.[23] It would only be a matter of time, however, before they returned to finish their job.

In the meantime, Castellanos confided in one of his Masonic colleagues that Garza was hidden in his house, hoping somehow to save Garza's life. The Mason confidant, Solís, was a Spanish consul who also represented Mexico in Key West. Thus, rather than helping Garza, Solís informed the U.S. authorities where Garza was hiding, presumably because he expected to receive the thousands of dollars promised by the U.S. and Mexican governments as a reward for the Mexican revolutionary's capture. It seems that Castellanos had hoped that Solís would assist Garza because he was a fellow Mason and, in doing so, take the heat off the Key West Cuban community that was under suspicion of hiding Garza.[24]

One might imagine that after so many brushes with death Garza would have given up or at least have tempered his revolutionary zeal. Danger produced the opposite effect, however, and Garza became ever more committed to his cause the closer he came to death. While hidden in Gerardo Castellanos's house, Garza even hatched a bold plan to invade Cuba and fight for its independence against Spain. To discuss his proposal, Garza organized a meeting with the most prominent Cuban exiles, generals Serafín Sánchez y Roloff, Gerardo Castellanos, and José Martí. This was a moment of fervent organizing among the Cuban exile community: the Cuban Revolutionary Party had been formed in January 1892 in Tampa and Key West, and serious plans to overthrow the Spanish were underway. Martí, the journalist, poet, and independence fighter, had also just been elected as the leader of the Cuban Revolutionary Party. According to Castellanos, Garza's invasion plan was not supported because Martí still had hope for "moral and financial" support from Mexico's Porfirio Díaz.[25] Joining forces with Garza, Díaz's personal enemy, would have meant sacrificing the support of Díaz, and Martí might have pragmatically decided that Díaz was a more powerful and hence more important ally. Under other circumstances it seems quite likely that these two liberal revolutionaries who plotted their movements from "inside the monster" would have become close friends and co-conspirators.[26] Before he could solidify his alliance with the Cuban independence leaders, however, and before he could be captured, Garza set sail again for Nassau.

Even though Martí apparently rejected Garza's offer, Catarino would remain in touch with Cuban exile leaders, and he continued to entertain the possibility of joining their struggle all the way up to 1895 when the Cuban insurrection began. During his time in Costa Rica, Garza befriended Antonio Maceo, the Afro-Cuban hero of Cuba's Ten Years' War (1868–1878) against Spain. Like Garza, Maceo was living in exile in Costa Rica, where he had established a successful colony of Cuban farmers. In June 1893, Martí visited the "Bronze Titan" Maceo in Costa Rica, where he convinced him to join the revolution.[27] Even at this late date, Garza considered signing on with Maceo and the Cuban independence movement.[28] The available sources do not allow us to ascertain whether it was Martí who rejected the participation of Garza because he could not afford to offend Mexico's president, or if it was Garza who declined to be part of the Cuban movement if he couldn't play a leading role.

BETRAYAL

Trying to survive the psychological trauma and loneliness of exile and the material deprivation of poverty was difficult enough, but Garza's desperation mounted when he suspected that former friends and comrades had turned against him. On his arrival in Havana in 1892, he wrote to both his father-in-law and his wife asking them to arrange for his friend, Francisco Mendoza, to send him letters of introduction.[29] Mendoza was an exiled Cuban who published the pro-Garzista newspaper *El Internacional* at Palito Blanco. Garza hoped that Mendoza's Cuban friends could provide the cover that he needed to survive underground in Cuba. Although he only stayed in Havana a few days, when Garza went to Nassau Mendoza's brother hosted him. While at Mendoza's house in Nassau, Garza received word that his brother Encarnación had been arrested in Key West. Although Garza's Cuban friends in Key West failed to prevent the arrest, they received assurances that Encarnación would be released after he had given the police the information they wanted. Garza believed that it had been Francisco Mendoza, whom he described as "the wretched coward and traitor," who had provided the authorities with Garza's letters thus leading them to his brother in Key West. Garza fumed at Mendoza's betrayal, and exhorted "Wretch! It's going to cost him in ways he can't even imagine."[30] Captain Bourke's diary entries from this period confirm Garza's suspicion that Mendoza had turned against him. A month after Encarnación's arrest, Mendoza provided Bourke with information about Garza's whereabouts and even offered to arrange for the rebel's return so that he could be arrested. He also informed Bourke that Garza had no money left and that he could not get any from his father-in-law, whose legal fees and hotel bills had left him bankrupt and bitter.[31] It is unclear why Mendoza suddenly turned on Garza, although the lack of money in the revolution may help explain the change of heart.

This was not the first betrayal, nor would it be the last. Garza's letters also accused the "sell-out" Longoria and the "reptile" Juan Antonio Flores, both former comrades, with cooperating with the army to squash his rebellion. Bourke's diary corroborates Garza's accusations, at least for Longoria, who after being arrested provided Bourke with detailed information about the revolution.[32] Although he was angry, Garza seemed almost resigned to Mendoza's turning against him. Referring to the "Judases" who surrounded him, Garza framed the incident within the Christian paradigm of Jesus Christ being betrayed by one of his disciples. Like Jesus foreshadowing the final betrayal that would lead to his crucifixion, Garza predicted "there is something else in the final pages of my turbulent and sad history, a secret betrayal that breaks my soul; but because I have been granted an exceptional brain by Nature, I have not yet been defeated. My brain conceives ideas that are still superior to those that betray me."[33] Garza did not reveal the identity of the secret traitor, and it is not even clear if he was speaking metaphorically or literally. In any case, he warned his wife not to let Mendoza know where he was, because he had been told that there was a plot against his life.

PUERTO LIMÓN, COSTA RICA

By February 1893, after passing through Jamaica, Garza ended up in Puerto Limón on the Atlantic Coast of Costa Rica.[34] Adopting the pseudonym Erasmo González Betancourt, he established himself in the small banana town of Matina, twenty-two miles from Costa Rica's main port city of Puerto Limón. Today there is not much evidence that Matina was anything but a provincial outpost for the extensive banana plantations that cover the whole area. After just ten days there, according to Garza's letters, he was appointed provisional judge and also began working as a land lawyer, settling disputes, drafting mortgage contracts, and filing property titles.[35] In addition to practicing law, Garza wrote about the local industry in newspapers and began his own small trading business. By his own account, which seems to be rather optimistic given his situation, everything was going exceedingly well.[36]

Writing to his father-in-law and brother-in-law, Alejandro and Mauricio González, Garza emphasized the success that he had achieved in Costa Rica, even though nobody knew of his illustrious past. "I am appreciated, I am listened to, and I am consulted as if my head were a public fountain in which all of the peoples of the nations could drink and quench their thirst."[37] Even though Garza provides evidence that he achieved some level of respectability in this small town, his overblown sense of his importance as a fount of knowledge for "all of the peoples of the nations" suggests that his letters exaggerated his position. Sometimes explicitly, and oftentimes just implicitly, Garza compared the assistance he received from other Latin Americans to the lack of response by the Mexican people. He noted that he had even managed to please the local hacendados with his articles that had inspired them to raise the price of their fruit, and he had high hopes that his business prospects would earn him "a considerable bonus." At one point, according to his letters, he was offered a job in the Finance Ministry, but he turned it down fearing that his identity would be discovered if he went to the capital. Rather than put himself at risk, he decided to dedicate himself to business endeavors and enjoy his status in Matina as a "cacique absoluto" (absolute ruler).[38]

Garza went to great lengths to prove to his family that he had influential friends in Costa Rica, such as the treasury minister. In one letter, he even printed his stationary with the official government stamps of the police and the administrator of the post office to show them that he had powerful friends. After setting himself up as a man of importance, Garza pitched a business proposition to the Gonzálezes. His request for $497 in cash and a $373 line of credit was only one in a long line of business propositions. The idea was to open a trading house to import clothes and groceries from New Orleans and to export wood, rubber, and fruits from Costa Rica. An investment of less than $621, Garza assured them, would easily earn $6,210 in just one year. And if the Gonzálezes were unable to raise the necessary funds, Garza suggested that they ask for the money from his friends and other relatives "who know how to appreciate the sacrifices of a patriotic Mexican."[39] A month later Garza wrote to his brother Encarnación, telling him that Valentín González should stop being a "scared mouse." With only $621, Garza promised that they could buy a cacao, coffee, or banana plantation in Costa Rica, from which they could make a 40 percent profit every month. Garza also wanted the other González brothers, Jesus and Hesiquio, to set up an import-export business so that they could ship cheap rubber from Costa Rica to New Orleans where it was considered to be "ground gold." Although the Costa Rican government controlled the rubber trade, as a judge Garza could obtain the official certificates.[40]

Garza's aborted revolution cost the González family a fair sum of money, both to supply the revolutionists and to defend themselves in court. Even today, some members of the González family blame Catarino for Alejandro's losses and the subsequent sale of parts of the family property. The fact that Alejandro González sold two large tracts of land totaling over 4,300 acres to the King ranch in 1893 and 1894 suggests that the rebellion took its toll on the family's wealth and property.[41] Perhaps Garza felt like he owed it to them, as he put it, to "replace in one year the loss of ten years."[42] Garza expressed sorrow to his wife that her family had been financially ruined by the revolution, but ever the eternal optimist he predicted that soon he would be able to help his father-in-law. "My hopes do not evaporate in the tropical sun, because I have been and will continue to succeed in my business dealings and my thoughts."[43]

After months of repeated begging for Chonita to come and join him in Costa Rica, he proclaimed defensively that he would "never return to Texas, even if they arrange a thousand things. I will never return, and the day that I would return it would be to my country, but never again to Texas."[44] When it became clear that his father-in-law would never allow his wife to join him, Garza changed tact by declaring that if she were not coming then he would "return to Texas to oblige everyone." "I can't be in exile and forgotten by everyone," he proclaimed desperately. "If so, it would be better to end everything once and for all."[45] None of Garza's strategies, including threatening never to return to Texas or to return immediately, convinced González to send his son-in-law money or to allow his daughter to join him.

While fighting for his liberal principles and against tyranny remained the main topic of Garza's letters, the separation from his wife and baby daughter, Amelia, also occupied his thoughts. "I am hungry, thirsty and etc. to see you," he plaintively wrote to his wife. When she arrived, he promised to be on the pier waiting for her with open arms. However, it appears as if either Concepción's father did not want her to leave Texas or that she herself was reluctant to drag herself and her toddler to an uncertain life of poverty and danger in Central America. Garza accused Chonita of using the uncertainty of his final residence as an excuse not to join him, and he was adamant that after establishing himself permanently in Costa Rica he expected her to come. If she insisted on remaining separate, Garza remarked dramatically, "then . . . I don't know what I would do."[46]

It was difficult for Garza to balance his political and personal commitments. His political activities had not only physically forced him away from his family but also put them in great danger. As Garza was allegedly enjoying his status as a "cacique absoluto" in Costa Rica, his family faced charges in U.S. federal courts and his father-in-law's financial reserves had been seriously drained. Even though Garza claimed he had secured a peaceful and successful life in Costa Rica, he also complained that his life was "difficult because I do not have at my side the loved ones who will be the only ones who will stop me from my political activities." After several months in Costa Rica without his family, Garza grew impatient with their epistolary relationship: "In truth," he concluded, "it is high time to see each other and not just write."[47] After two years of separation, Garza pleaded with his wife for an honest answer about her plans: "I hope that you tell me with plain frankness what you have decided with respect to your trip and the printing press. If [your family] continues to put obstacles in your way, I beg you to not say anything more to them about me."[48]

Garza suspected that Chonita's family prevented her from leaving and joining him. While he had written directly to Alejandro twice in two years of exile, he had not heard back from his father-in-law even once in all of that time.[49] Finally on April 4, 1894, Garza wrote again to his father-in-law to break the silence that had developed between them. While Garza understood that his father-in-law was upset because he had not written to him in over a year, he explained that "you [Alejandro] prohibited me from writing and even from mentioning your name." In an effort to heal whatever wounds existed, Garza declared that he had always thought of Alejandro as a "verdadero padre" (true father), even if he may have seen Garza as a "mal hijo" (bad son)." Offering the olive branch of peace, Garza wrote "now there is no danger — there will be no pretexts for us to stop writing." However, even in this conciliatory letter his frustration showed through: "I recommend nothing," he said, "because I have already made so many suggestions or requests that, pardon the frankness, I feel very deceived."[50]

At the end of April Garza wrote yet again to Alejandro, this time to request money to resuscitate the revolution in Mexico. From his detailed plans it seems that Garza had serious intentions to return to Mexico to complete his aborted insurrection. He planned to take a circuitous route to avoid detection, traveling first to San Francisco and from there to the northern Mexican states of Chihuahua or Sonora. With just $621 from González, he promised to arrive on the border within forty days, and even bring with him the revolutionary proclamations "to raise the spirits of the border people." "Ah," Garza mused, "my second apparition on the Chihuahua border would cause an extraordinary panic."[51]

Although he made it clear that his revolutionary services were in high demand by four different countries, Garza preferred to fight in Mexico. As a foreigner, he realized that he could not rise to any prominence in other countries without adopting their nationality. In any case, he had always maintained that he would only join the other rebellions if there were no possibility to continue the insurrection in Mexico. Garza also bristled that he, a revolutionary with an international reputation, was almost penniless while the other revolutionaries in Central America had hundred of thousands of pesos at their disposal. His letter therefore challenged Alejandro to become more active in planning his "second apparition," even implying that a failure to do so would show a lack of masculine honor. As Garza put it, "the men who don't insist with energy in a cause are not men." In contrast to such indecisive "men," Garza declared his own willingness to "gamble [his] life for the future of all of us." Like a moth to fire, he was drawn to revolution, and with the same suicidal and tragic results. Garza admitted that even hearing the word revolution "agitates my brain and irritates my fighting blood."[52]

It was not just Alejandro's lack of revolutionary zeal that frustrated Garza, but also the general lack of energy and rebelliousness in all Mexicans. In a poem to his wife, Garza rhetorically asked where all the "mexicanos valientes" (valiant Mexicans) had gone, the ones who had fought against the U.S. and French invasions "with the valor of Spartans." They refuse to call themselves "independent," Garza chided, "for fear of the despot or temerity of the *man*."[53] While some had actively betrayed Garza and collaborated with the U.S. Army, others who were supposed to be friends and family simply refused to help him. As Garza said, "good friends are as scarce as garbanzos by the pound."[54] Like he did in his autobiography, Garza tended to criticize other Texas Mexicans as cowards in order to inflate his own importance as the sole defender of Mexicans and liberalism.

Three months had passed since Garza wrote to Alejandro in April, and yet he had not received any mail from his wife. In the meantime he had become actively involved in local politics and was being solicited, according to his letters, to help in several different liberal movements in Latin America. Garza wanted to clarify his relationship with his wife to know whether or not he should risk his life and devote himself to these struggles: "If you are not coming let me know because I cannot be here without involving myself in some campaign, especially if I do not even have the excuse of family." Now that he had been declared an outlaw in Mexico and his family had abandoned him, he had nothing but the revolution to live and die for. To "continue the work that was begun," Garza decided, "it would be necessary to first help other people, so that later they would help me." "Tell me what you have decided," he pleaded; "I cannot exist without doing something big: Is there no trip? Is there no printing press? It appears not."[55]

"I AM C. E. GARZA"

At the same time that he was trying to jump-start the revolt on the border, Garza's letters show him becoming more and more ensconced in the political life of Costa Rica. By late September 1893, he had accepted a position as interim secretary of the police in Puerto Limón.[56] A few months later, in a private meeting with the secretary of war, Garza confessed his true identity. The secretary had apparently read a great deal about him beforehand and was very pleased, Garza claimed, to finally meet the famous revolutionary Mexican general. Although newspapers continued to refer to him as Erasmo G. Betancourt, "in the great centers, in the ministries, in the lodges, and other prestigious circles they know that I am C. E. Garza." As well as being offered a top position in the Costa Rican Army, Garza wrote to his wife that he had been treated to elegant dinners with leading intellectuals and Latin American military chiefs from El Salvador, Nicaragua, and Ecuador. According to the letters, the generals enthusiastically greeted Garza by toasting and applauding "the Mexican who is enemy of the *Yankees*."[57]

By February 1894, Garza ascended in the state bureaucracy, becoming chief of police of Puerto Limón and also being named *jefe político* (political boss); he now had the power to judge cases in the lower courts. The Costa Rican military also apparently bestowed honor on Garza, granting him the rank of division general. At this point, the *Gaceta oficial* published Garza's real name along with his appointment, and thus he could no longer hide under an alias. However, given the warm welcome he had received by the Costa Rican government and military, he confidently stated that "there is no longer any danger, I am finally only Garza."[58]

As soon as he was appointed as a military commander in Limón, Garza faced a rebellion led by friars who wanted to install a bishop as president. Acting quickly, Garza suffocated the movement, but not before six people were killed and five wounded in violent confrontations between clerics and liberals. Garza believed, mistakenly as it turned out, that his decisive action in putting down the clerical uprising would indebt the Costa Rican government to him.[59]

Garza had good reason to feel secure, for even when Díaz attempted to extradite him the Costa Rican government refused and instead placed him at the head of a political movement to unify the five Central American countries.[60] Garza also boasted that liberal revolutionaries from Guatemala to Chile called on him to help them with their revolutions, thereby suggesting to his wife that his reputation had spread throughout Latin America. When the former president of Ecuador wrote from Chile to ask Garza for help in his struggle to regain power, Garza wrote to his wife that he had responded eagerly: "As a man of universal ideas, my sword is always at the disposition of the people who moan under the heavy yokes of tyrannies, no matter what nationality they may be."[61]

These years in Costa Rica broadened Garza's geographical scope and solidified his revolutionary persona. More than simply being a Mexican nationalist revolutionary, he had visions of becoming a pan–Latin Americanist hero. Indeed, exile made Garza more defiant and more confident than ever. Such claims seem exaggerated for the purpose of convincing his wife that he was indeed the revolutionary hero that he believed himself to be. In a letter to Chonita he boasted that, even in Africa, "I am certain that with my character or my word, I attract the popular masses and I am placed in distinguished circles."[62] Further, Garza was beginning to see himself as a universal savior. In another letter home he recounted a spontaneous speech he gave to a crowd of over one thousand, in which he proclaimed, "Jesus Christ was the first democrat; he died on the cross to redeem us as free people and he left us his liberal doctrines so that we would never profane them."[63] In this speech not only did Garza explicitly use Jesus as a symbol of the fight for democracy and liberalism, but he implicitly draws a parallel between himself and the Christ figure. That Garza felt himself to be somewhat of a martyr to the liberal movement should not be surprising given his willingness to sacrifice and even die for the cause. In June 1894, when he discovered that the United States was pursuing his extradition, Garza made what would prove to be an ominous prediction: "Soon the blood of martyrs will run."[64]

In addition to corresponding with his wife, Garza remained in contact with his brother Encarnación and other political supporters in the United States. Hoping to continue his political activities in Costa Rica, he repeatedly asked his wife to send him his printing press, a collection of local newspapers, and all of his personal papers.[65] However, from Garza's safe haven in Costa Rica it proved extremely difficult to inspire people in Texas to rebel. Not only was communication sporadic but most of his supporters spent the latter part of 1893 in Texas courts and jails defending themselves against charges of violating neutrality laws. In spite of their suffering under the weight of repression in Texas Garza felt betrayed by his own people because, he claimed, they had not appreciated the sacrifices he had made for his "sainted causes." In a letter to his father-in-law, Garza wrote that "other people, perhaps strangers, will raise the thought to immortalize the memory of a man who did good for the oppressed collective."[66]

The religious imagery that Garza invoked in these letters to describe his "sainted causes" and his desire to be "immortalized" shows that he had begun to think of himself as a revolutionary martyr. His letter thus not only anticipated his own death but attempted to shape the meaning of it as well. He asked his wife to pray to God "that your exiled and persecuted husband live a few more years, because I foresee that when I hold up my political ideals I will be the chosen one to topple the Throne of Porfirio Díaz."[67] The feelings of mortality and immortality coursed through him, simultaneously fearing death yet sensing that he would be the "chosen one" to overthrow Díaz.

Garza thought of himself as a courageous hero, at least since the time he wrote his autobiography. After his revolt and his exile, his cultivation of that persona only grew stronger. Writing to his brother, Garza declared that in all of the Central and South American countries "the name of Garza embodies the principle of Mexican socio-political regeneration; this name has filled these atmospheres with a free environment, a democratic breeze."[68] In another letter, Garza called on his brother to prepare for insurrection in Texas, noting that now he had the support of all of the countries to the south of Mexico. As soon as they initiated their struggle, "the press from all of the nations on the American Continent will raise their voice in favor of Garza."[69] The rebellion had become a personal struggle between himself and Díaz, and he even suggested that a Garzista party be reorganized to act as the "rejuvenating emblem." The battle lines between liberal, freedom-loving Garzistas and authoritarian, tyrannical Porfiristas crystallized in Garza's mind. The equation was simple: " 'Garcistas' means 'free ones' and 'Porfiristas' signifies 'abject slaves.' "[70] Garza saw himself as Díaz's most significant rival because supposedly he had granted amnesty to all of his political enemies, with the exception of Garza.[71] However, while there is plenty of evidence that Díaz worried about Garza when he was on the border, and even pursued his extradition when he was in Costa Rica, the notion that Garza was Díaz's greatest rival is probably a stretch. There were many other Díaz rivals within Mexico, among them high-ranking military officers and wealthy hacendados, who posed a far greater threat to the Porfirian regime than this one poor rebel struggling to survive in exile in Costa Rica.

"YOUR INDISPENSABLE AND CONSTANT POLITICAL ENEMY"

Although Garza fantasized about his popularity in private letters, he was more circumspect in his public pronouncements. In a political pamphlet written during his exile in Costa Rica, Garza tried to paint a picture of humility, insisting, "I never had the crazy ambition to govern my country, because I understand that Mexico needs governors of a much better stature than the humble stature of my personality."[72] This pamphlet, titled *La era de Tuxtepec: O sea Rusia en América* (The era of Tuxtepec: in other words, Russia in America), excoriated Díaz and his administration for leading Mexico astray from its path of enlightened liberalism to a dark, tyrannical dictatorship. The reference to Russia was meant to imply that Díaz had become what Garza called an "eternal czar."

The pamphlet, published in San José, Costa Rica, in September 1894

23. Inscription from Catarino Garza to Porfirio
Díaz, September 30, 1894, in *La era de Tuxtepec:
O sea Rusia en América*. (Courtesy of Tulane
University, Latin American Collection)

was meant to justify Garza's rebellion to a broader Latin American audience as well as to help foment resistance to Díaz on the Texas-Mexico border. To prove his continued faith in the revolution, Garza sent his wife a few copies of *La era de Tuxtepec* and asked her to have them "circulate among those who judge me morally and politically dead."[73] Garza also mailed President Díaz a copy of the pamphlet; the handwritten inscription in the front explained that he had written the tract so that "my judgments, with respect to your lifetime Tyranny and Indefinite Dictatorship do not die with me, your indispensable and constant political enemy" (fig. 23).[74] At least one thousand copies were published, and according to Garza, the press received his pamphlet warmly. By mid-October, Garza claimed that more than fifty letters had streamed in from enthusiastic readers throughout Central and South America.[75]

The thirty-two page essay criticized the Porfirian regime for being corrupt and authoritarian. Except for the secretary of foreign relations, Ignacio Mariscal, whom Garza found "somewhat honorable," the other ministers were described as "scoundrels" who pilfered the public coffers for their personal benefit.[76] Garza also accused Díaz of personally masterminding several schemes to defraud the country, including paying off imaginary public debts that would actually end up in the president's pockets, and dispossessing Indians of their land in Sonora in order to sell it to U.S. surveying companies.[77] Beyond Díaz's financial improprieties, Garza listed a series of political assassinations carried out by the president, including a well-known case where Díaz sent a telegram to one of his generals in Veracruz ordering the execution of nine suspected coup plotters. Díaz's telegram gave the order succinctly: "Kill them in cold blood."[78]

More than just a critique of Porfirian abuses, *La era de Tuxtepec* was also a justification of the 1891 revolution. Garza insisted that his revolt was "spontaneous" rather than artificial; he pointed to his ability to raise a large army of "honorable men" as evidence that his was a popular cause. To prove that he had a large army, he claimed that more than six hundred Garzistas, almost certainly an exaggerated number, were tried in San Antonio for violation of neutrality laws. He also contended that the state's district attorney absolved the Garzistas, thus implying that their enemies also recognized the righteousness of their movement. There is no evidence, however, that any of the rebels were absolved as Garza claimed.[79] While *Harper's Weekly* reported that the Mexican government had offered $300,000 for Garza's capture, Garza contended that the Mexican government had given the U.S. government $760,000 to kill him and, if he were captured, the U.S. would receive Baja California as a prize.[80] These exaggerations and false statements were meant to inflate Garza's own significance by making him seem more dangerous to the U.S. and Mexican governments than he actually was.

Garza also tried to downplay Díaz's strength. It was the U.S. Army, not the Porfirian regime, Garza argued, that had crushed his revolt. He left after several months, he further stated, not because of cowardice but because he did not want to be responsible for an "international conflict" and because he had been badly wounded.[81] With this pamphlet, Garza sought to legitimize his crusade and prove that he was a "lawful revolutionary and not a criminal bandit."[82]

Although Garza situated his revolution within a longer trajectory of liberal struggle in Mexico, there was an element of personal rivalry in his critique. At one point, he compared his comportment to that of Díaz, asking rhetorically which one of them was more of a bandit: "He who executed without pity when he revolutionized, he who never paid a cent for what his army consumed, he who burned towns and railroad bridges, or I who paid even for my horse's hay, who never executed anyone, . . . I that never kidnapped anyone, nor violated any of the rights of the citizen, I who never had the resources of government."[83] Beyond the revolutionary rhetoric, the essay reveals a bitter tone of a poor, failed revolutionary who was stuck in exile, far from his country and his family. Rather than breaking his spirit, Garza argued that his bitterness made him more committed than ever to his revolutionary ideals, even if that meant opposing the United States, which he had tried so diligently not to offend during his revolution. As he wrote toward the end of his pamphlet, "I am a revolutionary in Mexico, the bitter enemy of the tyrants and enemy also of the Americans who dream of Baja California and the annexation of the border states of Mexico."[84]

While U.S. courts had refused to extradite Garza to Mexico in 1887 because it would have meant certain execution, in 1894 it was the U.S. government that was requesting Garza's extradition from Costa Rica. There were few places left to hide. Only fatalism and faith sustained him: "Whomever it may be, here I am, ready to sacrifice my life in favor of the cause that I defend and will defend."[85] By August, Garza confirmed that the Costa Rican government will "reject that pretense of the *yankees* and Díaz," and deny their extradition request because of his popularity among the masses.[86] Contrary to Garza's belief, however, the Costa Rican government eventually gave in to pressure by the United States and turned against Garza.

With the publication of *La era de Tuxtepec*, Garza claimed that he became a highly sought-after public speaker for national holidays and other official functions. In September 1894, Garza gave a one-hour speech at a banquet commemorating Central American independence. According to Garza, the captains of a British steamship and a U.S. warship who attended the banquet even lauded the speech. The U.S. Navy officers, Garza explained to his wife, said that "Garza had the most advanced ideas of any Mexican they had met — that Garza not only belonged to Mexico, but to all of America." The British captain allegedly declared Garza "a man of arms, of the rostrum and of letters: in the first he is a genius, in the second a hurricane and in the third a machine-gun or dynamite." The U.S. Navy captain was also apparently so impressed with Garza that he invited him to his ship for a banquet complete with "good champagne" and an eleven-gun salute in his honor. Garza politely declined, replying, "I don't want to commit suicide yet, I want to live a little longer to stir up disorganized movements among Mexicans and 'Americans.'" Whether or not this was a trap to lure Garza aboard the U.S. Navy ship and arrest him, Garza was not going to gamble with his life, "not even for millions of pesos."[87]

Avoiding the U.S. Navy was one thing, but there were other potentially more deadly threats. Garza imagined that President Díaz could easily hire an assassin to kill him, but he boasted that the assassin would be unable to finish the job "because in this country even the most common blacks love me and pay homage to me." Although he was always aware of the dangers posed by various enemies, he began to develop a false sense of security that his reputation among "all of the popular masses" would protect him. Writing to his wife, Garza even suggested that his sex appeal had helped him gain admirers. "I am sure," he wrote, "that if you had seen me [giving the speech] that you would have fallen in love with Garza — Truly? — Ca . . . ramba. . . . He made the girls' mouths water — Don't get jealous — you know well that I am very honorable."[88] As portrayed in his autobiography, Garza's self-depiction as a romantic, desirable, and honorable male hero was part of his political persona.

"THE HOUR IS GETTING CLOSER"

At the same time that his personal fame was supposedly growing, Garza decided to join the Colombian insurrection. After several meetings with exiled Colombian liberals, Garza became an official member of the Directorate of the Colombian Liberal War, and he took the position of commander of the Federal Restoration forces on the Atlantic Coast.[89] He also began raising funds and collecting arms for his intended reappearance in Mexico, and he corresponded with his fellow insurrectionists in Texas, including his brother Encarnación, as well as Paulino Martínez, Manuel Flores Chapa, and García Granados. When his coconspirators responded to his call, Garza enthusiastically exclaimed that they were "waking up with his letters." For the Mexican insurrection, he had supposedly secured promises from the vice president of El Salvador for one thousand rifles and twenty thousand bullets; had arranged a meeting with a "wealthy American entrepreneur" to obtain a large quantity of arms and munitions; and had hopes that the government of Guatemala would also provide assistance.[90] Garza's decision to join the Colombian struggle thus did not imply that he had forgotten or abandoned the Mexican revolution. In fact, Garza only agreed to help the Colombian liberals, he argued, after he secured their promise to help him fight Díaz once they had triumphed. The quid pro quo involved Garza leading Colombian troops that would land on the Pacific coast of Mexico. Garza also asked his brother to begin quietly organizing a guerrilla army on the Texas border. "Speak to the most prestigious people," Garza implored, "and tell them that I guarantee to lead them whenever they want." Given his defeat in Texas and lack of financial support in exile, Garza can be viewed either as an eternal optimist or as pathologically unrealistic, or both. "I have blind faith," Garza wrote, "that if I appear there again, all of the people will rise up with true enthusiasm."[91]

Meanwhile, the Mexican government kept a close watch on Garza in Costa Rica and attempted to extradite him before he could stir up trouble again. San Antonio's Mexican consul informed Bernardo Reyes that Garza resided in Puerto Limón, and that he received frequent letters from Texas and had definite plans to return there at some point.[92] While it is not exactly clear how much organizing occurred in Texas, the insurrectionists had written a revolutionary proclamation that they sent to Garza in Costa Rica for his approval. Garza responded that he was not that concerned about the form of the proclamation as long as it "toppled the Tyrant to raise up a popular representative that deserves to be called Constitutional President." He added, "my only ambitions, my only dreams are to free my people from the wicked tyranny that reigns in Mexico."[93] Clearly he was not being completely honest by glossing over his personal ambitions to be the protagonist in this epic battle against tyranny.

During the last few months of his stay in Costa Rica, the letters Garza sent to his wife focused more on his political activities in Central America and on his hope for a renewal of the rebellion in Mexico than on his personal feelings. After Concepción complained to him about the brevity of his recent correspondence, Garza responded defensively that he always wrote long letters. If he had been "laconic" at times, he explained, it was only because of his busy work schedule, which had forced him to employ two scribes and a personal secretary. He continued to send kisses and hugs to his "very dear wife," but he filled his letters more and more with details about the various revolutions he was planning to lead. Garza also noticed his own metamorphosis during his time in exile. Whereas before he had complained in his letters that he was deceived and forgotten by everyone, now he was writing "animated proclamations and sentences of hope," and he felt that everyone remembered and believed in him. His letters thus recast his earlier suffering as a necessary rite of passage that had enabled him to change "from a midget into a giant."[94]

In November 1894, Garza had heard that Mexicans in the capital were planning to write a biography about him, and he viewed it as proof of their "patriotic gratitude" for all that he had done for Mexico. He laid out some of the important points of his life story that he wanted Mauricio González (his brother-in-law) to relate to the authors. His biography should focus, he insisted, on "his humble crib" as a lesson to new generations that any poor child "with sufficient energy" could rise to the top. In addition to his image as a self-made man, Garza wanted the biography to include studies about his work for the good of the "*raza* mexicana" in Texas, and about the "chains, shackles, and the assassination attempts that I suffered." He also reminded his wife to mention that a [musical] march, Adelante, had been dedicated to him. Garza predicted that the authors of his story would become rich given the wide circulation that the book would have in all of the Americas.[95] In the end, however, not only did the biography not become a best-seller, it apparently was never written.

Garza's last few months in Costa Rica were ones of great uncertainty as he began to suspect that his comrades in Texas were not organizing anything. One letter chided "Los famosos!!! Revolucionarios" Garcia Granados, Paulino Martínez, Manuel Flores Chapa, and Victor Ochoa for their silence and fear. He needed every ally he could find, however, and so a month later he named these same people as the principal organizers of the insurrection in Texas. After celebrating his thirty-fifth birthday in late November, Garza was anxious to see his revolutionary seeds bear fruit. By the end of December his letters to Texas took on a more urgent tone as he sent official papers naming Encarnación Garza and Manuel Flores Chapa as officers of the Restoration Army of Mexico.[96] He informed his brother Encarnacíon that when he arrived in the north, he would give the "grito" (yell) and distribute the revolutionary proclamation. In the meantime he issued orders for Encarnación, including: go to Randado ranch and obtain one hundred to two hundred rifles, sell the printing press to buy supplies, tell the González's to prepare themselves, and contact the other revolutionaries as well. "The hour is getting closer."[97]

Just before Christmas 1894, Garza finally confided to his wife that whatever happened with the Colombian revolution, he was going to arrive in Chihuahua on Cinco de Mayo.[98] In subsequent letters, he warned Chonita to keep quiet and watch out for suspicious characters: "The thing is serious and your hide is on the line." This time, he predicted, "I have high hopes to reach the capitol with my sword held high, challenging the hatred of the tyrants." Encouraging her, he wrote, "don't lose faith nor hope, soon we will see each other and perhaps never again separate."[99]

By the end of January 1895, Garza announced that he was waiting for a French or German steamship so that he could begin his journey to Curacao via Colombia and Venezuela. Garza claimed that he had arranged a meeting with the ex-president of Venezuela, Dr. Rojas Paul, and the "liberal caudillo" of Colombia, General Avelino Rosas, to sign a reciprocal pact against "the three wicked tyrants of our countries." The trip and his public farewell party were also designed to confuse Díaz. Knowing that Díaz's spies would inform him about Garza's abrupt departure from Costa Rica, the trip would have Díaz believe that he was headed for Mexico when he was really off to Colombia. "¡Ah! Estupido," Garza exclaimed, Díaz "will put them on alert and will make his agents run off on disorganized searches for Garza, but I will head in the opposite direction," toward Colombia. By the time these "bandidos" exhausted themselves and relaxed again, Garza would already be on his way back to Mexico to surprise them.[100]

Garza sent off the first of his boats to Colombia on January 20, on a vessel flying the Norwegian flag. Writing to Chonita on February 5, he told her that he was busy preparing two more boats loaded with weapons on which he would travel himself. The reports he had received indicated that people in Colombia had already risen up in arms in four states, and that whole villages had been burned to the ground. Garza was sanguine about the violence: "Forward! You need to instill terror in the tyrants."[101]

"TO BE OR NOT TO BE"

Two days after Garza penned his letter to Chonita, he was almost killed by government agents. The Costa Rican government, having been pressured by Colombia, Mexico, and the United States, began prosecuting Garza on the pretext that he was arming an expedition on the Atlantic coast (which of course he was). They first ordered Garza to remain in the capital under close watch, then they prohibited him from leaving the country, and finally they wanted him captured "dead or alive." Garza hid in the house of a family in Puerto Limón until February 7, when the authorities surrounded the house and began to search inside. Having run out of all other options Garza jumped out of the window, which was eighteen feet above the ground, and even though he injured his leg he was able to hobble to a nearby bakery. After remaining in the bakery all day, Garza painted his face with a burned cork so that he would look black, and escaped at night in the company of an Afro–Costa Rican man. With the city's large black population it was easy for Garza in blackface to blend in with the crowd; he passed by a policeman and a barber without them suspecting him at all, and an hour later he managed to escape to the jungle. Meanwhile, the police were scouring Puerto Limón for Garza, and had even shot and killed someone who looked like him as well as wounding another innocent person.[102]

Garza remained in the jungle for three days with three of his supporters. Using his contacts in Limón, he finally managed to arrange for a canoe in which he escaped northward. "It was a miracle," Garza wrote to his wife, "that in the high sea [the canoe] was not swallowed by an alligator." After finally landing at San Juan del Norte, just north of the border on the Nicaraguan coast, Garza regrouped forces and pulled together 500 Remington rifles, 125 Winchesters, and a "magnificent boat." It was now February 20, and Garza was writing Chonita what would be his last letter. That night he raised anchor and headed south.[103] After leaving Nicaragua, Garza set up camp in the thick jungle next to Cahuita beach, about twenty-five miles south of Puerto Limón. He had with him between fifty and seventy-five well-armed men. By March 4, the Costa Rican Army was aware of Garza's presence near Puerto Vargas, and officials began collecting information from people in the area who had seen or heard about the rebel camp and their impending attack on Colombia.[104] Two days later, 250 Costa Rican "bare footed soldiers" were dispatched to Garza's camp, but they arrived too late. Garza and his men had departed on a boat for Bocas del Toro, Panama, just two hours earlier.[105]

In his final letter home, Garza mused at the cowardice of tyrants and the fear that he had inspired in them. As soon as the newspapers reported his leaving Costa Rica, the Spanish minister asked that Garza be watched because he worried that he would be heading to Cuba with the independence leader General Antonio Maceo. The Colombians were sure that Garza would head for their Atlantic coast, and the Mexicans insisted that he would invade their country through Guatemala. "Wretched cowards!" Garza exclaimed. "The truth is that the *garza* [heron] flapped her wings in the middle of the evil hunters who wanted to kill her."[106] In spite of his ability to confuse his enemies, the noose was tightening around Garza.

After years of indecision, and after years of waiting for his wife and child to join him, waiting for his fellow insurrectionists in Texas to organize themselves, and waiting for the Colombians to begin their revolt, it was finally time: "The moment has arrived, my Chonita, to fight hand to hand for the liberties of a brotherly people, who will later help liberate mine, or raise on my tomb a symbol of remembrance." He knew he was facing death, but facing death was the only way for him to live. " 'To be or not to be' — I am resolved to fight like a Lion to prove to the mercenaries of Latin America that they have or will have reason to cowardly tremble before my arm that holds the regenerating sword of Continental America." Garza ended his letter asking everyone to have faith in God that he would triumph. He sent kisses to his nearly four-year-old daughter Amelia, and he asked his wife to receive his heart that would never forget her. "At last the moment to be in battle has arrived, and I carry before the enemy a steady thought of you." His last line read: "A loving hug and goodbye my adored Chonita. Yours Always, C. E. Garza."[107]

On March 4, 1895, Chonita penned a letter to her husband from Palito Blanco, but she did not even know where to send it. It began formally, "my beloved and always remembered husband. This is to greet you and tell you that everyone here is well, wishing you a thousand warm wishes." Chonita had not heard from her husband in over a month. The last she knew from his letters was that he was heading to Curacao and would proceed from there to Colombia. The newspapers had reported that Garza had arrived on Colombia's border, but for fifteen days, she lamented, "there is a profound silence." In her letter she informed Catarino that his brother Encarnación had arrived safely in Texas and that his mother and the rest of their family were well. Of their daughter, she wrote simply, "Amelia sends you many kisses." In the end, however, Chonita never mailed the letter, because in the next few days Catarino's profound silence would finally be broken with the tragic news of his death.[108]

TO DIE FIGHTING

In the early morning hours of March 8, 1895, Garza led a small band of men in an attack on Bocas del Toro, a small town on an island off the Caribbean coast of northern Panama, which at that time was still a province of Colombia. The element of surprise was crucial, yet even before Garza set off in a small sailboat from Cahuita, the imminent raid was being reported in major U.S. newspapers. As early as March 5, the *Times Democrat* in St. Louis announced that Bocas del Toro would be taken by "revolutionaries without a known leader."[109] On the 6th, the *New York Herald* indicated that Garza had seized an armed ship and was planning an attack with the assistance of Venezuelan exiles in Curacao.[110] Meanwhile, the Mexican ambassador, Matías Romero, briefed the U.S. secretary of state on Garza's background and urged him to send forces to stop the attack.[111] A day after the meeting, the U.S. warship *Atlanta* set sail from Colón, Panama, to Bocas del Toro. Authorities claimed that the *Atlanta* was heading to Porto Bello for a fresh paint job and target practice, but the press questioned the official story, contending that the ship was probably heading to Bocas del Toro to head off Colombian rebels.[112] On that same day a cable from Puerto Limón warned that Bocas del Toro "has been or is going to be attacked one of these nights."[113] With all of this advance warning, the Panamanian and U.S. forces had plenty of time to prepare a strong defense, and the crucial element of surprise that the rebels counted on had been completely lost.

With the arrival of the *Atlanta* in Bocas del Toro and rumors running rampant about the impending rebellion, most of the foreigners and conservatives fled town. Meanwhile, the local liberals, who comprised a majority of the populace, waited anxiously for the arrival of the rebels.[114] The only detailed description of the attack on Bocas del Toro was published in 1896 by Donaldo Velasco, a Colombian conservative who witnessed the battle.[115] Although clearly biased against the liberals, this eighty-page booklet, based on Velasco's eyewitness account along with official reports and newspaper articles, provides a blow-by-blow description of Garza's last battle and the final hours of his life. Although Velasco opposed the Colombian liberals, he recognized that Garza was not the "bandido vulgar" (vulgar bandit) that the North Americans had portrayed. For him, Garza was like a brave "lion," a man who could fight ferociously, but who also had "a marked gentlemanly spirit."[116]

Velasco's account corroborates Garza's story of how he escaped from Puerto Limón under the darkness of night disguised as a soot-covered, shoeless coal miner. It is unclear whether Garza intended to appear like a "black" man or, as Velasco contended, like a "carbonero" (coal miner) whose face would be blackened by work in the mines. In either case, both versions have Garza escaping to the Atlantic coast of Nicaragua. It was there that Garza met up with several exiled Colombian liberals and began to prepare for the attack on Bocas del Toro.[117] Evidence gathered after the attack showed that the governor of Miskito Province in Nicaragua provided Garza with arms.[118] Finally, on the appointed day, Garza set off on a small sailboat named *Favor de Dios* (God's will) with thirty or forty armed men. According to Velasco, one was an "Americano," one was a Jamaican from Bluefields, seventeen were Nicaraguan officers, and only seven were Colombians.[119] It is important here to remember that Garza's raid was only one part of a much larger coordinated effort by Colombian liberals that had begun on January 22 in Bogotá.[120]

On the way to Bocas, Garza began to doubt that they would be successful given the small size of their band and the generally low quality of the soldiers. According to Velasco, most of Garza's men were mercenaries and therefore could not necessarily be counted on to fight with great courage and valor. Pereira Castro, another leader of the expedition, calmed Garza's fears by arguing that with the support by liberals in Bocas and with the element of surprise on their side, they would be victorious. Even if Castro's pep talk had not convinced him, after seeing the smoke from the ship that the Costa Rican government had sent after them Garza knew there was no turning back. Velasco explained Garza's dilemma: "To die fighting or die after being delivered to the Mexican government if they were imprisoned by the small steamship."[121] Needless to say, Garza chose to fight.

Just before midnight on March 7, Garza's group landed north of Bocas del Toro and began their trek along the coast. At 2 A.M., after a long march interrupted by bouts of rum drinking, the band arrived at a hilltop overlooking their final destination. A "sepulchral silence" enveloped the early morning air. Everything seemed to be on the rebels' side, except for the bright moonlight that forced them to delay their attack. As the moon set, the hazy light gave way to an impenetrable darkness. Following an interior path through the dense jungle instead of walking along the coastline, the rebels began a two-and-a-half-mile march to reach the military barracks. Once they arrived at the edge of town, the rebels were received with open arms at a brothel. It was here, according to Velasco, that the band of liberal revolutionaries received their last libation.[122]

The rebels attempted to capture the political chief of the town, but when they broke into his house they only found his sick wife. It was 4 A.M., and they decided not to wait any longer. They would simultaneously assault the police headquarters and the military barracks, with Castro leading the former attack and Garza the latter.

Crossing the street with three large steps, Garza shot five bullets point-blank into the head of the sentinel guarding the military barracks. A firefight broke out immediately as government soldiers woke from their slumber, grabbing their arms and taking aim at the rebels. In spite of taking a bullet in his thigh Garza rallied his troops, jumping from one point to another "with the elasticity of a panther." He also tried to rouse the local radicals to the fight by shouting the agreed-on slogan "Viva el General Ruiz."[123] Garza had earned the personal enmity of General Ruiz after calling him a coward in an article in the *Panama Daily Herald*. In fact, General Ruiz had requested to be sent to Bocas to fight Garza, and he was waiting there for him with 350 soldiers.[124] Velasco's account indicates that Garza stopped for a moment to ask a black sentinel guarding the barracks if he were injured. In that moment of hesitation a bullet hit Garza's knife, smashing it into four pieces, but Garza continued on. When his men asked if he was hurt, Garza replied that "it was nothing." Then, seeing one of his soldier's bullets miss the mark, Garza exclaimed in English, "this brut [*sic*] shot too high." It was in the heat of the battle with Garza's guns still blazing away that two bullets from the windows above struck him. He immediately fell to the ground, blood gushing out of his chest and belly. The fighting continued for awhile before the rebels realized that Garza had been killed. By 5 A.M., after only half an hour of battle, the guns fell silent.[125]

In the first moments of battle Castro successfully overtook the police station. Even after he saw that Garza and others had been killed, and that many more of their band had been captured, he still had hope. Taking one of his prisoners at gunpoint, Castro forced him to pour petroleum on a house near the military barracks. With a gun to his head, the prisoner was about to light a match to set the building ablaze when a bullet hit Castro in the chest, killing him instantaneously. With their two leaders dead, the rest of the rebels scattered. Only four managed to escape, however, one of whom died soon thereafter on a deserted beach. With the help of a steamboat lent by the Wilson merchant house, the authorities captured the *Favor de Dios* with the escaping rebels onboard; in this situation even God was not on their side.[126]

The muscles on Garza's cadaver were frozen in the active flexing pose he held at the moment of his death. Velasco described the moribund Garza as seeming almost alive with his "fixed and penetrating look, his clever and notably beautiful forehead and his hands withdrawn like a gladiator in a combat position." The body, with the black wool shirt, pants rolled up, and boots covered in dirt, testified to his grueling final hours. On his breast, near his biggest wound, lay two pictures of his wife Chonita and a packet of love letters. Garza had kept his promise to always keep Chonita close to him. "Even after death," Velasco commented, "[Garza] inspired respect."[127]

At four in the afternoon, Garza, Castro, and three of their comrades were buried in a deep grave in Bocas del Toro.[128] An informant from Puerto Limón commented on the funeral: "They say he [Garza] was buried like a dog." The informant continued, "Garza is dead and is no more to be dreaded by Mexico. He fell fighting like a man. He was shot 16 times through and through the body." The author of this letter, presumably written to either the U.S. or Mexican government, was very precise about documenting Garza's death and indicated that a Mr. Alberger from Limón, along with several others, positively identified Garza when he was buried on Friday evening.[129] Díaz, who in Velasco's estimation, "spent many long insomniac nights with his tenacious suitor" could finally rest easy now that the Mexican rebel was safely within his grave.[130]

No matter where we went or whom he was fighting, Garza always came up against the military might of what he called "the foreign invader to the North."[131] Here he was, a Mexican in a remote corner of Panama fighting against conservative Colombians and the U.S. marines were on hand to stop him. The *San Francisco Examiner* explained that the U.S. cruiser *Atlanta* was "landing marines at Bocas del Toro to protect the American interests there."[132] The commander of the *Atlanta* defended such intervention, claiming that it was "deemed necessary for the proper protection of American life and property." There must have been a "serious state of affairs," one newspaper reasoned, to warrant the landing of U.S. troops on foreign soil.[133] Landing the marines had a direct connection to U.S. interests in the Panama Canal and railway. Specifically, the U.S. government worried about the danger of a widescale uprising by disgruntled canal workers who had already threatened to "destroy property." As the *San Francisco Examiner* wrote: "The unemployed—the starving men who were set adrift by the canal company, having nothing to hope for from the Colombian government, made common cause with the insurgents."[134] Another newspaper attempted to calm investors' fears by proclaiming that "the US is pledged to prevent the interruption of traffic across the isthmus, and warships have been sent there to fulfill that pledge." If need be, they warned, "troops will be landed and distributed along the route as was done by Admiral Jouett several years ago when the property was similarly threatened."[135] Following the attack, the Colombian government declared a state of emergency in all of Panama.

While it seems clear that Panamanian authorities shot the fatal bullets into Garza's body, he can be said to have achieved the ultimate Latin American revolutionary martyrdom by being killed under the watchful eyes of the U.S. military while fighting for the liberal cause.[136] Once again, although Garza directed his revolt against "tyrants" in Latin America, he ended up facing U.S. troops. The economic interests that tied the United States and Latin America together could not be so easily separated. Therefore, even if Garza had no intent to antagonize U.S. interests in Panama, rebellion was not viewed kindly by Washington. Ironically, it would be the United States that provoked Panama's separation from Colombia in 1903 as a way to assure "in perpetuity the use, occupation and control" of the ten-mile-wide interoceanic canal zone.[137]

RESURRECTION

As a good revolutionary, Garza believed that his cause would continue after his death: "My disappearance or my death would not constitute the death of the sainted cause that I defended and will defend as long as I am alive."[138] Not only did the liberal struggle continue to rage throughout Latin America in the coming years and decades, but Garza was resurrected as a symbol of that enduring fight. In October 1895, seven months after his death in Bocas del Toro, a report by the Mexican consul in Havana cited several sources that indicated Garza was alive and fighting with the Cuban independence movement.[139] In fact, one informant told Consul A. C. Vasquez that Garza had not been killed in Colombia. Instead, the story went, after he had been defeated in Panama he crossed over to Ecuador and helped the exiled president of that country to reassume power. Vasquez added that Cuban newspapers described him as "a very valiant, very able, and extraordinarily bold Mexican. He was reputed to be a first class commander."[140]

While Vasquez referred to Garza as a "bewildering enemy of the tranquillity and progress of his country," he hinted at a degree of sympathy for Garza as a fellow Mexican. The consul requested "concrete instructions" in the form of a classified note or a confidential letter about whether to intervene and send Garza to Veracruz or allow the Spanish to execute him in the eventuality that they captured the rebel leader. Ultimately, Vasquez decided that if faced with the decision he would advocate on Garza's behalf, "seeing in him [more of] a compatriot, than an enemy of order in the Mexican Nation." With war operations about to begin in the region where Garza had been spotted, the possibility remained open for a quicker and possibly more sinister resolution to this dilemma. Therefore, although Vasquez felt some solidarity he was also prepared to get rid of the "disgraceful Mexican" if those were his "instructions."[141]

Reports and rumors circulated throughout the rest of 1895 that the Mexican general fighting the Spanish in Cuba was Catarino E. Garza. *La Discusión* of Havana and *La Defensa* of Monterrey both published accounts by captured Cuban independence fighters, testifying that they had been led by Catarino Garza. *La Defensa* concluded: "It seems that Garza did not die as was said; on the contrary, he is full of life and more ready than ever to show his turbulent and fighting character."[142] The Havana newspaper *Diario de la Marina* even reported that Garza's wife had recently received a letter from her husband who had been killed months earlier in Bocas del Toro. In the 1960s, one sixty-five-year-old resident of Palito Blanco claimed that Garza had been living at his mother-in-law's house since the rebellion. "I saw him many times," the old-timer said.[143] Not everyone, however, believed in Garza's magical resurrection. A Spanish-language St. Louis newspaper, for instance, was highly skeptical about reports that Garza appeared "to be alive and well in Cuba, fighting in the columns of the patriotic Cubans."[144]

Beyond the physical issue of whether or not Garza came back to life, which seems unlikely, lies the more important metaphysical question about why the press and other liberal revolutionaries felt a need to repeatedly resurrect him. Garza fulfilled a role that was not satisfied at the time of his death. Therefore, even if he had died he lived on as a symbol. Other figures, such as Antonio Maceo and José Martí in Cuba, and Ricardo Flores Magón, Pancho Villa, and Emiliano Zapata in Mexico, would rise to prominence in the coming years and supplant Garza as the embodiment of Latin America's liberal and anti-imperialist ideals. These struggles for national liberation and pan–Latin American unity would continue to reverberate throughout the hemisphere for quite some time, culminating in the ultimate symbol: Che Guevara. Just as Garza's life ended, the final war for Cuban independence began, and three years later Cubans succeeded in overthrowing Spanish rule. Fifteen years after Garza's death, liberal Mexicans organized a rebellion that toppled Porfirio Díaz and initiated a long social revolution whose echoes are still being heard today. Both the Cuban and the Mexican insurrections stopped short of fulfilling their revolutionary promise. The United States filled Spain's boots as the neocolonial lord in Cuba, and the ruling party in Mexico put the brakes on radical change and began pursuing many of the same policies fostered during the Porfiriato. Nonetheless, this liberal anti-imperialist movement changed the face of Latin America forever.

EPILOGUE

When my wife talks about him,

she says, "He's a communist. He

should have stayed at home and

taken care of his family."

—Carlos Pérez

In July 1999, I met with Catarino Garza's grandson, Carlos Pérez, on his ranch outside of Alice, Texas. The tall (6′6″), gaunt, seventy-seven-year-old rancher had kept alive the memory of his grandfather, preserving letters, photographs, and most important, the stories of the revolution. At first he was reluctant to be interviewed, but after encouragement from his nephew he held forth for the rest of the day, regaling me with stories about his family's roots in Texas and about Catarino's insurrection. At the end of the interview, he reached for a framed map of Spanish land grants that hung on the wall of his trailer, and proudly pointed out his ancestor's parcels. Over the years, the family's large grant has steadily dwindled in size, being subdivided among relatives and sold in hard times, as was done after Catarino's revolt failed. The family is not poor by any means, but neither are they rich, especially in comparison to the immense wealth of the nearby King ranch. More than a claim to property once held and now lost, however, the map symbolizes the family's deep roots in South Texas and their connection to the land. These are the roots that gave rise to Garza's revolution. Although the revolt was crushed before it could bloom the roots are still intact, preserved and nurtured all of these years in the memories of border Mexicans.

As the sun was about to set I visited the cemetery at Palito Blanco, the ranch that served as Garza's revolutionary headquarters a century ago. The gravestones called out the names of many Garzistas, and even the names of some who had opposed the rebellion. And in one corner, a small unassuming granite slab marked a memorial site for Catarino Erasmo Garza. In spite of the diligent efforts of Garza's grandson to memorialize Catarino, there is no monument or historical marker in Texas to record the 1891 revolution. In Matamoros, Mexico, one room in the city hall is named in honor of Garza, but few Mexicans today would have any idea of who he was. Garza's name is also unknown in Costa Rica and on the Panamanian island where he was killed. On the Texas border there are a few people who still remember stories about their fathers, grandfathers, and great-grandfathers "who rode a raid or two with Catarino Garza," but the memory is fading quickly as the older generations pass away.[1] Several months after I visited him at home near Alice, Carlos Pérez died. In doing so he took with him a lifetime of knowledge and passion about his grandfather and the revolution he led.

Stories about the past are powerful. They remind us about our connections to the land, to our ancestors, to political ideals, and to our cultures. Stories and narratives were also at the center of Garza's revolution. As I have shown, there were many motivating factors behind Garza's rebellion, including the dispossession of Mexican landholders, industrialization and commercial agriculture, demographic shifts, an international economic crisis, and a severe drought. However, understanding these objective or material conditions will not by themselves explain why some people on the border chose to pick up arms and fight with Garza, while others chose to side with the U.S. or Mexican governments. In order to answer these questions, the revolution needs to be understood through the competing stories and narratives about the border and about the revolt itself. Garza's autobiography, "La lógica de los hechos," along with his newspaper articles, helped him to make sense of the twelve years he lived in the United States and to situate himself and Mexicans in general in relation to the broader socioeconomic transformation of the time. Captain Bourke's diaries, articles, and books construct a very different narrative about the border, its history and its future. These stories were not, however, simply ways that each individual came to terms with their place in their world but rather efforts to convince and persuade others. Key intellectuals like Catarino Garza and Ignacio Martínez, or Army Captain John G. Bourke and the Mexican Ambassador Matías Romero, play fundamental roles in constructing these narratives and disseminating them to a wider audience. The ability of Bourke and Romero to reach a large audience in both English and Spanish, while Garza and Martínez spoke to a more limited Spanish-language public, illustrates the importance of having access to the means of communication and the means of legitimizing and disseminating one's story. The Garzistas were very able and articulate communicators, publishing their own newspapers, writing books, and giving moving speeches. However, the Garzista versions of events was ultimately suppressed and superceded by the official government position. It is symptomatic of this unequal balance of power that Garza's auto-biography remained unpublished; that so few of the Spanish-language border newspapers have been preserved in archives; and that most histo-rians have chosen to ignore or dismiss the Garza revolution.

Although the official story won out in the national and international arenas, popular culture on the border provided an alternative memory about the revolt. In corridos and in stories passed down from generation to generation, the memory of Garza's rebellion and how it fits into a larger framework of Mexican resistance in the borderlands has been preserved. Over time, these memories have faded, the corridos are no longer sung, and the storytellers die. Fortunately, the same institutions — the military, the foreign ministry, and the diplomatic corps — that worked so hard to squash the rebellion and suppress the Garzista version of events also pre-served the traces of the movement in their archives. The only remaining copies of Garzista newspapers are in the official archives of those who were most obsessed with crushing the revolt. Ironically, while the diligent surveillance operations of the Porfirian regime and the U.S. government undermined Garza's movement, they have also enabled me to write this history. The struggle over this particular story continues, therefore, as the luxury of time permits us to break below the smooth surface and examine the tangled underground made up of competing and clashing narratives.

THE NEW WORLD BORDER

One of the narratives that Garza challenged was that of U.S. imperialism, both within its borders and beyond. He questioned the U.S. usurpation of half of Mexico's territory in 1848, and the continued dispossession of Mexican landholders through the rest of the century. His critique proved to be prescient as the United States emerged as a global empire at the dawn of the twentieth century. With the U.S. triumph in the 1898 war, and with the occupation of Cuba, Puerto Rico, and the Philippines, the battle to "civilize" the frontier suddenly went global. While the colonization effort on the Texas-Mexico border had taken a long time, stretching back to the Mexican-American War, the Spanish missions, and perhaps even as far back as Cabeza de Vaca's sixteenth-century wanderings through the borderlands' desert, the process seemed complete by the early twentieth century. From a relatively isolated frontier outpost, the border became a center of economic and military activity. Mines, railroads, and irrigation drove up land values and opened up the area's natural resources to exploitation by outsiders. Garza was not opposed to modernization and free trade, and many of his supporters benefited from the region's economic integration, but they were against the socially destructive consequences of these changes.

By embracing foreign capital the Porfirian regime revolutionized agriculture, built factories, dug mines, and constructed railroads at an unprecedented rate. As railroads arrived, land prices skyrocketed, leaving a few wealthy families with most of the land and most of the rest of the people with no land at all. In the decade leading up to Garza's rebellion, a land grab of unsurpassed proportions transferred one-fifth of the total surface area of the country (roughly the size of California) from public to private hands. When it was all done, 1 percent of rural families owned 85 percent of the land in Mexico.[2] The same people who lost their land or had it threatened by encroaching haciendas were the first to raise arms against the government when the revolution was declared in 1910.[3] Land was a central concern for the Garzistas in 1891, just as it would be for their successors two decades later.

The economic "progress" that Díaz bought for his country was paid for dearly with a loss of political freedom and democracy. By 1891, many Mexicans were fed up with the regime's heavy-handed censorship of the press, with electoral fraud, and with the violation of the sacred liberal principle of no reelection for presidents. The centralization of virtually all power in the dictator's skillful and often bloody hands was simply too high a price to pay for thousands of miles of railroad tracks, high growth rates, and the image of being modern. The Garzistas welcomed modernization but they would not just stand aside as the *patria* was surveyed and sold off to foreigners at bargain rates while Díaz and his cronies reaped all of the rewards.

The caudillos of northeastern Mexico, men like generals Geronimo Treviño, Francisco Naranjo, and Luis Terrazas, supported the rebellion, albeit covertly, because Díaz had usurped their political power and autonomy. The poor ranchers and farm hands did not rise up en masse when the pronunciados crossed the river to declare their revolt. Perhaps they still had hope that their lives would improve with Díaz at the helm. Or, more likely, they were wisely waiting for a more opportune moment. The common folk who did join the rebels were slaughtered without mercy. The year 1891 was not an auspicious one to be a Mexican rebel. Twenty years later these same poor folk and their children filled the ranks of another rebellion against Díaz, this one led by Francisco I. Madero, the ambitious son of a wealthy Coahuilan hacendado. This time, however, the revolution succeeded, not only because masses of poor people joined but because the ruling elite was already badly fractured. Even though the northern Mexican elite fared well during the Porfiriato, at least economically, they, like their Garzista predecessors, grew tired of the corrupt and increasingly decrepit dictatorship, and some of them defected to join the ranks of the opposition.[4]

Texas underwent an economic structural adjustment similar to Mexico, but the racial implications were slightly different in the United States. As happened in Mexico, capitalist development in the U.S. Southwest attracted outside investment and drove up the prices of land. However, while there was a racial inflection to the economic transformation in Mexico, with most of the capital coming from Anglos in the United States and England, this racial bias was even more pronounced on the Texas border. A few South Texas elites diversified their economic activity and thus maintained economic and political power, but many others, most of whom were Mexicans, ended up losing their land as well as their social status in the new order. Wealthy Texas Mexican landowners like Garza's father-in-law were being forced by the market, natural disasters, and other forms of coercion to sell their land at deflated prices, often to wealthy Anglo owners like those of the famous King ranch. Small Mexican ranchers and farm owners fared even worse, losing all of their land and being forced into low-paid wage labor. While the details of this process of land dispossession are complex and vary according to county, the result was fairly straightforward: a few Anglo landowners took over the bulk of the Mexican land base by the beginning of the twentieth century. Even though the Garzista manifestos say nothing about fighting Anglo Texan landowners, Garza's other writings condemned the dispossession of Mexicans in Texas. The fact that wealthy Anglo ranchers like N. G. Collins spearheaded the anti-Garza effort, and that virtually all Mexicans in Texas supported the rebels, illustrate the extent to which the rebellion expressed racial tensions on the border. It was not a "race war" as some newspapers claimed, but race was as inescapable a part of the landscape as the omnipresent chaparral.

Anglos and Mexicans in South Texas not only struggled over land but also over a related valuable resource: cultural respectability and honor. Both the Garzistas and anti-Garzistas shared a belief in the developmentalist ethic, including hard work, moral propriety, and honor, and each side claimed it for themselves. In his autobiography, Garza argued that the increasing presence of Anglos had led to a coarsening of daily life on the border. Not only were they rude but in Garza's view these Texan "cowboys" lacked courage and masculine honor. Similarly, Garza's condemnation of Díaz, Reyes, and other Porfirian officials often focused on their laziness, immorality, and lack of masculine honor. At the same time, Captain Bourke was busy painting border Mexicans as lazy, dirty, treacherous, illiterate, and diseased. The stakes in this cultural duel were high because claiming the mantle of "civilization," honor, and manliness justified ownership of land and political control. The "Americanization" of the Rio Grande Valley that Bourke envisioned was therefore about not only building railroads and turning the region into a profitable "garden" but about de-Mexicanizing the border. Fearing for their way of life, the Garzistas ultimately turned their weapons on the U.S. soldiers, crying out in anger, "kill the damned Gringos."

It took over half a century to fully incorporate the border into the nation. While the U.S. Army made some headway in the mid-nineteenth century by physically occupying the region and forcing a feeble Mexico to sign away nearly half of its land, by the end of the century Mexicans still predominated in South Texas. Soldiers (and often religious missionaries) were the frontline of imperialism, but even after the settlers arrived, the colonization project remained incomplete. By 1900, the percentage of Anglos versus Mexicans in South Texas had actually decreased, and even if Anglos were taking over in the bigger towns, Spanish was still the lingua franca and Mexican national holidays were far more popular than the Fourth of July.[5] Bourke lamented that the tens of thousands of troops massed on the border during the Mexican-American and U.S. Civil wars "left scarcely any impression upon the general tone of thought, the manners or customs of the population."[6] Thus, as Bourke chased the Garzistas through the chaparral, he simultaneously engaged in a campaign to "open the valley" to Anglo settlers and investors. In his official reports, and in his articles in newspapers, academic journals, and popular magazines, he mapped and described the region in order to make it legible to the outside world. This ideological construction of the border was just as important a part of the colonizing mission as was suppressing the armed rebellion.

The physical battles of Garza's insurrection remained in a circumscribed area a few hundred miles on either side of the Rio Grande, but the larger ideological struggle was carried out in a more expansive geography. Newspapers in New York, San Francisco, Chicago, Monterrey, Mexico City, Havana, and even London and Frankfurt assiduously tracked the progress of the rebellion and the efforts to suppress it. At the same time, Bourke applied the knowledge he gained from imperial adventures in Africa, Asia, and the Middle East to the colonizing mission in South Texas. The captains of empire kept up-to-date on the latest "discoveries" and colonial techniques through their geographical societies and professional journals. While they did not have the same access to a publishing apparatus, anti-imperialists like Garza, Martínez, Maceo, and Martí communicated through smaller newspapers, mutual-aid societies, Masonic lodges, and exile revolutionary organizations. This anti-imperial network sustained Garza during his years in exile, and although he always seemed to be undermined at the end of the day by the U.S. military, the struggle against "Yankee" domination continued throughout the next century.

PATRONS AND PROGRESSIVES

Even though the border was linked to the international market and to global movements for and against imperialism, the region maintained its particular character. Thus, while race and class divided borderlands society, another cleavage, at times more profound, separated insiders (those from the borderlands) from outsiders. It was this strong regional identification and a distrust of outsiders that made it difficult for U.S. soldiers to apprehend the Garzistas. Texas Mexicans quite reasonably feared men in army uniforms given their fresh memories of the U.S. military invasion less than half a century before. It was not only Mexicans, however, who viewed the troops as foreigners. Soldiers found themselves being led astray, deceived, and sabotaged by a broad multiethnic and multiclass alliance, including Anglos and Italians, as well as judges, sheriffs, marshals, merchants, ranchers, and vaqueros. Even Sheriff Sheley, who eventually helped to capture the rebels, remained highly critical of the U.S. troops, and he wrote letters against Captain Bourke and even arrested him for harassment.

Border residents on the Mexican side of the river showed a similar disdain toward the meddling of outsider Porfirian military officers and political bosses. While most of the Garzistas were eventually arrested (or in Garza's case, forced into exile), the U.S. Army should not be given all of the credit for the suppression. It was only after border people decided to cut their losses and cooperate, in part to protect themselves from hotheaded soldiers and Rangers, that significant numbers of Garzistas were arrested. The fact that Captain Bourke was run out of South Texas speaks to the impotence of outside authorities and the limits of the army's power.

Nonetheless, while Bourke did not live to see it, his plan to gain political control over the region succeeded roughly three decades after he was booted out. In the name of good government, Bourke recommended appointing trustworthy Mexicans who spoke English to act as the intermediaries with the local population. From his perspective, local politicians, sheriffs, and judges were all corrupt and dangerously dependent on the Mexican vote, and an alternative "loyal" government needed to be established. His vision became a reality in the first and second decades of the twentieth century as the progressive-era movement hit South Texas. Independent Democrats and Republicans unseated the corrupt Democratic Party "bosses" who kept a stranglehold on power. While the accusations of embezzlement, manipulation of the legal system, and electoral fraud were well founded, once the progressive reformers gained power they proceeded to disenfranchise the Mexican electorate.[7] Sheriff Buddy Deeds in John Sayles's film *Lone Star* typifies the paternalistic boss who is corrupt but who also has the respect of the locals because he provides jobs and he is one of them. In the end, the paternalistic bosses probably did more for Mexicans than the progressive reformers ever would.

THE MAGIC VALLEY AND THE PLAN DE SAN DIEGO

Captain Bourke was also prescient in his prediction that the region would become a garden for commercial farmers. The process of the dispossession of Mexicans and the concentration of land in a few Anglo hands reached a fevered pitch by the beginning of the twentieth century. In 1900, the King ranch reached one million acres, a few thousand of which were excised from Garza's father-in-law's land. Furthermore, Jim and Jane Crow segregation undermined the relatively harmonious Anglo-Mexican borderland society that had briefly flourished along the border. This meant that the family ties that had bound Anglos and Mexicans together through intermarriage, and which were so important in sustaining Garza's rebellion, began to diminish in the twentieth century. In Cameron and Hidalgo counties the mixed-race population, those with Anglo and Mexican parentage, declined precipitously from roughly half to a quarter of the inhabitants between 1900 and 1920.[8] The racial tensions caused by the breakdown of what historian David Montejano calls the "peace structure," combined with growing economic inequalities, ultimately led to a radical revolt in South Texas in 1915.

The Plan de San Diego, named for the town just a few miles from Garza's former headquarters at Palito Blanco, responded to similar conditions of immiseration among the Mexican folk as did Garza's, but there were important differences between the two movements. Garza's insurrection was organized primarily in Texas and it was aimed at overthrowing the Mexican government, while the Plan de San Diego, notwithstanding its name, was organized mostly in Mexico and targeted the U.S. government. While Garza had a hard time rallying people to his cause in Mexico, the Plan de San Diego leaders had a difficult time recruiting Mexicans in Texas. The 1915 revolt also had a more explicit racial focus, restricting participants in the "Liberating Army for Races and People" to "the Latin, Negro or the Japanese race," and attempting to reclaim land taken by the United States during the Mexican-American War. The section of their manifesto demanding the execution of every North American male over sixteen years of age indicates the extent to which this rebellion was an act of racial revenge. After an aborted launch, the uprising began on July 4 and lasted through the summer, with raiders crossing into Texas to blow up railroad tracks, destroy irrigation pumping stations, burn automobiles, and kill Anglos.[9]

The raids and the inflammatory manifesto sent the Texas Rangers and vigilante posses on a massive killing spree. By the time the violence had subsided, between three hundred and five thousand Mexicans lay dead, compared to only sixty-two U.S. civilians and sixty-four soldiers.[10] By mid-September, the number of U.S. troops in the region had grown to four thousand, and Rangers had fanned out through the countryside, methodically eliminating "bad" Mexicans. As one longtime border resident said, "a campaign of extermination seemed to have begun in those days. The cry was often heard, 'we have to make this a white man's country!' "[11] After the militarization of the border, the killing of hundreds of innocent Mexicans, and the general terror imposed throughout the region, the "Americanization" that Bourke envisioned was finally being achieved. When the Border Patrol was established in 1924, many of the old Texas

Rangers signed up. Throughout the rest of the twentieth century, the Border Patrol had functioned very much like the Rangers, guarding the boundaries between Anglos and Mexicans and instilling fear in Mexicans and Mexican Americans alike.[12]

Along with the Plan de San Diego, the threat posed by violence from the Mexican Revolution spilling over into the United States sparked a massive military build-up on the border. In March 1916, revolutionary leader Pancho Villa attacked Columbus, New Mexico. Although it is unclear whether or not German support for Villa had anything to do with the attack on Columbus, diplomatic correspondence indicates that the Germans wanted to provide arms and ammunition to Villa and probably succeeded in doing so.[13] The fear of a German conspiracy on the U.S. border, together with an antipathy for the populist Villa, provoked the Punitive Expedition, a U.S. military invasion of northern Mexico to capture the "bandit" rebel. Troops on the border were once again put on full alert in 1917 when the Zimmerman telegram was decoded, which spoke of a military alliance between Mexico and Germany. By that time the border had become so fortified that there were twenty-four army posts in Texas alone, with Brownsville and El Paso boasting the largest cache of army ordnance in the whole country. Like the contemporary build-up on the border, the massing of thousands of troops and technologically advanced military equipment served to control the "foreign" enemy within the nation as much as it did to defend against foreign invaders. When revolutionary violence finally subsided in Mexico in 1920, the U.S. military presence was relaxed.[14] In addition to preventing Mexican revolutionaries from spilling into the United States, army troops oversaw the transfer of power on the border to Anglo hands. The 1915 Plan de San Diego proved to be the last armed insurrection on the border.

In the 1920s Texas Mexicans continued to struggle, but they began to emphasize their rights as U.S. citizens over their Mexican ethnic identity. In the place of revolutionary manifestos and plans to overthrow Mexican regimes, a new generation of leaders sought legal protections from discrimination and formed fraternal organizations such as the Order of the Sons of America (1923) and the League of United Latin American Citizens (LULAC; 1929). José T. Canales, a prominent Texas Mexican lawyer who was also a politician in Brownsville, a Texas legislator (1917–1920), and a founder of LULAC, was emblematic of the new civil rights movement. As a young teenager Canales followed closely the news of Catarino Garza's revolt, not only because it occurred near his family's ranch but also because Catarino's wife, Concepción González, was his cousin. However, unlike Catarino, who fought the U.S. Army, Canales organized a company of Mexican American scouts to collect intelligence for the army during the border raids following the Plan de San Diego in 1915. Although Canales and other LULAC leaders went out of their way to exhibit their U.S. patriotism and loyalty, they were not shy about defending Mexican Americans. The same Canales who helped the army against the border raiders in 1915–1916 filed charges against the Texas Rangers in 1918 for their abuses against Mexican Americans and demanded a legislative investigation and a reorganization of the force.[15]

NEW POSSIBILITIES

The U.S.-Mexico border is more fortified and policed today than ever before, yet every day the line is transgressed as Mexicans continue to swim across the river, jump the fence, or crawl through sewer pipes and tunnels for a chance to earn a decent living. While border revolts like Garza's and the Plan de San Diego ended a long time ago, there are still shoot-outs on the border with the U.S. and Mexican police and the military. These days the thriving drug cartels, some of whose members have family histories that stretch back a century to border smuggling and "banditry," are the ones doing battle with the Mexican Federal Judicial Police and the U.S. Drug Enforcement Agency. While these latter-day "bandits" have none of the political goals and motivations of their nineteenth-century predecessors, one senses a cross-border alliance at work similar to the one that sustained the Garzistas. Some of the narcocorridos (ballads about the drug trade) praise the traffickers as latter-day Robin Hood characters, and others question the U.S. war on drugs. A recent song by Los Invasores de Nuevo León criticizes the "super capos" (big bosses) like George Bush for their involvement in CIA drug trafficking to finance the Contra war against the Sandinistas in Nicaragua. In addition to condemning U.S. imperialism and the blockades on Cuba, Iraq, and the Palestinians, the corridos provide an alternative narrative about the "drug war." In this version of events, the U.S. government directs the drug trade, sponsors imperialist wars, and watches while young people suffer the consequences:

La droga inunda sus calles y el congreso lo sabe,
Pero como es buen negocio, a los güeritos les vale,
Que los chamacos adictos casi no asistan a clases.

(Drugs flood the [United States's] streets, and Congress knows it,
But since it is good business, the little white guys couldn't care less
That the addicted kids hardly even go to classes.)[16]

Corridos continue to provide a counterdiscourse by allowing border Mexicans a space in which to articulate their own view of the border and the larger world.

The "Americanization" plan pushed by Bourke aimed to erode Mexican American connections to Mexico, including its culture, language, and political life. A century later, even after periodic bouts of xenophobic attacks (1910s, 1930s, 1990s), Bourke's brand of "Americanization" seems as unlikely as ever to succeed. The participation of so many Mexicans living in the United States in the 2000 Mexican elections suggests that immigrants are as concerned today about the political life of their country as they were a century ago. The recent electoral defeat of the Institutional Revolutionary Party, a party that had ruled in Mexico for more than seventy years, opens up new possibilities for change, particularly on the border. The fact that remittances from migrants in the United States to their families in Mexico constitute one of the leading sources of foreign exchange, and that one out of nine Mexicans live in the United States, is strong evidence of ongoing cross-border connections. With an estimated 15 percent of the Mexican electorate in the United States, Mexicans abroad are even becoming an important target for Mexican politicians. In 2000, a Mexican residing in the United States was elected to the Mexican Congress for the first time.[17] Beyond changes in party politics, the emergence of cross-border labor organizing efforts in the wake of NAFTA indicate that these alliances are not only occurring at the level of government and corporate elites but among workers as well.

Garza's history is fundamentally a border story. He began by defending Mexicans in Texas against Anglo Texans, and then he took on the strongest president that Mexico had seen. Although he lost both of these fights, Garza continued his continentwide struggle against tyranny and empire and carried his liberal ideals with him to Central America and, ultimately, to his grave. The local political battles on the South Texas border, he discovered, were part of a much larger struggle, one that could be fought in Cuba and Panama just as in Mexico and Texas. By joining the Colombian struggle, he attempted to unify liberals across national boundaries in Latin America to defeat the authoritarian governments that "sold out" their countries to the "foreign invader to the North."[18]

Latin America was never able to achieve unity in the following century, and the omnipotence of the United States only grows stronger. Garza's dream of building alliances across borders is still unfulfilled. Yet the irrepressible interchange across the U.S.-Mexico border shows no signs of letting up. Garza's dream is one worth remembering. It is a dream worth fighting for.

INTRODUCTION

1 "El último de los periodistas independientes, el más humilde de todos, abandona hoy la pluma para empuñar la espada en defensa de los derechos del pueblo." Catarino Garza, "Proclama," Colección de Porfirio Díaz, Universidad Ibero-americana, Mexico City (hereafter cited as CPD), leg. 16, docs. 10951, 11418. If not included in the text, all Spanish-language quotes are given in the notes. To be as faithful to the original as possible, I have kept the original spelling and accents, which frequently do not conform to today's standard.

2 "Versos de despedida," collected in Brownsville in the 1980s, in Celso Garza Guajardo, ed., *En busca de Catarino Garza* (Monterrey, Mexico: Universidad Autónoma de Nuevo León, 1898), 53. It is not clear when this corrido first appeared or where it circulated. Sound recordings of several corridos about the Garza revolt were recorded by Américo Paredes in 1954 and can be found at the Center for American History at the University of Texas, Austin.

3 Walter Benjamin, "Theses on the Philosophy of History," in *Illuminations: Essays and Reflections*, trans. Harry Zohn (New York: Schocken Books, 1969), 255.

4 "Plan Revolucionario," in Gabriel Saldívar, *Documentos de la rebelión de Catarino E. Garza en la frontera de Tamaulipas y sur de Texas, 1891–1892* (Mexico City: n.p., 1943), 13–16.

5 John Gregory Bourke, "An American Congo," *Scribner's* (May 1894): 599.

6 "A Border Ruffian?" *Gate City*, 18 Sept. 1891, in Archivo Histórico de la Secretaría de Relaciones Exteriores de México (hereafter cited as SRE), leg. 11–10–44, exp. 1, f. 88.

7 For a more contemporary analysis of the power of narratives on the formation of border identities, see Pablo Vila, *Crossing Borders, Reinforcing Borders: Social Categories, Metaphors, and Narrative Identities on the U.S.-Mexico Frontier* (Austin: University of Texas Press, 2000), 15.

8 Michel-Rolph Trouillot, *Silencing the Past: Power and the Production of History* (Boston: Beacon Press, 1995), 28.

9 For a recent example of someone who tries to link the two genres, see Louis Gerard Mendoza, *Historia: The Literary Making of Chicana and Chicano History* (College Station: Texas A&M University Press, 2001).

10 Américo Paredes, *With His Pistol in His Hand: A Border Ballad and Its Hero*

(Austin: University of Texas Press, 1990 [1958]); Gloria Anzaldúa, *Borderlands/ La Frontera: The New Mestiza* (San Francisco: Aunt Lute, 1987).

11 Three recent books from different perspectives illustrate this trend: José David Sal-dívar, *Border Matters: Remapping American Cultural Studies* (Berkeley: University of California Press, 1997); David Spener and Kathleen Staudt, eds., *The U.S.-Mexico Border: Transcending Divisions, Contesting Identities* (Boulder: Lynne Rienner, 1998); and Claire F. Fox, *The Fence and the River: Culture and Politics at the U.S.-Mexico Border* (Minneapolis: University of Minnesota Press, 1999).

12 I do not mean to suggest that Cuba will eventually be annexed by the United States, although that was a very real prospect in the nineteenth century, but rather the historical economic, cultural, and political ties, not to mention the familial relationships, will eventually erode the U.S. government's long-standing policy of isolating Cuba. For an excellent history of U.S.-Cuban relations, see Louis A. Pérez Jr., *On Becoming Cuban: Identity, Nationality, and Culture* (Chapel Hill: University of North Carolina Press, 1999).

13 The term "borderlands" was coined by Herbert Eugene Bolton in the 1920s to refer to the northern frontier of the Spanish Empire (what is now mostly U.S. territory). My usage of the term extends beyond the colonial period, recognizing that one can speak of a transborder cultural community even after 1821, or 1848, or 1900.

14 In *Seeing Like a State: How Certain Schemes to Improve the Human Condition Have Failed* (New Haven: Yale University Press, 1998), James C. Scott explores the process of how the state "sees" and makes the world "legible" according to its own registers.

15 I discovered a stencil of these hatbands in the U.S. Army records in the National Archives relating to the revolt.

16 *Pax porfiriana* refers to the supposed period of peace and stability in Mexico achieved under President Porfirio Díaz. For an insightful critique of the Porfirian peace, see Paul J. Vanderwood, *Disorder and Progress: Bandits, Police, and Mexican Development* (Wilmington, Del.: Scholarly Resources, 1992), esp. ch. 8.

17 Daniel Cosío Villegas, *Historia moderna de México. Vol. 2: El Porfiriato: La vida política interior* (Mexico City: Hermes, 1972), 678–79. Cosío Villegas uses the term *chabacanos* (worthless) to refer to Garza's plans.

18 Saldívar, *Documentos de la rebelión*, 10. Saldívar also surmises that Mariscal kept these papers from Díaz because they implicated important generals in Díaz's inner circle, including Sóstenes Rocha, Francisco Naranjo, Sebastían Villareal, Francisco Estrada, Luis Terrazas, and Luis E. Torres (9). A letter from Díaz to Reyes, which includes a copy of these documents and discusses the complicity of some of these generals, shows that Díaz was well aware of what was happening but chose not to openly confront his generals. Díaz to Reyes, 2 Feb. 1892, in Archivo de Bernardo Reyes, Fondo DLI, Centro de Estudios de Historia de México, CON-DUMEX, Mexico City (hereafter cited as ABR), doc. 3037. The ABR collection is divided in two sections: the *copiadores*, where copies of letters sent to Reyes are noted by "cop." followed by the document number, whereas the second section, which includes letters sent to Reyes, is referred to with just the document number.

19 Scholarship by regional authors includes the article by Gilbert M. Cuthbertson, "Catarino E. Garza and the Garza War," *Texana* 12 (1974): 335–47, and the compilation of documents by Garza Guajardo, *En busca*. For positive accounts, see Arnoldo De León, *They Called Them Greasers: Anglo Attitudes toward Mexicans in Texas, 1821–1900* (Austin: University of Texas Press, 1991), 60–61, 93; and David Montejano, *Anglos and Mexicans in the Making of Texas, 1836–1987* (Austin: University of Texas Press, 1987), 89.

20 For a particularly good example of a border history that does mine archival sources on both sides of the border, see Linda B. Hall and Don M. Coerver, *Revolution on the Border: The United States and Mexico, 1910–1920* (Albuquerque: University of New Mexico Press, 1988).

21 Germans were not targeted as part of the 1915 raids, leading many to infer that the Plan de San Diego was part of a German government plot against the United States. See James A. Sandos, *Rebellion in the Borderlands: Anarchism and the Plan de San Diego, 1904–1923* (Norman: University of Oklahoma Press, 1992), 96.

22 For an excellent discussion of the contemporary militarization on the border, see Timothy J. Dunn, *Militarization of the U.S.-Mexico Border, 1978–1992: Low-Intensity Conflict Doctrine Comes Home* (Austin: University of Texas Press, 1996).

23 There is an extensive body literature on José Martí. For the best translation of his writings to date, see *José Martí: Selected Writings*, trans. Esther Allen (New York: Penguin, 2002); for an analysis of his political thought, see John M. Kirk, *José Martí: Mentor of the Cuban Nation* (Tampa: University Presses of Florida, 1983). For an insightful reading of Martí's writings on the United States, see Laura Lomas, "American Alterities: Reading between Borders in José Martí's 'North American Scenes,'" Ph.D. diss., Columbia University, 2001.

24 Michael Hardt and Antonio Negri, *Empire* (Cambridge: Harvard University Press, 2000), xi–xiv.

25 Guillermo Gómez-Peña, *The New World Border: Prophecies, Poems, and Loqueras for the End of the Century* (San Francisco: City Lights, 1996), 7. For an insightful discussion of both the positive and negative aspects of globalizing border art, see Fox, *The Fence and the River*, esp. 122–38.

26 See David J. Weber, *The Mexican Frontier, 1821–1846: The American Southwest under Mexico* (Albuquerque: University of New Mexico Press, 1982), 284. See also William Robbins, *Colony and Empire: The Capitalist Transformation of the U.S. West* (Kansas: University Press of Kansas, 1994), 25; although his comparison with the United States seems accurate, Robbins's emphasis on the absence of a Mexican frontier myth may be overstated. I am thinking of revolutionary leaders like Francisco Madero, Pancho Villa, Venustiano Carranza, and Alvaro Obregón, the infamous neoliberal President Carlos Salinas, and the enigmatic Subcomandante Marcos.

27 Ramón A. Gutiérrez, *When Jesus Came the Corn Mothers Went Away: Marriage, Sexuality, and Power in New Mexico, 1500–1846* (Stanford: Stanford University Press, 1991); Sara Deutsch, *No Separate Refuge: Culture, Class, and Gender on an*

Anglo-Hispanic Frontier in the American Southwest, 1880–1940 (New York: Oxford, 1987); Montejano, *Anglos and Mexicans in the Making of Texas*; Neil Foley, *The White Scourge: Mexicans, Blacks, and Poor Whites in Texas Cotton Culture* (Berkeley: University of California Press, 1997); David Gutiérrez, *Walls and Mirrors: Mexican Americans, Mexican Immigrants, and the Politics of Ethnicity* (Berkeley: University of California Press, 1995).

28 The growing literature on the so-called New Western history is too large to cite here in full. However, Patricia Nelson Limerick's *The Legacy of Conquest: The Unbroken Past of the American West* (New York: Norton, 1988), and the compilation of essays edited by William Cronon, *Under an Open Sky: Rethinking America's Western Past* (New York: Norton, 1992), provide an introduction to this growing field.

29 Emilio Zamora, *The World of the Mexican Worker in Texas* (College Station: Texas A&M University Press, 1993); Armando C. Alonzo, *Tejano Legacy: Rancheros and Settlers in South Texas, 1734–1900* (Albuquerque: University of New Mexico Press, 1998); Gilberto M. Hinojosa, *A Borderlands Town in Transition: Laredo, 1755–1870* (College Station: Texas A&M University Press, 1983).

30 Although provincial histories have been written since the 1910 revolution, a true florescence of professional regional studies has emerged since the late 1960s. For a good overview, see Thomas Benjamin, "Regionalizing the Revolution: The Many Mexicos in Revolutionary Historiography," in *Provinces of the Revolution: Essays on Regional Mexican History, 1910–1929*, ed. Thomas Benjamin and Mark Wasserman (Albuquerque: University of New Mexico Press, 1990), 319–57.

31 For the northeastern region, see Mario Cerutti, *Burguesía, capitales e industria en el norte de México: Monterrey y su ámbito regional, 1850–1910* (Mexico City: Alianza Editorial, 1992), and Alex M. Saragoza, *The Monterrey Elite and the Mexican State, 1880–1940* (Austin: University of Texas Press, 1988). Friedrich Katz, William Beezley, and Mark Wasserman, among others, have given us an especially deep understanding of politics and land in Chihuahua: see Friedrich Katz, *Secret War in Mexico: Europe, the United States, and the Mexican Revolution* (Chicago: University of Chicago Press, 1981), as well as his *The Life and Times of Pancho Villa* (Stanford: Stanford University Press, 1998); William H. Beezley, *Insurgent Governor: Abraham Gónzalez and the Mexican Revolution in Chihuahua* (Lincoln: University of Nebraska Press, 1973); and Mark Wasserman, *Capitalists, Caciques, and Revolution: The Native Elite and Foreign Enterprise in Chihuahua, Mexico, 1854–1911* (Chapel Hill: University of North Carolina Press, 1984), and his *Persistent Oligarchs: Elites and Politics in Chihuahua, Mexico, 1910–1940* (Durham: Duke University Press, 1993). Evelyn Hu-DeHart's *Yaqui Resistance and Survival: The Struggle for Land and Autonomy, 1821–1910* (Madison: University of Wisconsin Press, 1984) is a notable exception to the historiography, focusing on an indigenous rebellion in northwestern Mexico.

32 Daniel Nugent's *Spent Cartridges of Revolution: An Anthropological History of Namiquipa, Chihuahua* (Chicago: University of Chicago Press, 1993), and Ana Alonso's *Thread of Blood: Colonialism, Revolution, and Gender on Mexico's Northern Frontier* (Tucson: University of Arizona Press, 1995) depart significantly

from the political and economic histories of the countryside and offer insightful anthropological analyses of the gendered meaning of collective land ownership in a small village in Chihuahua. William French's *A Peaceful and Working People: Manners, Morals, and Class Formation in Northern Mexico* (Albuquerque: University of New Mexico Press, 1996), analyzes the inculcation of the work ethic in a mining district in Chihuahua by raising important questions about the culture of work and by taking labor history beyond a strictly materialist level. Paul Vanderwood's *The Power of God against the Guns of Government: Religious Upheaval in Mexico at the Turn of the Nineteenth Century* (Stanford: Stanford University Press, 1998), opens up the complex issue of the significance of faith and spirituality in social movements in northern Mexico.

33 Juan Mora-Torres, *The Making of the Mexican Border: The State, Capitalism, and Society in Nuevo León, 1848–1910* (Austin: University of Texas Press, 2001).

34 José E. Limón. *Dancing with the Devil: Society and Cultural Poetics in Mexican American South Texas* (Madison: University of Wisconsin Press, 1994), esp. ch. 1.

35 José T. Canales, *Juan N. Cortina: Two Interpretations* (New York: Arno Press, 1974); Jerry Thompson ed., *Juan Cortina and the Texas-Mexico Frontier, 1859–1877* (El Paso: Texas Western Press, 1994).

36 Sandos, *Rebellion in the Borderlands*; Juan Gómez-Quiñones, *Sembradores: Ricardo Flores Magón y el Partido Liberal Mexicano, a Eulogy and Critique* (Los Angeles: Aztlán Publications; 1973); Dirk W. Raat, *Revoltosos: Mexico's Rebels in the United States, 1903–1934* (College Station: Texas A&M University Press, 1981).

37 Hall and Coerver, *Revolution on the Border*; see also Oscar J. Martínez, *Troublesome Border* (Tucson: University of Arizona Press, 1988).

38 Saldívar, *Border Matters*, xiii. A good example of this trend is the collection of essays edited by Amy Kaplan and Donald E. Pease, *The Cultures of United States Imperialism* (Durham: Duke University Press, 1993), which illustrates the intimate linkages between U.S. culture and its global empire.

39 Gilbert M. Joseph, Catherine C. LeGrand, and Ricardo Salvatore's collection, *Close Encounters of Empire: Writing the Cultural History of U.S.-Latin American Relations* (Durham: Duke University Press, 1998), takes up this challenge of examining the "deployment and contestation of power," within the " 'contact zones' of American empire" (5).

40 Katz, *The Secret War in Mexico*, 7.

41 I want to thank Sam Truett for the long discussions that have contributed to this argument, a more developed version of which can be found in an introductory chapter by Samuel Truett and Elliott Young, "Making Transnational History," in *Continental Crossroads: Remapping U.S.-Mexico Borderlands History* (Durham: Duke University Press, 2004). Also, see William Cronon, George Miles, and Jay Gitlin, "Becoming West: Toward a New Meaning in Western History," in Cronon, ed., *Under an Open Sky*, 3–27. For a critique of this shortcoming in New Western history, see Richard White, "*It's Your Misfortune and None of My Own*": *A New History of the American West* (Norman: University of Oklahoma Press, 1991), 3.

42 Jeremy Adelman and Stephen Aron, "From Borderlands to Borders: Empires,

Nation-States, and the Peoples in Between in North American History," *American Historical Review* 104, no. 3 (June 1999): 841.

43 For an interesting theoretical exploration of transnational space, see Roger Rouse, "Mexican Migration and the Social Space of Postmodernism" in *Between Two Worlds: Mexican Immigrants in the United States*, ed. David Gutiérrez (Wilmington, Del.: Scholarly Resources, 1996), 254. While Rouse argues that this transnational experience is a new "social space of postmodernism," I would argue that such "postmodern" spaces existed on the border in the nineteenth century.

44 The laws enacted in the 1990s against legal and illegal residents in the United States, along with the infamous anti-immigrant Proposition 187 in California, are just some of the measures that have been used to stamp out transnational identities and enforce a homogenous national culture.

45 James Scott's discussion of public and hidden transcripts is instructive here. He argues that the positions that subalterns adopt in coercive public settings say nothing about how they truly feel or the ideas they may or may not express in private and safer contexts. See James C. Scott, *Domination and the Arts of Resistance: Hidden Transcripts* (New Haven: Yale University Press, 1990).

46 For more on the idea of the nation as an imagined community, see Benedict Anderson, *Imagined Communities: Reflections on the Origin and Spread of Nationalism* (London: Verso, 1983).

47 The lower Rio Grande Valley, which was part of the province of Nuevo Santander, was much more successful than Texas in attracting settlers, and by 1790 it had roughly 25,000 Hispanic inhabitants — about ten times the population of Texas. See David J. Weber, *The Spanish Frontier in North America* (New Haven: Yale University Press, 1992), 194–95.

48 For the most complete picture of the Porfirian regime, see Cosío Villegas, *Historia moderna de México. Vol. 2: El Porfiriato*. For a slightly shorter analysis in English, see Alan Knight, *The Mexican Revolution. Vol. 1: Porfirians, Liberals, and Peasants* (Lincoln: University of Nebraska Press, 1986), esp. ch. 1.

49 For more on the 1915 revolt, see Sandos, *Rebellion in the Borderlands*, and Benjamin Johnson, *Revolution in Texas: How a Forgotten Rebellion and its Bloody Suppression Turned Mexicans into Americans* (New Haven: Yale University Press, 2003). For a brief history of Cortina, see Charles William Goldfinch, *Juan N. Cortina, 1824–1892: A Re-appraisal*, and for a useful collection of Cortina's proclamations and biographical information, see Thompson, *Juan Cortina and the Texas-Mexico Frontier*.

50 For an overview of Murieta's story, see Ireneo Paz, *Life and Adventures of the Celebrated Bandit Joaquin Murieta: His Exploits in the State of California*, trans. Frances P. Belle (Houston: Arte Público Press, 2001 [1925]). For a more recent analysis, see Bruce Thornton, *Searching for Joaquin: Myth, Murieta, and History in California* (San Francisco: Encounter Books, 2002).

51 For more on Cortina, see *Reports of the Committee of Investigation Sent in 1873 by the Mexican Government to the Frontier of Texas* (New York: Baker and Goodwin, 1875).

52 Johnson, *Revolution in Texas*, 94, 113.

53 See Sandos, *Rebellion in the Borderlands*; and Charles C. Cumberland, "Border Raids in the Lower Rio Grande Valley, 1915," *Southwestern Historical Quarterly* 57 (January 1954): 285–311.

54 "Plan de San Diego," in *U.S.-Mexico Borderlands: Historical and Contemporary Perspectives*, ed. Oscar J. Martínez (Wilmington, Del.: Scholarly Resources, 1996), 139–41. The Plan de San Diego was named for a small town in South Texas where the manifesto was supposedly signed; San Diego is only a few miles from where Garza's headquarters at Palito Blanco was located. Once the rebels had established an independent republic out of Texas, New Mexico, Arizona, Colorado, and upper California, they proposed helping the liberated blacks seize six more states from the U.S., from which they would be able to form their own independent republic. The Plan de San Diego also mentioned the possibility that the rebels would request annexation to Mexico.

55 Robert Case, "La frontera texana y los movimientos de insurrección en México, 1850–1900," *Historia Mexicana* 30, no. 3 (January–March 1981): 415–52.

56 For an analysis of the Reyes plan, see Charles Harris III and Louis R. Sadler, "The 1911 Reyes Conspiracy: The Texas Side," in *The Border and the Revolution*, comp. Charles Harris III and Louis R. Sadler (Las Cruces: New Mexico State University Press, 1988), 27–50. Pascual Orozco and Victoriano Huerta also launched their ill-fated revolt against the Constitutionalist forces of Venustiano Carranza and Alvaro Obregón from Texas, but from the West Texas city of El Paso. See Hall and Coerver, *Revolution on the Border*, 25–27.

57 This analysis of the role of the Mexican North in the revolution comes from Katz, *Secret War*, 7–21. For the most thorough description of U.S. investments in mining, railroads, and land in Mexico during this period, see John Mason Hart, *Empire and Revolution: Americans in Mexico since the Civil War* (Berkeley: University of California Press, 2002), esp. 46–69, 140–43, 167–200.

58 I refer here to Michel de Certeau's use of the term "everyday practices" in *The Practice of Everyday Life*, trans. Steven Rendall (Berkeley: University of California Press, 1988). James Scott's *Domination and the Arts of Resistance* makes a similar point about the everyday forms of resistance that remain hidden or barely perceptible to those in power.

59 I use the term "ethnoracial" to blur the boundaries between biological notions of race and cultural notions of ethnicity and to highlight to constructedness of both of these terms. For a more in-depth discussion of this term and the ethnoracial pentagon, see David A. Hollinger, *Postethnic America: Beyond Multiculturalism* (New York: Basic Books, 1995).

60 For a survey of racial ideology in Porfirian and revolutionary Mexico, see Alan Knight, "Race Revolution and Indigenismo," in *The Idea of Race in Latin America*, ed. Richard Graham (Austin: University of Texas Press, 1990), esp. 71–78. Linda Gordon's *The Great Arizona Orphan Abduction* (Cambridge: Harvard University Press, 1999), 53–54, 96–105, contains a very insightful discussion about how Mexican and Anglo views of whiteness clashed in Arizona at the beginning of the twentieth century. For a discussion of Mexican claims to whiteness in 1930s El Paso, see Mario García, "Mexican Americans and the Politics of

Citizenship: The Case of El Paso, 1936," *New Mexico Historical Review* 59, no. 2 (1984): 187–204. Nancy Leys Stepan's *"The Hour of Eugenics": Race, Gender, and Nation in Latin America* (Ithaca: Cornell University Press, 1991) provides an excellent comparison of how flexible Latin American Lamarkian eugenics differed from the rigid Mendelian version in the United States and England. Gary Nash argues convincingly that there has been a great deal of racial mixing in the United States, far more than the official racial discourse admits. See Gary Nash, "The Hidden History of Mestizo America," *Journal of American History* (December 1995): 941–64.

61 Anti-Anglo sentiment among Irish Americans makes it awkward to label them Anglo Americans. Furthermore, the Irish had a tenuous claim to whiteness in the nineteenth century. For a discussion of how and why the Irish became "white" see David R. Roediger, *The Wages of Whiteness: Race and the Making of the American Working Class* (London: Verso, 1991), esp. ch. 7. French and Italians on the border were neither Anglos nor were they Mexicans, but they often stressed their common Latin heritage with Mexicans.

62 Martin Ridge argues against the use of the term "Anglo" as a surrogate for white European, but his solution to use "a more modernized neutral term, 'American,'" ignores the racialized meaning of that label. I choose not to use "American" to refer to white people of European ancestry because such usage implicitly gives a particular ethnoracial group monopoly over a national identity that should be multiethnic. The use of "America" to denote the United States similarly monopolizes a term that applies to an entire continent. See Martin Ridge, "Who's Who — or Western Name Calling," *Journal of the West* 38, no. 4 (October 1999): 3–4.

63 For the origins of the word "greaser," see De León, *They Called Them Greasers*, 16. According to the *Oxford English Dictionary*, the first recorded use of the word "gringo" occurred in 1849. Linda Gordon finds the same tendency toward a racial binary — either Anglo or Mexican (gringo or greaser) in Arizona by 1904 (Gordon, *The Great Arizona Orphan Abduction*, 102).

64 French, *A Peaceful and Working People*. For an analysis of this culture in a border town, see Elliott Young, "Deconstructing *La Raza*: Culture and Ideology of the *Gente Decente* of Laredo, 1904–1911," *Southwestern Historical Quarterly* (October 1994); 226–59.

65 This twilight perspective is similar to the metaphor used by the cultural critic Homi Bhabha to describe the "ambiguity," "inclarity," and "ambivalence" that he saw in the 1992 Los Angeles riot/rebellion. Bhabha argues that in twilight "the hard outlines of what we see in daylight, that make it easier for us to order daylight, disappear. So we begin to see its boundaries in a much more faded way. That fuzziness of twilight allows us to see the intersections of the event with a number of other things that daylight obscures for us, to use a paradox. We have to interpret more in twilight, we have to make ourselves part of the act" (Bhabha, *Twilight Los Angeles, 1992*, ed. Anna Deavere Smith (New York: Anchor, 1994), 233. Also see Homi Bhabha's discussion of ambivalence in "Signs Taken for Wonders: Questions of Ambivalence and Authority under a Tree Outside Delhi, May

1817," *Critical Inquiry* 12 (autumn 1985): 144–65; and his chapter "DissemiNation: Time, Narrative, and the Margins of the Modern Nation," in *Nation and Narration* (London: Routledge, 1990), 291–322.

1. THE MAKING OF A REVOLUTIONARY

1 Said, *Culture and Imperialism* (New York: Vintage, 1993), xii–xiii.
2 Zamora, *The World of the Mexican Worker*.
3 French, *A Peaceful and Working People*, chs. 3–4, esp. 91–97, 135–39. For more on women in Porfirian Mexico, see Carmen Ramos Escandón, "Señoritas porfirianas: Mujer e ideología en el México progresista, 1880–1910," in *Presencia y transparencia: La mujer en la historia de México*, ed. Ramos Escandón (Mexico City: El Colegio de México, Programa Interdisciplinario de Estudios de la Mujer, 1987). For a discussion of how honor and gender worked together in northern Mexico, see Alonso, *Thread of Blood*, esp. ch. 3.
4 "No en las aptitudes de mi pluma, sino en la seguridad de que cumplo fielmente como mexicano en extrangero suelo, al narrar las circunstancias de nuestros nacionales en este país." Catarino Garza, "La lógica de los hechos: O sean observaciones sobre las circunstancias de los mexicanos en Texas, desde el año 1877 hasta 1889," Misc. MS 73, Garza Papers, 1859–95, Benson Latin American Collection, University of Texas, Austin (hereafter referred to as BLAC), 19. The manuscript, which remained incomplete and unpublished, was donated to the University of Texas in 1927 by Garza's son-in-law, Frank Pérez, of Alice, Texas. There has been some confusion over whether Garza's papers were purchased by the university or donated by the family; however, the letters between Carlos Castañeda, librarian at the university, and Frank Pérez show clearly that the papers were donated by the family (see, particularly, Castañeda to Pérez, 8 Aug. 1927, Carlos Castañeda Papers, Correspondence, BLAC). In 1989, the Universidad Autónoma de Nuevo León published a compilation of documents relating to Garza's revolt, including Garza's autobiography (see Garza Guajardo, *En busca*). On close examination I found errors in this transcription; words have been changed and in some instances whole lines are missing. I have therefore cited only the original manuscript.
5 "Suscitar el celo entre los representantes de mi país." Garza, "La lógica," 20.
6 John G. Bourke, *Our Neutrality Laws* (Fort Ethan Allen, Vt.: privately printed [1895 or 1896]), 21.
7 "La ciencia que enseña a discurrir y razonar exactamente por medio de duducciones metódicas. . . . Disposición natural para discurrir y juzgar sin el auxilio del arte." Garza, "La lógica," 295.
8 "Hijo del pueblo." "Educar las masas." Ibid., 21.
9 "No se encontrará en todo el concurso de mis escritos, una sola frase galana, ni imágines [*sic*] delicadas, ni erudición, ni mucho menos pinturas literarias; por que mi pluma no sabe pintar, pero sí, reproducir, fotografíar y estampar verdades." Ibid., 29. Mary Louise Pratt notes a similar scientific and antiaesthetic stance on the part of travel writers in the 1820s, in contrast to the richly poetic descriptions

of earlier writers such as the preeminent Alexander Von Humboldt. See Mary Louise Pratt, *Imperial Eyes: Travel Writing and Transculturation* (London: Routledge, 1991), 148–49.

10 Like social critic Walter Benjamin, Garza saw the "aura of the work of art" withering in the age of mechanical reproduction. See Benjamin, "The Work of Art in the Age of Mechanical Reproduction," in *Illuminations*, 226.

11 For a good overview of *testimonio* literature, see George M. Gugelberger, ed., *The Real Thing: Testimonial Discourse and Latin America* (Durham: Duke University Press, 1996).

12 Mendoza, *Historia*, 21.

13 Garza included a brief sketch in a letter he wrote to his wife because he heard that someone was writing a biography about him and he wanted it to be written "sin exageraciones sobre la humildad de mis nacimientos" (without exaggerations about the humility of my origins). Garza to Concepcíon Garza de González, Puerto Limón, 21 Nov. 1894, in Garza Correspondence. The Garza Correspondence includes over 130 letters and poems written between 1886 and 1895. Most of the letters were sent from Garza to family and friends in Texas after he went into exile in 1892. They are currently in the possession of Garza's family in Alice, Texas.

   For another brief biography of Garza, see also Agnes G. Grimm, *Llanos Mesteñas: Mustang Plains* (Waco: Texan Press, 1968), 140–41.

14 The following description of events in Garza's life is culled from "La lógica."

15 Information about Bloomberg and Raphael from advertisement in the *Daily Herald* (Brownsville), 20 Dec. 1892, and from Garza, "La lógica."

16 In her engaging essay "Fieldwork in Common Places," Mary Louise Pratt discusses the way the arrival scene allows anthropologists to insert themselves within an otherwise objectified and "scientific" study of others. By recognizing themselves as part of the history of the people they study as well as part of the discursive traditions that preceded them, anthropologists can, she argues, come closer to the goal of fusing "objective and subjective practices." (Pratt, "Fieldwork in Common Places," in *Writing Culture: The Poetics and Politics of Ethnography*, ed. James Clifford and George E. Marcus [Berkeley: University of California Press, 1986], 50).

17 "Visto el desorden en que dejó mi ropa." Garza, "La lógica," 30. Garza inserted English phrases like "all right" throughout his text.

18 "Las costumbres de aquellos habitantes, no se puede decir que son ní mexicanas, ní americanas, pues son tan incultas, que a semejanza de los salvajes, se manejan unos con otros." Ibid., 33–34.

19 "Presididos por mexicanos de origen y gobernados por distintos círculos americanos, quienes escudados con los directores del pueblo siempre lo han convertido en instrumento servil." Ibid., 33. The Democrats (blue) and Republicans (red) chose colors to represent their parties to facilitate recognition by illiterate Mexican voters. The color affiliations for the parties were revised in Starr County. (See Evan Anders, *Boss Rule in South Texas: The Progressive Era* [Austin, University of Texas Press, 1987], 5, 43.)

20 For a detailed look at how James B. Wells forged a political machine in South Texas, see Anders, *Boss Rule*, 3, 25.

21 See Anders, *Boss Rule in South Texas*, esp. 168–69, for an interesting analysis of Texas Mexican Progressives. See also Johnson, *Revolution in Texas*.

22 Especuladores con la política." Garza, "La lógica," 35.

23 "Que vergüenza de decir que México ha sido la patria de seres tan degradados. México está mal juzgado por los emigrantes á este país." Ibid., 39.

24 French, *A Peaceful and Working People*, 75–84.

25 "Gran número de mexicanos que han sabido conservar su nacionalidad y que por sus intereses ó familias residen en el Estado sufriendo injustamente las deprivaciones de centenares de tejanos ambiciosos; que por medios ilegales y con el apoyo de funcionarios públicos de mal fé, se echan sobre sus propiedades." Garza, "La lógica," 39.

26 Mexican protests against intrusive public health measures continued on the border, sometimes leading to full-scale riots. In 1899, a group of Mexicans threw rocks and fired shots at the city marshal in Laredo, who was attempting to forcibly quarantine people exposed to smallpox (De León, *They Called Them Greasers*, 95–96).

27 Sí el pueblo obrero se perjudica ó se muere de hambre nada nos importa; lo que debemos ver es que no nos invada la fiebre amarilla, por que bien puede morir alguien americano, y como 'un blanco vale mas que diez mexicanos'; así es que yo protesto contra la idea de levantar la cuarentena." Garza, "La lógica," 43.

28 For a persuasive argument linking Western medical science to imperialism, see Andrew Cunningham and Birdie Andrews, *Western Medicine as Contested Knowledge* (Manchester: Manchester University Press, 1997), 1–23.

29 "No merecen penetrar en la sociedad culta; porque desde luego atropellan á la cortesía, á la delicadeza y al respeto á simismo." Garza, "La lógica," 47.

30 "Sepa ese abogado blanco que miente villanamente al asegurar que un americano vale más que diez mexicanos, pues en la casa de los Señores Bloomberg and Raphael está un mexicano (sin ser negro) que puede probarle en el terreno que quiera que vale tanto como él ó cualquiera otro de sus correligionarios." Garza, "La lógica," 47. Garza did not indicate the name of the Spanish-language newspaper, but he noted that the editor's name was Ramón Rodríguez.

31 "Arrojarle el guante." Ibid., 48.

32 Ibid., 43, 44, 47.

33 "De corteses maneras á pesar de ser moro, es decir de Marrueco, Tanger." Ibid., 84.

34 Ibid., 45, 48.

35 José Limón notes the differences between the English- and Spanish-language newspaper coverage of the Primer Congreso Mexicanista in Laredo in 1911, and suggests that the English-language press tailored their representation of the speeches for their audience (José E. Limón, "El Primer Congreso Mexicanista de 1911: A Precursor to Contemporary Chicanismo," *Aztlan* 5, nos. 1–2 (1974): 96–97. Américo Paredes also shows how a mistranslation of *yegua* (mare) for *caballo* (horse) led to the fatal shoot-out between Gregorio Cortez and Sheriff Morris (Paredes, *With His Pistol in His Hand*, 61).

36 "Tuve amor a la escabrosa carrera del periodismo." Ibid., 49.

37 For the most comprehensive treatment of mutualistas in South Texas, see Zamora, *The World of the Mexican Worker.*

38 "El derecho de ciudadanía." Garza, "La lógica," 51–52.

39 "En unos el entusiasmo, en otras la curiosidad y en la mayor parte el odio." Ibid., 57.

40 "Cuando éste vió que el cañón de mi pistola estaba en contacto con su pecho hizo lo que la mayor parte de los texanos hacen, gritó y se arrepintió de la manera mas cobarde." Ibid., 58–59.

41 "Elevar socialmente la raza mexicana." Ibid., 60.

42 For a survey of Anglo racism toward Mexicans in Texas, see De León, *They Called Them Greasers.*

43 Si los españoles no hubieran conquistado a México, aún sería fecha que anduvieramos con pabico y chimal huyendo por los campos." Garza, "La lógica," 32. Special thanks to Homero Vera for helping me discover the meaning of *pabico*, a local South Texas idiom for diaper.

44 "En México nuestra tradición fué de servidumbre y errores nacida del poder colonial, que se basó ó quizo basarse en la incommunicación con el extrangero, en la legitimidad de la esclavitud . . . mas no estamos obligados a seguir cargando el yugo de aquellas tradiciones por que es preciso convenir que tales errores, tales vicios morales producen en esta escala el malestar social; así como al entranarse estos errores en las clases imbéciles enjendran falsas opinions ante un pueblo que juzga por las apariencias, así pues, el pueblo americano nos ha dado calificativos impropios e insultantes." Garza, "La lógica," 69.

45 "Insultos a la gran nación civilizada, intrépida y valerosa conquistadora, a la madre de mi Patria, 'España.' No señores, nuestras dos naciones, ligadas de antemano por los vínculos sagrados de afecto y simpatía, fundados en su comunidad de orígen y lengua están llamados a ser una misma . . . España es México y México, España. No idénticas instituciones, pero sí iguales costumbres." Ibid., 86–87.

46 Another border intellectual who rose to prominence in Mexico as secretary of education in the 1920s, José Vasconcelos, made a similar argument in his tract glorifying mestizaje in Latin America. Vasconcelos praised the initial conquistadores, men like Pizarro and Cortez, for their ability to join the "destructive impetus to creative genius." However, he argued that the colonial bureaucrats who followed were servile and lacked the spirit necessary to foster progress. See José Vasconcelos, *The Cosmic Race/La Raza Cósmica* (Los Angeles: Centro de Publícaciones, California State University, 1979), 1–12.

47 Garza noted that this woman was of Mexican American heritage, but he did not mention her name (Garza, "La lógica," 60–61). Further information about this woman is from an untitled excerpted typescript in Coalson Collection, "Garza, Catarino," South Texas Archive, Texas A&M, Kingsville, Texas.

48 "Un error de mi juventud." Garza, "La lógica," 60.

49 "Garza the Revolutionist," *Examiner* (San Francisco), 18 Jan. 1892, in SRE, leg. 11-10-44, exp. 4, f. 58. This article contains a brief biography of Garza's life, and puts Caroline's surname as "Conner" and not "O'Conner."

50 Garza, "La lógica," 61–62.

51 Ibid., 62.

52 Ibid., 63.

53 "Laredo, TX." *The Handbook of Texas Online*, http://www.tsha.utexas.edu/handbook/online/articles/view/LL/hdl2.html.

54 "Disgustos familiares que me reservo, me obligaron abandonar aquella poblacíon para siempre." Garza, "La lógica," 65.

55 "Garza the Revolutionist," *Examiner* (San Francisco), 18 Jan. 1892, in SRE, leg. 11-10-44, exp. 4, f. 58.

56 For brief biographies that mention Garza having fathered two children with Caroline O'Conner, see "Garza the Revolutionist," *Examiner* (San Francisco), 18 Jan. 1892, in SRE, leg. 11-10-44, exp. 4, f. 58; "Another Garza Band Routed by Our Troops," *Herald*, 17 Jan. 1892, in SRE, leg. 11-10-44, exp. 3, f. 62; and untitled excerpted typescript in Coalson Collection, "Garza, Catarino," South Texas Archive, Texas A&M, Kingsville, Texas.

57 Garza, "La lógica," 69–70.

58 "Un ángel en mi defensa." "Por respeto al bello sexo, se moderaban un tanto cuanto los escándalos." Ibid., 75. William French found a similar ideal for Porfirian women in northern Mexico. They were seen as "guardian angels" who would be good wives and mothers and not sexually threatening (French, *A Peaceful and Working People*, 102–3).

59 "Armonía." Garza, "La lógica," 246.

60 "De los más populares en la frontera del estado de Coahuila y de los más queridos por el pueblo obrero." "Fiel y verdadero amigo." Ibid., 246. Pages marked to be set aside for biographical entries and photographs for Ignacio Martínez and others also remained blank.

61 Ibid., 76–79.

62 Ibid., 79, 91–92.

63 Ibid., 94–97.

64 "El destino me lleva a conocer la capital de mi patria; quizá no tarde tenga la satisfacción de abrazar una carrera que sin duda alguna me abrirá paso en la via pública." "No olvido que nací en un rancho me crié y me eduqué en el; pero sin embargo la humildad de mi cuna es probable que sea una estrella precursora que mas tarde me guíe al punto que ambiciono." Ibid., 100.

65 Ibid., 112–13.

66 Ibid., 119–20.

67 After Díaz served a four-year term as president (1876–1880), Manuel González was elected (1880–1884), and then Díaz retook the reins of power and would remain president until 1911.

68 Garza, "La lógica," 123–65.

69 "Haya aceptado a esa chusma de escritores mexicanos sin precaver si puedan traer piojos." Ibid., 127.

70 Alonso, *Thread of Blood*, 80–84. See also Mathew C. Gutmann, *The Meanings of Macho: Being a Man in Mexico City* (Berkeley: University of California Press, 1996), for an insightful analysis of Mexican masculinity. In his study of a working-

class community in Mexico City, Gutmann finds that the stereotype of the typical macho existed, but that the macho behavior, for the most part, did not.

71 "Como a una hermana." Garza, *La lógica*, 167–68, 171.

72 Ibid., 182–83.

73 "Entre estos *primos* son costumbres avolidas ayudar el huérfano o proteger a las viudas." Ibid., 168.

74 "Exponer la vida por una señorita o por un amigo, nada valía para un mexicano." Ibid., 174.

75 "Para ser un héroe entre los americanos se necesita muy poco, y para serlo entre nosotros los mexicanos, necesitamos morirnos defendiendo a la Patria." Ibid., 175.

76 See Paredes, *With His Pistol in His Hand*, which describes the portrayal in corridos of another Mexican border hero, Gregorio Cortez. See also Limón's *Mexican Ballads, Chicano Poems: History and Influence in Mexican-American Social Poetry* (Berkeley: University of California Press, 1992), for a gender analysis of Paredes's characterization of Cortez.

77 "Los mexicanos eran lo mismo que los perros, que por un hueso se peleaban." "Miserable difamador." "Demasiado violento." Ibid., 176–77.

78 "De la manera más cobarde." Ibid., 59.

79 "Las americanas aman por conveniencia, así como son fáciles para amar, son fáciles para olvidar y abandonar." Ibid., 180.

80 "De todo un poco." "Necesario distraer un tanto cuanto mi pluma para narrar acontecimientos que al paracer son de poca importancia." "En mi carrera de historiador, los recuerdo, y no puedo menos que mesclarlos con otros de mas interés." Ibid., 166.

81 Ibid., 183.

82 Ibid., 184. Garza ran this paper with an exiled Mexican journalist from Monterrey, Adolfo Duclós Salinas, who later published a stinging critique of Bernardo Reyes and Porfirio Díaz, titled *Méjico pacificado: El progreso de mejico y los hombres que lo gobiernan* (St. Louis: Hughes and Co., 1904).

83 "Editor Garza's Case," *San Antonio Express*, 16 Aug. 1887, in SRE, leg. 834, exp. 1; "Editor Garza's Case," *New York Times*, 14 Aug. 1887, in SRE, leg. 834, exp. 1, f. 19; "From Eagle Pass," *San Antonio Express*, 17 Apr. 1887, in SRE, leg. 834, exp. 1.

84 "Se dedicara exclusivamente a combatir los supremos abusos." Garza, "La lógica," 265.

85 "Un criminal." Ibid., 192.

86 "Editor Garza's Case," *San Antonio Express*, 16 Aug. 1887, in SRE, leg. 834, exp. 1.

87 "From Eagle Pass," *San Antonio Express*, 17 Apr. 1887, in SRE, leg. 834, exp. 1.

88 "Editor Garza's Extradition," *New York World*, 23 Aug. 1887, in SRE, leg. 834, exp. 1; "From Eagle Pass," *San Antonio Express*, 18 Aug. 1887, in SRE, leg. 834, exp. 1.

89 "Lo que sí sentimos es que nuestro pueblo tenga que regar su sangre con la de los mexicanos, cuya bajeza no merece tal distinción." Garza, "La lógica," 198.

90 "Estúpidos editors." "Los Veteranos Voluntarios borrachos." Ibid., 199. Garza also refers to "yanquees comedores de beyotas." Assuming that the "y" is "ll," then the reference to *bellota* could mean "acorn." However, the *Diccionario de mejicanismos* gives another meaning, "testicles of a young horse," which seems to fit this context and Garza's intent more closely than "acorn-eating yankees."

91 "Nos consideramos los mexicanos con más pureza de sangre que los americanos, supuesto que en nuestro país, sólo hay una mezcla, la de español e indio y entre ellos la generalidad son de aventureros irlandeses, mendigos polacos, suizos, prusianos, rusos y más que todo, africanos asquerosos." Ibid., 200.

92 "Jamás acostombro contrariar mis principios o convicciones." "Yo resido en un país libre y soy tan hombre como ustedes para responder en cualquier terreno por mis acciones." Ibid., 204.

93 "Mejores amigos y protectores." Ibid., 210.

94 "Defender la instituciones de un país no es marchar de acuerdo con su gobierno. Nosotros defendemos a México pero no así a sus actuales gobernantes. Atacamos á los filibusteros americanos, no á los hombres dignos y honrados." Ibid., 214.

95 José María Caloo, consul in Eagle Pass, to Sec. Rel. Ext., 2 Sept. 1886, in SRE, leg. 11–10–16, f. 64.

96 "Convertir aquel círculo de obreros, en un instrumento servil." Garza, "La lógica," 225.

97 "Si el Cónsul en estos momentos de convulsiones políticas internacionales, le da vergüenza y miedo decir que es mexicano, á mí por el contrario, me dá honra y valor decir que soy hijo de Anáhuac, de esta patria de Hidalgo, Morelos, Abasolo, Allende, Matamoros y otros de igual temple, que es la más envidiada por los filibusteros ambiciosos y miserables. . . . Se me dirá que ataco a los gobernantes; pero señores, estos no son la patria, ni son las leyes, ni son el pueblo; sino unos verdaderos sirvientes. Defiendo a la República Mexicana y no a los tiranos que la gobiernan." Ibid., 235–36.

98 "El sol se opacó y la opresión reinó." Ibid., 244.

99 Ibid., 418–20.

100 Ibid., 424–26.

101 Ibid., 426–29. Cinco de Mayo celebrates the battle of Puebla led by General Ignacio Zaragoza, a native Tejano. Although the Mexicans won the battle, they lost the war against the French; as a result, the Hapsburg Maximilian ruled as emperor in Mexico for the next five years (1862–1867). Cinco de Mayo is celebrated with much greater enthusiasm among Mexican Americans than in Mexico.

102 "Garza the Revolutionist," *Examiner* (San Francisco), 18 Jan. 1892, in SRE, leg. 11-10-44, exp. 4, f. 58.

103 There is an abundance of Ranger biographies. See, for example, Jack Martin, *Border Boss: Captain John R. Hughes — Texas Ranger* (Austin: State House Press, 1990 [1942]). For an academic version, see Walter Prescott Webb, *The Texas Rangers: A Century of Frontier Defense* (Austin: University of Texas Press, 1965 [1935]).

104 "Abandona la pluma para empuñar la espada." Catarino Garza, "Proclama," in CPD, leg. 16, docs. 10951, 11418. Garza repeats this line in a pamphlet he wrote in exile in Costa Rica, *La era de Tuxtepec en México: O sea Rusía en América* (San José, Costa Rica: Imprenta Comercial, 1894), 26. A copy of this pamphlet, with an inscription from Garza to Porfirio Díaz, can be found at the Latin American Library, Tulane University.

2. RESISTING THE PAX PORFIRIANA

1 Hart, Empire and Revolution, 129. Also, see Knight, *The Mexican Revolution*, vol. 1, 80.

2 For a discussion of the violence and repression during the pax porfiriana, see Vanderwood, *Disorder and Progress*, esp. ch. 8; and Knight, *The Mexican Revolution*, vol. 1, 15–18. For an analysis of the image of the Mexican rural police, see Vanderwood, *Disorder and Progress*, 54–55.

3 This quote specifically refers to how Díaz sent Bernardo Reyes to the northeast in 1885 to balance the power of generals Treviño and Naranjo, and then appointed Treviño as military commander in the region in 1909 to eliminate Reyes as a political threat (Knight, *Mexican Revolution*, vol. 1, 17).

4 For a detailed description of the events surrounding Reyes's assumption of power in the northeast by an avowed anti-Reyista, see Duclós Salinas, *Méjico pacificado*, esp. 100–5.

5 For more on Treviño and Naranjo, see Cerutti, *Burguesía, capitales e industria*, 253–59, 268–281. For an excellent discussion of how Díaz's system of co-optation and repression worked in relation to Evaristo Madero, see Romana Falcón, "Raices de la revolución: Evaristo Madero, el primer eslabón de la cadena," in *The Revolutionary Process in Mexico: Essays on Political and Social Change, 1880–1940*, ed. Jaime E. Rodríguez O. (Los Angeles: University of California Press, 1990), 33–56.

6 Falcón, "Raices de la revolución," 33–34.

7 Vanderwood, *The Power of God*, esp. 266–77.

8 For the most thorough analysis of the Yaqui struggle, see Hu-DeHart, *Yaqui Resistance and Survival*.

9 Manuel Treviño to Rel. Ext., 30 June 1886, in SRE, leg. 11-10-16, f. 46; "Proclama," *El Mundo*, 24 June 1886.

10 Treviño to Rel. Ext., 30 June 1886, in SRE, leg. 11-10-16, f. 45–46; Matías Romero to Rel. Ext., 28 June 1886, in SRE, leg. 11-10-16, f. 11-13. Treviño to Rel. Ext., 21 Sept. 1886, in SRE, leg. 11-10-16, f. 85; Copy of testimony, 21 Sept. 1886, in SRE, leg. 11-10-16, f. 89.

11 Cosío Villegas, *Historia moderna. Vol. 2: El Porfiriato*, 120.

12 Biographical data culled from *Diccionario histórico y biográfico de la revolución mexicana*, vol. 7 (Mexico, D.F.: INEHRM, 1992), 142–43; and *Rasgos biográficos del general y doctor Ignacio Martínez: Asesinado alevosamente en esta población el martes 3 de febrero del presente año entre 9 y 10 de la mañana* (Laredo: Tip. El Mundo, 1891), 3, 7. The publisher of this pamphlet, *El Mundo*,

was also the press for the newspaper that Martínez owned and edited. For an analysis of Martínez's travel writings, see Elliott Young, "Imagining Alternative Modernities: Ignacio Martínez's Travel Narratives," in Truett and Young, *Continental Crossroads*.

13 "La paz vergonzosa." "Aquí teneis a tu pueblo listo y entusiasta por la guerra contra el invasor francés." *Rasgos biográficos*, 9.

14 Ibid., 9–10.

15 Ibid., 12.

16 Ibid., 14.

17 Ibid., 15.

18 "Por catequizar a las Señoras, las que con ferviente perseverancia tornaban a sus maridos, padres ú hermanos del lado de Don Porfirio y de sus principios de no reelección." Ibid., 18.

19 "Expediente personal," in SRE, leg. 1867, part 11, f. 519.

20 "Mexican Revolt Is Spreading," [?], 17 July 1886, in SRE, leg. 11-10-16, f. 23. See also "The Uprising in Mexico," *New York Times*, 18 July 1886, in SRE, leg. 11-10-16, f. 23.

21 *El Mundo*, 17 July 1886, as quoted and translated in "Mexican Revolt Is Spreading," [?] 17 July 1886, in SRE, leg. 11-10-16, f. 23.

22 "Mexican Revolt Is Spreading," [?], 17 July 1886, in SRE, leg. 11-10-16, f. 23.

23 "Mexico Is Not Afraid," *Mexico Star*, 19 July 1886, in SRE, leg. 11-10-16, f. 23.

24 Lauro Cejudo to Reyes, 18 Nov. 1885, in ABR doc. 273.

25 "The Uprising in Mexico," *New York Times*, 18 July 1886, in SRE, leg. 11-10-16, f. 23.

26 Rodríguez to Cejudo, 10 Nov. 1885, in ABR, doc. 290.

27 "Continuan las concesiones fraudulentas, la malversación de los caudales públicos; los impuestos de aduanas y del timbre han sido recargados al extremo de hacer imposible el trafico; los favoritos y especuladores se reparten el territorio en inmensos girones a pretexto de colonización de terrenos baldíos; se ha consumado el fraude de la deuda inglesa; y el heroe del 2 de Abril capitaliza sus laureles y sus servicios patrióticos en barras de oro, en acciones ferrocarriles y en billetes de banco." "Ha hollado todas las libertades de los ciudadanos con la infame leyva, con las prisiones y asesinatos de los periodistas, con las persecuciones a cualquiera demostración de descontento." "Plan político." *El Mundo*, 22 Aug. 1886, in SRE, leg. 11-10-16, f. 101.

28 Ibid.

29 For an in-depth analysis of Zapata's part in the Mexican Revolution, see John Womack Jr., *Zapata and the Mexican Revolution* (New York: Vintage, 1970). For a more recent analysis, see Samuel Brunk, *Emiliano Zapata: Revolution and Betrayal in Mexico* (Albuquerque: University of New Mexico Press, 1995).

30 Garza's newspaper endorsed the Texas Mexican Independent Party slate of candidates, including seven Anglo-surnamed candidates and five Spanish-surnamed candidates. See Luis Pueblo, *El Comercio Mexicano*, San Diego, 18 Aug. 1888, in SRE, leg. 9-1-45.

31 Anders, *Boss Rule in South Texas*, 43.

32 Martin, *Border Boss*, 44–47.

33 I have not found any evidence for the charge that Garza had killed anyone, either in Mexico or in Texas.

34 "Origins of Dispute," *San Antonio Express*, 22 Sept. 1888, in SRE, leg. 18-27-112, f. 42.

35 "Cold Blooded Assassination at Rio Grande City," *Gate City*, 22 Sept. 1888, in SRE, leg. 18-27-112, f. 9.

36 "The Capital Cullings," *San Antonio Express*, 26 Sept. 1888, in SRE, leg. 18-27-112, f. 42. Agustín de la Peña denied that he had hired Garza to make speeches. He also clarified that on April 16, the Club Político-Progresista Méjico-Tejano de Rio Grande City was organized under the leadership of Andres Mancillas and Luciano López. See Agustín de la Peña, letter to editor, *La Colonia Mexicana*, 3 Oct. 1888, in SRE, leg. 18-27-112, f. 61.

37 "Origins of Dispute," *San Antonio Express*, 22 Sept. 1888, in SRE, leg. 18-27-112, f. 42.

38 Ignacio Martínez, "Ignacio Martínez: Informe sobre dicho emigrado político enemigo del Sr Gral. Porfirio Díaz," *El Mundo*, 26 Aug. 1888, in SRE, leg. 1-1-90.

39 "Un cuestionable delito de imprenta." "Como a un asesino o ladrón de caballos." "Cuanto no se sublevara nuestra sangre al ver tratado así a un escritor mexicano?" "El Sr. Catarino Garza," *El Mundo*, 9 Sept. 1888, in SRE, leg. 9-1-45.

40 "Ley linch tan en boga en este país." "Entre nosotros," *La Colonia Mexicana*, 8 Sept. 1888, in SRE, leg. 9–1-45, f. 20.

41 Patricia A. Schecter, *Ida B. Wells-Barnett and American Reform, 1880–1930* (Chapel Hill: University of North Carolina Press, 2001), 256 n.1, 274 n.16.

42 For an excellent discussion of the different ways in which vigilantism and lynching have been written about, and the sexualized nature of the lynching ritual, see Gordon, *The Great Arizona Orphan Abduction*, 261–68. See also Danalynn Recer, "Patrolling the Borders of Race, Gender, and Class: The Lynching Ritual and Texas Nationalism, 1850–1994," master's thesis, University of Texas, Austin, 1994.

43 "Un fin moral: la defensa de las hijas de familia comntra ataques de una raza degradada y grosera." Ironically, Duclós Salinas makes this distinction between the United States and Mexico to show the depravity of the Mexican government, while he seems to accept the moralistic and racist justification of mob lynching in the United States (Duclós Salinas, *Méjico pacificado*, 115–16).

44 José F. González to Rel. Ext., Rio Grande City, 22 Sept. 1888, in SRE, leg. 18-27-112, f. 11.

45 "Origins of Dispute," *San Antonio Express*, 22 Sept. 1888, in SRE, leg. 18-27-112, f. 42; *Brownsville Times*, 4 Oct. 1888, as transcribed in SRE, leg. 18-27-112, f. 69. Another account cited by Agnes Grimm quotes Garza as saying that he was "in the barber chair leaning back being shaved when that Rinche fired this shot at me from the sidewalk." Garza then got up and walked outside where he proceeded to beat the *rinche* (Ranger) with his bare fists. While this is certainly the most colorful version, none of the other contemporaneous sources corroborate it (Grimm, *Llanos Mesteñas*, 140). The Ranger Hughes biography asserts that both men went

for their weapons simultaneously, but Sebree was "quicker on the draw" (Martin, *Border Boss*, 51).

46 "Rio Grande City," *San Antonio Express*, 22 Sept. 1888, in SRE, leg. 18-27-112, f. 21.

47 *Laredo Times*, 22 Sept. 1888, in SRE, leg. 18-27-112, f. 21.

48 "Maldición! el que hace el bien; siempre encuentra como premio el martirio." *El Diablo Predicador*, 23 Sept. 1888, in SRE, leg. 18-27-112, f. 21.

49 Tel., Collector of Customs, Brownsville, 22 September 1888, reprinted in "At the Mercy of a Mob," *Washington Post*, 25 Sept. 1888, in SRE, leg. 18-27-112, f. 29.

50 Tel., John P. Kelsey to Governor Ross, Rio Grande City, 22 Sept. 1888, reprinted in *San Antonio Express*, 23 Sept. 1888, in SRE, leg. 18-27-112, f. 21.

51 "At the Mercy of a Mob," *Washington Post*, 25 Sept. 1888, in SRE, leg. 18-27-112, f. 29.

52 "Rio Grande City Trouble," *San Antonio Express*, 25 Sept. 1888, in SRE, leg. 18-27-112, f. 42.

53 "Proceder en el presente caso con total arreglo a lo prevenido por las leyes de este pais; de modo que se haga estricta y recta justicia." José F. González, consul, to Rex Ext; Rio Grande City, 22 Sep 1888, in SRE, leg. 18-27-112.

54 "¿No les parece a nuestros lectores que es un magnífico modo de hacer justicia?" "Arrestados," *La Colonia Mexicana*, 10 Oct. 1888, in SRE, leg. 18-27-112, f. 68; "Rio Grande City Trouble," *San Antonio Express*, 23 Oct 1888, in SRE, leg. 18-27-112, f. 76. "Remitido," *La Colonia Mexicana*, 28 Oct. 1888, in SRE, 18-27-112, f. 76

55 "Rio Grande City Trouble," *San Antonio Express*, 25 Sept. 1888, in SRE, leg. 18-27-112, f. 42; a Monterrey, Mexico, newspaper made a similar distinction in "El desorden del Rio Grande," *La Revista del Norte*, 26 Sept. 1888, p. 2, c. 2-3. Hemeroteca del Fondo Reservado, Biblioteca Nacional, Universidad Autonoma de México.

56 "Rio Grande City Notes," *San Antonio Express*, 24 Sept. 1888, in SRE, leg. 18-27-112, f. 42.

57 "Anarchy on the Border," *New York Herald*, 26 Sept. 1888, in SRE, leg. 18-27-112, f. 34.

58 At the Mercy of a Mob," *Washington Post*, 25 Sept. 1888, in SRE, leg. 18-27-112, f. 29. The *Washington Post* reported that a "mob" of 400 had taken over the city, and 200 had gone to Fort Ringgold. The *San Antonio Express* put the number of the mob at 100, "State Capital Cullings," *San Antonio Express*, 26 Sept. 1888, in SRE, 18-27-112, f. 42. Another newspaper citing one of two white men in the crowd, put the number at 500, "The Border Troubles," *Times Democrat* (New Orleans), 27 Sept. 1888, SRE, 18-27-112, f. 53.

59 "No ha vuelto a alterarse la tranquilidad pública." José F. González to Rel. Ext., Rio Grande City, 26 Sept. 1888, in SRE, leg. 18-27-112, f. 36.

60 Tel., Col. Clendennin to Gen. Stanley, 26 Sept. 1888, as transcribed in "State Capital Cullings," *San Antonio Express*, 28 Sept. 1888, in SRE, leg. 18-27-112, f. 60.

61 "Se han suscitado graves dificultades; al grado de que el pueblo mexicano; de por

sí sufrido y tolerante; se haya puesto en armas; decidido a castigar por su mano al criminal; que en el corto periodo de dos meses o tres ha asesinado alevosamente a dos mexicanos; y es una amenaza constante para el resto de la colonia mexicana de aquel condado de Starr." "La cuestión Garza, grande exitación," *La Colonia Mexicana*, 26 Sept. 1888, in SRE, leg. 18-27-112, f. 41.

62 "Los mexicanos avecinados en la frontera de Texas; conozcan perfectamente la falta de garantias de que adolecen; el cinismo y audacia exasperantes con que las autoridades del Condado de Starr toleran los desafueros cometidos con los mexicanos; y aun los estimulan indirectamete; facilitando a los criminales los medios de evadir el castigo de la justicia; y de seguir sembrando el terror entra la gente honrada de las poblaciones." "El atentado contra el escritor mexicano C. E. Garza," *La Colonia Mexicana*, 26 Sept. 1888, in SRE, leg. 18-27-112, f. 41.

63 "Result of Lawless Examples," *Laredo Times*, 26 Sept. 1888, in SRE, leg. 18-27-112, f. 43.

64 "Garza Killed," *Gate City*, 25 Sept. 1888, in SRE, leg. 18-27-112, f. 44.

65 Sociedad Mexicana, "Protesta," Laredo, 4 Nov. 1888, in Garza Correspondence.

66 " 'Si Uds. son ciudadanos americanos; es decir; tejanos; nada tengo que ver con Uds.; pero si entre Uds. se encuentran algunos ciudadanos mexicanos; cumple con mi deber en advertirles que estan infringiendo gravamente las leyes de este pais; mezclandose en la política . . . puesto que Uds. me piden un consejo; yo con el caracter oficial que tengo; leg digo que se retiren tranquilos para sus casas y no vuelvan a mezclarse en política en un pais extrangero.' " González to Rel. Ext., Rio Grande City, 22 Sept. 1888, in SRE, leg. 18-27–112, f. 13.

67 "Me ábstuve de hablar una sola palabra." González to Rel. Ext., Rio Grande City, 25 Oct. 1888, in SRE, leg. 18-27-112, f. 88–89.

68 "Las autoridades estan convencidas que los individuous que formaron el motín en su mayor parte son tejanos y algunos mejicanos naturalizados en este pais; y cuando más dos o tres verdaderos mexicanos." González to Rel. Tex., Rio Grande City, 1 Oct. 1888, in SRE, leg. 18-27-112, f. 27.

69 M. Treviño to Rel. Ext., Brownsville, 15 Nov. 1888, in SRE, leg. 18-27-112, f. 101.

70 "Han venido aqui para comer y dormir a pierna suelta?" "Las autoridades mexicanas en Texas," *El Comercio Mexicano*, 29 Sept. 1888, in SRE, leg 18-27-112, f. 56.

71 "Vergonzoso." "El hombre que tal hace no merece otra cosa que el epiteto de traidor." Trenidad J. Rodríguez, "Más infamias," *La Palanca*, 7 Nov. 1888, in SRE, leg. 18-27-112, f. 98.

72 *Brownsville Times*, 4 Oct. 1888, in SRE, leg. 18-27-112, f. 103.

73 *San Antonio Express*, 26 Sept. 1888, in SRE, leg. 18-27-112, f. 42.

74 *Brownsville Times*, 4 Oct. 1888, in SRE, leg. 18-27-112, f. 71.

75 In 1875, the Mexican government published a report that detailed various incursions into Mexican territory from Texas beginning in 1851; see *Reports of the Committee of Investigation*, translation of original report entitled *Informe de la Comisión Pesquisadora de la Frontera Norte al Ejecutivo de la Unión* (Mexico City: n.p. 1874).

76 Bourke, *Our Neutrality Laws*, 3.

77 "Que el del americano; el del francés y en resumen; menos que el hombre de color." "¡Para mayor garantizar de sus hermanos de raza! ¿Porque pues se dejan gobernar por americanos que odian extremadamente a la raza? ¿A caso no hay en este y otros distritos mayoría de México-texanos? ¿O se cree que puede haber superioridad de raza?" C. E. Garza, "Editorial," *El Comercio Mexicano*, 29 Sept. 1888, in SRE, leg. 18-27-112, f. 29.

78 Anders, *Boss Rule in South Texas*, 280–83. Anders notes that once the elections were "purified" and reform measures implemented to prevent abuses such as the corralling of voters, the practical result was the "disenfranchisement of the mass of Hispanic voters" (63).

79 "Entre ciertos abogados y unos cuantos aventureros americanos poseen en la actualidad los principales derechos; habiendo dejado en la mas completa ruina a infinidad de viudas y huerfanos mexicanos; que la desgracia quiso asignarles sus derechos en la parte del territorio que nos usurparon valiendose de la injusta guerra de 46 y 47." "Para que los mexicanos en Texas y texanos conozcan el origen de sus actuales ciurcunstancias; estudien la manera de salir de ellas y voten con dignidad el yugo que los oprime." Garza, "Editorial," *El Comercio Mexicano*, 29 Sept. 1888, in SRE, leg. 18-27-112, f. 29.

80 Garza, "Soneto," 16 Sept. 1888, Rio Grande City, Garza Correspondence.

81 There is a rich and growing literature about corridos. See the seminal work by Paredes, *With His Pistol in His Hand*, and the more recent analysis by Limón, *Mexican Ballads, Chicano Poems*.

82 Catarino Garza, "Estrofa dedicada al bandido Sebree," n.d., written in Garza's handwriting and found among Garza Correspondence.

83 Ibid. Even though the corrido was not signed by Garza, the way in which the story is told and the place where it was found suggests that Garza is the author.

84 Frank H. Bushwick, *Glamorous Days* (San Antonio: Naylor Co., 1934), 242. Agnes Grimm credits the heavy watch chain with stopping Sebree's bullet. Garza's wife had the bullet and watch chain encased in gold as a memento for her husband (Grimm, *Llanos Mestenas*, 140). Until recently the family still had the watch fob (Carlos Pérez, personal interview with author, 26 July 1999).

85 "¡Ah! Cobarde y miserable asesino. Crees que quitando a Garza la existencia; se acabarían los defensores de la raza mexicana? ¿Cuan engañado estás? A Garza le sucederá otro no menos acérrimo; y a este otro; y otro hasta ver coronados nuestros deseos." "Las autoridades mexicanas en Texas," *El Comercio Mexicano*, 29 Sept. 1888, in SRE, leg. 18-27-112, f. 56.

86 "Sandoval's Raid," *New York Herald*, 27 June 1890, in SRE, leg. 11-9-35, f. 116.

87 Paulino Martínez had a long and interesting revolutionary career that began with Garza on the border and ended with the Zapatistas in central Mexico. As well as his involvement with Garza and Sandoval in the early 1890s, Paulino Martínez supported the anarchist Flores Magón brothers when they came through Laredo in 1904, then joined Francisco Madero's antireelection campaign in 1909, and rode with Madero on his ill-fated raid into Coahuila in November 1910. Unsatisfied with Madero's agrarian program, Martínez plotted with the Vazquez Gómez brothers in their October 1911 revolt against Madero, and then finally

joined the Zapatista cause. Martínez was assassinated in December 1914 by Villistas after having led the Zapatista delegation to the aguascalientes convention. For more information, see Paulino Martínez, *Diccionario histórico y biográfico de la revolución mexicana*, 547–48; and for Martínez's role in the aguascalientes convention, see Vito Alessio Robles, *La convención revoluciónaria de aguascalientes* (Mexico City: INEHMR, 1979), 217, 411–12.

88 Reyes to Díaz, 29 Apr. 1890, in ABR, cop., doc. 870, f. 215.

89 Reyes to Díaz, 14 June 1890, in ABR, cop., doc. 931, f. 291; Reyes to Romero, 20 June 1890, in ABR, cop., doc. 320, f. 365–66.

90 "No podemos tolerar que una horda de rufianes siga traficando escandalosamente con los intereses nacionales." Paulino Martínez to Silviano Gómez, Tulancingo, 31 May 1890, in SRE, leg. 11-9-35, f. 17.

91 Díaz to Matías Romero, 12 June 1890, in SRE, leg. 11-9-35, f. 6.

92 Ornelas to Reyes, 21 June 1890, in ABR, doc. 2314.

93 *Laredo Times*, 25 June 1890, in Sutton to Asst. Sec. State, 24 June 1890, National Archives, Washington, D.C., General Records of the Department of State, RG 59, "Despatches from United States Consular Officials in Nuevo Laredo, Mexico, 1871–1906," Microcopy no. 280, Roll 2 (hereafter cited as DNL), f. 2.

94 *El Chinaco*, as cited in Sutton to Asst. Sec. State, 3 July 1890, in DNL, f. 4.

95 "Planes revolucionarios," *El Correo de Laredo*, 19 Sept. 1891, p. 2, c. 1. (Consulted at the Center for American History, University of Texas, Austin).

96 Sutton to Asst. Sec. State, 3 July 1890, in DNL, f. 2.

97 Reyes to Díaz, 26 June 1890, in ABR, cop., doc. 951, f. 316.

98 "The Size of a Revolution," *Laredo Times*, 1 July 1890, in SRE, leg. 11-9-35, f. 168.

99 "Protectores de la raza mexicana." Varrios to Rel. Ext., 4 July 1890, in SRE, leg. 11-9-35, f. 199–203.

100 "Comprado." Varrios to Reyes, 25 Sept. 1890, in ABR, doc. 2529, f. 2.

101 The Laredoan journalist Luis Bruni exemplifies the shared Latin identity between Mexicans and Italians (or French). Bruni, whose first name originally was Luigi and who was Italian, wrote for the Spanish-language newspaper *El Demócrata Fronterizo* in Laredo in the early twentieth century. For more on Bruni, see Young, "Deconstructing *La Raza*," 240–43.

102 "Una fianza ridícula y anti-legal." Justo Cárdenas, "La cuestión política," *La Colonia Mexicana*, 5 July 1890, in SRE, leg. 11-9-35, f. 131.

103 Reyes to Carlos C. Price [*sic*], 20 June 1890, ABR, cop., doc. 327, f. 372.

104 Varrios to Rel. Ext., 8 July 1890, in SRE, leg. 11-9-35, f. 203–8.

105 Ibid., f. 255.

106 Ibid., f. 233–35.

107 Reyes to Cerón, 30 June 1890, ABR, cop. doc. 37, f. 437.

108 Testimony of Juan Valadez in transcript of court proceedings sent by Rafael Varrios to Rel. Ext., 8 July 1890, in SRE, leg. 11-9-35, f. 238.

109 "Algunos auxilios pecuniarios y algunas esperanzas para el porvenir." "Explotables." Reyes to Ornelas, 19 July 1890, in ABR, cop., doc. 560, f. 559.

110 Ornelas to Rel. Ext., 17 Dec. 1890, in SRE, leg. 42-29-93, f. 71.

111 Varrios to Rel. Ext., 8 July 1890, in SRE, leg. 11-9-35, f. 258.

112 Ibid., f. 259–65.

113 McLeary and Flemming to Ornelas, 22 Dec. 1890, in SRE, leg. 42-29-93, f. 79.

114 Ornelas to McLeary and Fleming, "Memorandum Regarding Case against Ruíz Sandoval," 30 Aug. 1890, in SRE, leg. 15-3-120, f. 30.

115 Ibid.

116 "The Mexican Invasion," *Banner*, 19 Dec. 1890, in SRE, leg. 42-29-93, f. 102.

117 Ornelas to McLeary and Fleming, "Memorandum Regarding Case against Ruíz Sandoval," 30 Aug. 1890, in SRE, leg. 15-3-120, f. 28.

118 Ibid., f. 30.

119 "El hecho aparecería como un plagio verificado en territorio de Estados Unidos por agentes nuestros y ello daría margen a serias reclamaciones internacionales que además de traer reclamaciones a nuestro gobierno, provocaría grande escandalo en la prensa de los dos paises." [Reyes] to Cerón, in CPD, leg. 15, doc. 9898, f. 1. Although the copy of the letter in Díaz's archive does not contain the name of the sender, it is fairly obvious that it was Bernardo Reyes because of the type of information transmitted and its similarity to other correspondence between Reyes and Cerón. Reyes sent several letters to Cerón between September 1890 and January 1891, in which he referred explicitly to this plan to bring Sandoval to Mexico. See especially Reyes to Cerón, 8 Oct. 1890, in ABR, cop., doc. 2457, f. 124–25.

120 The details of the conspiracy can be found in [Reyes] to Cerón, in CPD, leg. 15, doc. 9898, f. 1–5. [Reyes] to Cerón, 11 Aug. 1890, in CPD, leg. 15, doc. 9900, f. 2. Reyes also procured a letter that Sandoval had sent to a friend in Mexico, asking him to join the insurrection. See Sandoval to Valencia, 7 Aug. 1890, in CPD, leg. 15, doc. 9901.

121 "Está muy sobre aviso y rodeado de precauciones." Reyes to Díaz, 29 Apr. 1890, ABR, cop., doc. 870, f. 215.

122 My request to consult Mexico's Defense Ministry archive was denied, even after the U.S. Embassy in Mexico made such a request on my behalf. The Defense Ministry wrote that they had no documentation on any of the people that I listed in my letter. These names included army officers such as Colonel Nieves Hernández, who was sentenced by a military court, and revolutionaries, such as Martínez and Garza, against whom extensive military campaigns had been launched.

123 The phrase "manufacturing consent" is borrowed from Edward S. Herman's book *Manufacturing Consent: The Political Economy of the Mass Media* (New York: Pantheon, 1988). Also, see Scott's *Domination and the Arts of Resistance* for an insightful discussion of what he refers to as the "hidden transcripts." Eminent historian of Mexico Daniel Cosío Villegas only devoted a paragraph to the rebellion in a section entitled "Notas Sueltas" (Loose notes). His citations for this section are *El Universal, El Monitor Repulicano, El Diario del Hogar, El Demócrata*, and *El Diario Oficial* (See Cosío Villegas, *Historia moderna de México*, 678–79). For the most part, this "official" interpretation has been the one to make it into the histories of Mexico. Thankfully, a boom in regional

histories has altered the Porfirian or centralist view of Mexican history, allowing for a more complex picture of "many Mexicos" and a heterogeneous revolutionary process. For an overview of this historiographical shift, see Benjamin, "Regionalizing the Revolution," 319–57.

124 Reyes to Cerón, 1 July 1890, in ABR, cop., doc. 417, f. 453.

125 Reyes to Felix González Vera, Nuevo Laredo, 25 July 1890, ABR, cop., doc. 580, f. 579.

126 Aplaudo o te mato." Reyes to Díaz, 3 Oct. 1890, ABR, cop., doc. 1047, f. 431.

127 Varrios to Rel. Ext., 2 Mar. 1891, in SRE, leg. 1-14-1649, f. 44.

128 Reyes to Díaz, 1 Sept. 1888, in ABR, doc. 1568.

129 Reyes to Díaz, 3 Jan. 1889, and Díaz to Reyes, 9 Jan. 1889, in ABR, doc. 1717.

130 "Es importante que los periodicos americanos hablen de la mala conducta con que se porta Ignacio Martínez con Ruíz Sandoval y sus cómplices, y con todos los demás que estaban en la conspiración después de que él los ha estado precipitando a las vías de hecho. Aun podrían agregar esos periódicos que los hombres que se han comprometido, al ver aquella conducta de Martínez, naturalmente se sentiran lastimados por él. De este modo, es probable que consigamos apartarlo las pocas simpatias que tiene el predicho Martínez y aun es posible que se tomen en antipatía. Hablé sobre este particular con Ornelas pues creo que él podra hacer que se lleven a efecto las publicaciones deseadas." Reyes to Cerón, 1 July 1890, ABR, cop. doc. 417, f. 453.

131 "Es un individuo cualquiera, que ni es General, ni es Mexicano." Reyes to Díaz, 25 Sept. 1890, in CPD, leg. 15, doc 11313.

132 Reyes to Díaz, 3 Oct. 1890, in ABR, cop. doc. 1047, f. 431.

133 "Los patrioteros de allende del Bravo, envidiosos de no sabemos que, pues ante el público sensato todos son iguales, están diciendose por la prensa unas verdades que . . . demuestran que la armonía más completa reina entre ellos." "Vagos estafadores que quieren vivir como parásitos del trabajo de los demás cubriendose con las máscaras de patriotas." "Un miserable, un cobarde, un asesino, villano, ambicioso, falso patriota y loco." *El Orden*, 23 Jan. 1891, in SRE, leg. 42-29-93, f. 136.

134 "Los revoltosos de allende el Rio Bravo pintados por sí mismos." "Tienen un comerciantillo que los dirige y recoge sus giros, un militarcillo que representa la empresa, un abogadillo que les defiende, una prensa inmuda que los ensalza y a la vez calumnia a los que no se dejan desplumar." "Nos profesan un odio entrañable, nos insultan y calumnian." "Ni proteger o tolerar a esos bribones chantagistas y miserables, que sin valor, sin gratitud, sin honra, ni vergüenza insultan como mujeres y se dejan abofetear como madrias, desgraciados que se fingen revolucionarios de Mexico, para estafar al producto de su trabajo a los hombres honrados y echar una mancha de infamia y de baldón a nuestra colonia mexicana en esta frontera." Ignacio Martínez, "Grupo de estafadores," *El Mundo*, 18 Jan. 1891, reprinted in *La Voz de Nuevo León*, 31 Jan. 1891, p. 1, c. 4, Capilla Alfonsina, Universidad Autónoma de Nuevo León (hereafter cited as UANL).

135 "Esperamos que ahora se dedique a trabajar en algo, pues cerca de un año ha vivido aquí con todo y familia sin ganar tres centavos en ningún trabajo honesto,

y sacando muchas sumas de este vecindario por medios más ó menos astutos."
"Vivía escandalizando en las cantinas sin capital y sin ningún conocido honesto
modo de subsitir." Ignacio Martínez, "Grupo de estafadores," *El Mundo*, 25 Jan.
1891, reprinted in *La Voz de Nuevo León*, 31 Jan. 1891, p. 2, c. 1, UANL.

136 "Los puercos nunca salen de su revolcadero." "La hora de justicia ha llegado. Yo
soy el eco de la voz de justicia. Yo vengo a gritarle, lo que otros no han tenido el
valor de decirle. Vd. es un miserable que se arodilla a limpiar el calzado de los
magnates de la población, y desprecia a los humildes mexicanos que no tienen
bienes ni influencia que poner a la disposicion de vd." "Soberbio con los humildes, humilde con los soberbios." Paulino Martínez, "Al Sr. Ignacio Martínez,
conocido con los sobrenombres Gral. y Dr.," *El Chinaco*, 18 Jan. 1891, reprinted
in *La Voz de Nuevo León*, 31 Jan. 1891, p. 2, c. 1, UANL.

137 "Solo prueban impotencia y rabia en el que los prodiga." Justo Cárdenas, *La
Colonia Mexicana*, reprinted in *La Voz de Nuevo León*, 31 Jan. 1891, p. 2, c. 3,
UANL.

138 "Sería bueno que la prensa de Nuevo Laredo reprodujera todos esos parrafos y
enciendiera los animos de una contra otros." Reyes to Cerón, 24 Jan. 1891, in
ABR, cop., doc. 2647, f. 323.

139 "Era bastante caballero para presentarse al primer llamado que le hiciese la
autoridad." "Quebrantado la paz." "Agresión violenta,"*La Colonia Mexicana*,
31 Jan. 1891, in SRE, leg. 1-14-1649, f. 3; "Localidades," *El Mundo*, 1 Feb.
1891, in SRE, leg. 1-14-1649, f. 4. Both of these articles were reprinted in *La Voz
de Nuevo León*, 7 Feb. 1891, p. 2, c. 1-2.

140 "Murder," *Gate City*, 4 Feb. 1891, in SRE, leg. 1-14-1649, f. 2, UANL.

141 "Para entenderse como hombres." Interview with Francisco Ruíz Sandoval, *El
Chinaco*, 24 Jan. 1891, reprinted in *La Voz de Nuevo León*, 31 Jan. 1891, p. 2, c.
2, UANL. According to Martínez's biographical pamphlet, he was attacked in
Brownsville by a "negro" who tried to kill him. In defending himself, Martínez
killed the attacker (*Rasgos biográficos*, 29).

142 There is a wide range of literature on the issue of masculinity and honor. For two
excellent discussions of honor and gender in the colonial and postcolonial context of the New Mexico–Chihuahua frontier, see Alonso, *Thread of Blood*, 80–
82, and Gutiérrez, *When Jesus Came*, 209–15. Pablo Piccato provides an insightful examination of honor and violence in Mexico City, especially among the
poor, in *City of Suspects: Crime in Mexico City, 1900–1931* (Durham: Duke
University Press, 2001), 80–94. For a classic discussion of honor in the Mediterranean context, see Julian Pitt-Rivers, "Honor and Social Status," in *Honor and
Shame: The Values of Mediterranean Society*, ed. J. G. Peristiany (Chicago: University of Chicago Press, 1965).

143 *El Duende*, 1 Feb. 1891, in SRE, leg. 1-14-1649, f. 3.

144 "Quebrantado la paz." "Agresión violenta," *La Colonia Mexicana*, 31 Jan.
1891, in SRE, leg. 1-14-1649, f. 3; "Localidades," *El Mundo*, 1 Feb. 1891, in
SRE, leg. 1-14-1649, f. 4. Both of these articles were reprinted in *La Voz de
Nuevo León*, 7 Feb. 1891, p. 2, c. 1–2, UANL.

145 "Localidades," *El Mundo*, 1 Feb. 1891, in SRE, leg. 1-14-1649, f. 4.

146 "Gran sensación . . . aun se espera algo serio." "Agresión violenta," *La Colonia Mexicana*, 31 Jan. 1891, in SRE, leg. 1-14-1649, f. 3.

147 "Localidades," *El Mundo*, 1 Feb. 1891, in SRE, leg. 1-14-1649, f. 4; Copies of court records and bonds for Martínez are in Rafael Varrios to Rel. Ext., 1 Feb. 1891, in SRE, leg. 1-14-1649, f. 15–21.

148 "Bold Assassination: General Martínez Shot Dead on a Public Street," *Laredo Daily Times*, 4 Feb. 1891, in SRE, leg. 1-14-1649, f. 2.

149 "Antiguo soldado de la libertad." "Nosotros enlutamos las columnas de nuestro periódico en testimonio de dolor por la sentida muerte de un mexicano que había ocupado un lugar respetable por sus servicios a la patria, por sus conocimientos científicos y literarios y por su inquebrantable fé política." "Un crimen más: El Gral. Ignacio Martínez," *La Colonia Mexicana*, 4 Feb. 1891, in SRE, leg. 1-14-1649, f. 1.

150 "Murder," *Gate City*, 4 Feb. 1891, in SRE, leg. 1-14-1649, f. 2.

151 Ibid.

152 "Assassinated Gen. Ignacio Martínez by Stealth," *Gate City*, 3 Feb. 1891, in SRE, leg. 1-14-1649.

153 "Martínez fue el alma de la joven generación fronteriza, el motor de los modernos principios en los estados de Nuevo León, Coahuila y Tamaulipas. Lo que otros no pudieron hacer con armas, el lo intentó y consumó con la fuerza de la propaganda: cada uno de sus condicipulos fue un nuevo apostol, y cada apostol hizo innumerables sectarios del dogma constitucional y reformista." *Rasgos biograficos*, 8.

154 "Un crimen más: El Gral. Ignacio Martínez," *La Colonia Mexicana*, 4 Feb. 1891, in SRE, leg. 1-14-1649, f. 1. "Bold Assassination: General Martínez Shot Dead on a Public Street," *Laredo Daily Times*, 4 Feb. 1891, in SRE, leg. 1-14-1649, f. 2.

155 *Gate City*, 5 Feb. 1891, in SRE, leg. 1-14-1649, f. 8.

156 "Assassinated Gen. Ignacio Martínez by Stealth," *Gate City*, 3 Feb. 1891, in SRE, leg. 1-14-1649.

157 "Almost a Tragedy," *Gate City*, 6 Feb. 1891, in SRE, leg. 1-14-1649, f. 8.

158 *Laredo Times*, 7 Feb. 1891, in SRE, leg. 1-14-1649, f. 8.

159 "Asesinato del Dr. Ignacio Martínez," and reprint of *El Monitor Republicano* "La muerte del General Martínez," *La Voz der Nuevo León*, 7 Feb. 1891, p. 2, c. 1–4, UANL.

160 "Monterrey sabe bien que Manuel no ha cometido el crimen." *El Duende*, 22 Feb. 1891, in SRE, 1-14-1649, f. 35.

161 "Si éste se ponía al frente de Martínez de una manera decidida y prestaba algun servicio de importancia contaría con la protección de las autoridades del lado mexicano." Reyes to Díaz, 1 Sept. 1888, in ABR, doc. 1568.

162 Varrios to Rel. Ext., 23 Apr. 1891, in SRE, leg. 1-14-1649, f. 72–75.

163 "Si Don Porfirio Díaz puede lavarse las manos como Pilatos que lo haga cuanto antes, porque muchos creerán ver en ellas manchas de sangre." "Un asesinato sospechoso," *El Progreso*, as cited in *Rasgos biográficos*, 34. Other newspapers that carried the news of Martínez's death included *El Diario del Hogar* (México), *El Día* (Lampazos, Nuevo León), *El Regidor* (San Antonio), the New York *World*, the New York *Tribune*, and the Chicago *News* (32–40).

164 "Jamás se les había presentado mejor oportunidad a los asesinos oficiales de México, para limpiarse las manos con los enemigos locales, supuesto que estos retaban a cada momento al finado Gral. Martínez, llamandolo cobarde, villano y asesino." "Esos viles asesinatos han cumplido con la misión encomendada por el autor de 'mátalos en caliente,' a quien ahora puede atribuírsele la nueva sentencia de 'matalos en el extranjero, yo te protejo.'" "No ha muerto aun," *El Libre Pensador*, 12 Feb. 1891, in SRE, leg. 1-14-1649, f. 25. Díaz became famous for this phrase "mátalos en caliente" which was issued as an order to General L. Mier y Terán to put down a revolt in Veracruz in 1879. His concise order resulted in a bloody massacre of nine oppositionists.

3. REVOLUTION AND REPRESSION

1 "El mas furioso, cobarde e insano de los asesinos uniformados." "Instintos bestiales y de espíritu sanguinario." "Voluptuosa y de temperamento linfático." "Mas amantes que dedos." "Gustaba embriagarse con el ardiente tequila." G. A. Cezar (an obvious anagram for C. E. Garza], "Bernardo Reyes," *El Libre Pensador*, 30 July 1891, in CPD, leg. 16, doc. 14347.

2 "Nunca hubieramos imaginado que un periódico que se publica en castellano, ofendiera el honor de una dama respetable y virtuosa." "Manchar la honra de una señora." "Cobarde acción," *El Cronista Mexicano*, 8 Aug. 1891, p. 2, c. 3. This newspaper can be found at the Hemeroteca of the Biblioteca Nacional at the Universidad Nacional Autónoma de México (hereafter cited as BN).

3 "Desgarró el siempre sagrado velo de la vida privada y rayando en lo monstruoso, mancillo con su lengua viperina el honor de la esposa, del esposo y del hijo." "Un cobarde difamador," *El Heraldo*, 9 Aug. 1891, in SRE, leg. 1-15-1724, f. 8. "Catarino E. Garza," *El Duende*, 9 Aug. 1891, in SRE, leg. 1-15-1724, f. 9.

4 "Oposición razonada y decente que hiciera a algunos malos gobernantes de nuestra patria; protestamos enérgicamente contra el lenguaje soez usado por ese periódico." "Insultos a una dama," *Don Pacasio*, 9 Aug. 1891, in SRE, leg. 1-15-1724, f. 21.

5 *Gate City*, 15 Aug. 1891, in SRE, leg. 1-15-1724, f. 21.

6 "Carta de Laredo," *El Cronista Mexicano*, 15 Aug. 1891, p. 2, c. 1–2, in BN.

7 McNeel to Mabry, 9 Aug. 1891, Texas State Archives, Adjutant General's Records, General Correspondence (hereafter cited as AGC), 401–20, f. 12–17.

8 "Carta de Laredo," *El Cronista Mexicano*, 15 Aug. 1891, p. 2, c. 1-2, in BN.

9 "Después de haber vomitado su inmundo veneno huye como los reptiles." El libelista Garza," *El Cronista Mexicano*, 15 Aug. 1891, p. 2, c. 5, in BN.

10 "On the Verge of War," *San Antonio Express*, 1 Sept. 1891, in SRE, leg. 11-10-44, part 9, f. 44.

11 "Is Díaz in Danger?" *Washington Post*, 2 Sept. 1891, in SRE, leg. 11-10-44, part 1, f. 26.

12 *San Antonio Express*, 2 Sept. 1891, in SRE, leg. 11-10-44, part 1, f. 27.

13 "Americans in Mexico," *San Antonio Express*, 14 Sept. 1891, in SRE, leg. 11-10-44, part 1, f. 128.

14 Varrios to Rel. Ext., 11 Sept. 1891, and Robert Bolton to [?], 9 Sept. 1891, in SRE, leg. 11-10-44, part 1, f. 33-36, 40.

15 Ibid., f. 39–40.

16 "Según las noticias que tengo no puede ser cierto." Reyes to Díaz, 14 Sept. 1891, in ABR, cop. doc. 1144, f. 564.

17 This description is culled from several newspaper articles and the eyewitness testimony of one of Garza's lieutenants, Sixto Longoria. John Gregory Bourke Diary, 1872–1896, United States Military Academy Library, West Point, New York (hereafter cited as Bourke Diary), 1 Jan. 1892, Vol. 107, p. 159–60. "Hot on Garza's Trail," *San Antonio Express*, 22 Sept. 1891, and *Gate City*, 19 Sept. 1891, in SRE, leg. 11–10-44, part 1, f. 117. The *San Antonio Express* put the number of men crossing the border with Garza at forty. Sixto Longoria, a Garzista who was captured and interrogated by Bourke, put the number at sixteen.

18 "Lo fusilen sin hacer ostentación." Reyes to García, 1 Oct. 1891, in ABR, cop. doc. 3458, f. 28.

19 "Victims of Suspicion," *San Antonio Express*, 25 Oct. 1891, in SRE, leg. 11-10-44, part 2, f. 43.

20 "Comido los huesos de todos aquellos individuos." "Un antropófago," *El Cromo*, 21 Nov. 1891, in Bourke Diary, Vol. 107, p. 1.

21 Bourke Diary, Vol. 107, 14 Nov. 1891, p. 1–2.

22 Bourke Diary, Vol. 107, 22 Nov. 1891, p. 15.

23 Reyes to Cerón, 14 Oct. 1891, in ABR, cop. 7, doc. 3589, f. 90.

24 Estarke Nix and Sheley to Rel. Ext., 30 Oct. 1891, in SRE, leg. 11-10-44, part 2, f. 53–54.

25 González to Matías Romero, 29 Oct. 1891, Archivo de Matías Romero, Banco de México, microfilm copy at the Benson Latin American Collection, University of Texas, Austin (hereafter cited as AMR), doc. 39263, roll 54, f. 2-3. González to Romero, 27 Oct. 1891, in SRE, leg. 11-10-44, part 2, f. 44–49.

26 "A Mysterious Murder," *San Antonio Express*, 21 Nov. 1891, in Bourke Diary, Vol. 107, p. 1.

27 Bourke Diary, Vol. 107, 18 Dec. 1891, p. 9.

28 Bourke Diary, Vol. 107, 23 Nov. 1891, p. 16–17. Bourke later blamed Garzistas for killing two Americans who were also disemboweled and thrown into the Rio Grande. It is not clear from Bourke's reference whether he is speaking of the Castillo brothers (Bourke, *Our Neutrality Laws*, 31).

29 "Su fusilamiento se hizo de un modo clandestino y como si hubiera dádosele alcance en su huida." Reyes to Díaz, 28 Oct. 1891, in ABR, cop., doc. 1228, f. 636; and Reyes to Díaz, 30 Oct. 1891, in ABR, cop., doc. 1231, f. 639.

30 Bourke Diary, Vol. 106, 19 Oct. 1891, p. 98.

31 Bourke Diary, Vol. 107, 14 Nov. 1891, p. 1–2.

32 McNeel to Mabry, 21 Sept. 1891, in AGC, 401–21, f. 4–6.

33 Atanacio Gómez to Mabry, 13 June 1892, in AGC, 401–24, f. 1–6. Brooks to Mabry, 19 June 1892, in AGC, 401–24, f. 7–13.

34 George Schmitt to Hogg, 13 Jan. 1893, Governor James S. Hogg Papers, Texas State Archives (hereafter cited as Hogg papers), LR (letters received), 301–136, f. 182.

35 John J. Dix to Mabry, 3 Mar. 1892, Hogg Papers, LR, 301-133, f. 109.

36 John J. Dix to Mabry, 3 Mar. 1892, Hogg papers, LR, 301-133, f. 109.

37 Bourke Diary, Vol. 106, 11-12 Nov. 1891, p. 156-71.

38 Bourke Diary, Vol. 106, 13 Nov. 1891, pp. 172, 175–76.

39 Bourke Diary, Vol. 106, 13 Nov. 1891, pp. 172–76.

40 Bourke Diary, Vol. 106, 13 Nov. 1891, pp. 184–91.

41 "Capt. Bourke's Close Call," Omaha *Bee*, 27 Nov, 1891, in Bourke Diary, Vol. 107, p. 1. Arrests also covered in "Arresto del Capitan John C. Bourke," *El Cromo*, 21 Nov. 1891, and in *New York Times*, 16 Dec. 1891, p. 1, 15, both in Bourke Diary, Vol. 107.

42 José González, Consul, to Rel. Ext., 14 Oct. 1891, in SRE, leg. 11-10-44, part 2, f. 18–22; and "Would Be Revolutionist," *Republic*, 15 Oct. 1891, in SRE, leg. 11-10-44, part 2, f. 51.

43 Varrios to Rel. Ext., 18 Sept. 1891, in SRE, leg. 11-10-44, part 1, f. 78.

44 *Gate City*, 17 Sept. 1891, in SRE, leg. 11-10-44, part 1, f. 88; and *El Cromo*, 17 Oct. 1891, in SRE, leg. 11-10-44, part 2, f. 23.

45 "Por ejemplo hacer general de division a quien le presente con un jamón y dos botellas de Tequila. De brigada al que lleve un mole de guajalote y seis medidas de pulque. Coronel a quien se le presente con una gallina, propia o agena, y un borrego. Teniente coronel al que lleve las tortillas calientes y así por el estilo hasta promover a Capitan 2 al que se le presente un par de huevos." "Bufanadas de Catarino," *El Cromo*, 17 Oct. 1891, in SRE, leg. 11-10-44, part 2, f. 15. The phrase "un par de huevos" could also be colloquially translated as "a pair of balls," which makes perfect sense in this context.

46 "El último de los periodistas independientes, el mas humilde de todos, abandona hoy la pluma para empuñar la espada en defensa de los derechos del pueblo." Catarino Garza, "Proclama," in CPD, leg. 16, docs. 10951, 11418.

47 "Proclama," in CPD, leg. 17, doc. 632; "Manifiesto," in CPD, leg. 17, doc. 10661-A.

48 I have located six different revolutionary proclamations attributed to Garza or his followers. The "Plan Revolucionario" (leg. 16, doc. 11417), "Proclama" (leg. 16, doc. 11417), "Proclama" (leg. 16, docs. 10951 and 11418 [these two versions dated Sept. 1891, Tamaulipas, are virtually the same], and "Proclama" (leg. 17, doc. 632 [signed by Juan Antonio Flores and dated 1 Jan. 1892, Nuevo León]), are all located in the Colección de Porfirio Díaz. "Plan Revolucionario" (Sept 1891), "Manifiesto: Estado de Tamaulipas" (30 Sept. 1891), and "Manifiesto" (1 Nov. 1891) are in Garza Guajardo, *En busca*, 209–14, 215–16. Finally, "Manifiesto," signed by Francisco Benavides and translated by John G. Bourke, Tamaulipas, Mexico, Nov. 1892, is included in a report by George F. Chase to Asst. Adj. Gen., *San Antonio*, 31 May 1893 (hereafter cited as Chase Report), National Archives, Washington, D.C., Records of U.S. Army, RG 393, Garza Revolution Papers (hereafter GRP), p. 3h (the letter "h" refers to an addendum so labeled in the Chase Report). While each of these manifestos varies slightly, they all make similar demands.

49 Rodney D. Anderson, *Outcasts in Their Own Land: the Mexican Industrial Workers, 1905–1911* (Dekalb: Northern Illinois University Press, 1976), 322–23.

50 Julian Flores, "El derecho de seguridad personal, el derecho de libertad individual y el derecho de propiedad." Plan Revolucionario," in CPD, leg. 16, doc. 11417.

51 "Serán deslindados los terrenos baldíos y repartidos entre los mexicanos que se comprometan á cultivarlos." Ibid.

52 Benavides, "Manifiesto," in Chase Report, GRP, p. 3h.

53 The first PLM program published in 1906 was a fairly moderate document in comparison to the openly anarchist manifesto issued by Ricardo Flores Magón in September 1911. For a thorough examination of the development of the PLM's ideology, see James D. Cockcroft, *Intellectual Precursors of the Mexican Revolution, 1900–1913* (Austin: University of Texas Press, 1976), 130–33, 196–97. For an analysis of Zapata's Plan de Ayala, see Womack, *Zapata*, 393–404.

54 James Scott explains how the field for subaltern resistance is greater when surveillance is relaxed, for example, when a reformist regime comes to power or a revolution takes place. Thus, even if a new regime has a reformist strategy, once the peasants are armed and mobilized it is very difficult to stop or limit the momentum from below (Scott, *Domination and the Arts of Resistance*, esp. 192–97). In spite of the reformist tendencies of the political elites, pressure from below led to radical labor and agrarian reform during the Mexican Revolution. This is not to say, however, that the radical goals of Zapata, Villa, and Flores Magón were fully achieved.

55 "La humillante disposición del Gobierno de que companías extrangeras vengan á practicar medidas y á servir de jueces en el deslinde de nuestras tierras, ó á obligar á los propietarios que paguen una fuerte suma, como 'Contenta' para no ser molestados." "Negociantes norteamericanos inmensas fajas de terreno de nuestra frontera con los Estados Unidos." Catarino Garza, "Proclama," in CPD, leg. 16, docs. 10951.

56 "Nos coloca en peor condición que á esclavos ó animals domésticos, pues á unos y á otros sus dueños los cuidan y no los matan por no perder el capital en ellos invertido, mientras que á nosotros, al asesinarsenos nada pierde el Gobierno porque nada le hemos costado." Ibid.

57 "Destronar á esos enemigos de la Patria y corrompidos liberticidas." Catarino Garza, "Manifiesto," 1 Nov. 1891, in Garza Guajardo, *En busca*, 214.

58 "Una turba de proceres falcificados reparte, como hambrientos caníbales, el último resto de nuestra libertad." Benavides, "Manifiesto," Chase Report, GRP, p. 1h.

59 "Hoy al pobre se le quita lo poco que tiene, al libre pensador se le asesina, á la prensa se le amordaza. Todas nuestras libertades han desaparecido." Ibid., p. 2h.

60 "Adelante, mexicanos, marchemos á morir por la libertad. ¡Gloria inmortal para los que saben morir por ella! ¡Escarnio y desgradación para los que prefieren ser esclavos que patriotas!" Ibid., p. 3h.

61 Benavides, "Manifiesto," Nov. 1892, and Prudencio González et al., "Plan Revolucionario."

62 Karl Marx, "The Eighteenth Brumaire of Louis Bonaparte," in *Karl Marx and Frederick Engels: Selected Works* (New York: International Publishers, 1986), 97.

63 Catarino Garza, "Proclama," Sept. 1891, in CPD, leg. 16, docs. 10951, 11418.

64 "Otro Gral. Santa Ana." Julian Flores, "Plan Revolucionario," Sept. 1891, in CPD, leg. 16, doc. 11417.

65 "Libertad y soberanía." Juan Antonio Flores, "Proclama," 1 Jan. 1892, in CPD, leg. 17, doc. 8983.

66 Bourke Diary, Vol. 107, 19 Dec. 1891, p. 128–30.

67 Bourke Diary, Vol. 106, 14 Oct. 1891, p. 84.

68 Bourke Diary, 1 Oct. 1891, p. 70–71.

69 Reyes to Díaz, 8 Oct. 1891, in ABR, cop., doc. 1201, f. 613; and Reyes to Díaz, 11 Oct. 1891, in ABR, cop., doc. 1206, f. 617.

70 Lameda Díaz to M. Romero, 2 Dec. 1891, in AMR, doc. 39460, roll 54; "Garza Makes a Fight," *San Antonio Express*, 15 Nov. 1891, in SRE, leg. 11-10-44, part 2, f. 62; and "Garza's Crowd on Top," *San Antonio Express*, 16 Nov. 1891, in SRE, leg. 11-10-44, part 2, f. 67.

71 "Bien puede vérseles y hablárseles, que ninguno sabe nada, ni ha oido decir cosa alguno; y gastan tal astucia y disimulo, que aun teniendo en cuenta su vida entera de contrabandistas y ladrones de profesión, avezados a todo genero de audacias y engaños se hace muy dificil creer que sean realmente los criminales a quienes se busca." "Los envuelvan y los burlen a su antojo." Consul Díaz to Rel. Ext., 27 Nov. 1891, in SRE, leg. 11-10-44, part 2, f. 110–12.

72 Richard Harding Davis, *The West from a Car-Window* (New York: Harpers and Brothers, 1903 [1892]), 46.

73 "El Combate de las Tortillas," in Garza, *En busca*, 52–53.

74 Reyes to Romero, 23 Dec. 1891, in AMR, doc. 39601, roll 65; Bourke *Our Neutrality Laws*, 14–15.

75 Bourke Diary, 21 Dec. 1891, Vol. 107, p. 135–37; "An Official Report," *New York Times*, 24 Dec. 1891, in AMR, doc. 39613, roll 54; Bourke, *Our Neutrality Laws*, 15–16.

76 "No pregunte quien se lo pague chingado." Testimony given to Promoter Fiscal H. C. Silva, 10 Dec. 1891, in SRE, leg. 834, part 2, f. 9–13.

77 Testimony of Ambrosio González, 4 Jan. 1892, in SRE, leg 834, part 2, f. 15.

78 "Ten of Garza's Men Killed," *New York Times*, 13 May 1892, in SRE, leg. 11-10-44, part 7, f. 2. This raid is also described in L. Díaz to M. Romero, 14 May 1892, and "A Bloody Battle," [?], in AMR, doc. 40167, roll 55.

79 Tel. García to Ornelas, in Ornelas to Commanding General, Dept. of Texas, 13 June 1892, in SRE, leg. 11-10-44, part 7, f. 80.

80 Tel. Francisco Alegria, encargado del Consulado, to Rel. Ext., 2 July 1892, in SRE, leg. 11-10-44, part 7, f. 136.

81 Vanderwood, *The Power of God against the Guns of Government*, 184, 270–77.

82 Ibid., 152.

83 "To Attack President Díaz," *New York Herald*, 10 Mar. 1896, in SRE, leg. 730. For the full text of the "Plan Restaurador," see Francisco Mallén to Rel. Ext., El Paso, 21 Mar. 1896, in SRE, leg. 730, f. 100–26.

84 United States of America: Western District of Texas v. Lauro Aguirre and Manuel Flores Chapa, El Paso, 24 Mar. 1896, in SRE, leg. 730.

85 "Conviene que sin manifestar disgusto porque nos interesa tener enteramente contento a Hernández." Reyes to Cerón, 10 Sept. 1890, in ABR, doc. 2509.

86 "Diligencia." Reyes to Díaz, 14 Nov. 1891, in ABR, cop., doc. 1253, f. 653–57.

87 "The Garza Uprising," *St. Louis Globe Democrat*, 30 Jan. 1892, in Bourke Diary, Vol. 108, p. 10.

88 Reyes to Díaz, 14 Nov. 1891, in ABR, cop., doc. 1253, f. 653–57.

89 "Ruthlessly Shot Down," *Laredo Times*, 7 Dec. 1891, and "Another Lie Nailed," *Laredo Times*, 8 Dec. 1891, both in AMR, doc. 39499, roll 54.

90 Interview with Charles P. Markham, "Guns to Be Turned on Díaz," *World*, 10 Jan. 1892, in CPD, 1178.

91 "Rebelión de Catarino E. Garza en Tamaulipas," in SRE, leg. 30-26-169, f. 33; also cited in Saldívar, *Documentos de la rebelión*, 25.

92 "Con la prisión de Nieves Hernández y de los bandidos que lo acompañaban, las incursiones vandálicas de estas vagamundos están terminadas." Consul Díaz to M. Romero, 12 Dec. 1891, in AMR, doc. 39526, roll 54.

93 Reyes to Díaz, 23 Jan. 1892, in ABR, cop., doc. 4844, f. 128. Reyes to M. Romero, 30 Jan. 1892, in ABR, cop., doc. 1852, f. 613–15.

94 "Bien merece." Reyes to Díaz, 9 Feb. 1892, in ABR, cop., 4870, f. 155–57.

95 "Garza's Waning Power," *San Francisco Examiner*, 24 Jan. 1892, in SRE, leg. 11-10-44, part 4, f. 112.

96 Federico de los Santos to Díaz, 1 Oct. 1892, in CPD, doc. 16431.

97 *Laredo Daily Times*, 25 Sept. 1892, in CPD, doc. 16431.

98 "Indulto de Nieves Hernández," *La Voz de Nuevo León*, 18 Feb. 1893, p. 3, c. 1, in UANL.

99 Lt. P. W. West to Commanding Officer, 16 Dec. 1892, in GRP, p. 1–3.

100 Bourke, *Our Neutrality Laws*, 31.

101 *Galveston News*, 31 Dec. 1892, in Bourke Diary, Vol. 110, p. 1.

102 "Un asalto bárbaro," 17 Dec. 1892, *La Voz de Nuevo León*, p. 3, c. 2; "Bandidos," 24 Dec. 1892, *La Voz de Nuevo León*, p. 2., c. 2, in UANL.

103 Plutarco Ornelas to General Frank Wheaton, 20 Dec. 1892, GRP, p. 1.

104 Reyes to Díaz, 12 Dec. 1892, in ABR, cop., doc 5123, f. 411.

105 Reyes to Díaz, 14 Dec. 1892, in ABR, cop., doc. 5135, f. 432.

106 Hedekin to Ft. McIntosh Commanding Officer, 25 Dec. 1892. GRP, p. 2.

107 Ibid., 1–2.

108 Ibid.

109 John W. Foster to Matías Romero, 4 Jan. 1893, in SRE, leg. 834, part 3, f. 31.

4. BOOMS AND BUSTS

1 *General Directory of the City of Laredo, 1889* (San Antonio: Maverick Printing House, 1889), 4.

2 *Description of Laredo, Texas: The Acknowledged Gateway between the Two Republics* (Laredo: Gate City Printing House, 1888), 4.

3 Ibid.

4 *General Directory of Laredo*, 165–66.

5 Ibid., 166.

6 Ibid., 4.

7 *Description of Laredo*, 21.

8 *General Directory of Laredo*, 166.

9 *Description of Laredo*, 5.

10 W. H. Chatfield, *The Twin Cities of the Border and the Country of the Lower Rio Grande Valley* (New Orleans: E. P. Brandao, 1893; reprint, Brownsville: Harbert Davenport Memorial Fund, 1959), 3, 1–2.

11 Ibid., 3.

12 Ibid., 5.

13 Chatfield to Hogg, 17 Dec. 1892, Hogg Papers, LR, 301-136, no. 172.

14 French, *A Peaceful and Working People*, 66–67.

15 E. H. Tarver, *Laredo: The Gateway, between the United States and Mexico* (Laredo: Daily Times, 1889), 1; *General Directory of Laredo*, 166. Promotional pamphlets contain useful information about these shifts, but one must be aware that the authors had an interest in portraying border cities as larger and more Anglo than they may actually have been. U.S. census figures, although presumably more accurate, did not include people living on the Mexican side of the river, thus rendering these statistics of only limited use for understanding the border as a transnational region.

16 Laredo's population went from 3,811 in 1880 (before the railroads) to 11,319 in 1890 (after the railroads). The population continued to rise in subsequent decades: by 1900 it had reached 13,429 and by 1910 it climbed to 14,855 (Hinojosa, *Borderlands Town*, 123, 119, 98).

17 *Description of Laredo*, 26.

18 Hinojosa, *Borderlands Town*, 119.

19 Cerutti, *Burguesía, capitales e industria*, 86–87.

20 Chatfield, *Twin Cities*, p. 31. Chatfield also estimated that Brownsville's population in 1893 was about 7,000, which is only slightly higher than the almanac's statistics (*Twin Cities*, 2).

21 Brownsville only grew from a population of 6,000 in 1867 to 6,305 in 1904. *Texas Almanac and State Industrial Guide for 1867* (Galveston: Galveston News, 1867), 88; *Texas Almanac and State Industrial Guide for 1904* (Galveston: Galveston News, 1904), 10–44.

22 Tom Lea, *The King Ranch* (Boston: Little, Brown 1957), 544–45.

23 Cameron County's population rose precipitously from 16,095 in 1900 to 36,025 in 1909. *Texas Almanac and State Industrial Guide for 1910* (Galveston: Galveston News, 1910), 158; information based on the 1900 census and estimate for 1909. For an explanation of the connection between population shifts in Brownsville and the rise and fall of the steamboat monopoly, see Montejano, *Anglos and Mexicans*, 42–43, 96–98.

24 The percentage of Tejanos in South Texas increased in the latter part of the nineteenth century, from 72.8 percent in 1870 to 85.1 percent in 1900; the percentage of Anglos decreased correspondingly. See Arnoldo De León and Kenneth L Stewart, *Tejanos and the Numbers Game: A Socio-Historical Interpretation from the*

Federal Censuses, 1850–1900 (Albuquerque: University of New Mexico Press, 1989), 17, 25–27.

25 *Texas Almanac and State Industrial Guide for 1871–73* (Galveston: Galveston News, 1867), 148.

26 *Texas Almanac*, 1904, 366.

27 *Description of Laredo*, 4.

28 "Súbito desarrollo." "Multiplicado en una proporción asombrosa." *Boletín oficial*, 9 July 1863, as cited in Cerutti, *Burguesía, capitales e industria*, 83. That same document credits the foreign cotton trade with the tremendous commercial growth in the city.

29 *Población de Nuevo León: Desde 1603 hasta 1921* (Mexico: Publicaciones del Departamento de la Estadistica Nacional, 1929), 15. The 1824 population estimates is from Saragoza, *The Monterrey Elite*, 18. By 1910 Monterrey's population had increased to over 88,000. See "La ciudad de Monterrey," *El Espectador*, 16 June 1898, p. 2, c. 1; and "El problema resuelto," *El Trueno*, 13 Nov. 1910, p. 1. These newspapers may be found at the hemeroteca of the Archivo General de la Nacion, Mexico City (hereafter cited as AGN).

30 Immigration from foreign countries and from other parts of Mexico caused the population boom, with immigrants accounting for 16 percent of the state's residents and 30 percent of the city's populace in 1895 (Saragoza, *The Monterrey Elite*, 39). The percentage of immigrants, both foreign and Mexican, is most probably higher than that reported in the census. The "not insignificant number" of people in the floating population were not counted in the census, and neither were many other immigrants in the capital (*Memorias del estado de Nuevo León* [Monterrey: n.p., 1885], 33).

31 "Los privilegios y monopolios otorgados a los bancos y otras campanías . . . [y] el despojo de la propiedad a pretexto de deslinde de terrenos baldíos." Vicente Peña, "Plan Restaurador del Orden Constitucional," 18 Aug. 1886, in *El Mundo*, 22 Aug. 1886, in SRE, leg. 11-10-16.

32 Garza, "Proclama," in CPD, leg. 16, doc. 10951.

33 C. E. Garza, "Editorial," *El Comercio Mexicano*, 29 Sept. 1888, in SRE, leg. 18-27-112, f. 29.

34 For the transcript of the speeches at the congress, see *Primer Congreso Mexicanista, verificado en Laredo, Texas, EEUU de A. Los dias 14 al 22 de Septiembre de 1911* (Laredo: Tip. De N. Idar, 1912), esp. 39. For my analysis of the Congreso, see Young, "Deconstructing *La Raza*," 254–57; see also Limón, "El Primer Congreso Mexicanista," 85–106.

35 "Odios de la raza," *El Defensor del Obrero* (Laredo), 20 Jan. 1907. For my analysis of this strike, see Young, "Deconstructing *La Raza*," 248–54. On the strike, see also Zamora, *The World of the Mexican Worker*, 112–26.

36 "¿Tiene ud. La intención de continuar siendo esclavo del burgués? . . . ¿No desea ud. preparar los proyectiles que ha de usar mañana en la formidable lucha por la existencia?" "Union Obrera Federada, Número 11953," as cited in *El Demócrata Fronterizo*, 28 Feb. 1906, in CAH.

37 Jovita González, "Social Life in Cameron, Starr, and Zapata Counties," master's thesis, University of Texas, Austin, 1930, p. 102.

38 "Plan de San Diego," in *US-Mexico Borderlands*, ed. Martínez, 139–41. See also Sandos, *Rebellion in the Borderlands*, esp. 83.

39 Benjamin Harrison, 6 Dec. 1892, in *Public Papers and Addresses of Benjamin Harrison: Twenty-Third President of the United States, March 4, 1889, to March 4, 1893* (Washington: Government Printing Office, 1893), 138.

40 The keen interest on the part of international investors in stopping revolutionary movements became glaringly clear in a 1995 internal memorandum by a Chase Manhattan Bank advisor arguing that the Mexican government needed to "eliminate the Zapatistas" to restore investor confidence (*La Jornada*, 11 Feb. 1995).

41 "The Future of Mexico and Its Relations with the United States," in *Mexican Night: The Toasts and Responses at a Complementary Dinner Given by Walter S. Logan at the Democratic Club, New York City, December 16, 1891* (New York: Albert B. King, 1892), 18–20, in SRE, CRI, T 411, f. 545.

42 On April 14, 1849, the Mexican Federal Congress passed a law legitimizing this practice for a three-year period. Finally, on March 17, 1858, the governor of Tamaulipas issued a decree formally establishing the *zona libre*, a move subsequently approved by the Federal Congress on July 30, 1861. Matías Romero (Mexican consul) to Thomas F. Bayard, Washington, D.C., 10 Feb. 1888, in *Extension of Zona Libre in Mexico*, Senate Executive Doc. no. 130, 50th Cong., 1st sess. (hereafter cited as Sen. Exec. Doc. 130), p. 138.

43 Warner P. Sutton to Asst. Sec. State, 25 April 1890, in DNL, 3–7; these pages include an English translation of the Mexican importation law published as U.S. Senate, "Chapter XII of the General Traffic of Foreign Goods into Free Zone," Sen. Exec. Doc. no. 130, p. 67.

44 "Petition of Citizens of El Paso," 10 April 1884, in Sen. Exec. Doc. 130, pp. 3–4.

45 Romero expressed his personal disapproval of the free zone on the constitutional grounds that it granted special privileges to one section of the country, but he reaffirmed Mexico's right to make its own rules regarding domestic and foreign trade (Romero to Bayard, 10 Feb. 1888, in Sen. Exec. Doc. 130, p. 140). In a speech before Mexico's Federal Congress in 1870, Romero argued that the zone was justified at the time of its establishment in 1858 because the difference between the low U.S. importation duties (15 percent) and the high Mexican duties (30–35 percent) created a situation of extreme hardship for border residents and caused them to leave Mexico for Texas (Romero, "Verbal Report on the Free Zone," 28 Oct. 1870, in Sen. Exec. Doc. 130, p. 11). However, he also reasoned that given the equalization of the importation duties, the zone should no longer exist.

46 Sutton to Asst. Sec. State, 25 April 1890, in DNL, 18.

47 Ibid., pp. 14–15.

48 "Una región despoblada con uno que otro rancho miserable." "Esta población esparcida es el foco de todas las acciones ilícitas, del robo, del asesinato y del contrabando, que en esta frontera se perpetran." "Editorial: La Zona Libre y 'La

Semana Mercantil,' " *La Revista del Norte*, Matamoros, 13 Oct. 1889, p. 1, col. 2, in UANL.

49 "El contrabando más escandoloso." "Mercancías legitimamente internadas." "Editorial: Zona Libre," *La Revista del Norte*, 20 Oct. 1889, p. 1, col. 1, in UANL.

50 Ibid.

51 "Sería una reducción prudente de la tarifa." "Francamente hablando, es contra la naturaleza de las cosas pagar 15 o 16 centavos por una yarda de indianas, que a distancia de quinientos pasos se consigue en seis." "Editorial: Zona Libre," *La Revista del Norte*, 18 Oct. 1889, p. 1, col. 3, in UANL.

52 "Los contrabandistas contarían con un campo más amplio para sus operaciones." "Editorial: Zona Libre," *La Revista del Norte*, 3 Nov. 1889, p. 1, col. 4, in UANL.

53 "Editorial: Zona Libre," *La Revista del Norte*, 15 Nov. 1889, p. 1, col. 4, in UANL.

54 Sutton enclosed in his dispatch a pamphlet entitled *La Zona Libre*, by Pedro Argüelles, the collector of customs at Nuevo Laredo (Sutton to Asst. Sec. State, 14 Mar. 1890; Pedro Argüelles, *La Zona Libre* (Nuevo Laredo: Tip. de A. Cueva y Hno., 1890). An English translation of the pamphlet was sent in the 25 April 1890 dispatch. Argüelles insisted that the Chamber of Commerce in Monterrey, the merchants of El Paso, and Senator Reagan of Texas had raised the issue of abolishing the free zone. Senator Reagan introduced legislation to prevent European goods from entering Mexico through U.S. territory until the Mexicans had abolished the zone (Argüelles, *La Zona Libre*, 3, in Sutton to Asst. Sec. State, 14 March 1890, in DNL). Although Sutton's own arguments mirrored almost exactly those of Argüelles, Sutton believed that the "bitterest and most influential" enemies of the zone were in Mexico (Sutton to Asst. Sec. State, 25 April 1890, in DNL, 2). "If this Zone is ever repealed," he argued, it would be due to domestic Mexican pressure and not "because of the opposition of the merchants of El Paso or because of Mr. Reagan's Bill" (2).

55 Sutton to Asst. Sec. State, 25 April 1890, in DNL, 10.

56 Ibid., 11.

57 "La zona libre," *El Correo de Laredo*, 23 Sept. 1891, p. 2, col. 4, in CAH.

58 *Don Quijote*, 8 Oct. 1910, p. 3, in BN.

59 *Don Quijote*, 24 July 1910, p. 10, in BN.

60 "The State of Coahuila," *The Mexican Developer Illustrated*, p. 2, in CPD, leg. 40, doc. 587. *El Espectador* cited a government report indicating that $12,887,227 of minerals had been extracted in Sierra Mojada between January 1891 and October 1893 ("La producción de las minas de Sierra Mojada," *El Espectador*, 19 Jan. 1897, p. 2, c. 5, in AGN).

61 Mora-Torres, *The Making of the Mexican Border*, 88.

62 Guggenheim to Romero, 22 Dec. 1891, in SRE, CRI, T 404, f. 429–433.

63 Hart, *Empire and Revolution*, 141.

64 Chatfield, *Twin Cities*, 37.

65 Ibid., 37.

66 Ibid., 37.

67 Ibid., 6–7.

68 Ibid., 38.

69 Montejano, *Anglos and Mexicans*, 108–9.

70 Chapter 62, *General Laws of the State of Texas, 22nd Leg. 1891* (Austin: Henry Hutchings State Printer, 1891), 82–83.

71 "Treaty of Guadalupe Hidalgo," in *U.S-Mexico Borderlands: Historical and Contemporary Perspectives*, ed. Oscar J. Martínez (Wilmington, Del.: Scholarly Resources, 1996), 25–26.

72 Luis G. Bossero, "Cuestión importante," *El Cronista Mexicano*, 25 July 1891, p. 1–2, in AGN.

73 "Las operaciones de medición y deslinde se harán en interés del Tesoro de los EU, no en interés de los legítimos propietarios de los terrenos." Luis G. Bossero, "Cuestión importante," *El Cronista Mexicano*, 8 Aug. 1891, p. 1–2, in AGN.

74 Alonzo, *Tejano Legacy*, 158.

75 Chatfield, *Twin Cities*, 38. Chatfield's statistics only accounted for large ranches (1,000 or more acres), but he indicated that the total land base in private hands was over 1.6 million acres.

76 Montejano, *Anglos and Mexicans*, 72–73.

77 The percentage of Anglo ranch–farm owners rose from 2 percent in 1850 to 31 percent by 1900. See Arnoldo De León, *The Tejano Community, 1836–1900* (Albuquerque: University of New Mexico Press, 1982), 63, as cited in Montejano, *Anglos and Mexicans*, 73.

78 Alonzo, *Tejano Legacy*, 265.

79 The Corpus Christi, San Diego and Rio Grande Narrow Gauge Railroad Company, later known as the Texas Mexican Railway Company, began construction of this line in the late 1870s, whereas it took until 1904 until rail service reached Brownsville.

80 Alonzo, *Tejano Legacy* 257–58.

81 For the records of González's sales to the King ranch, see Montejano, *Anglos and Mexicans*, 65–66.

82 Out of several hundred loans secured by Starr County residents between 1880 and 1900, only sixty of these were for $1,000 or more. Of these sixty, Guerra received twenty-three, showing how the elite, both Anglo and Mexican, monopolized credit (Alonzo, *Tejano Legacy*, 238).

83 On moral economy, see E. P. Thompson, "The Moral Economy of the English Crowd in the Eighteenth Century," in *Customs in Common: Studies in Traditional Popular Culture* (New York: New Press, 1991); also see James C. Scott, *The Moral Economy of the Peasant: Subsistence and Rebellion in Southeast Asia* (New Haven: Yale University Press, 1976); on moral economy in northern Mexico, see French, *A Peaceful and Working People*, 127–28, 181–82.

84 "Todo esto hace que los hombres de trabajo material se encuentren ociosos y sin pan y que miren a uno como redentor al que les promete un peso diario y otras grandes ganga por andar en correrias revolucionarias." Diaz to Romero, 13 Feb. 1892, in AMR, doc. 39851, roll 55.

85 "Las familias a esos hombres ven al cielo abierto tras esa perspectiva y Catarino Garza por lo mismo se torna en objeto de adoración, y se exhibe a los ojos de la

generalidad que no estudia las causas de los fenomenos, con tal aureola de simpatía y prestigio que puede muy bien tomarse por un heroe." Ibid.

86   Monroe et al. to Hogg, 1 Mar. 1892, Hogg Papers, LR, 301-133, f. 109.

87   "An Appeal," *Laredo Times*, 19 Apr. 1892, in AMR, doc. 40096, roll 55.

88   Ibid.

89   Que después de haber . . . fomentado la agitación garcista los condados de
bajo Rio Grande se presentan ahora pelando a la caridad pública." L. Díaz to
M. Romero, 19 Apr. 1892, in AMR, doc., 40096, roll 55.

90   "An Appeal," *Laredo Times*, 19 Apr. 1892, in AMR, doc. 40096, roll 55. Four of
the committee members had Spanish surnames, seven had Anglo surnames, and
one, Judge Jas Barbour, had a French-sounding surname. Unlike the public appeal
for help, the petition to Governor Hogg for drought relief was signed by at least
one known Garza supporter, Manuel Guerra, and several others who were suspected of having Garzista sympathies because of their attacks against Bourke
(Monroe et al. to Hogg, 1 Mar. 1892, Hogg papers, LR, 301-133, f. 109).

91   *Herald* (Chicago) as reprinted in "Garza's Revolution," *San Francisco Call*, 18
Jan. 1892, in SRE, leg. 11-10-44, part 4, f. 58.

92   "Trouble Ahead in Durango," 4 Jan. 1892, [?], in SRE, leg. 11-10-44, part 4, f. 12.

93   "El hambre, que mala consejera, los precipitó a todos en esta última locura."
L. Díaz to M. Romero, 14 May 1892, in AMR, doc. 40167, roll 55.

94   "Garza's Revolution," *San Francisco Call*, 18 Jan. 1892, in SRE, leg. 11-10-44,
part 4, f. 58.

95   Chatfield, *Twin Cities*, 40; Alonzo, *Tejano Legacy*, 209, 236.

96   Alonzo, *Tejano Legacy*, 238–39. Alonzo explains that wool prices plummeted
when new producers such as Australia and Argentina entered the market. "The
once profitable twenty cents per pound for wool in 1870, decreased to 14 cents by
1887, seven cents in 1893 and three to four cents in 1897" (Alonzo, *Tejano
Legacy*, 237).

97   Hart, *Empire and Revolution*, 200.

5. THE GARZISTAS

1   Thompson, "The Moral Economy of the English Crowd," esp. 185–89.

2   For more on Anglo-Mexican class and race relations in Laredo, see Elliott Young,
"Deconstructing La Raza: Culture and Ideology of the *Gente Decente* of Laredo,
1904–1911," *Southwestern Historical Quarterly* (October 1994): 226–59.

3   Four years prior to his death, an article stated that "Bruni had become the owner
of more than four hundred thousand acres of land in Webb and adjacent counties,
stock ranches, oil wells, onion farms, citrus groves, compose only a few of the
interest of the man who is known as the wealthiest and yet the most accommodat-
ing man of Laredo" ("Bruni as Pioneer Merchant," *The Pioneer Magazine* (February 1927): 17. He was honored in Laredo by having a school, a street, and a plaza
named after him; also the town of Bruni was established on part of his ranch land.
Biographical information on Bruni may be found in Felix García, *The Children of
A. M. Bruni* (Laredo: n.p., 1984), and *Cattleman* 18 (April 1931): 31.

4 Anders, *Boss Rule in South Texas*, 43–64.

5 Bourke to Post Adj. Gen., 2 Apr. 1892, in GRP, p. 3. In particular, Bourke condemned the laws of Texas that allowed "foreigners . . . to vote upon 'declaration of intention' to become citizens" (Bourke, *Our Neutrality Laws*, 13).

6 "Esa intentona de revolución no puede contar con nuestras simpatías, ni con las simpatías del pueblo mexicano, que engañado mil veces por los revolucionarios por oficio, ha perdido completamente la fe en esos redentores gratuitos, y solo busca en la paz y en el trabajo la felicidad personal y de la patria." "Lo del Dia; Planes Revolucionarias," *El Correo de Laredo*, 19 Sept. 1891, p. 3, col. 3, in CAH. It should be noted that Justo Cárdenas, *El Correo de Laredo*'s editor, had sought a rapprochement with Mexican government officials during this time. Therefore, the anti-Garza and antirevolution bias appears to have been the quid pro quo for establishing better relations with the Díaz government. *The Correo de Laredo* article was reprinted in Reyes's *Voz de Nuevo León* on 23 Sept. 1891.

7 "Son sueños de locos, de vagos, y de gente sin oficio." "La verdadera revolución es el trabajo. . . . ¡ Viva el Trabajo! ¡Muera la Revolución!" *El Eco Liberal* (San Diego), as cited in *El Correo de Laredo*, 26 Sept. 1891, p. 3, col. 1–2, in CAH.

8 Anders, *Boss Rule in South Texas*, 10–11.

9 Petition by Citizens of Duval County to Governor Hogg, 3 Feb. 1892, in GRP. In a strange twist of fate, the same Glover who was cut down by Garzista rebels had signed Garza's marriage license two years earlier as part of his duties as the clerk for Duval County (State of Texas Marriage License, Catarino Erasmo Garza and Concepción Gonzales, 23 May 1890, in Garza Guajardo, *En busca*).

10 Davis, *The West from a Car-Window*, 8-11.

11 Petition by Citizens of Duval County to Governor Hogg, 3 Feb. 1892, in GRP.

12 Bourke to Asst. Adj. Gen., 11 Mar. 1892, in GRP, pp. 1–2.

13 Petition, 3 Feb. 1892, in GRP.

14 "Several Garza Papers," 23 Jan. 1892, *Galveston Daily News*, in SRE, leg. 11-10-44, exp. 4, f. 140.

15 A full copy of these captured documents can be found in the Bernardo Reyes archive (ABR). Díaz to Reyes, 2 Feb. 1892, in ABR, doc. 3037. A copy is also located in "Rebelión de Catarino E. Garza en Tamaulipas," in SRE, leg. 30-26-169. In the 1940s, a Mexican historian published these documents (see Salvívar, *Documentos de la rebelión*, 20–22). It is interesting to note that Matías Romero, the Mexican ambassador, cites this same list in his pamphlet about the Garza revolution, but arrives at slightly lower numbers (997 soldiers and 253 officers) (Romero, "The Garza Raid and Its Lessons," *North American Review* 155 [September 1892]: 328).

16 "Rebelión de Catarino E. Garza en Tamaulipas," in SRE, leg. 30-26-169; also cited in Saldívar, *Documentos de la rebelión*, 25–27. These documents indicate that donations came from individuals and groups of individuals in Camargo, Reynosa, Matamoros, Guerrero, Nuevo León, Chihuahua, Sonora, and New York. Of particular interest are the donations by "Americanos" of $2,940 and by W. S. Frank of New York for $3,500. Also included in these documents is a list of expenses for October 1891, which comes to a total of $5,878.50 (Saldívar, *Documentos de la*

rebelión, 22–23). Matías Romero's calculations of donations to Garza ($19,640) fall short of my own. On the other hand, his calculation for expenses ($6,541.75) exceeds mine (Romero, "The Garza Raid," 329).

17   J. J. North could have been Garza's pseudonym but, if so, he left Texas shortly after writing these letters. The last few letters, dated in March, were signed Juan Villa, but this was after Garza had already left the state (Díaz to Reyes, 2 Feb. 1892, in ABR, doc. 3037).

18   It is unclear why the Garzistas would still be corresponding with Hernández in February 1892 when he had been arrested for complicity with the rebels in December 1891.

19   "¿Si reunimos mil hombres para el mes de marzo próximo podemos contar en que se levante ud. en Chihuahua?" "Dic. 6/91 general Luis Terrzas aceptó gustoso proposición = Dic. 9/91 General Sóstenes Rocha contestó favorable carta proposición." These notes on letters received and replied to were also not included in the Saldívar collection. Saldívar relied on a copy of the papers from Ignacio Mariscal's private archive. The version he consulted and translated into Spanish was an English version prepared for the U.S. District Court in Brownsville and then passed along to Mexico's consul in San Antonio, Plutarco Ornelas (Saldívar, *Documentos de la rebelión*, 7–10, 30). The version I consulted is in the Bernardo Reyes archive, and is attached to a letter sent from Porfirio Díaz to Reyes (Díaz to Reyes, 2 Feb. 1892, in ABR, doc. 3037). Judging from the date on Díaz's letter, 2 Feb. 1892, and the later dates of the J. J. North letters, it looks like Reyes attached these other letters to the file after he had received it.

20   Knight, *Mexican Revolution*, vol. 1, 15. Guy Thomson, with David Lafrance, *Patriotism, Politics, and Popular Liberalism in Nineteenth-Century Mexico: Juan Francisco Lucas and the Puebla Sierra* (Wilmington, Del.: Scholarly Resources, 1999), 187.

21   Katz, *Secret War*, 10.

22   The Mexican historian who discovered the Garza papers in the private archive of Foreign Relations Secretary Ignacio Mariscal incorrectly hypothesized that Mariscal kept them from Díaz to protect his friends (Saldívar, *Documentos de la rebelión*, 9).

23   "Nos da derecho a dudar de lo demás." Díaz to Reyes, 2 Feb. 1892, in ABR, doc. 3037.

24   Bourke to Post Adj., Fort McIntosh, 2 April 1892, in GRP, p. 3.

25   Ibid.

26   "Garza's Dream Nearly Over," *Examiner*, 4 Mar. 1892, in SRE, leg. 11-10-44, part 5, f. 188.

27   Tel. Bourke to Asst. Adj. Gen, 23 Dec. 1891, in GRP.

28   Bourke, *Our Neutrality Laws*, 14. The original version of this article was published in the *Mexican Financier* in 1895.

29   "Una circunstancia que favoreció mucho su propaganda entre los mexicanos de la frontera de Texas es el lamentable estado de miseria que los aflije pues que la mayor parte procede de la frontera de los estados de Tamaulipas y Coahuila que se encuentra en un estado verdaderamente alarmante de decaimiento y de falta de

recursos para la clase jornalera." "Ha venido sufriendo por la sequia y decaimiento de la industria ganadera." Ornelas to Romero, 18 Mar. 1892, in AMR, doc.
40005, roll 55.

30 "Fueron materia dispuesta a seducirse por las promesas de Garza." "Aventurero
criminal." Ibid.

31 "Pueblo bajo." "Victimas." Lameda Díaz to M. Romero, 12 Feb. 1892, in AMR,
doc. 39846, roll 55.

32 "Se suspenden, vuelven a aparecer, cada vez conteniendo mayores falsedades, mas
descaradas calumnias, mentiras mas atroces; cada palabrota asusta; el gobierno es
un tirano infama; se azota a los escritores publicos en los bediondos calabozos, se
les asesina y envilice; los mas conotados personajes de la situación son ladrones
desvergonzados, traidores sanguinarios." "Ignorantes." "Sin indarse de la posibi-
lidad de que el tal Garza realice su ofrecimientos." Lameda Díaz to M. Romero,
12 Feb. 1892, in AMR, doc. 39846, roll 55. Bourke contradicts the consul on this
issue, claiming that while rebel soldiers would receive a gun and a horse and the
support of their family while they were gone, the soldiers received no money
(Bourke to Asst. Adj. Gen., 29 Dec. 1891, in GRP, pp. 2–3).

33 "Pobres y ricos, extranjeros y nacionales, mexicanos de origen y otros, todos
hacen su agosto, por la sencilla razon de que se desarolla el contrabando, que es
por aquí el gran negocio." "Todos han contribuido al boom, como sucede siempre." "Se presentó bien en la palestra, tenía dinero, pagaba con regularidad su
gente, [y] ostentaba grandes conexiones y grandes recursos." Ibid.

34 Prince Iturbide was the adopted son of the Hapsburg monarch Maximilian, who
ruled over Mexico from 1862 to 1865.

35 "Inconscientemente." "Ahora, después del crash nadie por aquí se acuerda de
Garza sino para recriminarlo y juzgarlo tal como es; un atolondrado sin cabeza,
sin valor, sin inteligencia que inspira solo burla y desprecio." "Los rancheros
mismos del bajo Rio Grande, tan simpatizadores y sostenedores hasta ayer no mas
de Garza, son los primeros en pedirnos que les quiten de encima la plaga de
criminales con causa abierta que quedan todavia ocultos por allá en los montes."
Lameda Díaz to M. Romero, 12 Feb. 1892, in AMR, doc. 39846, roll 55.

36 "No falta a [Garza] algun entusiasmo que le favorece entre el pueblo bajo, las
mujeres especialmente de esa condición despreciable por falta de civilización y
respeto propio." Ibid.

37 Bourke to Asst. Adj. Gen., 2 March 1892, in GRP, p. 9.

38 Bourke to Asst. Adj. Gen., 10 Dec. 1891, in GRP, p. 5.

39 Bourke, Our Neutrality Laws, 11.

40 Chase to Adj. Gen., La Purissima, 12 Mar 1893, in Chase Report, GRP, pp. 2–4d.

41 Bourke to Asst. Adj. Gen., Fort Ringgold, 23 March 1892, in GRP, 4.

42 Bernardo Reyes to Porfirio Díaz, 26 Oct. 1899, in ABR, cop. 36, doc. 7190;
Ignacio Mariscal, Foreign Minister, to Rel. Ext., in SRE, 28 Dec. 1894, leg.
11-10-44, part. 9, f. 60–61. For more on Manuel Guerra, see Anders, Boss Rule in
South Texas, 43–44.

43 Bourke to Asst. Adj. Gen., 2 Apr. 1892, in GRP, p. 4; also reported in McNeel to
Mabry, 4 Apr. 1892, in AGC, 401–23, f. 4–6.

44 Anders, *Boss Rule in South Texas*, 10–11.

45 "Another Garza Band Routed by Our Troops," *Herald*, 7 Jan. 1892, in SRE, leg. 11-10-44, part 3, f. 62; "Garza's Father-in-law Arrested," *New York Times*, 28 Feb. 1892, in SRE, leg. 11-10-44, part 5, f. 180; "Captura," *El Cronista Mexicano*, 15 Oct. 1892, p. 3, c. 1, in BN.

46 "Salinas and Flores," *Globe Democrat*, 21 Dec. 1892 [?], in Bourke Diary, Vol. 110. Dr. Mendoza provided Bourke with the information about González's financial situation, although he claimed that the mortgage was for $22,000 and not for $26,000 reported in the *Globe Democrat* (Bourke Diary, 21 Dec. 1892, Vol. 109, p. 186).

47 Bourke to Asst. Adj. Gen., 20 Dec. 1891, in GRP, pp. 2–3.

48 "Rebelión de Catarino E. Garza en Tamaulipas," in SRE, leg. 30-26-169; also cited in Saldívar, *Documentos de la rebelión*, 26–27.

49 S. A. Brito to Hogg, 27 Jan. 1891 [date probably 1892], in AGC, 401–418, f. 7.

50 Chase to Asst. Adj. Gen, 3 Feb. 1892, in GRP, p. 3.

51 Longoria actually named some of the merchants from Laredo who supplied them, but Bourke transcribed the names in code. Bourke Diary, 1 Jan. 1892, Vol. 107, p 163.

52 Bourke Diary, 18 Nov. 1892, Vol. 109, pp. 50–51.

53 Bourke to Asst. Adj. Gen., Fort Ringgold, 23 March 1892, in GRP, pp. 5–6.

54 Bourke to Post Adj. Gen., 2 April 1892, in GRP, p. 2.

55 Bourke to Asst. Adj. Gen., Fort Ringgold, 5 March 1892, in GRP, p. 1.

56 "La Revolución," *El Internacional* (Palito Blanco, Texas), 6 Feb. 1892, p. 2, c. 2–3, in GRP.

57 Bourke to Asst. Adj. Gen., 5 Mar. 1892, in GRP, p. 1.

58 Bourke Diary, 27 Jan. 1892, Vol. 108, p. 8.

59 "List of the Charges," *San Antonio Express*, 20 Feb. 1892, in Bourke Diary, Vol. 108.

60 Bourke to Asst. Adj. Gen., 2 Mar. 1892, in GRP, p. 2. This same report indicates that Longoria also said that he had seen Garza at a lodge meeting and a ball in Peña on the night of 26–27 Dec. 1891, talking with Sheriff Buckley. Ironically, Sheriff John Buckley, who sympathized with the Garza revolution, ended up with the neoconservative commentator William F. Buckley Jr. as his grandson, proving that political conviction is thus not hereditary and history does not always move forward.

61 Chase to Morris, 19 Jan. 1892, in GRP, p. 3.

62 Eugene Iglesias to Governor Hogg, 26 Dec. 1891, Hogg Papers, LR 301-132, f. 93.

63 Buckley to Hogg, 4 Jan. 1892, Hogg Papers, LR, 301–132, f. 98; Stanley to Hogg, 25 Feb. 1892, Hogg Papers, LR, 301–133, f. 108.

64 Chase Report, in GRP, p. 19.

65 Bourke Diary, 16 Mar. 1892, Vol. 108, p. 71; Bourke to Asst. Adj. Gen., 2 Apr. 1892, in GRP, pp. 4–5.

66 Lt. Stephen O'Conner to Asst. Adj. Gen., 9 Sept. 1893, in GRP, p. 4.

67 John W. Foster to Hogg, 8 Dec. 1892, Hogg Papers, LR, 301–136, f. 169.

68 Chase to Dept. of Texas, 12 Mar. 1893 in Chase Report, GRP, p. 4d.

69 Virgil N. Lott and Mecurio Martínez, *The Kingdom of Zapata County* (San Antonio: Naylor, 1953), 115.

70 Bourke Diary, 28 Dec. 1891, Vol. 107, pp. 150–51.

71 Ibid., 4 Feb. 1892, Vol. 108, pp. 14–15.

72 Ibid., 3 Aug. 1892, Vol. 109, p. 34.

73 "Assassination," *Aransas Beacon*, n.d., in Bourke Diary, Vol. 109, p. 147; assassination also reported in the Washington *Evening Star, 14 Nov. 1892, in Bourke Diary, Vol. 109, p. 147; and the Tucson Star*, 24 Nov. 1892, in Bourke Diary, Vol. 109, p. 163.

74 Bourke Diary, Vol. 109, p. 145; Bourke, *Our Neutrality Laws*, 27.

75 Ibid., 7–8 Dec. 1892, Vol. 109, p. 170–75.

76 Ibid., 10 Jan. 1893, Vol. 110, pp. 55–56.

77 G. M. Raphael, "Grand Jury Report, Brownsville, 21 January 1892," in Bourke, *Our Neutrality Laws*, 21–23.

78 "Trial of Múnoz," *San Antonio Express*, 2 May 1892; "Rest Their Case," *San Antonio Express*, and "Ended the Trial," *San Antonio Express*," both in Bourke Diary, Vol. 108.

79 "Ended the Trial," *San Antonio Express*," in Bourke Diary, Vol. 108.

80 Ibid.

81 "Chase Report," in GRP, appendix.

82 The statistical information about sentences received by Garzistas is culled from the final report made by Captain George F. Chase on 31 May 1893. While the list appears to be comprehensive, there were another fourteen people who had been arrested but were not yet sentenced at the time. The usefulness of this list is further limited by what appears to be misspellings of Spanish names and names that appear twice (Chase Report, in GRP, pp. 1–2a). Antonio Bruni, the wealthy landowner and merchant from Laredo, was also listed as having been arrested and under bond, although the outcome of his case is not indicated in the report (p. 1b).

83 Bourke Diary, 19–20 Dec. 1892, Vol. 109, pp. 181–83; "The Federal Court Business," [?], in Bourke Diary, Vol. 109, p. 184.

84 Brito to Mabry, 27 Jan. 1892, in AGC, 401-22, f. 9–10.

85 Chase Report, in GRP, pp. 18–19.

86 Ibid., pp. 16–18.

87 Ibid., 20.

88 Bourke, *Our Neutrality Laws*, 27.

89 Bourke Diary, 18 Feb. 1893, Vol. 111, p. 31.

90 Chase Report, in GRP, p. 20.

91 Chase Report, in GRP, p. 20.

92 "Tired of Waiting," *Weekly Caller*, 25 Mar. 1892, in Bourke Diary, Vol. 108, pp. 84–85.

93 Petition by Citizens of Duval County, 3 Feb. 1892, and Petition by Citizens of Laredo, 4 Feb. 1892, Hogg Papers, LR, 301-133, f. 104: Petition by Nueces and Rio Grande Livestock Association, 21 Dec. 1892, Hogg Papers, LR, 301-136, f. 173.

94 Nicholas Dunn to Mabry, 8 Oct. 1892, in AGC, 401-21, f. 7–9.

95 McNeel to Mabry, 24 Dec. 1891, AGC, 401-22, f. 4–6.

96 W. C. Bowen to Hogg, 28 May 1891, AGC, 401-419, f. 7–10.

97 Frank Jones to Mabry, 12 Aug. 1891, AGC, 401-20, f. 12–17.

98 "Petition of Stockraisers and Farmers of Hidalgo County to Governor Hogg," 1 Aug. 1891, in AGC, 401–420, f. 12–17.

99 William P. Dougherty to Mabry, [?], in AGC, 401-20, f. 18–21. For this period, 1891–1892, there is one other request by Ranger Captain Brooks to appoint M. A. Bañados, presumably a Mexican, as a Special Ranger. The final decision in this case could not be determined (Brooks to Mabry, 3 July 1892, in AGC, 401-24, f. 14–20). The only other Mexican American Ranger I have been able to identify during this period is Jesse Pérez, who also fought against Garza. For more, see Jeffrey Kirk Cleveland, "Fight Like a Devil: Images of the Texas Rangers and the Strange Career of Jesse Perez," master's thesis, University of Texas, Austin, 1992.

100 "Governor's Proclamation," *San Antonio Express*, 20 Feb. 1892, in Bourke Diary, Vol. 108.

101 "After the Violence?" *San Antonio Express*, 27 Feb. 1892, in Bourke Diary, Vol. 108, pp. 51–52.

102 Chase Report, in GRP, p. 6.

103 "Los ultrajes en nuestros ciudadanos por militares y otros empleados, cuyo deber era evitar la invasión de México, llegaron á tanto colmo que debieron ser castigados." Jesus T. Recío ed., *El Bien Público: La guerra contra la paz ó un nuevo atila* (Rio Grande City: Imprenta Jesus T. Recío, 1895), 49.

104 Edward Said notes a similar inability of the British to take seriously resistant nationalisms in India and Africa, belittling them as "self-interested" or at best an exaggerated and misplaced reaction to the brutality of colonial rule (Said, *Culture and Imperialism*, 206–6).

105 Tel., Chase to Asst. Adj. Gen., 18 Jan. 1892, in GRP, p. 2; also J. T. Knight to Asst. Adj. Gen., 21 Jan. 1892, in GRP, p. 1.

106 G. T. Langhorne to Post Adj. Gen., 2 Jan. 1892, in GRP, p. 5.

107 Chase Report, in GRP, p. 21.

108 In the raid on Garza's camp at Palito Blanco, Bourke first blames the "chaparral" for Garza's escape. On another occasion, described in the same report, Bourke argues that there is no doubt Garza would have been captured had it not been for the "heavy rain" (Bourke to Asst. Adj. Gen., 2 Mar., 1892, in GRP, p. 6, 8).

109 Bourke, "An American Congo," 599.

6. THE IDEOLOGICAL BATTLE

1 "The Garza Uprising," *St. Louis Globe Democrat*, 30 Jan. 1892, in Bourke Diary, Vol. 108, p. 10.

2 "The Garza Revolution," *San Antonio Express*, 9 Feb. 1892, in SRE, leg. 11-10-44, part 5, f. 117.

3 Nicolás Kanellos notes the distinction between immigrant and exile newspapers, suggesting that the former were oriented toward political change in Mexico

while the latter were more focused on the condition of Mexicans in the United States. Such a distinction is difficult to make for Ignacio Martínez's and Catarino Garza's newspapers, which dealt with politics both in Mexico and in Texas. See Nicolás Kanellos, *Hispanic Periodicals in the United States, Origins to 1960: A Brief History and Comprehensive Bibliography* (Houston: Arte Público Press, 2000), 21.

4   "Garza's Narrow Escape," *Evening Star*, 25 Sept. 1891, in SRE, leg. 11-10-44, part 1, f. 161.

5   *Evening Telegraph*, 21 Sept. 1891, in SRE, leg. 11-10-44, part 1, f. 128.

6   "Garza," *Courier*, 13 Jan. 1892, in SRE, leg. 11-10-44, part 4, f. 53.

7   "De lo mas tonto y desgraciado del mundo." "El Presidente Harrison no podría, con todos sus elementos mover la prensa con el acierto, uniformidad y compás que se ha agitado en esta vagamunderia de Garza." Lameda Díaz to Matías Romero, 24 Feb. 1892, in AMR, doc. 39898, roll 55.

8   Bourke, *Our Neutrality Laws*, 6.

9   "The Garza Revolution," *San Antonio Express*, 9 Feb. 1892, in SRE, leg. 11-10-44, part 5, f. 117.

10 "Desesperados de la decadencia del Carnaval, querian resucitar con sus grotescas payasadas." "Ridícula intentona," *El Cronista Mexicano*, 19 Sept. 1891, p. 1, c. 3, in BN.

11 "Lays Down the Pen for the Sword" and "Border Ruffian?" both in *Gate City*, 18 Sept. 1891, in SRE, leg. 11-10-44, part 1, f. 88.

12 "Los hombres de negocios reprueban todo movimiento que tienda a entorpecer el tráfico mercantil; los hombre políticos tienden a favorecer al Gobierno de Mexico." "Sin proceso, sin ley, sin nada, algo como una justicia Lynch." "Ecos de la revolución," *El Correo de Laredo*, 20 Sept. 1891, in SRE, leg. 11-10-44, part 1, f. 32.

13 "No Further Developments," *Laredo Times*, 20 Sept. 1891, in SRE, leg. 11-10-44, part 1, f. 30.

14 "Que muchísimos desgraciados que han dado cabida a los cuentos y a las promesas de esos imbéciles han pagado y están pagando tal vez culpas agenas. Que no dejen su hogar, que no abandonen su familia y el trabajo honrado por seguir una causa vergonzosa." "Infamia," *El Cromo*, 24 Oct. 1891, in AMR, doc. 39262, roll 54.

15 "A fin de impedir en cuanto alcancen nuestros pobres fuerzas, la ruina, el deshonor, la muerte acaso de hombres que con solo fijar un poco su atención en la opinion pública aun pudieron ser útiles y honrados por la patria a quien todos tenemos un deber de consagrarnos." Ibid., p. 2, col. 1.

16 "Redundaría en perjuicio de los ciudadanos mexicanos adictos a los poderes públicos, de las autoridades de la otra margen del Rio, que cuentan con el periódico para repeler la agresión de otros periódicos y de los Jefes Militares, que desde el principio de la campaña han hallado en esta publicación un factor apreciable y un aliado utíl, sinceramente adicto y desinteresado." A. García del Tornel to Matías Romero, 29 Oct. 1891, in AMR, doc. 39262, roll 54.

17 Romero, "The Garza Raid," 333–35.

18 Ibid., 336.

19 Romero to Rel. Ext., 5 Dec. 1891, in SRE, leg. 11-10-44, part 2, f. 144. "Minister Romero Makes a Correction," 8 Dec. 1891, *Washington Post*, in SRE, leg. 11-10-44, part 2, f. 144.

20 "The Garza Revolt," *San Francisco Chronicle*, 12 Jan. 1892, in SRE, leg. 11-10-44, part 3, f. 115.

21 "He dejado correr . . . y aun le he dado calor porque ellos hacen aparecer a los que han formado la gavilla expresada, como vendidos en contra de los intereses de su patria." "Intereses de los enemigos del crédito de nuestro país." Reyes to Romero, 14 Jan. 1892, in ABR, cop., doc. 1839, f. 597.

22 Ibid., f. 598.

23 "Muy maliciosa." Reyes to Romero, 8 Jan. 1892, in ABR, cop., doc. 1829, f. 587–88.

24 "No hay de quien pueda sospecharse que represente algún bando político, facción religiosa, banco o asociación financiera, en suma organización seria de algun genero protegida por la bolsa, por el clero o por algún otro importante cuerpo social." "Pero de todas maneras esos exiguos recursos no vinieron de lejos sino que procedieron de la Frontera misma de Texas y de Mexico." Ornelas to Romero, 18 Mar. 1892, in AMR, roll 55, doc. 40005.

25 "Only a Paper Rebellion," *Evening Star*, 26 Sept. 1892, in SRE, leg. 11-10-44, part 8, f. 94.

26 Some Mexicans believed that the 1994 EZLN rebellion in Chiapas was organized by former President Salinas de Gortarí to scare away the electorate from the opposition party, the Partido Revolucionario Democrático, and insure the ruling Partido Revolucionario Institucional victory in the elections. This argument makes no sense, however, given that the Chiapas rebellion had seriously crippled the already decrepit ruling party, but it shows how the notion of an omnipotent regime still holds sway in Mexico.

27 "Garza and President Díaz," *Boston Herald*, 29 Sept. 1892, in SRE, leg. 11-10-44, part 8, f. 97.

28 "Shepard Backing Garza," *Chicago Times*, 9 Jan. 1892, in SRE, leg. 11-10-44, part 4, f. 55.

29 "Ripe for Revolt," *Globe Democrat*, 16 Feb. 1892, in L. Díaz to M. Romero, 23 Feb. 1892, in AMR, roll 55, doc. 39884.

30 "No hiciera elogios de personalidades de este país, para que revistiendo carácter imparcial, defendiera con mejor éxito los intereses de nuestro Gobierno." Reyes to Díaz, 8 Apr. 1891, in ABR, cop., doc. 1109, f. 506; Reyes to Obregón, 1 Feb. 1891, in ABR, cop., doc. 2660, f. 339; Reyes to Obregón, 11 Aug. 1891, in ABR, cop., doc. 2851, f. 565; Reyes to Cerón, 6 Aug. 1891, in ABR, cop., doc. 2844, f. 557.

31 "De convertir en simpatizadora esa fuerza que ahora tan acervamente antagoniza los intereses de nuestro país y de nuestro Gobierno." "Multitud de periodiquillos publicados de este lado del Rio Grande . . . logrando en gran parte enajenarles las simpatías de la remota frontera de Texas." Ornelas to Mariscal, 12 Dec. 1894, f. 7, in ABR, doc. 4291.

32 "Cuando necesario." Ornelas to Rel. Ext., 3 Jan. 1892, in SRE, leg. 11-10-44, part 3, f. 17.

33 Lameda Díaz to Ornelas, 14 Jan. 1892, in AMR, roll 54, doc. 39721.

34 "Conditions in Mexico," *Laredo Weekly Times*, 4 Apr. 1892, in AMR, roll 55, doc. 40053.

35 "Siempre fui uno de los escritores de Nuevo León que sostuvieron su candidatura de Ud. para Presidente . . . jamás he sido enemigo de su gobierno de Ud, que tantos bienes ha traido al pais." Justo Cárdenas to Porfirio Díaz, 25 Oct. 1891, in CPD, leg. 16, doc. 14348-49.

36 "Hemos formado el propósito de apartarnos de cierta gente que nos deshonra, y nos hemos propuesto no ser mas tiempo juguete de caballeros de industria, y por eso nos hemos retirado del campo oposicionista." "No necesitamos vendernos para vivir." "Nuestra independencia está asegurada con nuestros propios recursos, y no será el hambre la que nos ponga al borde del abismo, ni el estomago el que dicte nuestros escritos." "Causa nauseas." "Lo que son los oposicionistas," *El Cronista Mexicano*, 5 Sept. 1891, in p. 3, c. 1, in BN.

37 Cárdenas to Arnulfo García, 25 Oct. 1891, in CPD, leg. 16, doc. 14350; Cárdenas to García, 13 Nov. 1891, in CPD, leg. 16, doc. 14344.

38 Reyes to Díaz, 1 Feb. 1892, ABR, cop., doc. 4856, f. 137.

39 "Un arreglo . . . para que su publicación siga una marcha distinta de la que ha tenido." "Un elemento de hostilidad." Manuel Romero Rubio to Reyes, 18 Mar. 1892, ABR, doc. 6108.

40 "Su periodico no sólo tiene carácter de imparcial sino que ha llegado a atacar los papeles que allende el Bravo propagan ideas subversivas." Reyes to Romero Rubio, 21 Mar. 1892, ABR, cop., doc. 1890, f. 656.

41 "Que el Centro no le convendra hostilice al Gobierno de un Estado." Reyes to Consul Lameda Díaz, 3 Dec. 1892, in ABR, doc. 6130, f. 314.

42 Reyes to Consul Díaz, 13 Dec. 1892, in ABR, cop., doc. 6188, f. 364.

43 Lameda Díaz to Romero, 5 Apr. 1892, in AMR, roll 55, doc. 40053.

44 Alberto Leal, Consul Rio Grande City, to Rel. Ext., 13 July 1896, in SRE, leg. 1-15-1724, f. 16.

45 "Garza a Patriot, Not a Bandit," *Los Angeles Herald*, 19 Jan. 1892, in SRE, leg. 11-10-44, part 5, f. 27.

46 Matamoros: *El Eco de la Frontera, El Cronista, El Barbero*; Laredo: *La Constitucion, El Mutualista, Fray Tiburcio*; Nogales: *El Monitor Fronterizo*; Eagle Pass: *El Comercio Mexicano*; San Antonio: *El Observador*; San Francisco: *La Republica*; San Diego: *El Pueblo*; Brownsville: *El Defensor del Pueblo, El Mundo*. Note the inclusion of two nonborder sites, San Antonio and San Francisco ("Crece el numero," *El Mundo*, 22 Aug. 1886, in SRE, leg. 11-10-16, f. 101).

47 For a full listing, see the thorough bibliography of Hispanic periodicals in Kanellos, *Hispanic Periodicals in the United States*, 300–306.

48 Reyes to José María Garza Galán, 16 Apr. 1889, ABR, doc. 15, f. 17.

49 Reyes to Manuel Romero Rubio, 21 July 1890, ABR, cop., doc. 1502, f. 226; Reyes to Díaz, 6 Jan. 1893, ABR, cop., doc. 5189, f. 479.

50 "Mexico's Despotic Rule," *Journal* (Milwaukee), 31 Dec. 1891, in SRE, leg. 18-27-10, f. 10.

51 "Garza and his Gang," *San Francisco Examiner*, 1 Feb. 1892, in SRE, leg. 11-10-44, part 5, f. 11.

52 "Situación," *El Internacional*, 9 Jan. 1892, in "Garza's Men Evasive," *San Antonio Express*, 17 Jan. 1892, in SRE, leg. 11-10-44, part 4, f. 66. The *San Antonio Express* published a regular section in Spanish that included translated articles from the English section as well as other articles presumably of more interest to Spanish-speaking readers.

53 "Garza and his Gang," *San Francisco Examiner*, 1 Feb. 1892, in SRE, leg. 11-10-44, part 5, f. 11.

54 Ibid.

55 Ibid.

56 "Garza Tells His Story," *New York Times*, 4 Jan. 1892, in CPD, leg. 17, doc. 193.

57 Ibid.

58 "After the Head of Díaz," *Omaha Bee*, 4 Jan 1892, in SRE, leg. 11-10-44, exp. 4, f. 5. The *New York Times* article published the interview without additional commentary such as appeared in the *Bee* article.

59 "Garza Tells His Story," *New York Times*, 4 Jan. 1892, in CPD, reg. 17, doc. 193.

60 Ibid.

7. COLONIZING THE LOWER RIO GRANDE VALLEY

1 For a powerful critique of the connection between racism and empire, see Richard Drinon, *Facing West: The Metaphysics of Indian-Hating and Empire Building* (New York: New American Library, 1980).

2 Michel Trouillot argues that "silences enter the process of historical production at four crucial moments: the moment of fact creation (the making of *sources*); the moment of fact assembly (the making of *archives*); the moment of fact retrieval (the making of *narratives*); and the moment of retrospective significance (the making of *history* in the final instance)." Trouillot, *Silencing the Past*, 26–30.

3 Bourke Diary, Vol. 99, p. 76–78; Vol. 102, p. 18, as cited in Joseph C. Porter, *Paper Medicine Man: John Gregory Bourke and His American West* (Norman: University of Oklahoma Press, 1986), 280–82.

4 Bourke to J. H. Porter, 2 May 1894, Bourke Papers, United States Military Academy Library, West Point, New York.

5 Bourke to Asst. Adj. Gen., 6 Oct. 1891, in GRP, pp. 2–3.

6 Bourke, *Our Neutrality Laws*, 6–7.

7 Stephen O'Conner to Asst. Adj. Gen., 26 Feb. 1893, in GRP, p. 3.

8 O'Conner to Post Adj., 7 Jan. 1893, in GRP, p. 1. Wilfred Dudley Smithers photographed Mexican *avisadores* (signalers) along the Rio Grande at the beginning of the twentieth century. For photographs, see the Smithers (W. D.) Collection at the Harry Ransom Center, University of Texas, Austin.

9 Bourke to Asst. Adj. Gen., 6 Oct. 1891, in GRP, p. 4.

10 Bourke to Asst. Adj. Gen., 10 Dec. 1891, in GRP, p. 8.

11 Mills to Adj. Gen., 19 Mar. 1892, in GRP, pp. 1–2.
12 Ibid., 2.
13 General Orders No. 28, Adjutant General's Office, 25 Nov. 1884, noted in Post Return, Fort Brown, Dec. 1884; and General Orders No. 24, Adjutant General's Office, 19 June 1896, noted in ibid., July 1896; as cited in Richard Tandy Marcum, "Fort Brown, Texas: The History of a Border Post," Ph.D. diss., Texas Technological College, 1964, p. 219.
14 Mills to Adj. Gen., 19 Mar. 1893, in GRP, p. 2.
15 Ibid.
16 Bourke Diary, Vol. 109, 31 July 1892, pp. 31–32.
17 Bourke Diary, Vol. 108, 29 Jan. 1892, p. 11.
18 Bourke to Asst. Adj. Gen., 4 Nov. 1891, in GRP, f. 2.
19 Bourke to Asst. Adj. Gen., 10 Dec. 1891, in GRP, p. 3.
20 Ibid., pp. 2–3.
21 In her book on the Cristero rebellion in Mexico in the mid-1920s, Majorie Becker shows how peasants in Michoacán resisted the revolutionary state by boycotting state schools and killing teachers. See Majorie Becker, *Setting the Virgin on Fire: Lázaro Cárdenas, Michoacán Peasants and the Redemption of the Mexican Revolution* (Berkeley: University of California Press, 1995), 125–28.
22 Bourke to Asst. Adj. Gen., 10 Dec. 1891, in GRP, f. 3.
23 Ibid., pp. 4.
24 Bourke Diary, Vol. 106, 3 Nov. 1891, p. 130.
25 Bourke to Asst. Adj. Gen., 10 Dec. 1891, in GRP, f. 4.
26 Ibid.
27 Ibid.
28 Ibid., 4–5.
29 Edward Said makes a similar argument in *Culture and Imperialism*, xii–xiii. For a good discussion of the correlation between disease and imperialism, see Sheldon Watts, *Epidemics and History: Disease, Power, and Imperialism* (New Haven: Yale University Press, 1997).
30 Sigmund Freud, in John G. Bourke, *Scatalogic Rites of All Nations* (New York: American Anthropological Society, 1934 [1891]), ix. also cited in Porter, *Paper Medicine Man*, 274.
31 Bourke, *Scatalogic Rites of All Nations*, 29.
32 Ibid., 3–6.
33 Ibid., 467.
34 In his insightful book, Robert Young explores the connection between sexual desire and colonialism, arguing that a simultaneous repulsion and attraction to racial mixing was at the core of nineteenth-century racial thinking and colonialism. For his discussion of Homi K. Bhabha's conceptualization of "ambivalence," see Robert J. C. Young, *Colonial Desire: Hybridity in Theory, Culture, and Race* (London: Routledge, 1995), 160–62. I am reminded of U.S. Republican Representatives who must spend a great amount of time analyzing and studying "pornography" and "obscene" music so that they can condemn and censor it.
35 Bourke, "An American Congo," 604.

36 Bourke to Asst. Adj. Gen., 10 Dec. 1891, in GRP, f. 3.

37 Ibid.

38 Bourke to Asst. Adj. Gen., 20 Nov. 1891, in GRP, f. 4.

39 Bourke, "An American Congo," 594.

40 Ibid., 592.

41 Ibid.

42 Ibid., 601–2. George Brulé built the first irrigation system in the valley in 1876 (Sandos, *Rebellion in the Borderlands*, 66).

43 Bourke, "An America Congo," 603.

44 Ibid.

45 Ibid., 592.

46 Ibid., 592–94.

47 Matthew Arnold, "On the Study of Celtic Literature," as cited in Limón, *Dancing with the Devil*, 33.

48 Limón, *Dancing with the Devil*, 33.

49 Bourke to Asst. Adj. Gen., 24 Dec. 1892, in GRP, p. 1.

50 Ibid., 2.

51 Ibid., 1.

52 Ibid., 2.

53 Ibid., 3.

54 "Capital Attention," Brownsville *Herald*, 16 Jan. 1893, in Bourke Diary, Vol. 110, p. 81

55 The same quote from Bourke comparing Mexicans to "coyotes and wild hogs" appeared in "Road along the Border, *San Antonio Express*, 6 Mar. 1893, in Bourke Diary, Vol. 111, p. 5. It also appeared in "The Southwestern Border," Boston *Herald*, n.d., in Bourke Diary, Vol. 111, and in "The Rio Grande Situation," *Washington Star*, 27 Dec. 1892, in Bourke Diary, Vol. 110, p. 23.

56 *San Antonio Express*, 19 Dec. 1892, in Bourke Diary, Vol. 109, p. 184.

57 "Extermination the Only Remedy," *Gazette* (Fort Worth), as coded in San Antonio Express, 23 Dec. 1892 [?] in Bourke Diary, Vol. 110, p. 1.

58 Bourke to Asst. Adj. Gen., 20 Nov. 1891, in GRP, pp. 1, 4.

59 Ibid., p. 2.

60 Bourke to Asst. Adj. Gen., 10 Dec. 1891, in GRP, p. 8.

61 Ibid., p. 9.

62 Bourke to Asst. Adj. Gen., 23 Dec. 1891, in GRP, p. 5.

63 Bourke Diary, Vol. 107, 22 Dec. 1891, p. 142. Years later Bourke insisted that the killing of Edstrom marked a turning point. This incident proved, he argued, that they were "enveloped with an atmosphere of war," and that they "must not only defend their own lives, but those of their fellow citizens, order or no orders" (*Our Neutrality Laws*, 16).

64 Bourke Diary, Vol. 107, 22 Dec. 1891, p. 143.

65 Bourke to Asst. Adj. Gen., 23 Dec. 1891, in GRP, p. 6.

66 Ibid.

67 Porter, *Paper Medicine Man*, 263.

68 Bourke Diary, Vol. 110, 27 Dec. 1892, pp. 27–31.

69 Bourke, *Our Neutrality Laws*, 18.

70 "Corporal Edstrom's Funeral," *San Antonio Express*, 1 Jan. 1891, in Bourke Diary, Vol. 107, p. 146.

71 Bourke to Asst. Adj. Gen., 4 Nov. 1891, in GRP, p. 5.

72 Ibid.

73 F. H. Hardie to Post Adj., Fort McIntosh, 8 Dec. 1891, in GRP, p. 1.

74 Ibid.

75 James Scott, *Weapons of the Weak*. For his more recent and more theoretical elaboration of this argument, see *Domination and the Arts of Resistance*.

76 Chase to Adj. Gen., 12 March 1893, in Chase Report, GRP, p. 1d.

77 Chase to Adj. Gen., Palito Blanco, 12 Jan. 1892, in GRP, p. 3.

78 Bourke to Asst. Adj. Gen., 23 Dec. 1891, in GRP, pp. 5–6.

79 "Garza's Dream Nearly Over," *Examiner*, 4 Mar. 1892, in SRE, leg. 11-10-44, part 5, f. 188.

80 George K. Hunter to Post Adj., Los Angeles Ranch, 20 Jan. 1892, in GRP, p. 2.

81 Ibid.

82 Hardie to Post Adj., 8 Dec. 1891, in GRP, p. 3.

83 Bourke to Asst. Adj. Gen., 15 Dec. 1891, in GRP, p. 2.

84 Hedekin to Post Adj., 30 Dec. 1892, in GRP, p. 2.

85 Ibid., 2–3.

86 Ibid., 3.

87 Hardie to Post Adj. Gen., La Peña, 2 Jan. 1892, in GRP, p. 1.

88 Alberto Leal to Rel. Ext., 4 Aug. 1892, in SRE, leg. 11-10-44, part 7, f. 182–84.

89 Kenneth W. Porter, *The Black Seminoles: History of a Freedom-Seeking People* (Gainesville: University Press of Florida, 1996), 212–13.

90 Américo Paredes Folklore Collection, Center for American History, University of Texas, Austin, "Corrido de Capítan Hall," sung by Mecurio Martínez, 27 Aug. 1954. The lyrics for this corrido can also be found in Garza Guajardo, *En busca*, 52. Martínez's version substitutes the name of his father's ranch, "Los Cristales," for his father's name, "Don Proceso."

91 Ibid. This incident is also described in Lott and Martínez, *Kingdom of Zapata*, 114–15.

92 The libretto was published by the American Folk-Lore Society in 1907 as *Los Pastores: A Mexican Play of the Nativity*. For an in-depth anthropological analysis of the shepherd play in South Texas and Bourke's role in it, see Richard R. Flores, *Los Pastores: History and Performance in the Mexican Shepherd's Play of South Texas* (Washington: Smithsonian Institution Press, 1995), 106–10.

93 Bourke, "An America Congo," 609.

94 Flores, *Los Pastores*, 173.

95 "Rio Grande Situation," Washington *Evening Star*, 27 Dec. 1892, in Bourke Diary, Vol. 110, p. 23.

96 N. G. Collins to Hogg, 4 Feb. 1892, Hogg Papers, LR, 301-133, f. 104.

97 John J. Dix to Mabry, 16 Feb. 1892, in AGC, 401-22, f. 14–16.

98 Chase Report, in GRP, pp. 1–2a, 1b, 1c, 5–6d.

99 Bourke to Asst. Adj. Gen., 23 Dec. 1891, in GRP, p. 5.

100 "Texas and Texans," *San Antonio Express*, 4 Jan. 1892, p. 2, col. 6, in CAH.

101 "Kill Those Greasers," *Post* (Chicago), 28 Dec. 1892, in SRE, leg. 834, part 3, p. 62.11.

102 "The Old Spirit," [?], Evansville, Indiana, 29 Dec. 1892, in SRE, leg. 834, part 3, p. 39.17.

103 "Cuba and Mexico," [?], Newark, New Jersey, 30 Dec. 1893, in SRE, leg. 834 part 3, p. 39.5.

104 See Daniel J. Kelves, *In the Name of Eugenics: Genetics and the Uses of Human Heredity* (New York: Knopf, 1985), esp. ch. 6. Unfortunately, the widespread acceptability of the racist arguments made in Richard Hernstein and Charles Murray's best-selling book *The Bell Curve: Intelligence and Class Structure in American Life* (New York: Free Press, 1994) demonstrates that at the end of the twentieth century biological explanations for socially produced inequalities continued to carry weight for large sectors of the United States.

105 "Turbulent Mexico," [?], Davenport Louisiana, 28 Dec. 1892, in SRE, leg. 834, part 3, p. 39.13.

106 *Chaparral* (Laredo), 25 Feb. 1899, p. 2, c. 1 in CAH. For a detailed analysis of the complex relationship between British imperialism in India and Rudyard Kipling's literature, see Said, *Culture and Imperialism*, 132–62. Kipling was a popular author in the United States, even among the Texas Rangers chasing Garza through the chaparral in South Texas (Davis, *The West from a Car-Window*, 32).

107 For an excellent analysis of masculinity in the 1898 war, see Kristin L. Hoganson, *Fighting for Manhood: How Gender Politics Provoked the Spanish-American and Philippine-American Wars* (New Haven: Yale University Press, 1998). Also, see Amy Kaplan, "Black and Blue on San Juan Hill," in *Cultures of United States Imperialism*, ed. Amy Kaplan and Donad E. Pease (Durham: Duke University Press, 1993), 219–326. For another engaging analysis of how race, class, and masculinity worked together at the turn of the century, see Gail Bederman, *Manliness and Civilization: A Cultural History of Gender and Race in the United States, 1880–1917* (Chicago: University of Chicago Press, 1995).

108 Frederic Remington, "Trumpeter Tyler," "Captain Francis H. Hardie, G Troop, Third United States Cavalry," and "Third Cavalry Troopers—Searching a Suspected Revolutionist," in Davis, *The West from a Car-Window*, 29, 37, and 53. This chapter, "Our Troops on the Border," was originally published in *Harper's Weekly*, 26 Mar. 1892.

109 Davis, *The West from a Car-Window*, 41.

110 Bourke, "An American Congo."

111 Davis, *The West from a Car-Window*, 6.

112 Ibid., 41–42.

113 Ibid., 51–53.

114 Domingo F. Sarmiento, *Life in the Argentine Republic in the Days of Tyrants, or Civilization and Barbarism* (New York: Collier Books, 1961), 27.

115 Bourke Diary, Vol. 107, 3 Jan. 1892, p. 168–69.

116 The phrase "manufacturing consent" is borrowed from Herman's book *Manufacturing Consent*.

117 "Garza's Revolution," *Call* (San Francisco), 18 Jan. 1892, in SRE, leg. 11-10-44, part 4, f. 58. The article was originally published in the Chicago *Herald*.

118 Ibid.

119 Bourke to Asst. Adj. Gen., 10 Dec. 1891, in GRP, p. 3.

120 "Garza's revolution" *Call* (San Francisco), 18 Jan. 1892, in SRE, leg. 11-10-44, part 4, f. 58.

121 Bourke to Asst. Adj. Gen., 10 Dec. 1891, in GRP, f. 3.

122 Ibid., 7–8. "Garza's Revolution" *Call* (San Francisco), 18 Jan. 1892, in SRE, leg. 11-10-44, part 4, f. 58.

123 Bourke to Asst. Adj. Gen., 10 Dec. 1891, in GRP, f. 5.

124 Bourke to Asst. Adj. Gen., 6 Oct. 1891, in GRP, f. 1.

125 Bourke, "An American Congo," 603.

126 John G. Bourke, "Popular Medicine, Customs, and Superstitions of the Rio Grande," *Journal of American Folklore* 7 (April–June 1894): 125.

127 Bourke, "An American Congo," 603–4.

128 Said credits postcolonial writers' reinterpretations of Western culture as "not only an integral part of a political movement, but in many ways the movement's *successfully* guiding imagination." Many Westerners, he argues, see the natives' claims to such cultural territory as an "intolerable effrontery," and their repossession of it as "unthinkable" (Said, *Culture and Imperialism*, 212).

129 "Sr. Capitan John G. Bourke en lugar de traer la paz á estas regions, solo vino á hacer la Guerra á indefensos y pacíficos ciudadanos, y su marcha fué acompañada de la crueldad y la devestación, identificandose con aquel famoso Atila, ó sea el azote de Dios." "Calumnias . . . á toda la raza mexicana." Récio, ed., *El Bien Público*, 2.

130 "Simple viajero." "Sembrando el terror entre los pacíficos habitantes y atemorizando con amenazas y ultrajes á los ancianos, mujeres y niños ó indefensos vecinos, desórdenes y atropellos que hasta la misma soldadezca que lo acompañaba veía con indignación y reprochaba su conducta." Ibid., 40, 41–48.

131 "Socialmente lo estimamos como un fino y educado caballero." Ibid., 46.

132 "Protestamos enérgicamente contra la introduccion en territorio americano de unos métodos tan viciosos y corrompidos." "Mientras condenamos en los terminos mas enérgicos el movimiento desordenando de Garza y consideramos que ha ocasionado á esta seccion de nuestro Estado un mal grave y duradero, y mientras estamos dispuestos por todos los medios que nos sea possible ayudar para suprimirlo, consideramos que los actos de que ha habido queja (por aquellos que mas bien deberian ser los guardianes que los opresores del pueblo) no son menos subversivos de nuestros derechos civiles." Ibid., 47–48.

133 " 'Sotendremos estas verdades en sí mismo evidentes: que todos los hombres son creados iguales; que ellos son dotados por su Creador con ciertos derechos inalienables; que entre estos se encuentran la vida, la libertad y la aspiración a la felicidad.' " "El glorioso cuatro," *El Bien Público*, 3 July 1892, in ibid., 48–49.

134 "Reinado del terror," *El Bien Público*, 10 July 1892, in ibid., 51–53.

135 "Nuestros antecesores se hicieron libres." "El Glorioso Cuatro," *El Bien Público*, 3 July 1892, in ibid., 49.

136 Esperamos que el señor capitán no se enfadará porque le llamemos Nuevo Atila, pues del mismo modo que él compara primero al Rio Grande con el Nilo y ahora despues con el Congo, estamos seguros que mañana ó pasado podrá compararlo con el Rhin, el Sena ó el Manzanares, y entonces tendremos derecho de compararlo á él con Aníbal, Alejandro el Grande ó bien con Napoleón primero." Ibid., 57.

137 "¡Si un Negro de los soldados que traía á sus órdenes hubiese sido el Jefe, no habría cometido acciones tan vandálicas!" "Una parte de los los soldados que mandaba eran de raza africana, y seguramente á cada momento él *soñaba* en Africa." Ibid., 58–59.

138 Bourke sent the Smithsonian Institution samples of medicinal plants from the lower Rio Grande Valley of folk medicine. Among these samples was "Marijuan (keeps witches away)" and "Peyote . . . good for fevers." John G. Bourke to Smithsonian Institution, Washington, D.C., 11 Dec. 1891, Accession file 25282.

139 "Pues señor capitan, está Ud. Enmarihuanado. . . ?" "Y esa gente . . . no era mexicana, sino americanos de raza blanca nacidos y criados en Texas." "Los hijos de estos a leer eas páginas en donde se insulta á sus padres llamándolos gente degredada, no podrán menos que llenos de indignación maldecir al autor de esas calumnias." Récio, ed., *El Bien Público*, 60, 61, 63.

140 "Cansado de luchar para establecer en los pueblos una administración que destierre el compadrazgo y los monopolios." "No podiendo realizar sus propósitos han emigrado á este pais que cubre con su manto á todo ciudadano honrado y pacífico que viene y se escuda bajo el pabellón de las estrellas." Ibid., 64–66.

141 "Cierto ódio hácia los habitantes de esta region." Ibid., 70–78.

142 "Hemos empuñado la pluma para decir algo en favor de nuestros hermanos, porque nos pareció que dejando en silencio insultos tan groseros y gratuitos del famoso capitan, seria tanto como confirmarlos." Ibid., 77–78.

143 Among the many books listed in the bibliography to *Scatalogic Rites* was Henry M. Stanley's *Through the Dark Continent* (New York: Harper, 1878) and his book *Congo* (New York: Harper, 1885).

144 As cited in Norman R. Bennett, ed., *Stanley's Despatches to the New York Herald, 1871–1872, 1874–1877* (Boston: Boston University Press, 1970), xxx.

145 Ibid., xvi–xviii.

146 "Sprung a Sensation," *San Antonio Express*, 28 Feb. 1892, in Bourke Diary, Vol. 108. This story is also covered in "The Charges against Capt. Bourke," *Star* (Washington), 14 Mar. 1892, in Bourke Diary, Vol. 108, p. 80.

147 Bourke Diary, Vol. 108, 6 Mar. 1892, pp. 57–58.

148 J. R. Monroe, et al. to Hogg, 18 Feb. 1892, Hogg Papers, LR, 301-133, f. 107.

149 Bourke Diary, Vol. 108, 6 Mar. 1892, pp. 57–58.

150 "Will Indict Capt. Bourke," *World* (New York), 12 Mar. 1892, in Bourke Diary, Vol. 108, p. 81.

151 Ibid.

152 "Rest Their Case," *San Antonio Express*, [?] in Bourke Diary, Vol. 108.

153 "Sprung a Sensation," *San Antonio Express*, 28 Feb. 1892, in Bourke Diary, Vol. 108.

154 The witnesses were Alejandro González, Rumaldo Cadena Saens, Manuel Cadena, and Dr. F. S. Mendoza.

155 Bourke Diary, Vol. 108, 13 Mar. 1892, p. 65.

156 Bourke Diary, Vol. 108, 28 Mar. 1892, pp. 87–89.

157 "Captain Bourke's Accusers," *Omaha Bee*, 30 Mar. 1892, in Bourke Diary, Vol. 108, p. 100.

158 "Captain Bourke's Accusers," *Omaha Bee*, 1 Apr. 1892, in Bourke Diary, Vol. 108, p. 101.

159 "Bourke Investigation," [?] 15 Apr. 1892, in Bourke Diary, Vol. 108.

160 Bourke Diary, Vol. 108, 28 Mar. 1892, pp. 88–89.

161 "Grand Jury's Report," *Weekly Caller* (Corpus Christi), 13 Apr. 1892, in Bourke Diary, Vol. 108.

162 Bourke Diary, Vol. 108, 16 Apr. 1892, p. 125

163 Bourke Diary, Vol. 109, 9 Dec. 1892, p. 145.

164 Bourke, *Our Neutrality Laws*, 26–28.

165 Ibid.

166 "Down on the Lower Border," *San Antonio Express*, 3 Mar. 1893, in Bourke Diary, Vol. 111, p. 48; "Complain of the Troops," *San Antonio Express*, 6 Mar. 1893, in Bourke Diary, Vol. 111, p. 50.

167 *Wharton's Digest of International Law* (Washington, D.C.: Government Printing Office), pp. 340–51, in Bourke Diary, Vol. 110, 24 Jan. 1893, p. 87.

168 Quote from D. G. Brinton, *Journal of American Folk-Lore* (July–Sept. 1882): 182, in Bourke Diary, Vol. 111, 25 Feb. 1893, p. 38.

169 "Down on the Lower Border," *San Antonio Express*, 3 Mar. 1893, in Bourke Diary, Vol. 111, p. 48.

170 "The Curse of Texas," *San Antonio Express*, 28 Jan. 1893, in Bourke Diary, Vol. 110.

171 Bourke Diary, Vol. 111, 25 Feb. 1893, pp. 35–37.

172 Bourke Diary, Vol. 111, 27 Feb. 1893, pp. 38–41.

173 "Complain of the Troops," *San Antonio Express*, 6 Mar. 1893, in Bourke Diary, Vol. 111, p. 50.

174 Porter asserts that Bourke received a telegram on March 14 from the commander at Fort Ringgold saying that Starr County officials would drop all charges if he would not return to southern Texas (Porter, *Paper Medicine Man*, 291). The telegram to which Porter refers only indicates that Bourke agreed to be transferred to the Columbian Exposition, but it says nothing about an arrangement with Starr County officials (Bourke Diary, Vol. 111, 20 Feb. 1893, p. 32).

175 Based on Conrad's novella, Francis Ford Coppola's *Apocalypse Now* demonstrates how the U.S. war in Cambodia and Vietnam led to similar moments of Kurtzian "lack of restraint."

176 O'Conner to Asst. Adj. Gen., 22 July 1893, in GRP, p. 3.

177 Ibid.

178 Ibid.

179 Ibid., 3–4.

180 J. P. Martin to Asst. Adj. Gen., 3 Aug. 1893, in GRP.

181 Conrad, *Heart of Darkness*, 101.

182 O'Conner to Asst. Adj. Gen., 9 Sept. 1893, in GRP, p. 1.

183 Ibid., 2.

184 The diversity of labels to mark "outsiders" and justify violence against them was also noted by Conrad. When Marlow is told by Kurtz's admirer that the heads on the spikes were those of rebels, he laughs and then remarks "Rebels! What would be the next definition I was to hear? There had been enemies, criminals, work-ers — and these were rebels" (Conrad, *Heart of Darkness*, 96).

185 O'Conner to Asst. Adj. Gen., 9 Sept. 1893, in GRP, p. 2.

186 Ibid., 2.

187 Ibid., 3.

188 Ibid., 6–7.

189 Ibid., 6.

190 Ibid.

191 Conrad, *Heart of Darkness*, 83–84.

192 In his diary, Bourke noted that Major Louis Morris, Captain Michael Etling, First Lieutenant Joseph Dickman, and Captain Francis Hardie joined him in putting down the Pullman strike (Bourke Diary, Vol. 113, p. 189).

193 Bourke Diary, Vol. 114, 27 July 1894, p. 36.

194 Bourke Diary, Vol. 114, 11 Aug. 1894, p. 9.

195 Davis, *The West from a Car-Window*, 243.

8. EXILE, DEATH, AND RESURRECTION
IN THE CARIBBEAN

1 "Garza Has Surely Gone," *Chronicle* (San Francisco), 12 Nov. 1891, in SRE, leg. 11-10-44, exp. 2.

2 In January 1893, when Garza was most likely still in Nassau, he was sighted at the head of a large party in Zavalla County ("Garza on Deck," *St. Louis Republic*, 11 Jan. 1893, in Bourke Diary, Vol. 110, p. 86).

3 J. S. McNeel to General W. H. Mabry, 21 Apr. 1892, in AGC, 401-23, f. 7–10. Garza to Alejandro González, Havana, Cuba, 5 Mar. 1892, in Garza Correspon-dence. This letter to his father-in-law was the first one written after he was in exile that remains in the collection of family letters.

4 One Ranger report places Garza near New Orleans as late as May 1892. Sgt. Roberson [?] to Mabry, 1 May 1892, AGC, 401-23, f. 11–15. Garza to Alejandro González, Havana, Cuba, 15 Mar. 1892, in Garza Correspondence.

5 "Pues sin tí, no creo estar contento, ni [en] el paraiso mismo." Garza to Con-cepción González de Garza (wife), Havana, Cuba, 15 Mar. 1892, in Garza Cor-respondence.

6 "Que si me niegue el más grande de los favores que le he pedido, sería lo mismo que matarme moralmente, pues no creo poder vivir contento en el destierro sin tí, esposa mia. Contigo al lado no sería un destierro para mí porque todas mis

ilusiones por mi Patria las recordaré al verte a mi lado." Garza to Concepción González de Garza (wife), Havana, Cuba, 15 Mar. 1892, in Garza Correspondence.

7 Garza to Alejandro González, Havana, Cuba, 15 Mar. 1892, in Garza Correspondence.

8 Garza to Concepción González de Garza (wife), Havana, Cuba, 15 Mar. 1892, in Garza Correspondence.

9 "Con grandísima satisfacción." " 'El revolucionario mexicano' 'antagonista del Gral. Dn. Porfirio Díaz' 'Cuenta solamente 32 años de edad.' Me acerque á la vidriera y casi inmóvil me quedé ante el retrato de mi acrivllada persona." "Sentí orgullo al verme distinguido por todas las clases sociales. Ya veremos el porvenir que nos espera." Garza to Alejandro González, Havana, Cuba, 15 Mar. 1892, in Garza Correspondence.

10 Garza to Concepción González de Garza (wife), Havana, Cuba, 15 Mar. 1892, in Garza Correspondence.

11 " 'Si nosotros tuvieramos un hombre del temple de ese insurgente mexicano Garza, tiempo ha que fueramos independientes. Garza — decía el doctor — ha desafiado la ira de dos gobiernos, las traiciones de muchos de sus compañeros, y en fin ha luchado con el heroismo de los espartanos.' " "Elevado a distinguidos puestos sociales." Garza to Concepción González de Garza (wife), en route to Nassau, 23 Mar. 1892, in Garza Correspondence, f. 5.

12 "Grotesco, brusco, poco cortes, y algunas veces hasta grosero." "Considera sus súbditos como obedientes esclavos y no hombres libres." Ibid., 24 Mar. 1892, f. 7.

13 "Poética, romántica y preciosa." "Contaré con todo el pueblo cubano obrero y mason, así como con la influencia de varios capitalistas." Ibid., 27–28 Mar. 1892, f. 9–11.

14 Ibid.

15 "Es una isla de mucha aglomeración de negro que sirve por dos pesos al mes." Garza to Alejandro González, Key West, 1 Apr. 1892, in Garza Correspondence, f. 1.

16 "Una de las poblaciones pequeñas más hermosas que yo he conocido." Garza to Concepción González de Garza (wife), en route to Key West, 30 Mar. 1892, in Garza Correspondence, f. 9.

17 "De estar privado de la vista de mi familia en el destierro y estarlo en campaña, prefiero estar en campaña y no el destierro." "Sin un solo centavo." Garza to Alejandro González, Key West, 1 Apr. 1892, in Garza Correspondence, f. 1–2.

18 Garza to Concepción González de Garza (wife), Key West, 30 Apr. 1892, in Garza Correspondence, f. 2–4. Riva Palacio wrote the prologue to one of Ignacio Martínez's travel books, *Viaje universal: Visita a las cinco partes del mundo* (New York: n.p., 1886).

19 Garza to Concepción González de Garza (wife), Key West, 14 Apr. 1892, in Garza Correspondence, f. 1.

20 Ibid., f. 1–3. Some people in South Texas today speak about Garza having reached the rank of thirty-second-degree Mason, but according to Garza's own letter, by April 1892 he had only reached the rank of eighteenth-degree Mason.

21   Garza to Concepción González de Garza (wife), Key West, 30 Apr. 1892, in Garza
      Correspondence, f. 2–4.
22   "Caótica." "Criminal internacional peligroso." The account, based on the testi-
      mony of Gerardo Castellanos y Lleonart, was published by his son in 1944; see
      Gerardo Castellanos G., *Misión a Cuba: Cayo Hueso y Martí* (Havana: Alfa,
      1944), 143–44. Special thanks to Laura Benson for finding this reference.
23   "Como un león enjaulado." Castellanos G., *Misión a Cuba*, 144–45.
24   Castellanos G., *Misión a Cuba*, 145. Another description of Garza in Key West
      can be found in Gerardo Castellanos G., *Motivos de Cayo Hueso (Contribución) a
      la historia de las emigraciones revolucionarias cubanas en Estados Unidos* (n.p.,
      1935), 280.
25   "Esperanza moral y financiera." Castellanos G., *Misión a Cuba*, 145. While still a
      young boy, Castellanos's son describes stumbling into this secret meeting and
      finding himself face to face with "el maestro," Martí. Martí gently took a news-
      paper from the boy, gave him a hug, and returned to the meeting (Castellanos G.,
      Motivos de Cayo Hueso, 280).
26   The trajectories and discourse of Martí and Garza is strikingly similar. The phrase
      "in the monster" is borrowed from Martí's famous letter to Manuel Mercado in
      which he says, "I lived in the monster, and know its entrails." The monster is, of
      course, the United States (José Martí to Manuel Mercado, Dos Ríos, 18 May
      1895, in *José Martí*, 347).
27   Philip S. Foner, "Introduction," in *Our America: Writings on Latin America and
      the Struggle for Cuban Independence* by José Martí (New York: Monthly Review
      Press, 1977), 39.
28   Donaldo Velasco, *Asalto de Bocas del Toro por el general Catarino Erasmo
      Garza, con su retrato; relación histórica* (Bogotá: Tip. Salesiana, 1896), 74–75.
      Velasco credits Garza's friendship with Maceo and other well-placed individuals
      with Garza's ability to secure recognition from the Costa Rican government. Al-
      though I have found no other evidence, it would not be unreasonable to suspect
      that Garza, who already knew Martí from Key West, would have met him again
      when he visited Maceo on two occasions in Puerto Limón, Costa Rica. Martí's
      visits to Costa Rica occurred on June 30, 1893, and on June 13, 1894, at the same
      time that Garza resided there. The Cuban insurrection began on February 24,
      1895, just a few weeks before Garza launched his attack on Panama.
29   Garza to Concepción González de Garza (wife), Havana, Cuba, 15 Mar. 1892, f.
      7, and Garza to Alejandro González, Havana, Cuba, 15 Mar. 1892, f. 3, both in
      Garza Correspondence.
30   "Miserable cobarde y traidor." "¡Desgraciado! Le va a costar lo que no se ima-
      gina." Garza to Concepción González de Garza (wife), Nassau, 1 Nov. 1892, in
      Garza Correspondence, f. 2–3.
31   Bourke Diary, Vol. 109, 21 Dec. 1892, p. 185–86.
32   "Reptil." Garza to Concepción González de Garza (wife), Nassau, 1 Nov. 1892, in
      Garza Correspondence, f. 3–7. Bourke Diary, Vol. 107, 2 Jan. 1892, f. 163–67.
33   "Mas en las últimas paginas de mi turbulenta y triste historia una traición secreta
      que me llega al alma; pero que por estar yo dotado por la Naturaleza de un cerebro

excepcional, no me ha dominado aun. Mi cerebro concibe ideas todavía más superiores que con las que se me traicion." Garza to Concepción González de Garza (wife), Nassau, 1 Nov. 1892, in Garza Correspondence, f. 3–7.

34 Garza to Concepción González de Garza (wife), Puerto Limón, 8 Feb. 1892, in Garza Correspondence, f. 1.

35 Garza to Concepción González de Garza (wife), Matina, 28 Mar. 1893, and Garza to Concepción González de Garza (wife), Matina, 29 Mar. 1893, f. 1, both in Garza Correspondence.

36 Garza to Concepción González de Garza (wife), Matina, 14 June 1893, in Garza Correspondence, f. 2–3,

37 "Se me aprecia, se me oye y se me consulta como si mi cabeza fuera una fuente pública en la que los pueblos de las naciones todas pudieran beber ó mitigar su sed." Garza to Alejandro and Mauricio González, Matina, 28 Mar. 1893, in Garza Correspondence, f. 1–5. Garza signed this letter with the various aliases he used in exile: Galeno; G. A. Cezar; and C. E. G.

38 "Un pico considerable." Garza to Concepción González de Garza (wife), Matina, 14 June 1893, in Garza Correspondence, f. 2–3.

39 "Que sepan apreciar los sacrificios de un patriota mexicano." Garza to Alejandro and Mauricio González, Matina, 28 Mar. 1893, in Garza Correspondence, f. 1–5. Garza signed this letter with the various aliases he used in exile: Galeno; G. A. Cezar; and C. E. G.

40 "Ratón de un agujero." "Oro molido." Garza to Encarnacíon Garza, Matina, 26 Apr. 1893, in Garza Correspondence, f. 1–3.

41 For the records of González's sales to the King ranch, see Montejano, *Anglos and Mexicans*, 65–66. Carlos Pérez, Garza's grandson, suggested that some family members blamed Catarino for the land loss, but he contended that the sale of Alejandro González's land happened in 1906, years after Catarino had been killed (Carlos Pérez, interview with author, Alice, Texas, 26 July 1999). One member of the González family has indicated that Alejandro lost up to 32,000 acres on account of Catarino (Homero Vera, electronic communication, 16 Aug. 2000).

42 "Reponer en un año la perdida de diez años." Garza to Encarnación Garza, Matina, 26 Apr. 1893, in Garza Correspondence, f. 1–3.

43 "Mis esperanzas no se evaporan con el sol de los trópicos porque he sido y seré levantado en mis empresas y pensamientos." Garza to Concepción González de Garza (wife), Matina, 21 June 1893, in Garza Correspondence, f. 1.

44 "Yo no volveré a Texas aunque me arreglaran mil asuntos—jamás volveré y el dia que vuelva será á mi patria, pero nunca mas á Texas." Garza to Concepción de Garza (wife), Matina, 29 Mar. 1893, in Garza Correspondence, f. 3.

45 "Ir de vuelta a Texas para comprometer a todo mundo." "No puedo estar desterrado y olvidado de todos, pues mas vale acabar de una vez." Garza to Concepción González de Garza (wife), Limón, 1 Nov. 1893, in Garza Correspondence, f. 1–2.

46 "Tengo hambre, sed y etc. de verlas." "Entonces . . . no se que haría." Garza to Concepción González de Garza (wife), Matina, 28 March 1893, in Garza Correspondence, f. 3–4.

47 "Es pesada porque no tengo a mi lado los queridos seres que serán los unicos que

en lo sucesivo refrenen mis ímpetus políticos." "En verdad, ya es tiempo de vernos y no escribirnos." Garza to Concepción González de Garza (wife), Matina, 14 June 1893, in Garza Correspondence, f. 1, 4.

48 "Espero que tú, con llana franqueza me digas que determinación tienen respecto a tu viaje y a la imprenta. Si continuan poniendo obstaculos, te suplico no vuelvas a decirles nada más á mi nombre." Garza to Concepción González de Garza (wife), Limón, 31 Jan. 1894, in Garza Correspondence, f. 4.

49 In the two letters from Garza to Alejandro González up to that point, 1 Apr. 1892 and 28 Mar. 1893, Garza complained that he had not received any news from him.

50 "Me prohibió escribirle y hasta mencionar su nombre." "Ahora ya no hay peligro—no habrá pretextos para dejarnos de escribir." "Nada le recomiendo, pues ya son tantas las recomendaciones o súplicas que les he hecho que ya estoy bien decepcionado y perdone mi franqueza." Garza to Alejandro González, Limón, 4 Apr. 1894, in Garza Correspondence, f. 1-2.

51 "Para levanter el espíritu de los pueblos fronterizos. ¡Ah! Mi segunda aparición en la Frontera de Chihuahua causaría un pánico extraordinario." Garza to Alejandro González, Limón, 24 Apr. 1894, in Garza Correspondence, f. 1-3.

52 "Los hombres que no insisten con energia en una causa no son hombres." "Que yo voy a jugar mi vida por el porvenir de todos nosotros." "Mi cerebro se exacerba y se irrita mi sangre bélica." Garza to Alejandro González, Limón, 24 Apr. 1894, in Garza Correspondence, f. 4-6.

53 "Con el valor potente de espartanos." "Por miedo al despota ó temor al *hombre*." Garza to Concepción González de Garza (wife), Limón, 13 Mar. 1892, in Garza Correspondence, f. 1.

54 "Los buenos amigos son más escasos que los garvanzos [*sic*] de a libra." Garza to Hesiquio González, Key West, 12 Apr. 1892, in Garza Correspondence, f. 4.

55 "Si no han de venir avisénmelo, porque yo no puedo estar sin comprometerme en alguna campaña, en el supuesto que ni la excusa de familia tengo." "Para continuar la obra empezada, sea necesario ayudar otros pueblos primero, para que despues me ayuden a mi." "Digame que han acordado; no puedo estar sin determinarme a algo grande: ¿no hay viaje? ¿no hay imprenta? Nada parece." Garza to Concepción González de Garza (wife), Limón, 13 June 1894, in Garza Correspondence, f. 1-3.

56 Presidential Decree No. 80, San Jose, 30 Sept. 1893, in Garza Correspondence.

57 "En los grandes centros, en los ministerios, en las logias, y demas círculos de prestigio saben que soy C. E. Garza." "Mexicano que es enemigo de los *yankees*." Garza to Concepción González de Garza (wife), Limón, 31 Jan. 1894, in Garza Correspondence, f. 1.

58 "Ya aquí no hay ningun peligro, ya soy Garza puro." Garza to Concepción González de Garza (wife), Limón, 7 Mar. 1894, in Garza Correspondence, f. 1-2.

59 Garza to Concepción González de Garza (wife), Limón, 7 Mar. 1894, in Garza Correspondence, f. 2-3

60 Garza to Concepción González de Garza (wife), Limón, 13 June 1894, in Garza Correspondence, f. 1. Although the Costa Rican government rejected Mexico's extradition request at this point, they later acceded to the request when it came from the

United States. Corroborating Garza's account, Velasco argues that by March 1895, the Costa Ricans were prepared to hand over Garza to the Mexican authorities (Velasco, *Asalto de Bocas del Toro*, 49). I was, however, unable to locate any trace of the extradition communications in the Costa Rican national archive.

61 "Como hombre de ideas universalistas que soy, mi espada está siempre a la disposición de los pueblos que gimen con el pesado yugo de las tiranias, no importa de la nacionalidad que sean." Garza to Concepción González de Garza (wife), Limón, 31 Jan. 1894, in Garza Correspondence, f. 3.

62 "Tengo la última consciencia de que con mi carácter ó con mi palabra, atraigo las masas populares y me coloco en círculos distinguidos." Garza to Concepción González de Garza (wife), Limón, 31 Jan. 1894, in Garza Correspondence, f. 2.

63 "Jesus Cristo fue el primer demócrata que murió en el cadalzo para redimirnos como libres y nos dejó sus doctrinas liberales para que nunca las profanemos." Garza to Concepción González de Garza (wife), Limón, 1 Jan. 1895, in Garza Correspondence, f. 3.

64 "Correrá en breve tiempo la sangre de los mártires." Garza to Concepción González de Garza (wife), Limón, 26 June 1894, in Garza Correspondence, f. 1.

65 Garza to Concepción González de Garza (wife), Limón, 13 June 1894, f. 3, 15 Mar. 1892, f. 6, 1 Apr. 1892, f. 1, Nov. 1893, f. 1, in Garza Correspondence, f.

66 "Santas causas." "Otros pueblos, quizá extraños elevaran pensamiento para immortalizar un tanto cuanto la memoria del hombre que hace bien a la colectividad opresa." Garza to Alejandro González, Limón, 4 Apr. 1894, in Garza Correspondence, f. 1–2.

67 "Que tu desterrado y perseguido esposo viva unos cuantos años, pues yo presiento cuando remonto mis ideales políticos, de que seré el llamado a derrocar el Trono de Porfirio Díaz." Garza to Concepción González de Garza (wife), Limón, 13 June 1894, in Garza Correspondence, f. 2.

68 "El nombre de Garza encarna el principio de regeneración político-social mexicana; ese nombre ha llenado estas atmósferas de ambiente libre, de brisa democrática." Garza to Encarnación Garza, Limón, 12 July 1894, in Garza Correspondence, f. 1.

69 "La prensa de todas las naciones dé Continente Americano levantarán su voz en pro de Garza." Garza to Encarnación Garza, Limón, 7 Aug. 1894, in Garza Correspondence, f. 2.

70 "El emblema regenerador." "Garcistas quiere decir 'libres' y Porfiristas significa esclavos abyectos." Garza to Encarnación Garza, Limón, 12 Dec. 1894, in Garza Correspondence, f. 2–3.

71 Garza to Concepción González de Garza (wife), Limón, 13 June 1894, in Garza Correspondence, f. 1.

72 "Nunca he tenido la loca ambición de gobernar en mi patria, pues comprendo que México necesita gobernantes de talla muy superior á la talla humilde de mi personalidad." Garza, *La era de Tuxtepec*, 30.

73 "Circule entre los que me juzgan muerto en lo moral y en lo político." Garza to Concepción González de Garza (wife), Limón, 15 August 1894, in Garza Correspondence, f. 1.

74 "Para que no fenezcan conmigo los juicios, que respecto de su vitalicia Tiranía ó su Indefinida Dictadura, tiene su indispensable y constante enemigo político." Inscription in *La era de Tuxtepec* can be found in the copy of the pamphlet in the Latin American Library, Tulane University.

75 Garza to Concepción González de Garza, Limón, 27 Sept. 1894, f. 3, and 15 Oct. 1894, f. 2, both in Garza Correspondence.

76 "Algo honrado." "De más canalla." Garza, *La era de Tuxtepec*, 7–9.

77 Ibid., 13, 17.

78 "Mátalos en caliente." Ibid., 21, 20–26.

79 "Espontánea." "Hombres honrados." Ibid., 27. U.S. Army reports at the end of May 1893 indicate that around 130 men had been tried and convicted of violating neutrality laws, not the number claimed by Garza of over 600. I have found no evidence that any of these men were absolved by the district attorney, as Garza contended.

80 "$300,000 reward," *Harper's Weekly*, 23 Jan. 1892, p. 93; Garza, *La era de Tuxtepec*, 28.

81 Garza, *La era de Tuxtepec*, 29.

82 "Conflicto internacional." "Soy revolucionario de buena ley y no un bandido facineroso." Ibid., 32.

83 "El que fusiló sin piedad cuando revolucionaba, si él que nunca pagó un solo centavo de lo que consumía su ejército, si él que incendiaba poblaciones y puentes de ferrocarriles, ó yo que pagué hasta la pastura de mi caballada, que no fusilé jamás á nadie, . . . si yo que jamás secuestré á nadie, ni violé ninguno de los derechos del ciudadano, si yo que jamás dispuse de los elementos del Gobierno?" Ibid., 26.

84 "Soy revolucionario en México, enemigo acérrimo de los tiranos y enemigo también de los americanos que sueñan en la Baja California y en la anexión de los Estados fronterizos de México." Ibid., 32

85 "Uno ú otro que sea, aquí estoy, dispuesto al sacrificio de mi vida en pro de la causa que defiendo y defenderé." Ibid.

86 "Rechazara tal pretensión de los *yankees* y Díaz." Garza to Concepción González de Garza (wife), Limón, 7 Aug. 1894, in Garza Correspondence, f. 1–2.

87 "Garza era el mexicano de ideas mas avanzadas que conocian—que Garza no solamente pertenecía a México sino á toda la américa." "Garza es hombre de armas, tribuna y letras: en lo primero es un genio, en lo segundo un huracan y en lo tercero una metralla ó dinamita." "Muy buena champagne" "No quiero suicidarme todavía, quiero vivir un poco mas para poner en desordenados movimientos a mexicanos y americanos." "Ni por milliones de pesos." Garza to Concepción González de Garza (wife), Limón, 19 Sept. 1894, in Garza Correspondence, f. 1–3.

88 "Porque en este país hasta los negros mas ordinarios me quieren y me rinden homenaje." "Las masas todas populares." "Estoy seguro que tu te hubieras enamorado de Garza—Verdad?—Ca . . . ramba— . . .—a las muchachas se les hizo la boca agua. No te enceles—pues sabes tu bien que soy muy honrado." Garza to Concepción González de Garza (wife), Limón, 19 Sept. 1894, in Garza Correspondence, f. 4–5.

89 Garza to Encarnación Garza, Limón, 12 July 1894, in Garza Correspondence, f. 1.

90 "Están despertando con mis cartas." "Un rico empresario americano." Garza to Concepción González de Garza (wife), Limón, 12 Sept. 1894, in Garza Correspondence, f. 1–2.

91 "Habla con las personas de más prestigio y diles que les garantizo estar al frente de ellos cuando lo quieran." "Tengo la fe ciega de que si aparezco por allá de nuevo los pueblos todos abrazarán la causa con verdadero entusiasmo." Garza to Encarnación Garza, Limón, 12 July 1894, in Garza Correspondence, f. 1–2.

92 Ornelas to Reyes, 14 Feb. 1895, in SRE, leg. 9-1-45, f. 309.

93 "Derrocar al Tirano para levantar un representante popular qu merezca llamarse Presidente Constitucional." "Mis únicas ambiciones, mis solos ensueños es libertar mis pueblos de la Tiranía inicua que reina en México." Garza to Encarnación Garza, Limón, 20 Sept. 1894, in Garza Correspondence, f. 2–3.

94 "Lacónico." "Muy amada esposa." "Proclamas de animación y sentencias de esperanzas." "De un enano a un gigante." Garza to Concepción González de Garza, Limón, 21 Nov. 1894, in Garza Correspondence, f. 1–2.

95 "Humildad de mi cuna." "Suficiente energía." "Las cadenas que cargue y los grillos, de las privaciones y los atentados de asesinato." He estimated that in Central and South America the book would sell at least one hundred thousand copies. Garza to Concepción González de Garza, Limón, 21 and 22 Nov. 1894, in Garza Correspondence, f. 3–5.

96 Garza to Concepción González de Garza (wife), Limón, 29 Nov. 1894, f. 2; Garza to Encarnación Garza, Limón, 20 Dec. 1894, f. 1–5, both in Garza Correspondence.

97 "Ya la hora se acerca." Garza to Encarnación Garza, Limón, 20 Dec. 1894, in Garza Correspondence, f. 1–5.

98 Garza to Concepción González de Garza (wife), Limón, 24 Dec. 1894, in Garza Correspondence, f. 1.

99 "La cosa es seria y el pellejo va de por medio." "En esta vez tengo fundadas esperanzas de llegar al Capitolio con mi espada en guardia, desafiando los tiranos." "No pierdas la fe ni la esperanza, pronto nos veremos y tal vez para no volvernos a separar nunca." Garza to Concepción González de Garza, Limón, 1 Jan. 1895, in Garza Correspondence, f. 2–4.

100 "Las tres tiranías inicuas de nuestros paises." "¡Ah! Estúpido; se pondrá alerta y hará que sus esbirros se pongan en desordenadas carreras buscando a Garza, pero yo cojeré un rumbo opuesto." Garza to Concepción González de Garza, Limón, 23 Jan 1895, in Garza Correspondence, f. 1–3.

101 "!Adelante! El terror hay que infundírselos a los tiranos." Garza to Concepción González de Garza, Limón, 5 Feb. 1895, in Garza Correspondence, f. 1,

102 "Vivo ó muerto." Garza to Concepción González de Garza, San Juan del Norte, 20 Feb. 1895, in Garza Correspondence, f. 1–2.

103 "Fue milagro que en alta mar no se la tragara un caiman." "Un buque magnífico." Garza to Concepción González de Garza, San Juan del Norte, 20 Feb. 1895, in Garza Correspondence, f. 2. Garza told his wife that he was heading south to the port of Barranquila, on the Caribbean coast of Colombia. He ul-

timately ended up stopping first on the Costa Rican coast, and then launching his first attack in Panama.

104 There is surprisingly little information on Garza in the Costa Rican national archive, but I found one folder in the war department section relating to his rebel camp in Cahuita, and especially to Garza's collaboration with Miguel Angel Salazar (Archivo Nacional de Costa Rica, Secretaria de Guerra, doc. 2949).

105 "Extractos de dos cartas procedentes de Puerto Limón," 6 Mar. 1895 and 13 Mar. 1895, in SRE, leg. 9-1-45, f. 399–400. It is not clear who wrote these letters because only the extracts have been copied. The original English-language extracts can be found in the foreign ministry archive in Mexico City. The March 6 letter gives the number of Garza's men as 250, while the letter dated March 13 puts the number, probably more accurately, at 40.

106 "¡Miserables cobardes! El caso fué de que la garza batió sus alas enmedio de los inicuos cazadores que pretendieron matarla." Garza to Concepción González de Garza, San Juan del Norte, 20 Feb. 1895, in Garza Correspondence, f. 1–3.

107 "Llegó el momento, Chonita mia, de luchar cuerpo a cuerpo en pro de las liber-tades de un pueblo hermano, que despues me ayudará á libertar el mio, ó levantar en mi tumba un símbolo de recuerdo." " 'Ser ó no ser' — Estoy resuelto á luchar como león para probarles á los esbirros de la américa latina tienen ó tendrán razón para temblar cobardes ante mi brazo que empuña la regeneradora espada Americana continental." "Por fin llegó el momento de estar en campaña y llevo ante el enemigo fijo el pensamiento en ti." "Un abrazo amoroso y adios mi adorada Chonita. Tuyo Siempre, C. E. Garza." Garza to Concepción González de Garza, San Juan del Norte, 20 Feb. 1895, in Garza Correspondence, f. 2–4.

108 "Querido y siempre recordado esposo. Esta es con el fin de saludarte y decirte que por á quí todos estamos buenos deaseandote mil felicidades." "Un silencio profundo." "Amelia temanda muchos becitos." Concepción González de Garza to Catarino Garza, Palito Blanco, 4 Mar. 1895, in Garza Correspondence, f. 1–2. As elsewhere, I have preserved the orthography and misspellings that occur in the original letter.

109 Letter from Comandante Guerrero in *Times Democrat*, as cited by Velasco, *Asalto de Bocas del Toro*, 34. The Mexican consul in Havana also warned the Mexican government that Garza had set sail on an armed boat and was probably heading to Colombia but could have been going to Mexico (A. C. Vasquez to Rel. Ext., 7 Mar. 1895, in SRE, leg. 11-10-44, part 9, f. 96).

110 "Garza in Colombia," *New York Herald*, 6 Mar. 1895, in SRE, leg. 11-10-44, part 9, f. 69.

111 Romero to Sec. Rel. Ext., 6 Mar. 1895, in SRE, leg. 11-10-44, part 9, f. 68.

112 "Sailing of the Atlanta," *San Francisco Examiner*, 8 Mar. 1895, p. 1, c. 4.

113 "Ha sido o va a ser atacada en una de estas noches." Velasco, *Asalto de Bocas del Toro*, 35.

114 Ibid., 36–37.

115 Ibid.; Mexican Consul to Sec. Rel. Ext., Panama, Colombia, 11 Mar. 1895, in SRE, leg. 11-10-44, part 9, f. 101. For another announcement of Garza's death,

see "Catarino Garza Dead," *Weekly Caller* (Corpus Christi), 15 Mar. 1895, in SRE, leg. 11-10-44, exp. 9, f. 107.

116 "León." "Espíritu caballeresco marcado." Velasco, *Asalto de Bocas del Toro*, 75. While the lack of references makes it impossible to determine the source for particular pieces of information, it appears that detailed information about the rebels, including conversations had in the middle of the night prior to the attack, came from interrogations of prisoners after the insurrection had been crushed.

117 Velasco, *Asalto de Bocas del Toro*, 74–75.

118 Ibid., 71. The Atlantic coast of Nicaragua had historically been at odds with the government on the Pacific coast. The Spanish-speaking side of the country on the Pacific has tended to dominate the English-speaking Atlantic coast. This antagonism reemerged with the Miskito Indians on the Atlantic Coast joining the Contras in their struggle against the Sandinista Revolution in the 1980s. For an in-depth analysis of the racial and political antagonisms between the two Nicagaraguan coasts, see Charles R. Hale, *Resistance and Contradiction: Miskitu and the Nicaraguan State, 1894–1987* (Stanford: Stanford University Press, 1996).

119 Velasco, *Asalto de Bocas del Toro*, 71, 44–45, 67. British and Spanish diplomats in Guatemala had also received reports that residents of Guatemala had fought with the Colombian liberals (as reported by José F. Godoy to Rel. Ext., 13 Mar. 1895, in SRE, leg. 11-10-44, part 9, f. 109).

120 Jesús María Henao and Gerrardo Arrubla, *Historia de Colombia*, Vol. 2 (Bogotá: Plaza and Janes, 1984), 337. Although the government ultimately crushed the 1895 "revolution" by mid-March, such a public display of opposition demonstrated the weakness and vulnerability of the Colombian conservatives (338).

121 "Morir luchando o morir entregado al Gobierno mejicano, si eran apresados del vaporcito." Velaco, *Asalto de Bocas del Toro*, 49.

122 "Sepulcral silencio." Ibid., 50–52, 57–58.

123 Ibid., 59–61.

124 "Extractos de dos cartas procedentes de Puerto Limón," 13 Mar. 1895, in SRE, leg. 9-1-45, f. 399–400.

125 "Elasticidad de la pantera." "No es nada." "This brut shot too high!" Ibid., 60–63. Perhaps Garza used English to communicate with his Jamaican and Atlantic coast Nicaraguan comrades.

126 Velasco, *Asalto de Bocas del Toro*, 61, 64–69. According to another source, Garza and eighteen of his men were killed, eight to ten escaped, and the rest were captured ("Extractos de dos cartas procedentes de Puerto Limón," 13 Mar. 1895, in SRE, leg. 9-1-45, f. 399–400).

127 "Mirada fija y penetrante, frente despejada y de notable hermosura y sus manos recogidas como el gladiador en actitud de combate." "Aun después de muerto inspiraba respeto." Ibid., 76. The letters, photographs, and his watch were apparently sent to the governor of Panama.

128 Ibid., 71.

129 "Extractos de dos cartas procedentes de Puerto Limón," 13 Mar. 1895, in SRE, leg. 9-1-45, f. 400.

130 "Pasaba largas noches de insomnio con este pretendiente tenaz." Velasco, *Asalto de Bocas del Toro*, 73–74.

131 "Extrangero invasor del Norte." Garza to Vidal Canales, Limón, 7 Aug. 1894, in Garza Correspondence, f. 1.

132 "Battle in Colombia," *San Francisco Examiner*, 11 Mar. 1895, p. 3, c. 5.

133 "Troops Landed," *Evening Star*, 11 Mar. 1895, in SRE, leg. 11-10-44, part 9, f. 104.

134 "Proclaim Martial Law," *San Francisco Examiner*, 13 Mar. 1895, p. 4, c. 4.

135 "Troops Landed," *Evening Star*, 11 Mar. 1895, in SRE, leg. 11-10-44, part 9, f. 104.

136 "Extractos de dos cartas procedentes de Puerto Limón," in SRE, leg. 9-1-45, f. 400.

137 In 1978, the U.S. Senate ratified a new Panama Canal Treaty between U.S. President Jimmy Carter and Panamanian President Omar Torrijos, in which the United States agreed to cede control over the canal to Panama in the year 2000.

138 "Mi desaparición ó mi muerte no constituía la muerte de la santa causa que defendí y defenderé mientras viva." Garza, *La era de Tuxtepec*, 28.

139 A. C. Vasquez to Sec. Rel. Ext., Havana, 16 Oct. 1895, in SRE, leg. 11-10-44, part 9, f. 120–23.

140 "El Mejicano es muy valiente, muy hábil y extraordinariamente audaz. Se le reputa como un jefe de primer orden." Ibid., f. 121.

141 "Enemigo ofuscado de la tranquilidad y progreso de su patria." "Instrucciones concretas." "Viendo en ál a un compatriota, antes que a un enemigo del orden, en la nacion Mexicana." Ibid., f. 122–23.

142 "Parece que Garza no murió como se decía; sino por el contrario esta rebosando vida y dispuesto más que nunca a mostrar su carácter turbulento y batallador." "Prensa Extranjera: Catarino Garza en la guerra de Cuba," *La Discusión*, 9 Dec. 1895, in SRE, leg. 11-10-44, part 9, f. 127; *La Discusión*, 18 Nov. 1895, as cited by Vasquez to Rel. Ext., in SRE, leg. 11-10-44, part 9, f. 125.

143 Grimm, *Llanos Mesteñas*, 145.

144 "Estar en Cuba vivo y sano, peleando en la filas de los patriotas cubanos." *Las Dos Naciones*, 18 Nov. 1895, as cited by Vasquez to Rel. Ext., in SRE, leg. 11-10-44, part 9, f. 129. It is possible, given the delays in transportation and mail service, that Garza's wife received his letters months after he was killed. The last letter Garza's family has is dated 20 February 1895, more than two weeks before he was killed in Bocas del Toro.

EPILOGUE

1 The late Américo Paredes dedicated *With His Pistol in His Hand* to "the memory of my father/who rode a raid or two with Catarino Garza."

2 Knight, *Mexican Revolution*, Vol. 1, 95. Alonso, *Thread of Blood*, 127.

3 The price of public land in Chihuahua rose from about $1.50 per hectare in 1896, and then rose precipitously after the introduction of the first railroad, reaching $8 by 1908 (Wasserman, *Capitalists, Caciques, and Revolution*, 109–10).

4 For an interesting analysis of how the old Porfirian Chihuahua elite was able to maintain its power and wealth through the 1910 revolution, see Wasserman, *Persistent Oligarchs*. For a majestic account of the entire revolutionary process, see Knight, *The Mexican Revolution*.

5 In 1898, prominent Laredoans attempted to reverse the emphasis on Mexican holidays by launching a spectacular celebration of Washington's Birthday. To this day the Washington's Birthday celebration remains by far the largest and most important festivity in Laredo. See Elliott Young, "Red Men, Pocahontas, and George Washington: Harmonizing Race Relations in Laredo at the Turn of the Century," *Western Historical Quarterly* 29 (spring 1998): 48–85.

6 Bourke to Asst. Adj. Gen. 24 Dec. 1892, in GRP, f. 2.

7 For a full-length study, see Anders, *Boss Rule in South Texas*, 283.

8 Sandos, *Rebellion in the Borderlands*, 64.

9 Ibid., 79–96; "Plan de San Diego," in *US-Mexico Borderlands*, ed. Martínez, 139–41.

10 There is a wide range in the number of Mexicans killed, and given the extrajudicial manner of these executions we will never have an accurate body count. Montejano cites Walter Prescott Webb's figure of five hundred to five thousand, while Frank Pierce puts the number of summary killings at between one hundred and three hundred (Montejano, *Mexicans and Anglos*, 125; Frank C. Pierce, *Texas' Last Frontier: A Brief History of the Lower Rio Grande Valley* [Menasha, Wisc.: Banta, 1917; reprinted Rio Grande Historical Society, 1962], 103).

11 Emilio C. Forto "Actual Situation on the River Rio Grande: Information Rendered to Colonel H. J. Slocum of the American Forces at Brownsville," *Pan American Labor Press*, 11 Sept. 1918, as cited in Montejano, *Angelos and Mexicans*, 127.

12 Dunn, *Militarization of the U.S.-Mexico Border*, 12–13.

13 British secret agents claimed that Germans smuggled arms to Villa in coffins and oil tankers from the U.S. arms factories they owned. The head of the Mexican desk at the German foreign office recommended covertly sending arms and ammunition to Villa in March 1916 (Archiv de Auswartiges Amts, Bonn, Mexico I, vol. 56, Montgelas memorandum, 23 Mar. 1916, as cited in Katz, *Pancho Villa*, 662–63).

14 Hall, *Revolution on the Border*, 26–27.

15 Canales briefly mentions the Garza revolt in his "Personal Recollections" and indicates that he "followed the developments of this Revolution closely" (José T. Canales, "Personal Recollections of J. T. Canales," typescript, 1945, Canales, Joe T.," Vertical File, CAH). Thanks to Richard Ribb for locating this reference to Garza. For more on Canales, see Richard H. Ribb, "José Tomás Canales and the Texas Rangers: Myth, Identity, and Power in South Texas, 1900–1920," Ph.D. diss., University of Texas, Austin, 2001. See also "Canales, Jose Tomas," *The Handbook of Texas Online*, http://www.tsha.utexas.edu/handbook/online/articles/view/CC/fcaag.html.

16 Los Invasores de Nuevo León, "Los Super Capos," as cited by Elijah Wald, *Narcocorrido: A Journey into the Music of Drugs, Guns, and Guerillas* (New York: HarperCollins, 2001), 41–42.

17　In 1994, remittances to Mexico totaled $3.7 billion, a number that has certainly increased in subsequent years. See David E. Lorey, *The U.S.-Mexican Border in the Twentieth Century* (Wilmington, Del.: Scholarly Resources, 1999), 139. While Mexicans are not allowed to vote abroad and cannot hold dual citizenship, there are several proposals in Congress to enfranchise Mexicans in the United States. See Pam Belluck, "Mexican Presidential Candidates Campaign in US," 1 July 2000, *New York Times*, A3.

18　Garza to Vidal Canales, Limón, 7 Aug. 1894, in Garza Correspondence, f. 1.

BIBLIOGRAPHY

ARCHIVAL SOURCES

ABR: Archivo de Bernardo Reyes, Fondo DLI, Centro de Estudios de Historia de México, CONDUMEX, Mexico City. (The collection is divided in two sections: the *copiadores*, where copies of letters sent to Reyes are noted by "cop.," followed by the document number, whereas the second section, which includes letters sent to Reyes, is referred to with just the document number.)

AGC: Texas State Archives. Adjutant General's Records. General Correspondence.

AGN: Archivo General de la Nacion. Hemeroteca. Mexico City.

AMR: Archivo de Matías Romero, Banco de México. Microfilm copy at the Benson Latin American Collection, University of Texas, Austin.

BLAC: Benson Latin American Collection. University of Texas, Austin.

BN: Hemeroteca del Fondo Reservado. Biblioteca Nacional. Universidad Nacional Autónoma de México. Mexico City.

Bourke Diary: United States Military Academy Library, West Point, New York, John Gregory Bourke Diary, 1872–1896.

CAH: Center for American History. University of Texas, Austin.

Coalson Collection. South Texas Archive. Texas A&M, Kingsville, Texas

CPD: Colección de Porfirio Díaz. Universidad Iberoamericana, Mexico City.

DNL: National Archives, Washington, D.C. General Records of the Department of State. RG 59. "Despatches from United States Consular Officials in Nuevo Laredo, Mexico, 1871–1906." Microcopy no. 280. Roll 2.

Garza Correspondence. Pérez Family Private Collection, Alice, Texas.

GRP: National Archives, Washington, D.C. Records of U.S. Army. RG 393. Garza Revolution Papers.

Hogg Papers: Governor James S. Hogg Papers. Texas State Archives. Austin.

NA: National Archives. Washington, D.C.

SRE: Archivo Histórico de la Secretaría de Relaciones Exteriores de México.

TSA: Texas State Archives, Austin.

UANL: Capilla Alfonsina, Universidad Autónoma ele Nuevo León. Monterrey.

USMA: United States Military Academy, West Point, New York.

PERIODICALS

Aransas Beacon
Boston Herald
Brownsville Times
Cattleman
Chaparral, Laredo, Texas
Chicago Times
Corpus Christi Weekly Caller
Courier
Daily Herald (Brownsville)
Diario de la Marina, Havana, Cubua
Don Pacasio
El Bien Público, Brownsville, Texas
El Chinaco, Laredo, Texas
El Comercio Mexicano, Eagle Pass and Corpus Christi, Texas
El Correo de Laredo, Laredo, Texas
El Cromo
El Cronista Mexicano, San Antonio, Texas
El Defensor del Obrero, Laredo, Texas
El Demócrata Fronterizo, Laredo, Texas
El Diablo Predicador, Texas
El Diario del Hogar
El Duende
El Espectador, Monterrey, Nuevo León
El Ferrocarrilero, Mexico City
El Financiero
El Heraldo
El Imparcial
Gate City, Laredo, Texas
Mexican Developer Illustrated
El Internacional, Palito Blanco, Texas
El Libre Pensador, Corpus Christi and Laredo, Texas
El Mundo, Brownsville and Laredo, Texas
El Pendón Coahuilense, Saltillo, Coahuila
El Progresista. Ciudad Victoria, Tamaulipas
El Trueno, Linares, Nuevo León
El Universal
Evening Star (Washington)
Evening Star
Evening Telegraph
Fort Worth Gazette
Harper's Weekly
La Colonia Mexicana, Laredo, Texas
La Crónica, Laredo, Texas

La Defensa, Monterrey, Nuevo León
La Discusión, Havana, Cuba
La Frontera
La Palanca, Laredo, Texas
La Revista del Norte, Matamoros, Tamaulipas
La Revista Mexicana, St. Louis, Missouri
La Voz de Linares
La Voz de Nuevo León, Monterrey, Nuevo León
Laredo Times, Laredo, Texas
Los Angeles Herald
Los Dos Naciones, St. Louis, Missouri
Mexican Herald
Mexico Star
Milwaukee Journal
New York Herald
New York Times
North American Review
Omaha Bee
Pioneer Magazine
Saint Louis Globe Democrat
San Antonio Express
San Francisco Call
San Francisco Chronicle
San Francisco Examiner
Scribner's, New York
St. Louis Republic
Tucson Star
Washington Post

PRIMARY SOURCES

Alessio Robles, Vito. *La convención revoluciónaria de Aguascalientes.* Mexico: INEHRM, 1979.

Argüelles, Pedro. *La zona libre.* Nuevo Laredo: Tip. de A. Cueva y Hno., 1890.

Bennett, Norman R., ed. *Stanley's Despatches to the New York Herald, 1871–1872, 1874–1877.* Boston: Boston University Press, 1970.

Bourke, John G. "An American Congo." *Scribner's* (May 1894): 590–610.

——. *Our Neutrality Laws* (Fort Ethan Allen, Vt.: privately printed [1895 or 1896].

——. "Popular Medicine, Customs, and Superstitions of the Rio Grande." *Journal of American Folklore* 7 (April–June 1894): 119–46.

——. *Scatalogic Rites of All Nations.* New York: American Anthropological Society, 1934 [1891].

Chatfield, W. H. *The Twin Cities of the Border and the Country of the Lower Rio Grande Valley.* New Orleans: E. P. Brandao, 1893. Reprint, Brownsville: Harbert Davenport Memorial Fund, 1959.

Davis, Richard Harding. *The West from a Car-Window*. New York: Harpers and Brothers, 1903 [1892].

Description of Laredo, Texas: The Acknowledged Gateway between the Two Republics. Laredo: Gate City Printing House, 1888.

Garza, Catarino E. *La era de Tuxtepec en México: O sea Rusía en América*. San José, Costa Rica: Imprenta Comercial, 1894.

——. "La lógica de los hechos: O sean observaciones sobre las circunstancias de los mexicanos en Texas, desde el año de 1877 hasta 1889." Benson Latin American Collection. Garza Papers 1859–95. Misc. no. 73.

Garza Guajardo, Celso, ed. *En busca de Catarino Garza*. Monterrey, Mexico: Universidad Autónoma de Nuevo León, 1989.

General Directory of the City of Laredo, 1889. San Antonio: Maverick Printing House, 1889.

General Laws of the State of Texas, 22nd Leg. 1891. Austin: Henry Hutchings State Printer, 1891.

Harrison, Benjamin. *Public Papers and Addresses of Benjamin Harrison: Twenty-Third President of the United States, March 4, 1889, to March 4, 1893*. Washington, D.C.: Government Printing Office, 1893.

Martínez, Ignacio. *Viaje universal: Visita a las cinco partes del mundo*. New York: José Molina, 1886.

——. *Recuerdos de un viaje en América, Europa y Africa*. Paris: Lib. de P. Bregi, 1884.

Martínez, Oscar J., ed. "Treaty of Guadalupe Hidalgo." In *U.S.-Mexico Borderlands: Historical and Contemporary Perspectives*. Wilmington, Del.: Scholarly Resources, 1996.

Memorias del estado de Nuevo León. Monterrey, Mexico: n.p., 1885–1910.

Mexican Night: The Toasts and Responses at a Complementary Dinner Given by Walter S. Logan at the Democratic Club, New York City, December 16, 1891. New York: Albert B. King, 1892.

Pierce, Frank C. *Texas' Last Frontier: A Brief History of the Lower Rio Grande Valley*. Menasha, Wisc.: Banta, 1917. Reprint, Rio Grande Historical Society, 1962.

Poblacion de Nuevo León: desde 1603 hasta 1921. Mexico: Departamento de la Estadistica Nacional, 1929.

Primer Congreso Mexicanista, verificado en Laredo, Texas, EEUU de A. Los dias 14 al 22 de Septiembre de 1911. Laredo: Tip. De N. Idar, 1912.

Rasgos biográficos del general y doctor Ignacio Martínez: Asesinado alevosamente en esta población el martes 3 de febrero del presente año entre 9 y 10 de la mañana. Laredo: Tip. El Mundo, 1891.

Récio, Jesus T., ed. *El Bién Público: La guerra contra la paz ó un nuevo atila*. Rio Grande City: Imprenta Jesus T. Recio, 1895.

Reports of the Committee of Investigation Sent in 1873 by the Mexican Government to the Frontier of Texas. New York: Baker and Goodwin, 1875. Translation of original report entitled *Informe de la comisión pesquisadora de la frontera norte al ejecutivo de la unión*. Mexico City, 1874.

Romero, Matías. "The Garza Raid and Its Lessons." *North American Review* 155 (September 1892): 324–37.

Saldívar, Gabriel. *Documentos de la rebelión de Catarino E. Garza en la frontera de Tamaulipas y sur de Texas, 1891–1992.* Mexico City: n.p., 1943.

Stanley, Henry M. *Through the Dark Continent.* New York: 1978.

Tarver, E. H. *Laredo: The Gateway between the United States and Mexico.* Laredo: Daily Times, 1889.

Texas Almanac and State Industrial Guide for 1867. Galveston: Galveston News, 1867.

Texas Almanac and State Industrial Guide for 1871–73. Galveston: Galveston News, 1871–73.

Texas Almanac and State Industrial Guide for 1904. Galveston: Galveston News, 1904.

Texas Almanac and State Industrial Guide for 1910. Galveston: Galveston News, 1910.

United States Congress. Senate. *Extension of Zona Libre in Mexico.* 50th Cong., 1st sess. Senate Executive Doc. no. 130.

Velasco, Donaldo. *Asalto de Bocas del Toro por el general Catarino Erasmo Garza, con su retrato; relación histórica.* Bogotá: Tip. Salesiana, 1896.

SECONDARY SOURCES

Adelman, Jeremy, and Stephen Aron. "From Borderlands to Borders: Empires, Nation-States, and the Peoples in between in North American History." *American Historical Review* 104, no. 3 (June 1999): 814–841.

Alonso, Ana. *Thread of Blood: Colonialism, Revolution, and Gender on Mexico's Northern Frontier.* Tucson: University of Arizona Press, 1995.

Alonzo, Armando. *Tejano Legacy: Rancheros and Settlers in South Texas, 1734–1900.* Albuquerque: University of New Mexico Press, 1998.

Anders, Evan. *Boss Rule in South Texas: The Progressive Era.* Austin: University of Texas Press, 1987.

Anderson, Benedict. *Imagined Communities: Reflections on the Origin and Spread of Nationalism.* London: Verso Press, 1983.

Anderson, Rodney D. *Outcasts in their own Land: The Mexican Industrial Workers, 1905–1911.* Dekalb: Northern Illinois University Press, 1976.

Anzaldúa, Gloria. *Borderlands/La Frontera: The New Mestiza.* San Francisco: Aunt Lute Books, 1987.

Becker, Majorie. *Setting the Virgin on Fire: Lázaro Cárdenas, Michoacán Peasants, and the Redemption of the Mexican Revolution.* Berkeley: University of California Press, 1995.

Bederman, Gail. *Manliness and Civilization: A Cultural History of Gender and Race in the United States, 1880–1917.* Chicago: University of Chicago Press, 1995.

Beezley, William H. *Insurgent Governor: Abraham Gónzalez and the Mexican Revolution in Chihuahua.* Lincoln: University of Nebraska Press, 1973.

Benjamin, Thomas. "Regionalizing the Revolution: The many Mexicos in Revolutionary Historiography." In *Provinces of the Revolution: Essays on Regional Mexican History, 1910–1929,* ed. Thomas Benjamin and Mark Wasserman. Albuquerque: University of New Mexico Press, 1990.

Benjamin, Walter. *Illuminations: Essays and Reflections*. New York: Schocken Books, 1988.

Bhabha, Homi K. "DissemiNation: Time, Narrative, and the Margins of the Modern Nation." In *Nation and Narration*. London: Routledge, 1990.

———. *Twilight Los Angeles, 1992*. Ed. Anna Deavere Smith. New York: Anchor Books, 1994.

———. "Signs Taken for Wonders: Questions of Ambivalence and Authority under a Tree Outside Delhi, May 1817." *Critical Inquiry* 12 (autumn 1985): 144–65.

Brunk, Samuel. *Emiliano Zapata: Revolution and Betrayal in Mexico*. Albuquerque: University of New Mexico Press, 1995.

Bushwick, Frank H. *Glamorous Days*. San Antonio: Naylor Co., 1934.

Canales, José T. *Juan N. Cortina: Two Interpretations*. New York: Arno Press, 1974.

Case, Robert. "La frontera texana y los movimientos de insurrección en México, 1850–1900." *Historia Mexicana* 30, no. 3 (January–March 1981): 415–52.

Castellanos, G., Gerardo. *Misión a Cuba: Cayo Hueso y Martí*. Havana: Alfa, 1944.

———. *Motivos de Cayo Hueso (Contribución) a la historia de las emigraciones revolucionarias cubanas en Estados Unidos*. n.p., 1935.

Cerutti, Mario. *Burgesía, capitales e industria en el norte de méxico: Monterrey y su ámbito regional, 1850–1910*. Mexico: Alianza Editorial, 1992.

Cleveland, Jeffrey Kirk. "Fight Like a Devil: Images of the Texas Rangers and the Strange Career of Jesse Perez." Master's thesis, University of Texas, Austin, 1992.

Cockcroft, James. *Intellectual Precursors of the Mexican Revolution, 1900–1913*. Austin: University of Texas Press, 1976.

Conrad, Joseph. *Heart of Darkness with the Congo Diary*. London: Penguin, 1995 [1898–1899].

Cosío Villegas, Daniel. *Historia moderna de México*. Vol. 2: *El Porfiriato: La vida Política interior* Mexico: Hermes, 1972.

Cronon, William, ed. *Under an Open Sky: Rethinking America's Western Past*. New York: Norton, 1992.

Cumberland, Charles C. "Border Raids in the Lower Rio Grande Valley — 1915." *Southwestern Historical Quarterly* 57 (January 1954): 285–311.

Cunningham, Andrew, and Birdie Andrews. *Western Medicine as Contested Knowledge*. Manchester: Manchester University Press, 1997.

Cuthbertson, Gilbert M. "Catarino E. Garza and the Garza War." *Texana* 12 (1974): 335–47.

De Certeau, Michel. *The Practice of Everyday Life*. Trans. Steven Rendall. Berkeley: University of California Press, 1988.

De León, Arnoldo, and Stewart, Kenneth L. *Tejanos and the Numbers Game: A Socio-Historical Interpretation from the Federal Censuses, 1850–1900*. Austin: University of Texas Press, 1991.

———. *The Tejano Community, 1836–1900*. Albuquerque: University of New Mexico Press, 1989.

De León, Arnoldo. *They Called Them Greasers: Anglo Attitudes Towards Mexicans in Texas, 1821–1900*. Albuquerque: University of New Mexico, 1982.

Deutsch, Sara. *No Separate Refuge: Culture, Class, and Gender on an Anglo-Hispanic Frontier in the American Southwest, 1880–1940.* New York: Oxford, 1987.

Diccionario histórico y biográfico de la revolución mexicana. Mexico: INEHRM, 1992.

Duclós Salinas, Adolfo. *Mejico pacificado: El progreso de mejico y los hombres que lo gobiernan.* St. Louis: Hughes and Co., 1904.

Dunn, Timothy J. *Militarization of the U.S.-Mexico Border, 1978–1992: Low-Intensity Conflict Doctrine Comes Home.* Austin: University of Texas Press, 1996.

Drinon, Richard. *Facing West: The Metaphysics of Indian-Hating and Empire Building.* New York: New American Library, 1980.

Falcón, Romana. "Raices de la revolución: Evaristo Madero, el primer eslabón de la cadena." In *The Revolutionary Process in Mexico: Essays on Political and Social Change, 1880–1940,* ed. Jaime E. Rodríguez O. Los Angeles: University of California Press, 1990.

Flores, Richard R. *Los Pastores: History and Performance in the Mexican Shepherd's Play of South Texas.* Washington, D.C.: Smithsonian Institution Press, 1995.

Foley, Neil. *The White Scourge: Mexicans, Blacks, and Poor Whites in Texas Cotton Culture.* Berkeley: University of California Press, 1997.

Foner, Philips S. ed. *Our America: Writings on Latin America and the Struggle for Cuban Independence by José Martí.* New York: Monthly Review Press, 1977.

Fox, Claire F. *The Fence and the River: Culture and Politics at the U.S.-Mexico Border.* Minneapolis: University of Minnesota Press, 1999.

French, William. *A Peaceful and Working People: Manners, Morals, and Class Formation in Northern Mexico.* Albuquerque: University of New Mexico Press, 1996.

García, Felix. *The Children of A. M. Bruni.* Laredo: n.p., 1984.

García, Mario. "Mexican Americans and the Politics of Citizenship: The Case of El Paso, 1936." *New Mexico Historical Review* 59, no. 2 (1984): 187–204.

Geertz, Clifford. "Thick Description: Toward an Interpretive Theory of Culture." In *The Interpretation of Cultures.* New York: Basic Books, 1973.

Goldfinch, Charles William. *Juan N. Cortina, 1824–1892: A Re-apprisal.* Brownsville: Bishop Print Shop, 1950.

Gómez-Peña, Guillermo. *The New World Border: Prophecies, Poems, and Loqueras for the End of the Century.* San Francisco: City Lights, 1996.

Gómez-Quiñones, Juan. *Sembradores: Ricardo Flores Magón y el Partido Liberal Mexicano: A Eulogy and Critique.* Los Angeles: Aztlán Publications, 1973.

González, Jovita. "Social Life in Cameron, Starr, and Zapata Counties." Master's thesis, University of Texas, Austin, 1930.

Gordon, Linda. *The Great Arizona Orphan Abduction.* Cambridge: Harvard University Press, 1999.

Grimm, Agnes G. *Llanos Mesteños: Mustang Plains.* Waco: Texan Press, 1968.

Gugleberger, George M., ed. *The Real Thing: Testimonial Discourse and Latin America.* Durham: Duke University Press, 1996.

Gutiérrez, David. *Walls and Mirrors: Mexican Americans, Mexican Immigrants, and the Politics of Ethnicity.* Berkeley: University of Califorinia Press, 1995.

Gutiérrez, Ramón A. *When Jesus Came the Corn Mothers Went Away: Marriage,*

Sexuality, and Power in New Mexico, 1500–1846. Stanford: Stanford University Press, 1991.

Gutmann, Mathew C. *The Meanings of Macho: Being a Man in Mexico City*. Berkeley: University of California Press, 1996.

Hale, Charles R. *Resistance and Contradiction: Miskitu and the Nicaraguan State, 1894–1987*. Stanford: Stanford University Press, 1996.

Hall, Linda B., and Don M. Coerver. *Revolution on the Border: The United States and Mexico, 1910–1920*. Albuquerque: University of New Mexico Press, 1988.

Hardt, Michael, and Antonio Negri. *Empire*. Cambridge: Harvard University Press, 2000.

Harris, Charles, III, and Louis R. Sadler. "The 1911 Reyes Conspiracy: The Texas Side." In *The Border and the Revolution*, ed. Charles Harris III and Louis R. Sadler. Las Cruces: New Mexico State University Press, 1988.

Hart, John Mason. *Empire and Revolution: Americans in Mexico since the Civil War*. Berkeley: University of California Press, 2002.

Henao, Jesús María, and Arrubla, Gerrardo. *Historia de Colombia*, Vol. 2 Bogotá: Plaza and Janes, 1984.

Herman, Edward S. *Manufacturing Consent: The Political Economy of the Mass Media*. New York: Pantheon, 1988.

Hernstein, Richard, and Murray, Charles. *The Bell Curve: Intelligence and Class Structure in American Life*. New York: Free Press, 1994.

Hinojosa, Gilberto Miguel. *A Borderlands Town in Transition: Laredo, 1755–1870*. College Station: Texas A&M University Press, 1983.

Hoganson, Kristin L. *Fighting for Manhood: How Gender Politics Provoked the Spanish-American and Philippine American Wars*. New Haven: Yale University Press, 1998.

Hollinger, David A. *Postethnic America: Beyond Multiculturalism*. New York: Basic Books, 1995.

Hu-DeHart, Evelyn. *Yaqui Resistance and Survival: The Struggle for Land and Autonomy, 1821–1910*. Madison: University of Wisconsin Press, 1984.

Johnson, Benjamin Heber. *Revolution in Texas: How a Forgotten Rebellion and its Bloody Suppression Turned Mexicans into Americans*. New Haven: Yale University Press, 2003.

Joseph, Gilbert M., Catherine C. LeGrand, and Ricardo Salvatore. *Close Encounters of Empire: Writing the Cultural History of U.S.-Latin American Relations*. Durham: Duke University Press, 1998.

Kanellos, Nicolás. *Hispanic Periodicals in the United States, Origins to 1960: A Brief History and Comprehensive Bibliography*. Houston: Arte Público Press, 2000.

Kaplan, Amy, and Donald E. Pease, eds. *The Cultures of United States Imperialism*. Durham: Duke University Press, 1993.

Kaplan, Amy. "Black and Blue on San Juan Hill." In *The Cultures of United States Imperialism*, ed. Amy Kaplan and Donald E. Pease Durham: Duke University Press, 1993.

Katz, Friedrich. *Secret War in Mexico: Europe, the United States, and the Mexican Revolution*. Chicago: University of Chicago Press, 1981.

————. *The Life and Times of Pancho Villa*. Stanford: Stanford University Press, 1998.

Kelves, Daniel J. *In the Name of Eugenics: Genetics and the Uses of Human Heredity*. New York: Knopf, 1985.

Kirk, John M. *José Martí: Mentor of the Cuban Nation*. Tampa: University Presses of Florida, 1983.

Knight, Alan. *The Mexican Revolution*. 2 vols. Lincoln: University of Nebraska Press, 1990.

————. "Race, Revolution, and Indigenismo." In *The Idea of Race in Latin America*, ed. Richard Graham. Austin: University of Texas Press, 1990.

Lea, Tom. *The King Ranch*. Boston: Little, Brown and Co., 1957.

Limón, José E. *Dancing with the Devil: Society and Cultural Poetics in Mexican American South Texas*. Madison: University of Wisconsin Press, 1994.

————. "El Primer Congreso Mexicanista de 1911: A Precursor to Contemporary Chicanismo." *Aztlan* 5, nos. 1–2 (1974): 85–106.

————. *Mexican Ballads, Chicano Poems: History and Influence in Mexican-American Social Poetry*. Berkeley: University of California Press, 1992.

Limerick, Patricia Nelson. *The Legacy of Conquest: The Unbroken Past of the American West*. New York: Norton, 1988.

Lomas, Laura. "American Alterities: Reading between Borders in José Martí's 'North American Scenes.'" Ph.D. diss., Columbia University, 2001.

Lorey, David E. *The U.S.-Mexican Border in the Twentieth Century*. Wilmington, Del.: Scholarly Resources, 1999.

Lott, Virgil, and Mecurio Martínez. *The Kingdom of Zapata County*. San Antonio: Naylor, 1953.

Marcum, Richard Tandy. "Fort Brown, Texas: The History of a Border Post." Ph.D. diss., Texas Technological College, 1964.

Martí, José. *José Martí: Selected Writing*. Trans. Esther Allen. New York: Penguin Books, 2002.

Martin, Jack. *Border Boss: Captain John R. Hughes — Texas Ranger*. Austin: State House Press, 1990 [1942].

Martínez, Oscar J., *Troublesome Border*. Tucson: University of Arizona Press, 1988.

————. *U.S.-Mexico Borderlands: Historical and Contemporary Perspectives*. Wilmington, Del.: Scholarly Resources, 1996.

Marx, Karl. "The Eighteenth Brumaire of Louis Bonaparte." In *Karl Marx and Frederick Engels: Selected Works*. New York: International Publishers, 1986.

Mendoza, Louis Gerard. *Historia: The Literary Making of Chicana and Chicano History*. College Station: Texas A&M University Press, 2001.

Montejano, David. *Anglos and Mexicans in the Making of Texas, 1836–1986*. Austin: University of Texas Press, 1987.

Mora-Torres, Juan. *The Making of the Mexican Border: The State, Capitalism, and Society in Nuevo León, 1848–1910*. Austin: University of Texas Press, 2001.

Nash, Gary. "The Hidden History of Mestizo America." *Journal of American History* (December 1995): 941–64.

Nugent, Daniel. *Spent Cartridges of Revolution: An Anthropological History of Namiquipa, Chihuahua*. Chicago: University of Chicago Press, 1993.

Paredes, Américo. *With His Pistol in His Hand: A Border Ballad and Its Hero*. Austin: University of Texas Press, 1990 [1958].

Paz, Ireneo. *Life and Adventures of the Celebrated Bandit Joaquin Murieta: His Exploits in the State of California*. Trans. Frances P. Belle. Houston: Arte Público Press, 2001 [1925].

Pérez, Louis A., Jr. *On Becoming Cuban: Identity, Nationality, and Culture*. Chapel Hill: University of North Carolina Press, 1999.

Piccato, Pablo. *City of Suspects: Crime in Mexico City, 1900–1931*. Durham: Duke University Press, 2001.

Pitt-Rivers, Julian. "Honor and Social Status." In *Honor and Shame: The Values of Mediterranean Society*, ed. J. G. Peristiany. Chicago: University of Chicago Press, 1965.

Porter, Joseph C. *Paper Medicine Man: John Gregory Bourke and His American West*. Norman: University of Oklahoma Press, 1986.

Porter, Kenneth W. *The Black Seminoles: History of a Freedom-Seeking People*. Gainesville: University Press of Florida, 1996.

Pratt, Mary Louise. "Fieldwork in Common Places." In *Writing Culture: The Poetics and Politics of Ethnography*. Berkeley: University of California Press, 1986.

———. *Imperial Eyes: Travel Writing and Transculturation*. London: Routledge, 1991.

Raat, Dirk W. *Revoltosos: Mexico's Rebels in the United States, 1903–1934*. College Station: Texas A&M University Press, 1981.

Ramos Escandón, Carmen. "Señoritas porfirianas: Mujer e ideología en el México progresista, 1880–1910." In *Presencia y transparencia: La mujer en la historia de México*, ed. Carmen Ramos Escandón. Mexico City: El Colegio de México, Programa Interdisciplinario de Estudios de la Mujer, 1987.

Recer, Danalynn. "Patrolling the Borders of Race, Gender, and Class: The Lynching Ritual and Texas Nationalism, 1850–1994." Master's thesis, University of Texas, Austin, 1994.

Ribb, Richard H. "José Tomás Canales and the Texas Rangers; Myth, Identity, and Power in South Texas, 1900–1920." Ph.D. diss., University of Texas, Austin, 2001.

Ridge, Martin. "Who's Who — or Western Name Calling." *Journal of the West* 38, no. 4 (October 1999): 3–4.

Robbins, William. *Colony and Empire: The Capitalist Transformation of the U.S. West*. Lawrence: University Press of Kansas, 1994.

Roediger, David R. *The Wages of Whiteness: Race and the Making of the American Working Class*. London: Verso, 1991.

Rouse, Roger. "Mexican Migration and the Social Space of Postmodernism." In *Between Two Worlds: Mexican Immigrants in the United States*, ed. David Gutiérrez. Wilmington, Del.: Scholarly Resources, 1996.

Said, Edward. *Culture and Imperialism*. New York: Vintage, 1993.

Saldívar, José David. *Border Matters: Remapping American Cultural Studies*. Berkeley: University of California Press, 1997.

Sandos, James A. *Rebellion in the Borderlands: Anarchism and the Plan of San Diego, 1904–1923*. Norman: University of Oklahoma Press, 1992.

Saragoza, Alex M. *The Monterrey Elite and the Mexican State, 1880–1940*. Austin: University of Texas Press, 1988.

Sarmiento, Domingo F. *Life in the Argentine Republic in the Days of Tyrants or Civilization and Barbarism*. New York: Collier Books, 1961.

Schecter, Patricia A. *Ida B. Wells-Barnett and American Reform, 1880–1930*. Chapel Hill: University of North Carolina Press, 2001.

Scott, James. *Domination and the Arts of Resistance*. New Haven: Yale University Press, 1990.

———. *The Moral Economy of the Peasant: Subsistence and Rebellion in Southeast Asia*. New Haven: Yale University Press, 1976.

———. *Seeing Like a State: How Certain Schemes to Improve the Human Condition Have Failed*. New Haven: Yale University Press, 1998.

———. *Weapons of the Weak: Everyday Forms of Peasant Resistance*. New Haven: Yale University Press, 1985.

Spener, David, and Kathleen Staudt, eds. *The U.S.-Mexico Border: Transcending Divisions, Contesting Identities*. Boulder: Lynne Rienner, 1998.

Stepan, Nancy Leys. *"The Hour of Eugenics": Race, Gender, and Nation in Latin America*. Ithaca: Cornell University Press, 1991.

Thompson, E. P. "The Moral Economy of the English Crowd in the Eighteenth Century." In *Customs in Common: Studies in Traditional Popular Culture*. New York: New Press, 1991.

Thompson, Jerry D., ed. *Juan Cortina and the Texas-Mexico Frontier, 1859–1877*. El Paso: Texas Western Press, 1994.

Thomson, Guy, with David Lafrance. *Patriotism, Politics, and Popular Liberalism in Nineteenth-Century Mexico: Juan Francisco Lucas and the Puebla Sierra*. Wilmington, Del.: Scholarly Resources, 1999.

Thornton, Bruce. *Searching for Joaquin: Myth, Murieta, and History in California*. San Francisco: Encounter Books, 2002.

Trouillot, Michel-Rolph. *Silencing the Past: Power and the Production of History*. Boston: Beacon Press, 1995.

Truett, Samuel, and Elliott Young. "Making Transnational History." In *Continental Crossroads: Remapping U.S.-Mexico Borderlands History*, ed. Samuel Truett and Elliott Young. Durham: Duke University Press, 2004.

Vanderwood, Paul. *Disorder and Progress: Bandits, Police, and Mexican Development*. Wilmington, Del.: Scholarly Resources, 1992.

———. *The Power of God against the Guns of Government: Religious Upheaval in Mexico at the Turn of the Nineteenth Century*. Stanford: Stanford University Press, 1998.

Vasconcelos, José. *The Cosmic Race/La Raza Cósmica*. Los Angeles: Aztlan Publications, 1979.

Vila, Pablo. *Crossing Borders, Reinforcing Borders: Social Categories, Metaphors, and Narrative Identities on the U.S.-Mexico Frontier*. Austin: University of Texas Press, 2000.

Wald, Elijah. *Narcocorrido: A Journey into the Music of Drugs, Guns, and Guerrillas*. New York: HarperCollins, 2001.

Wasserman, Mark. *Capitalists, Caciques, and Revolution: The Native Elite and Foreign Enterprise in Chihuahua, Mexico, 1854–1911.* Chapel Hill: University of North Carolina Press, 1984.

———. *Persistent Oligarchs: Elites and Politics in Chihuahua, Mexico, 1910–1940.* Durham: Duke University Press, 1993.

Watts, Sheldon. *Epidemics and History: Disease, Power, and Imperialism.* New Haven: Yale University Press, 1997.

Webb, Walter Prescott. *The Texas Rangers: A Century of Frontier Defense.* Boston: Houghton Mifflin, 1935. Reprint, Austin: University of Texas Press, 1965.

Weber, David J. *The Mexican Frontier, 1821–1846: The American Southwest under Mexico.* Albuquerque: University of New Mexico Press, 1892.

———. *The Spanish Frontier in North America.* New Haven: Yale University Press, 1992.

White, Richard. *"It's Your Misfortune and None of My Own": A New History of the American West.* Norman: University of Oklahoma Press, 1991.

Womack, John, Jr. *Zapata and the Mexican Revolution.* New York: Vintage, 1970.

Williams, Raymond. "Base and Superstructure in Marxist Cultural Theory." In *Problems in Materialism and Culture.* London: Verso, 1981.

Wu, Yi-Li "Medicalizing the Monstruous: Ghost Fetuses (*guitai*) in Traditional Chinese Medical Thought." Paper prepared for Symposium on the History of Health and Beauty, Taipei, Taiwan, 1999.

Young, Elliott. "Before the Revolution: Catarino Garza as Activist/Historian." In *Recovering the U.S. Hispanic Literary Heritage,* vol. 2. Houston: Arté Público, 1996.

———. "Deconstructing *La Raza*: Culture and Ideology of the *Gente Decente* of Laredo, 1904–1911." *Southwestern Historical Quarterly* (October 1994): 226–59.

———. "Imagining Alternative Modernities: Ignacio Martínez's Travel Narratives." In *Continental Crossroads: Remapping U.S.-Mexico Borderlands History,* ed. Samuel Truett and Elliott Young. Durham: Duke University Press, 2004.

———. "Red Men, Princess Pocahontas, and George Washington: Harmonizing Race Relations in Laredo at the Turn of the Century." *Western Historical Quarterly* 29 (spring 1998): 48–85.

———. "Remembering Catarino Garza's 1891 Revolution: An Aborted Border Insurrection." *Mexican Studies/Estudios Mexicanos* 12, no. 2 (summer 1996): 231–72.

Young, Robert J. C. *Colonial Desire: Hybridity in Theory, Culture, and Race.* London: Routledge, 1995.

Zamora, Emilio. *The World of the Mexican Worker in Texas.* College Station: Texas A&M University Press, 1996.

French, William, 12, 27
French Revolution, 248
Freud, Sigmund, 220
Fricke, Paul (U.S. marshal), 171–176,
  255

Galán, Garza (governor), 48–54, 59–60,
  99, 205
García, Eusebio, 86–87, 91, 93
García, Lorenzo (general), 103–106, 111,
  122, 247
Garza, Amelia, 281, 295
Garza, Catarino Erasmo: assasination
  attempts on, 48–49, 65–78, 96, 116,
  290, 294–295; biography of, 4, 10, 16,
  18, 23, 30–32, 41–42, 292; Concepción Tobar (pseudonym), 269; in Costa
  Rica, 1, 261, 277–295; in Cuba, 271–
  278; death of, 2, 4, 10, 295–301;
  Erasmo Betancourt (pseudonym), 272,
  278, 283; in Florida, 270–276; as Journalist, 4, 25–27, 36–37, 48–54, 65–
  67, 74–75, 95–96, 192, 205–206, 244;
  *La era de Tuxetepec, O sea Rusia en
  América,* 286–289; *La Logica de los
  Hechos* (autobiography), 8, 13, 23–56,
  62, 85, 285, 290, 304, 308; in Mexico,
  117, 202; in Panama, 2, 4, 11; relations
  with father-in-law, 54, 103, 118, 171–
  172, 271, 274, 279–285; relations with
  wife, Concepción, 54, 268–271, 275,
  280–284, 290–294, 299, 313; relations with women, 23, 40–47; as Revolutionary, 12–13, 25–26, 47, 64, 79,
  97, 282–291, 296–301; in St. Louis,
  28, 35, 42–48, 213, 273; in Texas, 31–
  42, 66–67, 98, 102, 118, 156, 177,
  188, 195, 206, 213, 218, 268, 291–
  292; wedding of, 39
Garza, Concepción González (Chonita),
  54, 268–271, 291–295, 299, 313
Garza, Encarnación, 269, 277–278, 280,
  285, 290–295; Martín Ortíz
  (pseudonym), 269
Garza, Juan, 103

Garza Revolution: causes of, 3, 4, 18, 55–
  58, 65, 74–76, 95, 140, 150–156, 165,
  197, 242; goals of, 3, 9, 117, 129–130,
  139, 191, 208; manifestos, 80, 111–
  117, 121–126, 145,155, 164, 177;
  meanings of, 1–8, 14, 21–26, 57, 98,
  129–131, 193, 212, 301–315 origins
  of, 60, 103; supporters of, 8, 11, 21,
  27, 110, 123–129, 132, 145, 151–191,
  194–200, 206–207, 214, 227–235,
  246, 253, 261, 263, 288, 306–307,
  310
Garza, Tomás (U.S. deputy marshal), 120,
  175
Gender, 45; femininity, 27, 43, 47, 101,
  130, 225; masculinity, 12, 23, 27–28,
  34–35, 43–47, 100, 130, 225,
  308
Gente culta, 23, 27
Germany, 312
Geronimo, 212–213
Glover, Rufus, 159
Gómez, Doroteo, 106
Gómez, Manuel, 61
Gómez-Quiñones, Juan, 13
Gómez's Saloon, 170
González, Alejandro, 52, 100, 103, 150,
  169–170, 179, 207, 252–255, 269–
  274, 279, 283, 310
González, Jovita, 140
González, Manuel, 63–64, 207
González, Mauricio, 279, 292
González, Valentín, 280
Granados, Garcia, 290–292
Gran Liga Mexicanista, 140
Guajardo, Celso Garza, *En busca de Cat-
  arino Garza,* 8
Guardado de Arriba, 103
Guatemala, 294
Guerra, Manuel, 150–157, 169, 253
Guerrero, Mexico, 79, 108, 124
Guevara, Che, 301
Guerilleros de Coahuila, 160
Gulf of Mexico, 149
Gutiérrez, Ramón, 12

Uña De Gato, 118
United States Army, 3–6, 13–16, 22–23, 28, 74, 106–110, 119, 134, 157–163, 168, 173–188, 190, 198, 209–219, 225–233, 237–238, 247–256, 259, 266, 283, 288, 308, 310, 313; Punitive Expedition, 312
United States Border Patrol, 311
United States Civil War, 223, 308
United States Constitution, 226, 247
United States Declaration of Independence, 248
United States Department of Justice, 215
United States Drug Enforcement Agency, 313
Unites States Marshals, 180–182, 226–228, 252
United States-Mexican International Water Boundary Commission, 74, 215
United States Navy, 289–290
United States War Department, 224, 227
University of Texas, Austin, 25
Urrea, Teresa, 122

Valádez, Manuel, 82–83
Valverde, M.L., 159
Vallecillo, 119
Vanderwood, Paul, 12, 122
Vasquez, A.C. (consul), 300–301
Vela, Eulalio, 9
Velasco, Donaldo, 296–299
Venezuela, 293
Vera, José Angel, 103–104
Veracruz, Mexico, 33, 300
Vidaurri, Santiago, 60
Villa Garza Galán, 122

Villa, Juan, 160
Villa, Pancho, 301, 312; German support for, 312
Villareal, Lino, 81
Villareal, Sebastían (general), 160
Villastrigo, Tomás, 81
Villegas, Daniel Cosío: *Historia moderna de Mexico,* 8
Volunteer Veterans of Texas, 49–50
von Clausewitz, Karl, 130

War against Peace, or a New Attila, 246–251
Washington, D.C., 141
Webb County, 149, 157
Wells, James B., 158, 170
Wheaton, Frank (brigadier general), 231, 260
Whitman, Walt, 236
Wounded Knee, 227, 265
Wyoming, 242

Yaqui Indian rebellion, 21, 59–60
Yellow Journalism, 5
Young-MacAllen ranch, 222

Zamora, Emilio, 12, 27
Zapata, Emiliano, 64, 115, 301
Zapata County, 149–152, 168, 175, 228, 262
Zaragoza, Ignacio, 54
Zardeneta, Romulo, 81, 90, 95
Zerna, Eduardo (captain), 127
Zertuche, Rafael, 83–84
Zimmerman Telegram, 312
Zona Libre. *See* Free trade

Elliott Young is an associate professor in the
Department of History at Lewis & Clark College.

Library of Congress Cataloging-in-Publication Data
Young, Elliott.
Catarino Garza's revolution on the Texas-Mexico
border / Elliott Young.
p. cm. — (American encounters/global interactions)
Includes bibliographical references and index.
ISBN 0-8223-3308-2 (cloth : alk. paper)
ISBN 0-8223-3320-1 (pbk. : alk. paper)
1. Mexican-American Border Region — History — 19th century.
2. Garza, Catarino, 1859–1895. 3. Revolutionaries — Mexico —
Biography. 4. Journalists — Mexico — Biography. 5. Revolutions — Mexican-
American Border Region — History — 19th century. 6. Revolutions —
Mexican-American Border Region — Historiography. 7. Texas — Relations —
Mexico. 8. Mexico — Relations — Texas. 9. Díaz, Porfirio,
1830–1915. 10. Mexico — Politics and government — 1867–1910.
I. Title. II. Series.
F786.Y565 2004   972'.06 — dc22